Democracy and Deliberation

Democracy and Deliberation

THE LAW AND POLITICS OF SEX OFFENDER LEGISLATION

Cary Federman

UNIVERSITY OF MICHIGAN PRESS
ANN ARBOR

For questions or permissions, please contact um.press.perms@umich.edu

Published in the United States of America by the University of Michigan Press
Printed and bound by CPI Group (UK) Ltd, Croydon, CR0 4YY

First published June 2021

A CIP catalog record for this book is available from the British Library.

Library of Congress Cataloging-in-Publication Data

Names: Federman, Cary, 1963– author.
Title: Democracy and deliberation : the law and politics of sex offender legislation / Cary Federman.
Description: Ann Arbor : University of Michigan Press, 2021. | Includes bibliographical references and index.
Identifiers: LCCN 2021003603 (print) | LCCN 2021003604 (ebook) | ISBN 9780472132515 (hardcover) | ISBN 9780472128839 (ebook)
Subjects: LCSH: Sex offenders—Legal status, laws, etc.—United States.
Classification: LCC KF9325 .F43 2021 (print) | LCC KF9325 (ebook) | DDC 345.73/03—dc23
LC record available at https://lccn.loc.gov/2021003603
LC ebook record available at https://lccn.loc.gov/2021003604

To James Ceaser and Gerald DeMaio, and to the memory of Louis Henri (Tracy) Bolce III and Martha Derthick

Contents

Digital materials related to this title can be found on the Fulcrum platform via the following citable URL: https://doi.org/10.3998/mpub.11728464

Introduction

The purpose of this book is to describe the constitutional and political problems associated with sex offender legislation, with a focus on the social scientific critique of sex offender legislation. Sex offender legislation includes postconviction civil commitment laws, the registration and notification of sex offenders' whereabouts, and residency restrictions. Rather than extending time served in prison, states now impose commitment after conviction of a sex offense, a process called postconviction civil commitment. States also rely upon less exacting medical or psychological language for commitment purposes. Postconviction civil commitment is designed to treat offenders suffering not from a specific list of mental disorders but from a "mental abnormality"—a word without meaning in the psychiatric literature—and to protect "society from the sexually violent acts associated with that abnormality" (In re Young 1993, 21). Registration laws, which vary by state, require convicted sex offenders to register personal information with local police departments.[1] This information is available to the public on the Internet. Notification laws require local police departments to notify neighborhoods of the presence of released convicted sex offenders, whose dangerous levels are public and categorized by tiers (tier 3 being the most dangerous, tier 1 the least). Residency restrictions prohibit convicted sex offenders from living near schools, playgrounds, and other places where minors can congregate.[2]

This is the first book to study sex offender legislation from a constitutional and political perspective. I mean by this that this book is not strictly limited to legal interpretation. I place a distinct value on the constitutional structure, the political process, and the deliberations of legislators in making sex offender laws. Other works that tackle the legal problems of sex offenders tend to diminish the law's role in protecting the public and play up the harmful medical, psychological, and sociological aspects of the legislation. They focus, in other words, on social science data. There is also, among such works, a great emphasis on the rhetoric of angry state legislators who want to banish sex offenders to another state and the nondeliberative aspects—the moral panic view[3]—of sex offender legislation. I reject these views because they lack a comprehensive political and juridical understanding of lawmaking and governance. My view of constitutional law extends beyond the four corners of the Bill of Rights and includes the separation of powers, judicial restraint, democratic theory, and the deliberative aspects of legislation. My view of governance requires that legislators, judges, and the American people be treated as responsible persons, barring extenuating circumstances.

My main focus is to explain how the social sciences try to influence sex offender legislation. Social scientists claim to be objective in the study of social problems and stress efficiency in outcomes. A social scientist might oppose a law that bans all convicted sex offenders from entering parks because not all sex offenders offend against minors who might congregate in parks. Our social scientist would also point out that most sex offenders are not strangers to their victims, so laws that ban sex offenders from entering parks are useless—and vindictive. Legislators, in this view, are not objective; they are partisan. They respond to interest-group pressure and public opinion, which can be wrong and motivated by vengeance. Legislators pass general laws to protect the public safety, but they also co-opt and weaken medical terminology to ensure that the mentally ill are held responsible for their crimes.

In turning to the social scientific critique of sex offender legislation, I want to focus on the real impetus for judicial activism. Intellectual and partisan debates about judicial restraint and activism have much to teach us about jurisprudence and institutional politics. But social scientists exert a tremendous amount of influence on sex offender legislation and judicial decision-making. This is, then, an interdisciplinary study. The conflict between legislators who favor postconviction remedies, based on social science data, public opinion, and concerns about public safety, and social scientists and those in the legal profession who argue for individualized, therapeutic solutions, efficient lawmaking, and the fundamental rights of convicted sex offenders not to have restrictions imposed upon them, is the theme of this work.

The conflict over sex offender laws began in the 1990s. Traditional civil commitment refers to the incarceration of those who are incapable, because of mental or physical disease, of taking care of themselves. They may self-harm or harm others. I am not concerned with this type of commitment. From 1935 to the late 1960s, states had sexual psychopaths committed for society's and the individual's protection. Under both civil commitment and sexual psychopath laws, sex offenders were committed in lieu of imprisonment and in some cases in lieu of trials.[4] The care provided by asylums was not restoration but superintendence, in the same way that "day care" means the superintendence of children. During the 1970s, states moved away from a model of care and focused on public safety and individual therapy. They changed the language of civil commitment from "unsafe to be at large" to "dangerous to themselves or to others" (Bloom 2004, 433). This change reflects the increased influence of health-care professionals in policymaking at all levels of government, or what Edward Banfield (1980, 1, 3) has called "policy-oriented social science"—the attempt, that is, by professional problem solvers to "cure the ills of society."

Tamara Rice Lave (2009, 549) has written that "[b]etween 1937 and 1967, twenty-six states and the District of Columbia passed legislation calling for the indefinite civil commitment of so-called sexual psychopaths. By 1990—when the first sexually violent predator law was passed in the state of Washington—most of the sexual psychopath laws had fallen out of use or been overturned." By the 1990s, lawmakers believed that sex offenders posed a different threat to the public than in the past and that the legal and medical standards used to commit were in need of updating.

There is no medical or psychological definition of the term "sex offender." The legal meaning of what constitutes sex offending differs by statute. New Jersey determined that sex offenders "suffer from mental conditions that do not necessarily lend themselves 'to characterization under the existing statutory standard for involuntary civil commitment'" (In re Commitment of M.G. 2000, 371–72). Congress (2006, sec. 111(1)) defines a sex offender as someone who has been "convicted of a sex offense." In 2006, Congress passed the Sex Offender Registration and Notification Act (SORNA), also known as the Adam Walsh Child Protection and Safety Act. SORNA governs federal sex offenders and imposes requirements and restrictions on state sex offenders. Congress defines a "sexually dangerous person" as suffering "from a serious mental illness, abnormality, or disorder, as a result of which the individual would have serious difficulty in refraining from sexually violent conduct or child molestation" (Congress 2006, sec. 301 (e)(2)). The *Diagnostic and Statistical Manual* (*DSM*), a handbook of mental disorders, neither defines mental illness nor serious mental illness. Mental health professionals consider any mental illness that seriously impairs one's ability to function to be a serious mental disorder. Sex offenders, however, are rarely so impaired, and legislatures have used other terms in place of mental disorder, for example, insanity and mental abnormality. Insanity and mental abnormality have no medical meaning; they are juridical terms to determine levels of personal responsibility. Moreover, while "no definition adequately specifies precise boundaries for the concept of 'mental disorder,'" the *Diagnostic and Statistical Manual* defines mental disorder as a "clinically significant behavioral or psychological syndrome or pattern that occurs in an individual and that is associated with present distress . . . or disability . . . or with a significantly increased risk of suffering death, pain, disability, or an important loss of freedom" (DSM 2000, xxx–xxxi). The *DSM* warns against associating mental disorders with "deviant behavior" and "conflicts that are primarily between the individual and society." SORNA does not define "sexually violent conduct" (Timms v. Johns 2010, 771).

Convicted sex offenders are subject to postconviction civil commitment upon a finding of mental abnormality plus dangerousness. A finding of mental illness alone cannot be used for civil commitment (O'Connor v. Donaldson 1975, 575–76). Dangerousness itself cannot be the reason for postconviction civil commitment; the term has no medical or psychological meaning. It is a "term of art," describing "anyone who we would, all things considered, prefer not to encounter on the streets" (Millard v. Harris 1968, 1099). In law, the determination of dangerousness is not limited to past actions. It also refers to one's potential for future danger (Kansas v. Crane 2002, 418–19). Indeed, dangerousness is not limited to acts of violence (Project Release v. Prevost 1983, 973). In determining dangerousness, judges can weigh clinical assessments of an offender's past and potential for future dangerousness and rely upon actuarial instruments that take "into account the interrelationship of various risk factors and the population base rates," and that assign "weights to the individual risk factors" (Beecher-Monas 2003, 363). The state has to prove that the potential committee is dangerous, "despite the fact that such testimony is wrong two times out of three" (Barefoot v. Estelle 1983, 916). Jurors, not medical experts, decide who is dangerous to a community.

Because postconviction civil commitment is potentially for life, states have to narrow the distinction between those who are mentally ill and not dangerous and those who suffer "from a mental abnormality or personality disorder which makes the person likely to engage in predatory acts of sexual violence" (In re Young 1993, 12). States call such persons sexual predators or sexually violent predators, though these terms have no meaning in the psychological or medical literature. "The term 'sexual predator' is often applied to offenders who offend against strangers, have multiple victims, commit sexually violent offenses, have perhaps started their sexual offending at an early age, are sexually deviant, and may have had prior sex offense convictions." A "violent sexual predator" who has difficulty controlling the impulse to commit sexual violence is "eligible for [postconviction] civil commitment" (Fabian 2003, 390).

What Is Controversial about Sex Offender Legislation?

Sex offender laws provide a "vivid example of the conflict that . . . arises between the rights of individuals and the needs of society" (Doe v. Pataki 1996, 693). For reasons I develop throughout this work, I regard sex offender laws as constitutional, though not without public policy problems. I also regard the passage of sex offender legislation in the 1990s as signs of the health of democratic practices, rather than examples of rage, anger, and moral panic.

Sex offender legislation shines an important light on the problem of governance, for it raises questions about the relationship citizens have with legislators, with law, with their state and local governments, with the medical interpretations of behavior that inform social science research, and with the institutions that shape our views and behaviors. A study of sex offender legislation cannot avoid reflecting on the meaning of governance. By governance, I mean self-governance, which means that laws are directed at those free to choose their paths, that laws are passed after legislative deliberations, and that laws are designed to achieve "wise judgments about public policy," which are "firmly grounded in the interests and desires of the American citizenry" (Bessette 1994, 5; The Federalist 2001, nos. 10, 46, 57, 62). We can call this the public interest (it used to be called the public or common good), which "refers to the needs rather than to the wants of a particular community" (Storing 1995, 265).

My approach has the virtue of conforming judging to the aims of the separation of powers and takes seriously the important role the Constitution assigns to representation, majority rule, and public opinion (Weiner 2019; Bessette 1994). Sex offender legislation implicates democratic principles of deliberation and governance because it focuses attention on the deliberative procedures that enable majority rule, which entails a necessary concern for minority rights. It is this understanding of sex offender laws as governance—law as the product of the deliberative intentions of representatives informed by public opinion—that focuses my attention throughout this book.

Many studies of sex offenders focus on the individual sex offender who has been unjustly confined or has had his movements restricted. Such studies tend to dismiss the moral and political implications of majority rule in passing such laws and regulations. "It was majority rule—not significantly, individual liberty—that Madison called 'the vital principle of our free Constitution'" (Weiner 2012, 23, 6–7). We "govern by majority rule," Alexander Bickel (1975, 102) has written, but do so "with the consent of the minority." Majority rule means representative majority rule because there is no effective alternative for governance—unanimity and direct popular rule are impossibilities for a nation this size. The purpose of representation is to "refine and enlarge the public views" (The Federalist 2001, 58–59 [no. 10]). Refining popular opinion takes time, and time, as Greg Weiner (2012, 121) has demonstrated, "is what preserves the authority of fundamental law while ensuring its ongoing compatibility with popular sovereignty." I recognize that a defense of majority rule might appear controversial to some readers, given the rights claims involved in sex offending. Consider, however, four important facts of constitutional history: (1) the framers wrote the Constitution without a Bill of Rights; (2) James Madison and Alexander Hamilton regarded a Bill of Rights as harmful to the Constitution's meaning; (3) no one foresaw that the Supreme Court would become the translator of the Bill of Rights' meaning; and (4) the Supreme Court did not get around to protecting—and creating—individual rights until the 1960s (Berns 1985, 52). It is the unamended Constitution, Hamilton wrote, that secures the blessings of liberty (The Federalist 2001, 549 [no. 84]). Governance must begin with the Constitution and the structures it put in place. I do not claim that judges should ignore the Bill of Rights, only that we should acknowledge its place within the constitutional structure.

Governance does not mean an abstract commitment "to the principles of individual liberty and respect for personal autonomy" (Schulhoffer 1996, 93) that are presumably lodged in the Bill of Rights. Such a view (1) elevates minority rights over majority rule; (2) creates an abstraction without institutional linkages, which fosters extreme views of rights and public policies; (3) disturbs what Publius called "the public tranquility by interesting too strongly the public passions" (The Federalist 2001, 323 [no. 49]) toward questions of morality or conscience; and (4) implies that there are no other considerations for governance except personal experiences and desires, thereby denying a place for legislative deliberations regarding public safety based on public opinion and foundational principles of democratic governance.

Critics tend to overlook these institutional concerns and argue that sex offender legislation is the product of "outrage" (Lave 2011, 391), rather than a deliberative attempt by elected representatives to protect vulnerable members of a community. Critics also note that residency restrictions create stigmas, foster shame, and increase homelessness among an already ostracized group in American society. They argue that residency restrictions push those with mental illnesses and behavioral problems into areas of a state with meager supporting institutions and increase the possibility of recidivism.[5] Critics also regard registration requirements as invasions of privacy that ostracize and stigmatize members of a vulnerable population. The Alabama Sex Offender Registration and Community Notification Act (ASORCNA), for example, required registered offenders to have their driver's licenses state that they are sex offenders, which a federal district court ruled infringed upon First Amendment rights (Doe I v. Marshall 2019). Such public shaming devices, critics hold, are criminal in intent, if not effect, and therefore unconstitutional under the Eighth and Fourteenth Amendments. Critics also view notification laws as fostering moral panic, weakening the chances for rehabilitation, and creating opportunities for vigilantism. Postconviction civil commitment laws are particularly controversial. Because states impose commitment after conviction, they can violate the constitutional prohibition against ex post facto laws. This challenges the idea that prisoners have paid their debt to society (Roe v. Office of Adult Probation 1996, 1086). Postconviction commitment also raises the specter of preventive detention, thereby introducing into the American legal system practices used in the Soviet Union toward those with unorthodox opinions or idiosyncratic behavior.

Some of these claims have merit on two levels: public policy and constitutional law. They also have important limitations. These laws and regulations clearly inhibit the "liberty" of sex offenders to move about the country, if liberty has no meaning other than doing what one wants to do. The question is whether convicted sex offenders have a constitutionally recognized "liberty interest" (Doe v. Lee 2001) to enter parks where children are or to search the Internet for victims under the age of eighteen. Social scientific inquiry, I argue, cannot resolve the liberty question sex offenders raise because the philosophic and constitutional meaning of both "liberty" and "interest" is broader and more publicly spirited than sex offenders and their supporters suppose. Advocates for sex offenders argue that liberty is always individual liberty. But Publius wrote that "[t]he mild voice of reason" pleads the cause of "permanent" interests (The Federalist 2001, 270 [no. 42]), by which he meant the common good. Just as the founders spoke of the "interests of justice or the public good," which they contrasted with "personal and party attachments" (The Federalist 2001, 506 [no. 79]), they also spoke of "public liberty" and the "liberty of the people" (The Federalist 2001, 55 [no. 10]; 152, 155 [no. 25]; 47 [no. 9]; 332 [no. 51]) rather than of individual liberty.

The question sex offenders raise about liberty and public safety can only be resolved democratically, by legislatures concerned about the common good. In a democratic society, courts must be reluctant to invalidate laws passed by deliberative majorities "unless they are irreconcilable with a specific command of the United States Constitution" (Romer v. Evans 1995, 4). The social scientific proofs that demonstrate the collateral effects of these laws do not undermine what I believe are the constitutional aspects of these laws. Law in the United States has a broader function than the application of scientific findings that seek to promote efficiency. "[R]eliance on courts," Donald Downs (2005, 18) has written, can have a deleterious effect on civic participation: it "can diminish the development of political skills and mobilization dedicated to persuasion and changing minds." Judicial resolutions of scientifically unstable and controversial topics can also increase political polarization in the long term (Rosenberg 1993). Laws can coerce *and* educate (Lerner 1987, 91).

Governance means more than the administration of people and things; deliberation is more than discussion. Governance and deliberation are foundational concepts regarding democratic legitimacy and constitutional sustenance. I argue, then, that courts need to take a minimalist view of their powers over rights claims. For courts, the question is not "whether the legislature has made the best choice possible to address the problem it seeks to remedy, but whether the regulatory means chosen are reasonable in light of the nonpunitive objective" (Smith v. Doe 2002, 105). This is so because of the twin importance in our constitutional framework of institutional configurations, such as the separation of powers and legislative deliberation:

> It is a "well-settled principle that the legislative branch is entitled to deference from the courts because of the constitutional separation of powers." It also

> is hornbook law that courts are not authorized to second-guess the motives of a legislative body and that, if reasonable, legislation will not be disturbed. (Connecticut Indemnity Company v. Superior Court of San Joaquin County 2000, 814)

This is the essence of Cass Sunstein's claim about the importance of judicial minimalism, which I develop in depth in chapter 1.

The purpose of this book is to assess the constitutionality of sex offender laws and analyze the legal, philosophical, and social scientific critiques that question those objectives. This is an attempt at a comprehensive but not total study of the constitutional problems related to sex offender legislation. I do not address all the collateral consequences related to sex offender legislation, such as the "inability to vote, engage in certain businesses, hold public office, or serve as a juror" (Piasecki v. Court of Common Pleas 2019, 176; McPherson 2016). Nor do I discuss the role that global positioning devices can play in monitoring sex offenders (Park v. Georgia 2019). I also do not address the problem of juvenile sex offenders on the registry, a topic that would require an extra chapter at least, given the legal and psychological issues involved (In re C.P. 2012; Wind 2003). I do, however, thoroughly examine postconviction civil commitment laws, the registration and notification of sex offenders' whereabouts, and residency restrictions. To examine the constitutional questions raised by sex offender legislation, I rely on jurisprudential, institutional, and deliberative theories of law and politics. I explain these ideas in depth in chapter 1.

There is a sense among scholars and perhaps the American public that sex offender laws are unduly harsh and arbitrary. My constitutional support of these laws requires a brief defense. Although laws regulating sex offenders have their origins in the 1930s, under what critics call an era of moral panic, they gained popularity during the 1990s, a decade characterized as tough on crime by the passage of the Violent Crime Control and Law Enforcement Act of 1994 and the Antiterrorism and Effective Death Penalty Act of 1996. I think, however, there is a different way to understand the 1990s. I see the 1990s as a deliberative decade, as parents of abducted and murdered children and other interested individuals and groups began working with legislators to pass comprehensive legislation concerning sex offenders. "Between 1987 and 1991," John Kirwin (2003, 1141) writes, "Minnesotans were horrified by a number of rape/murders committed by sex offenders recently released from state prisons." In response, Minnesota passed a law that included postconviction civil commitment for sex offenders.

Alaska passed a similar law in 1994, in response to a child sex abuse "crisis" (Doe v. Otte 2001, 837). In 1993, in Kansas, Donald Gideon, on "supervised release" for a rape conviction, sexually assaulted and murdered Stephanie Schmidt. Gideon and Schmidt worked together, though Gideon's employer did not know about Gideon's criminal record. Following Schmidt's death, her parents "formed a task force that quickly proposed a package of legislation, including an 'Employer Notification' bill that would require parole officers to notify employers of violent felons' offense histories; an enhanced set of sentencing guidelines; and a 'sexually violent predator' civil commitment procedure" (Pearce 2007, 594). In 1998, Florida passed the Jimmy Ryce Involuntary Civil Commitment for Sexually Violent Predators' Treatment and Care Act, following the abduction, rape, and murder of nine-year-old Jimmy Ryce in 1995. Jimmy Ryce's parents played an active role in getting that legislation passed. Congress incorporated parts of Florida's Jimmy Ryce Act into the Adam Walsh Act in 2006.

In 1990, Washington State passed the first law in the nation that granted authorities the power to commit convicted sex offenders to psychiatric facilities who had served their time in prison but who remained dangerous and suffered from mental illness. Washington passed the law in response to numerous sexual assaults against women and children over the previous year and a half, which led to the creation of a number of victims' rights groups that lobbied the legislature for change. After the release of Donald Chapman, a violent sex offender, from prison in 1993, the New Jersey legislature tried to pass legislation confining dangerous sex offenders (Gladwell 1993). The bills failed. But in 1994, Jesse Timmendequas abducted and killed seven-year-old Megan Kanka in New Jersey. Timmendequas had two prior convictions for sex offenses, and unknown to the Kankas, lived on the same block as them. The legislature then passed "Megan's Law," which requires those convicted of sexual assaults to register their name and provide other information with the police. All of these laws were products of deliberative attempts by concerned parents to influence policy regarding sex offenders. To equate these laws with expressions of moral panic is to be Neronian.

At the national level, Congress, in passing the Adam Walsh Act, was not only influenced by John Walsh's advocacy on behalf of his son but was particularly influenced by Joseph Duncan's abduction and murder of the Groen family. Duncan was a sex offender in three states (Miner 2011). As the third circuit court of appeals has noted (E.B. v. Verniero 1997, 1081): "By May of 1996, forty-nine states had adopted sex offender registration laws and thirty-two states maintained some form of community notification program." Today, all fifty states and the federal government have sex offender registration laws. About thirty states have residency restrictions. Local governments also have residency restrictions, although they can be unconstitutional if state law preempts them (New York v. Diack 2015).

The Supreme Court has upheld challenges to postconviction civil commitment and to registration and notification laws at the state and federal levels. The Court, however, has not yet decided a residency restriction case, but it has refused to hold that there is a right to "intrastate" travel that would implicate so-called banishment statutes, i.e., laws that restrict how much distance must exist between where a person lives and a public school, playground, or daycare center. Federal courts have also refused to grant sex offenders the status of a "suspect class" or declare they constitute a "discrete and insular" minority, which would subject sex offender legislation to heightened scrutiny analysis (U.S. v. LeMay 2001, 1030; Doe v. Moore 2005, 1346; Weems v. Little Rock Police Department 2006, 1016; U.S. v. Carolene Products 1938; San Antonio Independent School District v. Rodriguez 1973).

The only notable victory for the critics of sex offender legislation in the Supreme Court is *Packingham v. North Carolina* (2017). *Packingham* is a First Amendment case involving a North Carolina law that restricted sex offenders from accessing social media websites, out of concern, as Congress noted in the Adam Walsh Act, that the "vast majority of child pornography prosecutions involve images contained on computer hard drives, computer disks, and related media" (Congress 2006, sec. 501 (2)(A); Tatelman 2014, 431). I discuss this case in chapter 1. Briefly, the Court held that the law was so broad that it not only banned offenders from using Facebook.com but that it could extend to Amazon.com, the washingtonpost.com, and webmd.com, because each site allows for comments, which could lead to interactions with others. *Packingham* is a sex offender case in name only. But critics of sex offender laws celebrate it as a victory of reason over emotion. *Packingham* embodies the kind of understanding of sex offender laws that I criticize, even though its lack of concern for the regulation of sex offender behavior says more about the Court's First Amendment jurisprudence than it does about the content of sex offender legislation.

Overview of the Book

In chapter 1, I introduce the reader to the three major themes of this book: deliberation, the defense of a limited role for the judiciary in sex offender legislation, and the social scientific critique of sex offender laws. Deliberation among legislators and judges requires an understanding of, and reflection upon, the constitutional design the law operates under. The social scientific critique, because it posits a universal and objective solution to a particular problem, is the enemy of deliberative politics and judicial restraint. In the first part of the chapter, I divide deliberativists into two camps, a theoretical group and an institutional group. Theoretical deliberativists stress the participatory aspects of democratic theory and emphasize equality, fairness, and dignity as sources of deliberation. The institutionalists stress the representative nature of our constitutional system, underscore the republican character of the American political system, and emphasize the deliberative aspects of legislation. In the second section, I make the case for judicial minimalism or deference. I borrow much from Cass Sunstein's book on judicial minimalism (1999), but I extend his arguments to the claims made by institutional deliberativists. To test my defense, I analyze the Supreme Court's decision in *Packingham v. North Carolina.* More than an exegesis of a case, I set out to explain the social scientific critique against sex offender legislation and make the case for judicial deference to state legislative attempts to regulate the postconviction status of sex offenders.

Chapter 2 introduces the theme of the social scientific critique of law, which threads its way throughout the book. Chapter 2 is an examination of the problems of law and psychology as they relate to sex offenders and civil commitment. I begin with *Foucha v. Louisiana,* a 1991 case about a man who, following his conviction for armed robbery, pleaded not guilty by reason of insanity. The trial judge found in Terry Foucha's favor and had him committed to a mental facility. After a couple of years, Foucha claimed he was free of his insanity, and the attending physicians mostly agreed. The Supreme Court held that a state may not detain in a mental facility someone found not guilty by reason of insanity if that person is no longer insane. The opinion contained language about the dangers of unlawful detentions, and it emboldened critics of postconviction civil commitment. I also discuss in this chapter the complex controversies over the meaning of mental illness, insanity, and public safety, and provide a historical overview of civil commitment cases.

I have two aims in chapter 3. One is to chart the movement of the equal protection clause from its limited understanding of equal application of the law to its more robust understanding as a substantive vehicle for the implementation of criminal protections in a series of postconviction civil commitment cases in the 1960s. The second focus is on the interplay that exists between the psychological and social sciences' understanding of risk and dangerousness and the law's understanding of public safety. My first aim involves a study of psychological disorders and their relation to legal concepts, such as equal protection and due process. My second aim requires an analysis of two cases (from the state and federal courts) that highlight the problem of what happens to legal analysis when it becomes too dependent upon psychological or social scientific concepts.

This is a deeply interdisciplinary chapter, as I show how much courts have come to rely upon psychological diagnoses to justify their decisions either to commit offenders or to release committees. The contest that exists between the law and psychology over the body of the prisoner/civil committee is not easily settled by resort to one discipline or the other. I argue that institutional considerations need to be taken into account because the psychological sciences rely on behavioral and neurological methods that are at odds with the deliberative intentions of legislators and the public.

Chapter 4 is an analysis of the first postconviction case the Supreme Court decided, and Kansas's attempt to rewrite the law to broaden protections for civil committees. In *Kansas v. Hendricks* (1997), Kansas moved to have Leroy Hendricks civilly committed to a mental facility following the completion of his criminal sentence for sexual assault. Hendricks sued, claiming the law violated double jeopardy, ex post facto, due process, and substantive due process. The Supreme Court upheld the Kansas statute in a 5–4 decision. In *Hendricks*, the Court muddled the problem of mental illness and deterrence, which they tried to resolve in *Kanas v. Crane* (2002). Justice Stephen Breyer's opinion in *Crane* was even less successful in its attempt to require the states to investigate the psychological state of the convicted offender than the *Hendricks* decision, and I examine this issue as well.

If the problem of sex offenders is a problem of neighborhood safety, why is Congress involved? Chapter 5 examines Congress's attempt to regulate sex offenders on a national scale, centered on the Supreme Court's decision in *U.S. v. Comstock* (2010), which upheld the Adam Walsh Act. Relying upon evidence that sex offenders travel the country and move away from the states in which their crimes were committed, Congress passed the Adam Walsh Protection and Safety Act (2006), named after a boy abducted by a convicted sex offender. The law separates offenders into tiers of dangerousness; requires registration of sex offenses; and creates a national sex offender registry. The law is not without its critics, from the left and the right, the former finding that civil commitment is a form of punishment, the latter holding that the federal government has no police power to commit civilly the mentally ill postconviction.[6] The Supreme Court upheld the act in a narrow victory. My overall idea in this chapter is to stress the importance of deliberation over the focus on rhetoric, narrative, and abstract questions of right and morality that encourage judicial interventions but that downplay and ultimately damage public participation in lawmaking. My in-depth analysis of congressional power is an attempt to show that sex offender legislation is not the product of moral panic but of deliberative interests seeking to influence public policy.

The purpose of chapter 6 is to examine residency restrictions through the lens of the social scientific critique of residency restrictions. Along with notification and registration laws, states have passed laws that restrict where convicted sex offenders can live and move about following their release from prison. These laws excite the most interest among social scientists because, it is argued, they are not only unconstitutional but create bad policy. In this chapter, I address the two most important conflicts facing judges over residency restrictions: one, the scientific uncertainty of the data about dangerousness and recidivism; and two, the democratic implications of laws that restrict where convicted sex offenders can live, which I view as legitimate expressions of the democratic character of local and state politics. I argue in this chapter for judicial deference or minimalism because judicial intervention in this area is fraught with enormous difficulties, not all of them juridical. I offer here a critique of the social scientific engagement in policy rooted in the democratic processes at work. The chapter engages in a full-scale examination of risk analysis, as well as of social scientific methods designed to make laws more rational and efficient.

If there is one question that plagues sex offender legislation it is whether it constitutes punishment and thus violates the Eighth Amendment. In chapter 7, I discuss the problem of residency restrictions as banishment and banishment as punishment. If residency restrictions do not formally constitute punishment, do they nevertheless resemble banishment or result in de facto banishment? First, I examine the varieties of theories of punishment that exist in the academic literature and then address the problems they pose for understanding the constitutionality of sex offender legislation. Second, I analyze the Supreme Court's understanding of punishment, focusing mostly on criminal justice cases, such as the "three-strikes" cases and conditions of confinement cases. My point is to define the aims and scope of what punishment is and is not and relate those aims to residency restrictions. Finally, I consider the claim that residency restrictions constitute actual banishment and thus violate the Eighth Amendment's prohibition against cruel and unusual punishment. What started out as an attempt at risk management in the public interest, akin to quarantine and curfew, is now considered an ancient and medieval practice unsuitable for a modern people. For this reason, I find the term banishment in the context of residency restrictions excessive and strained. This final chapter returns to the theme discussed in chapter 1, the important relationship that the Constitution created among democratic institutions setting policy, the deliberation of public policy by representatives, and the limited role that the social scientific critique of law and representative institutions should have.

NOTES

1. New Jersey, for example, requires fingerprints, the offender's vehicle and license plate numbers, as well as the "offender's name, Social Security number, age, physical description, sex, date of birth, address of legal or temporary residence, date and place of employment, date and place of each conviction, and a brief description of the crime or crimes for which registration is required." The attorney general can also request "criminal and correction records, nonprivileged personnel, treatment, and abuse registry records, and evidentiary genetic markers if available" (Doe v. Poritz 1995, 115).

2. These also vary by state. "At least thirty states" (Zandbergen, Levenson, and Hart 2010, 482) have residency restrictions that prevent convicted sex offenders from living within so many feet of a park or day-care center, but not all states prohibit convicted sex offenders from living next-door to their victims (CBS News 2017).

3. A term that refers to the moment when "societal values and interests" (Cohen 2011, 1) become threatened by perceived threats.

4. According to Tamara Rice Lave (2009, 572–73), "[s]eventeen states required that a person be convicted of some crime before he could be committed for treatment. Although some of the states required that the conviction be for a sex offense (Alabama, Colorado, Kansas, Massachusetts, New Jersey, Oregon, Pennsylvania, South Dakota, Tennessee, Utah, Virginia, Wyoming), others did not (California, Indiana, Ohio, Vermont, Wisconsin). Seven states required that the individual be charged with a crime (Florida, Illinois, Indiana, Iowa, Michigan, Missouri, and Washington). Of these, only Washington required that the charge be sex related. Four states and the District of Columbia did not require charges or a conviction;

instead, commitment could occur upon cause that the person was a sexual psychopath (District of Columbia, Minnesota, Massachusetts, New Hampshire, and Wisconsin)."

5. The definition of "residency" is unclear in some state statutes (Doe I v. Marshall 2019).

6. The word "police" in police power refers to the power of a state to maintain the people's health and safety through policies that promote peace. Police powers and the police function meet at the junction of a government's control over those who pose a threat or danger to public order or morals (The Federalist 2001, 102 [no. 17]).

REFERENCES

Banfield, Edward. 1980. "Policy Science as Metaphysical Madness." In *Bureaucrats, Policy Analysts, Statesmen: Who Leads?*, edited by Robert Goldwin, 1–19. Washington, DC: The AEI Press.

Beecher-Monas, Erica. 2003. "The Epistemology of Prediction: Future Dangerousness Testimony and Intellectual Due Process." *Washington & Lee Law Review* 60 (2): 353–416.

Berns, Walter. 1985. "The Constitution as Bill of Rights." In *How Does the Constitution Secure Rights?*, edited by Robert Goldwin and William Schambra, 49–73. Washington, DC: The AEI Press.

Bessette, Joseph. 1994. *The Mild Voice of Reason: Deliberative Democracy and American National Government.* Chicago: University of Chicago Press.

Bickel, Alexander. 1975. *The Morality of Consent.* New Haven: Yale University Press.

Bloom, Joseph. 2004. "Thirty-Five Years of Working with Civil Commitment Statutes." *Journal of the American Academy of Psychiatry and Law* 32 (4): 430–39.

CBS News. 2017. "Sex Offenders Can Live Next Door to Victims in 45 States because of Loophole." https://www.cbsnews.com/news/sex-offenders-live-next-to-victims-state-law-loophole

Cohen, Stanley. 2011. *Folk Devils and Moral Panics: The Creation of the Mods and the Rockers.* London: Routledge.

Diagnostic and Statistical Manual. 2000. 4th ed. Washington, DC: American Psychiatric Association.

Downs, Donald. 2005. *Restoring Free Speech and Liberty on Campus.* Cambridge: Cambridge University Press.

Fabian, John. 2003. "Kansas v. Hendricks and Beyond: 'Mental Abnormality,' 'Volition,' Dangerousness,' and the Debate between Community Safety and Civil Liberty." *University of West Los Angeles Law Review* 35 (4): 389–439.

The Federalist. 2001. Edited by Robert Scigliano. New York: Modern American Library.

Gladwell, Malcolm. 1993. "A Small Town Lives in Dread that Freed Rapist 'Could Snap' Again." *Washington Post.* https://www.washingtonpost.com/archive/politics/1993/02/07/a-small-town-lives-in-dread-that-freed-rapist-could-snap-again/fcbba049-1e60-4db8-9645-8d91aad73861/?utm_term=.8df307f4455d

Kirwin, John. 2003. "One Arrow in the Quiver—Using Civil Commitment as One Component of a State's Response to Sexual Violence." *William Mitchell Law Review* 29 (4): 1135–1220.

Lave, Tamara Rice. 2009. "Only Yesterday: The Rise and Fall of Twentieth Century Sexual Psychopath Laws." *Louisiana Law Review* 69 (3): 549–92.

Lave, Tamara Rice. 2011. "Throwing Away the Key: Has the Adam Walsh Act Lowered the Threshold for Sexually Violent Predator Commitments Too Far." *University of Pennsylvania Journal of Constitutional Law* 14 (2): 391–430.

Lerner, Ralph. 1987. *The Thinking Revolutionary: Principle and Practice in the New Republic.* Ithaca: Cornell University Press.

McPherson, Lori. 2016. "The Sex Offender Registration and Notification Act (SORNA) at 10 Years: History, Implementation, and the Future." *Drake Law Review* 64 (3): 741–96.

Miner, Matthew. 2011. "The Adam Walsh Act's Sex Offender Registration and Notification Requirements and the Commerce Clause: A Defense of Congress's Power to Check the Interstate Movement of Unregistered Sex Offenders." *Villanova Law Review* 56 (1): 51–95.

Pearce, Marc. 2007. "Civilly Committing Criminals: An Analysis of the Expressive Function of Nebraska's Dangerous Sex Offender Commitment Procedure." *Nebraska Law Review* 85 (3): 575–642.

Rosenberg, Gerald. 1991. *The Hollow Hope: Can Courts Bring About Social Change?* Chicago: University of Chicago Press.

Schulhofer, Stephen. 1996. "Two Systems of Social Protection: Comments on the Civil-Criminal Distinction, with Particular Reference to Sexually Violent Predator Laws." *Journal of Contemporary Legal Issues* 7 (1): 69–96.

Storing, Herbert. 1995. "Interest Groups and the Public Interest." In *Toward a More Perfect Union: Writings of Herbert J. Storing*, edited by Joseph Bessette, 259–68. Washington, DC: The AEI Press.

Sunstein, Cass. 1999. *One Case at a Time: Judicial Minimalism on the Supreme Court.* Cambridge, MA: Harvard University Press.

Tatelman, Laura. 2014. "Give Me Internet or Give Me Death: Analyzing the Constitutionality of Internet Restrictions as a Condition of Supervised Release for Child Pornography Offenders." *Cardozo Journal of Law & Gender* 20 (2): 431–57.

U.S. Congress. 2006. The Adam Walsh Child Protection and Safety Act. U.S.C. 42 secs. 16911 et seq.

Weiner, Greg. 2012. *Madison's Metronome: The Constitution, Majority Rule, and the Tempo of American Politics.* Lawrence: University Press of Kansas.
Weiner, Greg. 2019. *The Political Constitution: The Case against Judicial Supremacy.* Lawrence: University Press of Kansas.
Wind, Timothy. 2003. "The Quandary of Megan's Law: When the Child Sex Offender Is a Child" *John Marshall Law Review* 37 (1): 73–124.
Zandbergen, Paul, Jill Levenson, and Timothy Hart. 2010. "Residential Proximity to Schools and Daycares: An Empirical Analysis of Sex Offense Recidivism." *Criminal Justice and Behavior* 37: 482–502.

CASES

Barefoot v. Estelle, 463 U.S. 880 (1983).
Connecticut Indemnity Company v. Superior Court, 23 Cal.4th 807 (2000).
Doe v. Lee, 132 F.Supp.2d 57 (2001).
Doe v. Moore, 410 F.3d 1337 (2005).
Doe v. Otte, 248 F.3d 832 (2001).
Doe v. Pataki, 919 F.Supp. 691 (1996).
Doe v. Poritz, 142 N.J. 1 (1995).
Doe I v. Marshall, 2019 WL 539055 (2019) (slip opinion).
E.B. v. Verniero, 119 F.3d 1077 (1997).
In re Commitment of M.G., 331 N.J.Super. 365 (2000).
In re C.P., 131 Ohio St.3d 513 (2012).
In re Young, 122 Wash.2d 1 (1993).
Kansas v. Crane, 534 U.S. 407 (2002).
Kansas v. Hendricks, 521 U.S.346 (1997).
Millard v. Harris, 406 F.2d 964 (1968).
New York v. Diack, 24 N.Y.3d 674 (2015).
O'Connor v. Donaldson, 422 U.S. 563 (1975).
Packingham v. North Carolina, 137 S.Ct. 1730 (2017).
Park v. Georgia, WL 1006323 (2019).
Piasecki v. Court of Common Pleas, Bucks County, 917 F.3d 161 (2019).
Project Release v. Prevost, 722 F.2d 960 (1983).
Roe v. Office of Adult Probation, 938 F.Supp. 1080 (1996).
Romer v. Evans, 1995 WL 17008425 (U.S.) (Appellate Brief).
San Antonio Independent School District v. Rodriguez, 411 U.S. 1 (1973).
Smith v. Doe, 538 U.S. 84 (2002).

Timms v. Johns, 700 F.Supp.2d 764 (2010).
U.S. v. Carolene Products Company, 304 *U.S.* 144 (1938).
U.S. v. Comstock, 560 U.S. 126 (2010).
U.S. v. LeMay, 260 F.3d 1018 (2001).
Weems v. Little Rock Police Department, 453 F.3d 1010 (2006).

CHAPTER 1

Sex Offender Legislation and Judicial Minimalism

In this chapter, I offer an interpretation of sex offender laws from a jurisprudential and institutional perspective. Because reconciling competing interests is a legislative task, I take an institutional approach to sex offender legislation, which means I accord primacy to the elected branches of government over the judiciary and reject the application of social scientific evidence to politics.[1] The "proper forum for mediating a clash of feelings and rendering a prophetic judgment is the body chosen for those purposes by the people" (A.F.L. v. American Sash and Door Company 1949, 557).

Mine is not a legal, exegetical perspective, culling opinions from case law and thereby vindicating judicial supremacy. By a jurisprudential perspective, I mean I regard our constitutional system to be "composed not of legal rules but of political judgments" (Weiner 2019, 9). If constitutionalism is to maintain its meaning as something more than the application of law—as governance—then political judgments about the content of laws cannot easily be dismissed as the dead hand of the past. To preserve the role of public opinion and of institutions that shape public opinion, I favor judicial opinions limited by concerns found within our nation's history, legal traditions, and practices. My view contrasts with those who favor letting judges decide cases based upon "evolving conceptions of decency," the famous dicta from *Trop v. Dulles* (1958, 101), which granted the Supreme Court the power to take up "the cause of humanity, a cause unlimited by partial and parochial divisions" (Faulkner 1989, 93). My view also contrasts with those who ask judges to defer to social scientific studies that are, allegedly, free of normative commitments, but which seek to demonstrate the biases and harmful effects sex offender laws presumably have on individuals or a class. The problem with this approach, it seems to me, is that the Constitution does not invest judges with heightened insight into the nature of justice (or scientific studies) while denying that insight to legislators. As Justice Felix Frankfurter once noted, "Holding democracy in judicial tutelage is not the promising way to foster disciplined responsibility in a people" (1955, 229; U.S. v. Lovett 1946, 319). Judicial deference to legislative aims sets a tone about the limits of the judiciary to rectify society's ills. Judicial deference stresses the importance of elective deliberation and public consent as the vehicles for governance over a large and diverse nation; it also creates a need for the demonstration of personal responsibility among elected officials that can pervade civil society (Glendon 1991).

Our peculiar constitutional system, call it democratic republicanism based on a separation of powers scheme and federalism, places burdens on legislators to deliberate well, and on citizens, who need to participate in the formation of "public values," contribute to "the direction of public policy," and choose "the officials who manage public affairs" (Whittington 2018, 18; Bessette 1994, 13). I am arguing for the recognition of the need and necessity of judicial limits in a federal and separation of powers scheme of governance, particularly in instances where the science that influences policy is not settled or contradictory. The focus on fundamental rights (in the case of sex offenders, privacy and travel) leads to outcomes that require more of judges and less of legislators than is healthy for our democratic republic. The autonomy of the person and individual dignity, while important concepts in the maintenance of democratic ideals, do not fully comprehend the requirements of civic life. Indeed, they suggest an emphasis on private concerns: dignity is always individual, never national, and autonomy, by definition, is about one's self. As Alexander Hamilton wrote in *The Federalist*, it is peculiarly our fate, as Americans, to deliberate about public things, most especially about the form of government that best promotes "reflection and choice" (2001, 3 [no. 1]) regarding the content of our laws. It is our obligation as citizens to discuss the "*merits* of the competing policy alternatives . . . which we, as a self-governing people, are obliged to choose" (Kendall 1971, 336; italics in original).

It is in legislatures where real deliberation about policy outcomes occur. Legislators are "best adapted to deliberation and wisdom," *The Federalist* says, not judges, the people as a whole, or subgroups (2001, 449 [no. 70]). As Greg

Weiner (2012, 3) has made clear, Madison's notion of majority rule, which I follow, depends upon time, ensuring that when "passion" subsides, "transient appetites" yield "to long-term interests." Majorities "seasoned with time," are "'cool,' 'deliberate,' 'settled,' and focused on 'permanent' needs rather than immediate desires" (2012, 3).

Legal realism, the interdisciplinary movement known as "Law and" (Leff 1978; Lavi 2011), and the critical legal studies movement all downplay the role of law and legislation as an educator of societal norms, as a defender of constitutional and institutional principles and traditions, and as a reflection of the preferences of democratic majorities. These movements reject what Alexander Bickel called the Constitution of "structure and process." Bickel's structure and process view favors the electoral process, deliberation among representatives, and the separation of powers as the generators of part of the Constitution's meaning. He rejects "metaphysical privileges and immunities" found in "fashionable notions of progress" (1975, 29, 27). Bickel's view presupposes the right of majorities to govern—shaped by the wisdom of time and through representation. It is a view that regards judicial review—and a reliance on social science data—apprehensively. By contrast, critics of sex offender legislation celebrate what Bickel called the Constitution of "open texture" (1975, 29), which stresses moral rights encased in the Bill of Rights and the Fourteenth Amendment, filtered through John Rawls's notion of justice as fairness, and elements of critical legal theory that emphasize law's indeterminacy. The critics of sex offender legislation borrow from these (disparate) traditions and argue for the superiority of the social sciences in determining law's path toward progress and efficiency and away from the impositions of democratic deliberation and majority rule. As Timothy Fortney et al. write: "Public policies informed by scientific evidence are more likely to be effective in achieving goals of community protection" (2007, 2).

The essence of legislation is not wisdom but constitutionality. I do not say that all laws are good and wise that are democratically derived. There is "nothing in human nature," Joseph Bessette (1994, 246) has written, "or in how democratic deliberation is structured that can guarantee the wisdom of popular deliberations." The conclusion is fourfold: (1) there are limits to what democratic political systems can accomplish; (2) we have to trust government to exercise its powers wisely and with regard to constitutional limits, otherwise democracy and republicanism have no meaning; (3) elections, campaigns, and interest groups are the means by which the people show their approval and disapproval of laws; and (4) we have to encourage "statesmanship of the highest order" (Bessette 1994, 246) among elected representatives and the less-democratic branches. A republic based on interests uninformed by principles is not what the founders created. From the standpoint of democratic theory, it is better for representatives (and judges) to acknowledge the representative nature of our laws as the first order of politics and law. Opinions long held and expressed, however faulty from a moral point of view, have the virtue of being authentic expressions of democratic life in American communities.

Throughout this book, I argue for judicial restraint and for judicial deference to sex offender legislation. In this chapter, I argue for judicial minimalism in cases involving sex offending. The fact that sex offender laws (all laws, really) are the result of "the bumbling, compromising efforts of legislatures and political parties" (Elliott 1974, viii) does not translate into a mandate to replace legislators with judges, or the Constitution, the states, and political parties with empirical findings about equality, or to make laws informed by Rawlsian principles of fairness. If judges understand the law as the product of representative majorities operating under the constraints (and the possibilities) created by the Constitution, then the law works moderately and modestly, as a set of rules democratically derived. So I hold sex offender laws to be constitutional not because I necessarily agree with them as policy, but because they were legitimately passed by legislatures, and insofar as they conform to the requirements of due process, the equal protection of the laws, and our national traditions (Thayer 1893; Washington v. Glucksberg 1997). With Felix Frankfurter, whose judicial opinions, Gary Jacobsohn has written, "were intended to imbue the habits and sentiments of the people with a reverence and awe of the law and the judicial process" (1977, 151), I argue that the justices of the Supreme Court must not exercise their "judicial power unduly," confusing their power with "legislators." It is not the justices' job to hold "with too tight a rein the organs of popular government" (Mason 1956, 615). It is with this understanding of the limits of the judiciary that I offer this work on sex offender legislation.

After examining the important legal and theoretical themes in sex offender laws, principally deliberative democracy, I then discuss *Packingham v. North Carolina*, a case about the regulation of sex offenders' Internet use. *Packingham* highlights the disjunction between North Carolina's concern for safety and social scientists' emphasis on measurement and prediction as a way to produce justice. *Packingham* allows me to lay out my view of the pros and cons of sex offender laws, making special reference to Cass Sunstein's ideas on judicial minimalism. Sunstein offers a way to limit the powers of the judiciary while simultaneously defending individual rights and upholding our republican political structure. I have too many differences with Sunstein to call myself an adherent to his views, but I support the broad outline Sunstein sets forth.

Constitutional Limits and Theoretical Themes

A jurisprudential and institutional view of the law of sex offenders requires me to reject a key idea put forth by its critics: that the rights involved in sex offender laws are fundamental and beyond the reach of the political process (Dworkin 1978, 271). When rights are regarded as "immutable norms" (Gould 2005, 47) that cannot be reached by courts or legislatures, and majorities are regarded as inherently tyrannical, the democratic elements that support the institutionalization of rights are diminished; immoderation appears normal.

Critics of sex offender laws argue that there is a fundamental right to freedom from bodily restraint; to travel throughout neighborhoods, cities, and across the United States; and to live where one wants and to enter public spaces, even if children congregate there. The courts have given this view some victories, but the logic of the rulings present problems for democratic governance. By contrast, I favor an approach to rights that protects the deliberative intentions of legislators, a view that acknowledges that "state legislatures have constitutional authority to experiment with new techniques; [and that] they are entitled to their own standard of the public welfare." It is not the judiciary's proper function to "sit as a super-legislature to weigh the wisdom of legislation nor to decide whether the policy which it expresses offends the public welfare" (Day-Brite Lighting, Inc. v. Missouri 1952, 423). A bicameral deliberative system of lawmaking has no need of a "third legislative chamber" (Hand 1958, 42) that rules in the name of humanity, progress, or social science. Judicial review takes place within our tripartite system of government, and so courts are not in a position to claim the lexical priority of individual liberty as a precondition for justice (Rawls 1971, 4, 42–43, sec. 32; 1993, 358–63). The problem with isolating fundamental rights from deliberative concerns about public safety or the common good is that this arrangement assumes a hierarchy of rights that, with the exception of speech, has no basis in constitutional law or practice (Kovacs v. Cooper 1949, 89–97). It is worth recalling that the preamble to the Constitution requires of the people the same commitment to securing domestic tranquility as it does to justice.

The purpose of placing rights protections in legislatures that deliberate over time is to "enable reason to prevail over an impulsive will" (Weiner 2012, 103–4). For the founders, the "the cool and deliberate sense of the community" (The Federalist 2001, 403 [no. 63]) is reached not through a preordained or prefabricated "consensus" about abstract forms of liberty that imposes itself upon a newly unveiled society, but through a combination of statesmanship, "the functioning of a large, differentiated commercial society" (Storing 1995, 120), and an elaborate scheme of government designed to check, balance, inhibit, and produce consensus, however temporary. This is meant neither as an expression of the fullness of constitutional law nor as a defense of classical pluralism.[2] In our constitutional system, deliberation occurs within and across the political system, at the local, state, and national levels. The majorities created at these levels differ from each other, which was the founders' intention. Deliberation, in this view, is not the preserve of "the people" acting on their own behalf, because the Constitution excludes them from directly making laws (The Federalist 2001, 407 [no. 63]). The Constitution creates "constitutional distance between the government and the citizenry" (Gregg 1997, 60) to encourage deliberation, not thwart it. The purpose of representation is the refinement and enlargement of "the public views" by those "whose wisdom may best discern the true interest of their country" (The Federalist 2001, 59 [no. 10]). The people's will finds its expression through the separation of powers.[3]

The purpose of majorities is to govern, a fact we lose sight of when we focus on autonomy, dignity, and fairness as the elements that constitute a good society. A focus on fundamental rights, derived from authenticity or dignity, is precisely the kind of claim the framers feared from a certain kind of degenerate democracy. They warned against the creation of "a will in the community independent of the majority" (The Federalist 2001, 335 [no. 51]). What the framers wanted was an active and diverse citizenry—a "multiplicity of interests" (The Federalist 2001, 334 [no. 51]) spread across the nation—who elect representatives who then temper the passions of a majority possibly bent on oppression. As Robert Martin (2010, 209) has written, for James Madison "the solution to majority tyranny" lies in "reflective, deliberate and empowered public opinion." Sex offender laws are clear expressions of this Madisonian focus; it is the ground upon which the consent of the governed, the protection of rights, and public security lives.

Considerations on Deliberation and Sex Offender Legislation

According to James Bohman and William Rehg,

> *deliberative democracy* refers to the idea that legitimate lawmaking issues from the public deliberation of citizens. As a normative account of legitimacy, deliberative democracy evokes ideals of rational legislation, participatory politics, and civic self-governance. In short, it presents an ideal of political autonomy based on the practical reasoning of citizens (1997, ix; italics in original).

There are numerous and divergent strands of thought that constitute the field known as deliberation (Gutmann and Thompson 1996; 2004; Fishkin and Laslett, eds. 2003; Copp, Hampton, and Roemer, eds. 1993; Benhabib 1996; Bohman 1996; Parkinson and Mansbridge, eds. 2012). Deliberative democratic theorists are a disparate group of political and legal theorists. Some focus on social and moral problems, such as abortion and welfare, and rely upon the Kantian-infused ideas of autonomy and dignity to critique social policy and constitutional law; others more explicitly investigate political or procedural issues, such as elections. Much of the literature against sex offender laws and regulations is dependent upon this deliberativist critique, which I call the theoretical deliberativist critique (Barker 2006; Marteache 2012). Theoretical deliberativists support a set of key ideas about democracy, namely participation, consensus, mutual respect, and an openness to disagreement and difference. I contrast it with the institutional deliberativist critique. These are not mutually exclusive views. The theoretical position is not purely abstract and the institutional approach is not hostile to theoretical concerns (Ferejohn 2000). Nevertheless, there are substantive differences. I begin with the institutional approach.

The institutional approach takes its bearing from the Constitution's design, the founding documents, and the role of elections and elected representatives in articulating its meaning. Theoretical deliberativists negatively characterize this view as aggregative, adversarial, and interest-based; they call their view "communicative" (Young 1996, 120, 125; Dryzek 1990), "discursive," and "unitary" (Mansbridge 1980; Chambers 2012). We can agree that these descriptions touch upon certain truths about each group without passing judgment on the merits of these terms. For institutionalists, the Constitution creates a democratic and republican form of government and reconciles "the advantages of democracy with the sobering qualities of republicanism" (Diamond 1981, 8; Epstein 1984, chap. 3). This means that the institutionalists understand deliberation as the primary responsibility of legislators, whom Joseph Bessette calls "surrogate deliberators for their constituents" (1994, 218). Institutionalists acknowledge the "spirit" and "form" of our "popular government" but seek to rescue popular government from the "opprobrium under which it has so long labored" (The Federalist 2001, 57 [no. 10]). This view requires majorities to rule because it acknowledges the difficulty, if not impossibility, of unanimity, as well as the danger of minority rule.

A fair reading of our complex political system suggests that deliberation is not the end of government; it is an effect of the separation of powers. The Constitution does not exclude representatives from deliberating among themselves and with the executive department over the content of laws. The Constitution allows for decisions arrived through nondeliberative means (Bailey 2002). Deliberation extends to the public as well. As one federal court judge wrote, notification and registration requirements "contemplate[] public involvement in the state's police function; the public becomes an agent of law enforcement to the extent that heightened awareness will help prevent crime" (Artway v. Attorney General of New Jersey 1995, 690). For this reason, policymaking, properly understood, is the outcome of the Constitution's institutional design and not, as theoretical deliberativists argue, dependent upon "moral discussion in the political process" (Gutmann and Thompson 1996, 223).

Jeffrey Tulis clarifies the distinction between the two deliberative camps when he speaks of "institutionally induced deliberation," by which he means deliberation that occurs between or among national institutions. For Tulis, when deliberation occurs between or among institutions, it produces moderate forms of governance and moderate policies, because each branch's advocacy for a policy is "tethered to interest and institutional position." As each branch of government articulates an interest about a "democratically relevant concern[]," the separation of powers, as a political structure that influences both institutional and individual behavior, attempts to resolve "tensions by representing them in and among competing institutions" (Tulis 2003, 209). Sex offender legislation is a product of this system. It is an engagement in dialogue among competing institutional and noninstitutional interests. It begins at the local level, as a response to a crime or series of crimes, spreads across the country, where different local concerns alter the laws to fit their concerns, and circles back as national legislation. For this reason, I extend Tulis's idea of institutionally induced deliberation to include state legislatures and courts, who act in constitutional dialogue with the federal branches of government.[4]

The institutional view of deliberation has the virtue of connecting policies with American political thought in its principles and its practices as they have developed over time. By contrast, the intellectual background of the theoretical deliberativists is decidedly idealist and dependent upon a number of political theorists not specifically connected to American political thought, from the egalitarian musings of Jean-Jacques Rousseau to the liberal theories of John Stuart Mill, and from the discursive ideas of Jürgen Habermas to the moral philosophy of John Rawls. The takeaway from these thinkers is that decisions must not only be "broadly fair and democratic" (Bohman and Rehg 1997, xviii), they must be the outcome of deliberation "among equals" (Cohen 1997, 73).

Theoretical deliberativists stress substantively fair outcomes and dismiss the idea of foundational ideas or principles guiding deliberative politics. This requires setting aside the "animating principles and attitudes" (Ceaser 1986, 169) that inform our institutions and politics in favor of theoretical "concepts such as equality, fairness, liberty, and reciprocity" (Rosenblum 2006, 133). For institutional, spatial, and temporal reasons, James Madison thought that the "public voice" of "the representatives of the people will be more consonant to the public good than if pronounced by the people themselves" (The Federalist 2001, 59 [no. 10]). Theoretical deliberativists reject the complexity of the Madisonian system and its underlying theoretical premises. They conceive "of democracy as a process that creates a public, citizens coming together to talk about collective problems, goals, ideals, and actions" (Young 1996, 121). Benjamin Barber promotes his version of deliberative democracy as strong democracy, first by rejecting any metaphysical language concerning a pre-political beginning in the state of nature, then by replacing majority rule and representative institutions with new modes and orders, "rich in affect and commonality," and finally by calling for "public action based on community consent" (Barber 1984, 158, 161, 167). John Dryzek (1990, 43) emphasizes that citizens should come together as individuals and not as representatives of interests.

Most theoretical deliberativists are concerned about institutional considerations of justice, such as civic participation, political parties, and the distribution of goods and services. Institutions as presently constructed, in this view, are of limited value. Gutmann and Thompson (1996, 347), for example, write that "proceduralism" and "constitutionalism" are "obstacles" that ought to be overcome, so that "democracy" can be "made safe for deliberation." Dryzek (1990,

77) speaks of a "world beyond capitalism, interest group politics, and bureaucracy." These theorists understand political concerns to be guided "explicitly" by "moral principles" which are "independent of the preferences of citizens" (Gutmann and Thompson 2004, 18–19). Gutmann and Thompson argue that "deliberative accountability extends beyond electoral constituents" (1996, 227). Rejecting the separation of powers and other institutional constraints, theoretical deliberativists stress "equality, fairness, liberty, and reciprocity"—along with respect, publicity, and accountability (Rosenblum 2006, 133–34; Gutmann and Thompson 1996, chap 2; Gutmann and Thompson 2004, 133)—as the cornerstones of a just democracy.

An important theme that theoretical deliberativists focus on that institutionalists do not is domination and its relationship to inclusion. This is an important undercurrent in the criticisms of sex offender laws. Theoretical deliberativists favor outcomes derived not from the governing power of majority rule but from citizens coming together "regardless of social position or power" (Young 1996, 122). Theoretical deliberativists assert that institutions corrupt the innate equality of individuals because oppressive social forces psychologically operate upon individuals without their knowledge. Here is the greatest divide between the theorists and the institutionalists. I will isolate three implications of this divergence for sex offender legislation.

First, the theoretical deliberativists presuppose the possibility of greater popular participation in the political process without coming to terms with the historical problem of democracy and our nation's size and extent. The problems they see with the institutional view of politics are not, for them, "sown in the nature of man" (The Federalist 2001, 55 [no. 10]), and thus in accord with the principles of limited government, but the products of a wrong-turn in historical consciousness that greater participation by equals can correct. Second, theoretical deliberativists assume the possibility of a national or moral consensus, which acts on the people like a general will. Rather than seeing self-interest become enlightened by elected representatives deliberating about the public good (The Federalist 2001, no. 57), they attribute self-interest to a set of social and discursive forces operating within Western political practices that perpetuate "background inequalities" (Gutmann and Thompson 1996, 133) and limit democratic practices. For this reason, theoretical deliberativists focus on "micro-deliberative forums" as the beginning point in the creation of a truly deliberative democracy (Bohman 2012, 75). While the focus on local governance is admirable, theoretical deliberativists fail to acknowledge that it is the formation of a particular kind of government, a popular yet republican government, that is "essential to the happiness of the people of America" (The Federalist 2001, 293 [no. 45]). Third, theoretical deliberativists assume that our national institutions, and presumably the population as a whole, can be made more democratic by being more deliberative, but they make no concession to local governments as currently constituted, where democracy, minority rights, and majority rule live in constant contestation.

The two approaches also differ at the theoretical level, which affects their different understandings of institutions. The theoretical approach, as articulated by Gutmann and Thompson, regards all principles as "provisional" (2004, 116). This means that not only are principles always open to revision but there can be no foundational understanding of politics, as all principles are relative. Institutions, in this view, can only coerce; they cannot teach, shape, or inform public opinion. By stark contrast, the institutional approach explicitly has a "foundational" approach to politics, as it begins not with a theoretical construct that makes the lived experiences of the self the authentic expression of the aims and scope of democracy, but with "a foundational concept [that] is authoritative for the political community" because it was created within the political community. Foundational concepts are not mere abstractions that live on as myth. They need "to meet certain political requirements" of a polity that are subject to change (Ceaser 2006, 185, 88). The connection our national institutions have to local communities and individuals within communities has the virtue of not simply ratifying individual or group preferences but of moderating opinion, a mechanism that has no counterpart among theoretical deliberativists.

Institutional democratic theorists differ from their theoretical counterparts by beginning their inquiry with what is known or established, supported by, but not wholly dependent upon, public opinion. Institutional deliberativists are "guided by a body of thought—an understanding of individual rights, of the duties of citizenship, and of the means and ends of self-government—that is external to itself and that is the basis, at least occasionally, of popular statesmanship of the highest order" (Bessette 1994, 246). Rather than looking to create a homogeneous majority that promotes consensus, institutionalists argue that there is a "continuing dialectical relationship" (Kendall 1971, 220) between representatives and their constituents that is built into the constitutional design, which produces different majorities throughout the nation and among the institutions of government. The complexity of the institutional design teaches us to "accept and live with the fact of disunity"[5] (Kendall 1971, 125). The saving grace of this potential deadlock of democracy is neither judicial intervention to protect those marginalized by the political process nor a resort to "an overlapping consensus," as Rawls would have it, but the constitutional design itself and the majority-rule principle (i.e., elections), constrained by foundational principles and other institutional configurations. For this reason, the institutionalists are much more willing to defer to local majorities, in the name of democracy, than the theoretical deliberativists are. In Publius's view, "the genius of the American constitutional scheme was that the popular will would prevail on those issues on which it could make itself felt throughout the deliberative process" (Bolce, DeMaio, and Muzzio 1987, 567).

There are, in the critique against the utilitarian tendencies of sex offender legislation, theoretical deliberative sensibilities. Sex offender laws challenge basic notions of democratic theory (e.g., autonomy and dignity) because, it is said, they treat offenders as a means to a public safety end. On this view, the postconviction civil commitment of sex offenders (unlike treatment, presumably) has a sinister rhetorical purpose—it sends a message not just to offenders but to those who want to violate the law. Such configurations of laws, it is said, are denials of democratic, deliberative principles. Sex offender legislation, particularly residency and registration requirements, sweeps too broadly: they have little regard for individual differences, as they prevent convicted sex offenders from visiting parks and from picking up their children at school, even if such persons pose no risk to minors.

If residency and registration laws are examples of nondeliberative lawmaking, postconviction civil commitment is an example of the vengeful, rash, and nondeliberative instincts of voters. Vanessa Barker, in *The Politics of Imprisonment*, shares a conceptual framework with the theoretical deliberativists and attributes the punitive turn in the states to the institutional structure of state governments. She finds that states that promote participatory and deliberative forms of government, such as Washington, facilitate "networks of trust and reciprocity not only among social groups but between the state and civil society" (Barker 2006, 19). By contrast, the "populist mode of governance," typified by California's three-strikes law, which provides for twenty-five years to life for those convicted of a third felony, "creates a political context that encourages conflict rather than compromise" (Barker 2006, 15; 2009, chap 2).

Washington was the first state to require sex offender registration in the modern era (the law also included a postconviction civil commitment provision; Seling v. Young 2001). Washington did so in part because of Earl Shriner, who "had a 24-year history of killing, sexual assault, and kidnapping." Prior to his release from prison, in May of 1987,

> prison officials learned that he intended to torture children after he was released, and tried vigorously to detain him through the civil commitment laws covering mental illness. Unable to demonstrate the required "the recent overt act" to prove dangerousness, the state had no option but to release Shriner. Two years after his release, he raped and strangled a seven-year-old boy in Tacoma, Washington, severed his penis, and left him in the woods to die. (Lieb 1996, 1)

As I discuss in chapter 5, a popular uprising occurred in Washington that put enormous pressure on the governor and the state legislature to make it easier to confine sex offenders in psychiatric facilities postconviction. The movement for tougher laws spread across the country and finally to Congress. Barker writes that the deliberative process Washington enacted had a "cooling effect on crime victims' righteousness" (2009, 114). She attributes the moderate tone of the law to Washington's commitment to a legal regime of "parsimony" (2009, 7), which encourages finding the "least repressive sanctions possible," and contrasts that understanding of law and deliberation to California's passage of a three-strikes law, a clear example of retribution,[6] according to Barker.

There is a lot to admire in Barker's analysis of Washington's sex offender law. But the Washington Community Protection Act does not satisfy theoretical deliberative principles of justice (Morse 1996; Scheingold, Olson, and Pershing 1992; Bodine 1990; La Fond 1992). Postconviction civil commitment is an addition to a criminal sentence, not a replacement of it. This is controversial enough. Gary Gleb mentions two other problems with the law: the law requires proof of a "mental abnormality" or "personality disorder," terms with no meaning in the *Diagnostic and Statistical Manual* (*DSM*), but not of a mental disorder, a concept the *DSM* employs. In addition, the state "admits that no effective treatment exists for sexual predators" (Gleb 1991, 216), effectively incarcerating sex offenders indefinitely and twice for one crime.

Theoretical deliberativist critics argue that registration and civil commitment laws are examples of penal populism rather than the outcome of deliberation among equals seeking to foster equality. Penal populism is "the intentional attempt to exploit public anxiety about crime and public resentment toward offenders" (Roberts et al. 2002, 3). For example, elected representatives write psychiatric classifications of dangerousness that determine whether or not someone is suitable for civil commitment. These representatives, it is alleged, have their own narrow interests (reelection, for example), unlike trained medical practitioners, who presumably because they view sex offenders as ill, not criminals, are objective. Moreover, critics charge that these laws are criminal sanctions, masquerading as civil regulations, to avoid Eighth Amendment scrutiny.[7] Rather than deliberative expressions of the law's meaning, critics regard these laws as part of a structuralist mindset that seeks only to manage risk, social problems, and dangerous populations.

There is no doubt that the civil commitment of sex offenders, notification and registration laws, and residency restrictions impose heavy administrative, economic, and psychological burdens on convicted sex offenders, particularly minors who may have to stay on the registry for life (Human Rights Watch 2013), and upon those who are not dangerous to minors. These laws and regulations clearly interfere with personal liberty concerns, including domestic and international travel (Congress 2016). One cannot but feel sympathy for someone on a registry that anyone on the Internet can access. (Some states have laws against committing acts of vengeance against sex offenders.) However, by stressing the burdens these laws and regulations impose on offenders and their families, and by implying that heartfelt personal experiences are universal in their application of cruelty,[8] these stories, called narratives,[9] deflect thinking away from institutional and deliberative politics and toward judicial power, which is more centralized, elitist, and ultimately less deliberative and democratic than the view proposed here. The narrative view of law is monolithic and thin. Narratives focus on outcomes and ignore the personal and institutional compromises that go into framing legislation. Narratives are goal-oriented; they ignore important research that shows that parties, constituents' values, coalitions and interest groups, reelection concerns, federalism, gerrymandering, and money all provide reasons for the passage of legislation (Bishin and Smith 2013; Smith 2007; Fenno 1978; Mayhew 1974).

There are five kinds of critics of sex offender legislation and their ideas are deeply intertwined. First, there are those who favor narratives or discursive theories of justice. These critics tend to be sociologists, journalists, and philosophers concerned about social justice (Horowitz 2015; Nathan 2016; Rickard 2016).

The idea behind narratives is that a powerful story can cut through the formalities of law and the intricacies of institutional politics and reveal, on a personal level, how harmful these laws are. A narrative, Iris Marion Young writes, "reveals a source of values, culture, and meaning" (1996, 131). A narrative of a sex offender's time on the registry tells us more about the punitiveness of penal populism than any formal Eighth Amendment analysis can. Narratives are egalitarian and democratic. With narrative, no offender is better or worse than another offender—or the victim. But narratives cut both ways. Narratives have nothing to say about how or why democratic institutions mold and sanction behavior, and they fail to explain how and why institutions seek to deter bad behavior. Writing about "Brandon" (Human Rights Watch 2007, 5), who was put on the registry because, as a senior in high school, he had consensual sex with a fourteen-year-old girl, as a way to highlight the oppression inherent in having a registry, does not negate the importance of having registries for sex offenders. Indeed, it makes the case for it. For every Brandon there is an Earl Shriner, who cut off his victim's penis; for every fourteen-year-old girl who "consents," there is a Megan Kanka.[10]

A second type are libertarians. Libertarians hold that Congress's powers are strictly limited (U.S. v. Comstock 2010, 158–80; Morse 1982) and express concern that state sex offender laws trample on fundamental constitutional rights and liberties protected either by substantive due process or substantive equal protection. Libertarians are deeply concerned about postconviction civil commitments, as they veer toward the totalitarian instincts of the modern administrative state. A third view emanates from within the quantitative aspects of social science and finds support among sociologists, economists, and those who work in the mental health profession (Levenson 2004; Agan and Prescott 2014). These critics hold that policies should be informed by "evidence-based treatment," as it is "the most ethical approach" to legal policymaking (Fortney et al. 2007, 2; Mancini and Mears 2013). These critics stress the counterproductive aspects of sex offender legislation by relying on quantitative studies of danger and risk. They also emphasize the importance of judicial review but subordinate constitutional law to "empirical data to show that the laws have a punitive effect" (Moghaddam 2010, 237). And they dismiss public opinion as uninformed and unscientific (Anderson, Sample, and Cain 2015). A fourth type regards sex offender laws as symbolic, signifying nothing other than the appearance of being tough on crime (Pearce 2007, 619; Feeley and Simon, 1992; Edelman 1985; Lave and Zimring 2018). This "new order," Michael Campbell and Heather Schoenfeld write (2013, 1376, 1379), "is characterized by a set of ideas . . . that criminals are 'other' and not worthy of redemption, and that being labeled soft on crime is the ultimate political liability." A final type are the postmodernists in the legal profession and within the social sciences (Beckett and Herbert 2010; Feeley and Simon 1992; Simon 1998; Harcourt 2010; Garland 2001). These critics emphasize the socially constructed aspect of law. "In the social constructionist perspective," Ronald Weitzer has written (2007, 448), "social conditions become 'problems' only as a result of claims-making by interested parties, claims that may or may not reflect actual social arrangements. Claims about 'putative conditions' are more consequential than the conditions themselves."

This last critique raises serious concerns regarding the application of social science knowledge to policymaking. As there is no objective knowledge in this mode of thought, there can be no objective social problems. If all problems are relative and constructed only by interested actors, then it makes no sense to criticize the power "moral crusaders" or the general public have in shaping public policy. Yet this is what some non-postmodern critics of sex offender legislation and regulations do. They borrow from structuralist and social constructionist language the idea that there is a historical relationship between sex offender legislation and any governmental act that has imposed harsh regulations against "out" groups, regardless of the form of government, while maintaining a moral stance against such laws. In this structuralist view, notification laws cannot be the result of community interest in safety or a way to empower a community in the wake of a horrific crime. They must be the outcome of "neoliberal penality" and of a "vision of an ordered market delimited by the penal sanction" (Harcourt 2010, 77; McLeod 2014, 1581). Denying intentionality among legislators and citizens, these critics focus their attention on the effect big structures have on the psychic life of legislators and community activists. Thus they regard sex offender laws as part of the "punitive turn" in criminal justice—the idea that, during the 1970s, there was an application of political strategies that was only partly conscious to demonize and incarcerate the poor, racial minorities, and the underprivileged. While some critics of notification and registration laws go so far as to argue that these laws are the modern-day equivalent of the scarlet letter, an idea taken from Nathaniel Hawthorne's 1850 book, *The Scarlet Letter: A Romance*, others see notification laws as the equivalent of the Nazi requirement that Jews wear identifying armbands (Post 2016). Not to be outdone by symbols from the right, there are those who regard post-conviction civil confinement as akin to the Gulag archipelago (Erlinder 1993), a space where undesirables cannot be seen. The problem with this way of thinking about policy is that structuralist thought judges policy outcomes irrespective of the forms that constitute a regime. It flattens the historical (and moral) differences that clearly separate the insane imperatives of Nazism and communism from the democratic and deliberative processes of a liberal democracy (Brilliant 1989, 1370).

One example of this type of critique of knowledge is moral panics, which comes from "labeling theory" and is connected to structuralist thought. Stanley Cohen defines moral panics as the "set of ideas" each society has "about what causes deviation" and how "these conceptions shape what is done about the behaviour" (2011, 9; Jenkins 1998, 232). Moral panics are responses to changes in the way a society operates, usually involving the scapegoating of a particular group. Social scientists contend that sex offender legislation is classic moral panic. The traditional understanding of moral panics is that they ebb and flow. By the 1990s, as Keri Burchfield and her colleagues have noted (Burchfield, Sample, and Lytle 2014, 98), "rather than peaking and dissipating," the regulation of sex offenses "plateaued." Moral panics are now a critical part of the normal discourse about danger and a key idea among critics of sex offender legislation. Yet the logic of the critique turns on itself. If we are in a permanent state of moral panic, how do we discourse about moral panic in a discursive episteme of moral panic? Can we understand moral panic if all thought is irrational and unknowable because it is dependent upon moral panic?

Discourse is a popular concept in sex offending literature. It is more than just "issue framing." Issue framing is where legislators or lobbyists "spell out the essence of the problem, suggest how it should be thought about, and may go so far as to recommend what (if anything) should be done" (Filler 2001, 357). It assumes some degree of rationality and intentionality on the part of those doing the framing. Discourse, by contrast, "includes all the practices and meanings shaping a particular community of social actors" (Howarth 2000, 5). Discourse (not rational thought) frames the way humans speak about things, objects, and persons. At the same time, the things, objects, and persons of which we speak modify discourse. Mona Lynch argues (2002, 531) that "sex offender legislation" must "be understood in terms of the specific temporal, cultural, political, and moralistic settings in which they occur." But if ordinary people cannot understand a policy problem in ordinary, functional terms, then we teeter on the brink of nothingness: as we discourse through discourse, we conceptualize policymaking only as the result of irrational emotive concerns and sclerotic institutional designs. Among the discourse theorists and the theoretical deliberativists, notification and registration laws cannot be understood as legitimate deliberative responses to tragic events because they are linked with all prior events throughout history that have sought to control populations.

By stressing the discursive and noninstitutional factors that contribute to successful deliberation, the theoretical deliberativists fail to see the moderate influence that institutions and public opinion bestow upon democracies. What I find most troubling about the criticisms of sex offender legislation at the theoretical level is the denial of the common-sense observation that democratic politics is a continuing operation of process and engagement. When policy changes happen through the legislative process, their success ought not to be dismissed as a result of "profound transformation[s] in the nature of liberal governance," as Jonathan Simon writes (2000, 1113), just because the new policy may fit into a paradigm that regards all laws that restrict individual movements as rooted in the evils of Nazism and Puritanism. It is one thing to have a reasonable set of differences about policy goals and to expect that interest groups will form to influence legislation that other interest groups oppose. It is another to argue that sex offender laws are the result of "populist punitiveness" (Simon 1998, 455) or "punitive governance" (Lancaster 2011, 15), or the result of an "infantilized political community," committed only to extending the state's power over "those deemed 'monstrous'" (Simon 2000, 1137; 1998, 459), or the result of "law and order ideologues" (Scheingold, Olson, and Pershing 1994, 759). Such views are nothing more than a denial of the ability of representatives to reason about means and ends. The denial of intentionality and agency, key ideas in law, criminal justice, and political science, means that there can be no connection between individual responsibility and collective punishment, popular deliberation and legislative policymaking, the means to achieve accountability and the ends of safety and justice in democratic republics. At the end of this line of thought lies a Constitution devoid of meaning.

My own view of this matter—the view from being a citizen—is one of qualified support for these laws. I concede their need and note their connection to the crime victims' movement and expressive punishment theories (Cassell 2017; Adler 2000). They seem to bring a sense of peace and a feeling of safety to communities, ideas not to be dismissed if democratic theory were truly democratic. At the same time, I have no doubt that they are wrongly applied in some instances and that they sweep too broadly (Human Rights Watch 2013). This is particularly the case with minors on the registry. I agree with a leading critic of sex offender legislation, Eric Janus, who, with Wayne Logan, argues that "involuntary civil commitment . . . should be carefully policed by the courts" (Janus and Logan 2003, 370). Because postconviction civil commitment can last the offender's entire life, judicial scrutiny is required. Courts should be vigilant in ensuring that states are not simply locking up those with unorthodox views or behaviors. Other aspects of the civil regulation of sex offenders, residency restrictions, for example, which impose lesser burdens than lifetime commitment, need not be policed to the same extent.

Given my approach—this is not a work of policy but of constitutional and institutional analysis, though I concede there is some mixing—I am reluctant to advocate on behalf of specific legislation. But I find it necessary to say that sexually violent predator (SVP) laws are useful because (1) sentences for sex offenders are too short or ineffectual (Zgoba et al. 2008, 27); (2) there are weak informal social controls available to criminals, especially sex offenders, outside of prison (Kruttschnitt, Uggen, and Shelton 2000, 63; Tewksbury 2007; Petersilia 2003; Collateral Consequences Resource Center 2019), which increases the possibility of recidivism; (3) predicting recidivism and dangerousness is an inexact science and a thin reed upon which to overturn otherwise valid laws; and (4) there are constitutional limitations on states to regulate behavior postconviction (Peters-Baker 1998). In the absence of postconviction treatment, John M. Fabian argues that states should: (1) impose "harsher sentencing guidelines"; (2) use "consecutive criminal sentencing guidelines rather than concurrent sentencing guidelines" (this would increase time in detention); and (3) develop "comprehensive sex offender treatment programs" (2003, 391). Lifetime surveillance and supervision of some offenders is an option, though an expensive one (Wisconsin v. Muldrow 2018).

One possible alternative is to replace postconviction civil commitment with sentence enhancements for sex offending (Kirwin 2003, 1206). Iowa did this in 1996 (Peters-Baker 1998, 657–60; Iowa v. Oliver 2012; Kansas v. Allen 2006; 2007; Kansas v. Spinden 2002). Two risks, however, may not be worth the costs. There is the risk of the loss of treatment (Kingston 2016) and the loss of periodic review, which is required of all civil committees. Fabian writes that the legislative goal should be the elimination of "the need for the civil commitment of sex offenders" and the conservation of "state resources" (2003, 391), a view I do not disagree with but hope that treatment would not be abandoned. I would, however, stress the search for legal reform through legislatures not courts, in an effort to emphasize the deliberative aspects of policymaking. As Stephen McAllister has written (1997, 432), "the fixing of prison terms reflects a substantial penological judgment that is generally the province of legislatures."

An approach that favors legislatures over courts reinforces the core aims of our democratic polity. It situates the government's remedial powers in legislatures subject to election.

Judicial Minimalism

I would now like to examine how the ideas mentioned above look in practice. In this section, I analyze the Supreme Court's decision in *Packingham v. North Carolina*, a case that challenges the views I set forth in this chapter.

The idea that the judiciary should defer to the political branches is most closely associated with Felix Frankfurter on the Supreme Court and in the work of Alexander Bickel. For Bickel (1986, 16–17), "when the Supreme Court declares unconstitutional a legislative act or the action of an elected executive, it thwarts the will of representatives of the actual people of the here and now." For Frankfurter, "To fight out the wise use of legislative authority in the forum of public opinion and before legislative assemblies rather than to transfer such a contest to the judicial arena, serves to vindicate the self-confidence of a free people" (Minersville School District v. Gobitis 1940, 600).

For two important reasons, I think that courts should exercise restraint when considering sex offender legislation. One, the issues most central to sex offenders, that of mental illness and dangerousness, are elusive concepts, medically and legally, and too uncertain scientifically to lock-in legal doctrines about fundamental rights and dignity. Two, as Frankfurter noted, the Fourteenth Amendment neither enacts "Mr. Herbert Spencer's *Social Statics*" nor "does it enact the psychological dogmas of the Spencerian era." Frankfurter thought then, and I think it still applies, that the "Court is not ready . . . to pronounce on causative factors of mental disturbance and their relation to crime. Without formally professing to do so, it may actually do so by invalidating legislation dealing with these problems as too 'indefinite'" (Winters v. New York 1948, 676; Kansas v. Hendricks 1997, 359).

Unlike restricting the movement of sex offenders or requiring them to register with the police, both of which are connected to the states' police powers and are thus regarded as relatively uncontroversial and constitutional, *Packingham* involves the First Amendment. That amendment, lacking a due process clause, does not take a back seat to majority preferences (West Virginia v. Barnette 1943, 638). *Packingham*, however, is not the slam-dunk its proponents think it is, and I have no doubt that more cases like it will continue to burden the courts. With this caveat in mind, let us look at the case.

In 2005, North Carolina passed a law requiring the registration of sex offenders, noting that sex offenders "pose significant and unacceptable threats to the public safety and welfare of children" (North Carolina v. Packingham 2013, 294). In 2008, the North Carolina legislature passed, "as part of the Protect Children from Sexual Predators Act," a statute that "bans the use of commercial social networking Web sites by registered sex offenders" (North Carolina v. Packingham 2013, 294). According to the state's brief, the Internet allows predators "to gather intimate information about minors' social lives, families, hobbies, hangouts, and the like. They then used this information to target unwitting victims, either in person or online, in the guise of familiarity or shared interests" (Packingham v. North Carolina 2017a, 1). A police officer searching through Facebook noticed a picture of Lester Gerard Packingham, a registered sex offender, previously convicted at twenty-one years of age for having had sex with a thirteen-year-old female. Packingham had registered his Facebook page under a different name and posted a notice that a court had just dismissed a traffic ticket issued to him.[11] With some detective work, the police officer was able to connect Packingham's false page to his real one. Packingham was found guilty of "accessing a commercial social networking Web site" and sentenced to "six to eight months of imprisonment," which the court suspended. The court placed him on "supervised probation" (North Carolina v. Packingham 2015, 381–82), which did not contain a prohibition on Internet use.

Laws that regulate sex offenders' use of the Internet or social networking sites (SNS) apply different standards to those who have completed their sentences and are under no supervision and those who are on parole, probation, or some form of supervised release (U.S. v. Abregana 2008). Federal and state courts have discretion to impose restrictions on those subject to parole and probation, provided they are "reasonably related to the goal of deterrence, protection of the public, or rehabilitation of the offender, and 'involve no greater deprivation of liberty than is reasonably necessary for the purposes of supervised release'"[12] (U.S. v. Rearden 2003, 618). Moreover, courts are more willing to sustain "sweeping bans on Internet usage" in cases that not only involve convictions for possession of child pornography but also involve use of the Internet "to engage in direct exploitation of children" (Chan, McNiel, and Binder 2016, 369; J.B. v. New Jersey State Parole Board 2013; 2016). The North Carolina statute applied to sex offenders who have completed their terms and were not subject to parole or probationary regulations, which partly accounts for the Supreme Court's rejection of the statute.

Although the Supreme Court's decision was unanimous that the law was unconstitutional, there were disagreements about the power of the Internet (and not, interestingly, about the states' power to control the dangerousness of sex offenders). For Justice Anthony Kennedy, who wrote the majority opinion, the Internet is the "modern public square," offering the citizen a "powerful mechanism . . . to make his or her voice heard" (Packingham v. North Carolina 2017b, 1737). For Justice Samuel Alito, the Internet "provides previously unavailable ways of communicating with, stalking, and ultimately abusing children" (Packingham v. North Carolina 2017b, 1739–40).

North Carolina did not regard searching the Internet for illegal sexual purposes as a fundamental freedom. The legislature relied upon empirical data to support its regulatory power.

> The General Assembly recognizes that sex offenders often pose a high risk of engaging in sex offenses even after being released from incarceration or commitment and that protection of the public from sex offenders is of paramount governmental interest. (North Carolina v. Packingham 2013, 293–94)

Unfortunately, sex offending is not uncommon in the United States. In a 2013 report to Congress on sex offender legislation, the General Accounting Office noted that "about 1 in every 5 girls and 1 in every 7 to 10 boys are sexually abused by the time they reach adulthood, and about 1 in 6 adult women and 1 in 33 adult men experience an attempted or completed sexual assault" (2013, 1). Anthony Beech and his colleagues have shown that the Internet is not a neutral forum for speech. Sex offenders use the Internet "(1) to disseminate images for personal and/or commercial reasons; (2) to establish and engage in social networks with other individuals who have a sexual interest in children; and (3) to engage in inappropriate sexual communication with children and/or to locate children to abuse" (2008, 217). Cohen and Spidell (2016, 22), assessing a number of studies of online sex offenders, have noted that "many online child pornography offenders are involved in contact offending." Indeed, they note that among federal sex offenders "convicted of child pornography offenses, about a fourth of them had an official record of contact sexual offenses" (2016, 23). A 2013 PEW study of the Internet and teenagers found that "One in six online teens say they have been contacted online by someone they did not know in a way that made them feel scared or uncomfortable" (2013, 12).

There are numerous studies of the relationship between the Internet and sex offending that show: (1) that "arrests for Internet sex crimes have tripled in the United States"; (2) that "Internet sex offending is a new phenomenon that may not be influenced by the same factors as other sexual or violent crimes"; and (3) that "Internet offending outstrips law enforcement resources" (SMART). Prentky, Knight, and Lee, in a report written for the National Institute of Justice, found that "[s]exual offenses . . . are more likely than other types of criminal conduct to elude the criminal justice system." Indeed, the authors note that there is no "single 'molester' profile." Rather, "[c]hild molesters arrive at deviancy via multiple pathways and engage in many different sexual and nonsexual 'acting-out' behaviors" (1997, 2–3). Preventing states from regulating the Internet can only encourage more sex offenders to use that option. For example, researchers at the National Center for Missing and Exploited Children have found that

> 40% of arrested CP [child pornography] possessors were "dual offenders," who sexually victimized children and possessed child pornography, with both crimes discovered in the same investigation. An additional 15% were dual offenders who attempted to sexually victimize children by soliciting undercover investigators who posed online as minors. (Wolak, Finkelhor, and Mitchel 2005, vii)

Beech's research reveals that "[p]edophile networks by their very nature have typically operated covertly and the Internet, with its perceived anonymity, has to some extent allowed these networks to develop relatively unchecked" (Beech et al. 2008, 221). The National Center for Missing and Exploited Children (Wolak, Finkelhor, and Mitchel 2006, 15) has noted that the "dangers posed from people who use the Internet to make inappropriate and sometimes criminal sexual overtures to youth remain a primary concern of families, law enforcement, and others concerned with the welfare of youth." Ethel Quayle and her colleagues have found that sex offenders who use the Internet have a number of psychological and behavioral problems, "including intimacy deficits, distorted sexual scripts, emotional dysregulation, antisocial cognitions, and multiple dysfunctional mechanism" (Quayle, Vaugh, and Taylor 2006, 4; Wolak, Finkelhor, and Mitchel 2006, 1). And Justice Alito pointed to a number of federal and state cases that demonstrate the harm that can come to minors who think they are interacting with other minors but who are in fact talking with adults (Packingham v. North Carolina 2017b, 1740, n.3).

The Supreme Court rightly puts a high burden on laws that restrict speech, expression, and modes of communication (Ashcroft v. A.C.L.U. 2002; Reno v. A.C.L.U. 1997; Texas v. Johnson 1989). But it is of some constitutional importance that the state's highest court found the North Carolina law constitutional. It noted, correctly, that the Supreme Court will tolerate restrictions on speech when speech and "nonspeech elements are combined in the same course of conduct" (North Carolina v. Packingham 2015, 388; U.S. v. O'Brien 1968, 376). For the state supreme court, nonspeech factors outweighed speech factors because "protecting children from sexual abuse is a substantial governmental interest" (North Carolina v. Packingham 2015, 388; Congress 2006, sec. 501). Moreover, the law did not ban access to the Internet as such. Rather, the state "carefully tailored the statute in such a way as to prohibit registered sex offenders from accessing only those Web sites that allow them the opportunity to gather information about minors" (North Carolina v. Packingham 2015, 389).

In their brief on behalf of Packingham, the Association for the Treatment of Sexual Abusers (ATSA) and the National Association for Rational Sexual Offense Laws (NARSOL) and its North Carolina chapter argued that

> restrictions on registrants must have some basis in empirical reality to be effective. One such reality is the fact that registrants are not a homogenous group of "sex offenders" that should be monolithically managed. Rather, registrants comprise a diverse group of individuals, each different from the next in terms of past criminal history, behavioral patterns, and risk of recidivism. On top of the fact that the observed recidivism rates for "sex offenders" in the aggregate are far lower than what conventional folk wisdom suggests, differences in recidivism risk among the diverse registrant population require a tailored rather than uniform approach to crime prevention. (Packingham v. North Carolina 2016, 3)

Here is the essence of the social scientific critique of sex offender laws: they are too general and too much the product of uninformed public opinion, and sex offenders are constructs of fear and of generalizations about danger. The brief argues for "individualized risk assessments." Individualized risk assessments deny that laws should govern all citizens, equally and fairly. Individualized risk assessments raise the concern that the law paints with too broad a brush because not all convicted sex offenders pose threats to minors. This argument has weight because the Supreme Court dislikes overly broad laws, especially in free speech cases.[13]

The heart of the empirical criticism of sex offender legislation is that the state disregards evidence contrary to the state's purpose and instead "relies on misconceptions about sex offenders." This is a shorthand way of saying that public opinion is a dangerous tool to rely on when passing sex offender legislation because of the possibility of punitiveness. On this view, sex offender legislation promotes the wrong kind of deliberation and fails to focus on equality and justice. The preference for courts over legislatures, and for social science data over popular opinion filtered through representation, arises because most empirical studies say things that the public does not know. Research suggests, for example, that "(1) most victims of sexual crimes know their attacker; (2) most victims live with their attacker; and (3) most attacks are committed by first-time offenders, not registrants" (Packingham v. North Carolina 2016, 4). Presumably, North Carolina legislators ignored these studies or failed to understand them. The North Carolina law operates as if most sex offenders were strangers to their victims. Justice Kennedy adopted this critique in his opinion: "Imposing the restriction on all registrants ignores the fact that a substantial portion of the registrant population appears on the registry for reasons that have nothing to do with minors or social networking" (Packingham v. North Carolina 2016, 4).

To rely on empirical studies to expand constitutional rights is, in the language of Cass Sunstein, "maximalist" (Sunstein 1999, 9). A maximalist jurisprudence seeks "to decide cases in a way that sets broad rules for the future and that also gives ambitious theoretical justifications for outcomes" (Sunstein 1999, 9–10). Justice William Brennan's dissent in *McCleskey v. Kemp* (1987) is maximalist. In that case, the Court rejected relying on data that attempted to prove that a black person who kills a white person was four times more likely to receive a death sentence than if the killer was white and the victim black. Brennan not only wanted to overturn McCleskey's conviction, he wanted to alter the way prosecutors go about the business of filing death penalty cases (McCleskey v. Kemp 1987, 333–34).

Sunstein objects to maximalism because it forces judges to decide more than the case at hand. Maximalist judges look to make broad claims about fundamental rights and liberties, even as those rights and liberties may not have reached a settled level with the American public. Judicial minimalism's point is to create decisions that are narrow and shallow, rather than wide and deep. Narrowness preserves democratic uncertainty about the question of the fundamental nature of rights. Shallowness allows for "*the possibility of concrete judgments on particular cases, unaccompanied by abstract accounts about what accounts for those judgments*" (Sunstein 1999, 13; italics in original). Sunstein favors judicial decisions that (1) minimize abstract theorizing and (2) avoid turning social science data into hardened law because circumstances change, but which (3) emphasize clarity, democratic accountability, and popular participation, while (4) avoiding reliance on abstract conceptions of rights that the American public is either deeply divided over or not knowledgeable enough about. A key feature of minimalism is that "a simple rule" cannot "resolve all cases" (Sunstein 1999, 194).

It is striking that the Court in *Packingham* never acknowledged the need for deference to popular sentiment about community safety, the legitimacy of the state law in light of sex offenses in that state, or the legislature's general concerns about dangerous sex offenders and the Internet. It ignored the particular psychological effects sex offenses can have on victims, which distinguishes sex crimes from other types of crime (Lieb, Quinsey, and Berliner 1998). The opinion referred neither to cases that have upheld sex offender legislation on general police power grounds nor to statements about public safety. It is silent about the power of states to regulate Internet sex trafficking (Brown v. Entertainment Merchants Association 2011). It also ignored the United States Sentencing Commission's finding that "Internet-based child pornography communities . . . thrive in Internet chat-rooms and bulletin board systems" (2012, viii). And it does not refer to cases involving restricting the Internet for those on parole, probation, and other postrelease supervisory programs at the federal level. Finally, the decision says nothing about the fact that "many cases of sexual child abuse go unreported" (Broward County 2009, 5).

Although a unanimous decision, three justices (Neil Gorsuch did not participate) disagreed with the Court's reasoning, and Justice Alito touched upon some minimalist principles. According to Alito, the majority opinion engaged in "unnecessary rhetoric" (Packingham v. North Carolina 2017b, 1738). He was referring to the majority's notion that "'cyberspace' and 'social media in particular' are now 'the most important places (in a spatial sense) for the exchange of views'" (Packingham v. North Carolina 2017b, 1743). This idea is the centerpiece of Kennedy's majority opinion. Kennedy noted, for example, that the ban on social media prevents sex offenders from "knowing current events, checking ads for employment, speaking and listening in the modern public square, and otherwise exploring the vast realms of human thought and knowledge" (Packingham v. North Carolina 2017b, 1737). The law does no such thing. The "vast realms of human thought" are not limited to the Internet. The ban does not prevent sex offenders from talking to other informed citizens in public places, visiting libraries, watching television, listening to the radio, reading newspapers in libraries or at home, attending book clubs, or responding to help wanted ads in newspapers. Indeed, the law does not ban sex offenders from searching large portions of the Internet. Alito wondered whether Kennedy's broad defense of Internet freedoms means that the

> States may have little ability to restrict the sites that may be visited by even the most dangerous sex offenders. May a State preclude an adult previously convicted of molesting children from visiting a dating site for teenagers? Or a site where minors communicate with each other about personal problems? (Packingham v. North Carolina 2017b, 1743)

These are valid questions, and news reports about sex offenders preying on minors through social media validate Alito's questions (NJ.com). Alito should have said more, framing the case in light of legitimate governmental purposes, the history of sex offender legislation as a deliberative attempt to protect children and public safety, and the need for civic morality in such cases (Kingsley International Pictures Corp. v. Regents of the University of the State of New York 1959; Clor 1969). He also could have suggested, borrowing an idea from Judge Frank Easterbrook, that if no alternative to Internet regulations exist, then a judge could extend the convicted sex offender's sentence in the interest of public safety (U.S. v. Scott 2003, 737). Alito concluded in minimalist fashion: "if it is true, as the Court believes, that 'we cannot appreciate yet' the 'full dimensions and vast potential' of 'the Cyber Age,' we should proceed circumspectly, taking one step at a time" (Packingham v. North Carolina 2017b, 1744).

Despite *Packingham*'s holding, state and federal courts have upheld Internet regulations on sex offenders, noting that while *Packingham* prohibits banning registered sex offenders from using the Internet, the decision says nothing about regulating parolees' and probationers' access. The Supreme Court has granted courts much leeway to set conditions on parolees and probationers (U.S. v. Knights 2001; Griffin v. Wisconsin 1987). The Illinois court of appeals, for example, upheld a regulation on Internet access to a convicted sex offender on probation, even though the convicted sex offender's crime did not involve the Internet (Illinois v. Morger 2018). The United States court of appeals for the District of Columbia circuit upheld, as part of supervised release, a ban on a convicted sex offender's Internet access. The court noted that Brandon Rock's supervision was "imposed as part of his supervised-release sentence" (U.S. v. Rock 2017, 831). As the federal district court explained in *U.S. v. Farrell* (2018), "*Packingham* dealt with a lifetime, state-wide statute restricting the internet access of all registered sex offenders, while this case involves temporary, individual conditions, which are effective only for the duration of Farrell's supervised release" (U.S. v. Farrell 2018, 2). And the seventh circuit court of appeals upheld Indiana's prohibition on a convicted sex offender from entering any school—even to vote. Brian Valenti argued that this regulation involved a fundamental right that the state could not infringe upon. The court of appeals rejected that approach, holding that, under rational basis, "We must uphold the statute 'even if it is unwise, improvident, or out of harmony with a particular school of thought.'" As to Valenti's argument that voting is fundamental, the court held that Valenti's right was "statutory," that is, he was a convicted felon, and Indiana, like all states, has the right to disenfranchise convicted felons (Valenti v. Lawson 2018, 430).

These cases clearly demonstrate that there is room for states to regulate convicted sex offenders' Internet access. They also show why the *Packingham* decision is the poster-boy case for judicial minimalism. *Packingham* was decided too soon, written too broadly, and without any regard for the reasons why North Carolina passed the law. The essence of Sunstein's claims about minimalism is that courts should leave "many things undecided" because of "reasonable disagreement in a heterogeneous society," and because courts should be "intensely aware of [their] own limitations" (Sunstein 1999, ix). Viewing this case strictly through the categorical command of the First Amendment harms the content of laws that raise complex questions of public safety, morality, and the application of social science data. It also destroys the delicate balance between the individual's right to expression and the needs of a community to restrain various criminal behaviors. For this reason, Sunstein is an advocate of denying certiorari (Sunstein 1999, 39). Wisdom (or a better outcome) may result if the Court waits until an issue has had time to work its way through the electoral process and the court system. This should have been the case here. There was no pressing constitutional reason to accept this case. It did not come from a conflict among federal or state courts (Blaisdell 2009, 1174, n. 69, 1175,

n. 71). Rather than a minimalist decision, the Court offered an opinion that was so wide and deep that whatever benefits the decision has for First Amendment freedoms will be lost in the continuing debate over sex offenders' use of the Internet at the state level.

Conclusion

In this conclusion, I want to say a few words about how I understand the proper way to view sex offender legislation, which I offer in more detail throughout the book. While I agree with the thrust of Sunstein's minimalist argument, Sunstein's construct lacks a strong theoretical underpinning. Overall, I find Sunstein's theory of judicial review too beholden to Rawlsian philosophic principles to be successful across many issues (Sunstein 1999, 50–51). Sunstein accepts Rawls's defense of pluralism but is silent about Rawls's argument for distributive justice. Sunstein never tells us if we can have one without the other. Moreover, Sunstein makes no case for judicial review, for the virtue of a law (or a right) that needs judicial protection, for a law's political importance, and for its contributions to norm enforcements and the civilizing process. He is silent about the need to understand law as part of a larger political project, one tied to the aims of the regime (which, understandably, would violate the point of minimalism). His construct for laws that are shallow but narrow or wide, or deep but narrow or wide, is intriguing and useful as a heuristic, but it is not airtight (Sunstein 1999, 16–17). In addition, Sunstein's ideas are too dependent upon social science to serve the purposes of a sustained republican defense of sex offender legislation that criticizes the reliance on social science as a violation of judicial minimalism.

For these reasons, I find it most useful to turn to Antonin Scalia's understanding of textualism (and not, be it noted, originalism). I reject the idea that the Constitution's meaning is fixed in some originalist fashion, but I hold that it is authoritative. It is not "on a level with ordinary legislative acts," and therefore "alterable when the legislature shall please to alter it" (Marbury v. Madison 1803, 177). For Scalia, the purpose of textualism is to deny that the intent of a legislator has any purchase on the meaning of a law. In legislative debates over sex offender laws, it is not uncommon to find a legislator saying something like what Jerry Keen, then a member of the Georgia House of Representatives, said when debating a sex offender law that included a residency restriction:

"There is no place in our society for those who prey on innocent children," and added, "We don't want these types of people staying in our state" (Geraghty 2007, 517). A federal district court, reviewing New York's notification and registration law, stated that the law's intent was punitive because "members of the New York State legislature referred to sex offenders as 'depraved,' 'the lowest of the low,' 'animals,' and 'the human equivalent of toxic waste.' One member flatly stated: 'We are coming out to get them'" (Doe v. Pataki 1996, 605). And another legislator declared about residency restrictions in his state: "No sex offender is ever going to want to live here. I'd be mighty happy to see that happen" (Bains 2007, 486). Such quotes, which are more bark than bite, get widely disseminated in law reviews as instances of vengeance, passion, and prejudice. Indeed, in the individual case, they are instances of vengeance, passion, and prejudice. Surely, the retort goes, this was not the view of every legislator who voted, was it? With textualism, the judge's purpose is constrained to the evaluation of the law's meaning under the Constitution and from within the "the concept of ordered liberty" (Palko v. Connecticut 1937, 325). Judicial minimalism, properly understood, is a case-by-case method that seeks, above all, a moderate politics and constitutionalism.

Textualism, like Bickelian deference, is agnostic on the value of the law. "Words do have a limited range of meaning," Scalia writes, "and no interpretation that goes beyond that range is permissible" (Scalia 1997, 24). Textualism points to formalism and foundationalism, for the importance of institutions within a polity dedicated to a set of claims about nature, the human condition, and political life. Tocqueville tells us that democracies, which tend toward formlessness because of the alienating aspects of civic life, are greatly in need of forms (2000, 2: 4: 7). Decisions such as *Packingham* appear to uphold individual liberty because they appeal to our sense of autonomy and individuality. But *Packingham* is not a victory for individual rights. Decisions such as *Packingham* destroy the important role that the forms of deliberative justice play in sustaining democratic politics and individual rights.

NOTES

1. My approach resembles Keith Whittington's theory of "constitutional construction" (1999) and the work of Greg Weiner (2012; 2019) and George Edwards (2008). There are differences with Whittington's approach, but no disagreements. Whittington separates his method from a jurisprudential one, which is closer to my

approach, though I agree with his criticism of traditional jurisprudence. The jurisprudential approach, Whittington writes, is a "technical activity, concerned with employing a set of analytical tools to unearth the meaning inherent in the constitutional text" (1999, 7). My approach is not hermeneutic.

For Whittington, the weakness of the jurisprudential approach, which I agree with, is its lack of a "political" approach "that describes a distinct effort to understand and rework the meaning of a received constitutional text." "Construction," he writes, "provides for an element of creativity in construing constitutional meaning" (1999, 6).

This means that constitutional meaning can be had "outside of courts," a view I share and promote here. "The Constitution," he writes, "also delegates power from the people to their chosen representatives in order to realize positive constitutional values" (1999, 207). I not only agree with this, it is a central theme of this work. And I agree with his approach to political history, which demonstrates "how a political process gives meaning to the Constitution" (1999, 208). I am also in complete agreement with his notion that "Constitutional institutions structure political battles, and constitutional principles infuse political thought" (1999, 211).

I differ from Whittington in two ways, one formal, the other more practical, though informed by theory. At the formal level, this book is not concerned with regime-altering moments in political history, as Whittington's book is, so there is no need to adopt fully his approach to constitutional meaning. This study of sex offender legislation offers no opportunity to gain insight into the nature of political struggle or constitutional development, except to note how few studies there are of the republican and political process implications of sex offender legislation. At the practical level, I differ from Whittington because, while I agree that a jurisprudential approach can be limiting, I believe that constitutional meaning can be determined by combining a jurisprudential and institutional approach. In this, I follow Greg Weiner (2019) and George Thomas (2008), both of whom advocate a limited role for the judiciary and an expanded understanding of constitutionalism and republicanism. An understanding of institutions informed by principles derived from our founding texts and history can infuse jurisprudence with a wider scope and provide sufficient backdrop to understand the need for judicial limits and for deliberative democracy.

Whittington, Weiner (2019, 146–47, 152), and Edwards (2008, 17–19) accept that "the separation of powers is a source of positive action" (Whittington 1999, 224) in constitutional construction. For me, the separation of powers is the place to start thinking about the limits of judicial review, deliberative democracy, and sex offender legislation. I regard the separation of powers as "a doctrine designed chiefly to allocate the primary powers" of government, with a specific focus on governance rather than on policymaking (Ceaser 1986, 178–79).

2. Classical pluralism is hostile to deliberation, as it presupposes that interested actors have already thought through their interests.

3. *Marbury v. Madison* (1803, 176): "This original and supreme will organizes the government, and assigns, to different departments, their respective powers."

4. It is possible that the deliberative virtues of American politics are not well understood because they work in subtler ways than the idea that citizens should deliberate in public spaces and produce consensus through moral reasoning supposedly does. Yet even the theoretical deliberativists admit this rarely happens. The institutional view is the long view, and democrats, as Tocqueville recognized, can be impatient. Yet some reflection on the process the founders created demonstrates that it produces a more moderate view of politics and policy than the theoretic position on deliberation does, and for this reason it is the view I take of sex offender legislation.

5. Kendall should have said dissensus rather than disunity.

6. Three-strikes laws are examples of deterrence not retribution, if we follow the traditional understanding of theories of punishment. Barker means vengeance rather than retribution.

7. On the civil-criminal problem in sex offender cases, see *Kansas v. Hendricks* (1997, 372–73); *Seling v. Young* (2001, 275); *Allen v. Illinois* (1986).

8. Sex offender critics rely on the language of "lived experience," an idea derived from phenomenology. Experience is never the experience of a nation or a people, or even of a particular individual whose actions are instructive. Rather, it is an attempt to demonstrate the authenticity of a personal experience even if others have not witnessed the experience. Diana Rickard's book on sex offenders, which is based on interviews with sex offenders, is an example (2016, 2). On lived experience, see Rosenthal and Bourgeois (1977).

9. Narratives are attempts to explain phenomena without relying on positivist social science, with its assumptions of scientific accuracy and objective facts leading to correct interpretations. Narrative discourses reject the idea of an unbiased explanation of events. Narratives universalize the subjective by focusing on the "mutual relationships between actors and systems" (Stivers 1993, 413, 418).

10. Megan Kanka was a seven-year-old New Jersey resident who was raped and killed by a neighbor, a convicted sex offender. New Jersey named its sex offender law Megan's Law.

11. It is Facebook's policy to ban convicted sex offenders from their site. https://www.facebook.com/help/210081519032737?helpref=uf_permalink

12. At least four states have lifetime postrelease supervision for sex offenders, and other states are considering that option (Daugherty 2013, 673–74; Kansas v. Dull 2015; Kansas v. Mossman 2012). In 2017, New York State considered such a regulation: https://assembly.state.ny.us/leg/?default_fld=&bn=A02948&term=2017&Summary=Y&Actions=Y&Text=Y&Votes=Y

13. The problem with the overbreadth doctrine is that it, too, can be overbroad. It can act as a substitute version of substantive due process (Lewis v. City of New Orleans 1974, 136–37). While Justice Alito agreed that the broad sweep of the statute rendered it unconstitutional, he also acknowledged, which the majority did not, that "the social exchanges facilitated by these websites [e.g., Amazon.com, webmd.com] occur in the open, and this reduces the possibility of a child being secretly lured into an abusive situation" (Packingham v. North Carolina 2017b, 1743). In other words, the statute is not as broad as the majority say it is.

REFERENCES

Adler, Matthew. 2000. "Expressive Theories of Law: A Skeptical Overview." *University of Pennsylvania Law Review* 148 (5): 1363–1501.

Agan, Amanda, and J. J. Prescott. 2014. "Sex Offender Law and the Geography of Victimization." *Journal of Empirical Legal Studies* 11 (4): 786–828.

Anderson, Amy, Lisa Sample, and Calli Cain. 2015. "Residency Restrictions for Sex Offenders: Public Opinion on Appropriate Distances." *Criminal Justice Policy Review* 26 (3): 262–77.

Bailey, Michael. 2002. "Surrogates for Deliberation and the United States Constitution." *Polity* 34 (4): 533–52.

Bains, Chiraag. 2007. "Next Generation Sex Offender Statutes: Constitutional Challenges to Residency, Work, and Loitering Restrictions." *Harvard Civil Rights-Civil Liberties Law Review* 42 (2): 483–500.

Barber, Benjamin. 1984. *Strong Democracy: Participatory Politics for a New Age.* Berkeley: University of California Press.

Barker, Vanessa. 2006. "Deliberating Crime and Punishment: A Way Out of Get Tough Justice?" *Criminology & Public Policy* 5 (1): 37–44.

Barker, Vanessa. 2009. *The Politics of Imprisonment: How the Democratic Process Shapes the Way America Punishes Offenders.* Oxford: Oxford University Press.

Beckett, Katherine, and Steve Herbert. 2010. "Penal Boundaries: Banishment and the Expansion of Punishment." *Law and Social Inquiry* 35 (1): 1–35.

Beech, Anthony R., Ian A. Elliott, Astrid Birgden, and Donald Findlater. 2008. "The Internet and Child Sexual Offending: A Criminological Review." *Aggression and Violent Behavior* 13 (3): 216–28.

Benhabib, Seyla. 1996. "Toward a Deliberative Model of Democratic Legitimacy." In *Democracy and Difference: Contesting the Boundaries of the Political*, edited by Seyla Benhabib, 67–94. Princeton: Princeton University Press.

Bessette, Joseph. 1994. *The Mild Voice of Reason: Deliberative Democracy and American National Government.* Chicago: University of Chicago Press.

Bickel, Alexander. 1975. *The Morality of Consent.* New Haven: Yale University Press.

Bickel, Alexander. 1986. *The Least Dangerous Branch: The Supreme Court at the Bar of Politics.* New Haven: Yale University Press.

Bishin, Benjamin, and Charles Smith. 2013. "When Do Legislators Defy Popular Sovereignty? Testing Theories of Minority Representation Using DOMA." *Political Research Quarterly* 66 (4): 794–803.

Blaisdell, Krista. 2009. "Protecting the Playgrounds of the Twenty-First Century: Analyzing Computer and Internet Restrictions for Internet Sex Offenders." *Valparaiso University Law Review* 43 (3): 1155–1210.

Bodine, Brian. 1990. "Washington's New Violent Sexual Predator Commitment System: An Unconstitutional Law and an Unwise Policy Choice." *University of Puget Sound Law Review* 14 (1): 105–42.

Bohman, James. 1996. *Public Deliberation: Pluralism, Complexity, and Democracy.* Cambridge, MA: MIT Press.

Bohman, James. 2012. "Representation in the Deliberative System." In *Deliberative Systems: Deliberative Democracy at the Large Scale*, edited by John Parkinson and Jane Mansbridge, 72–94. Cambridge: Cambridge University Press.

Bohman, James, and William Rehg. 1997. "Introduction." In *Deliberative Democracy: Essays on Reason and Politics*, edited by James Bohman and William Rehg, ix-xxx. Cambridge, MA: MIT Press.

Bolce, Louis, Gerald DeMaio, and Douglas Muzzio. 1987. "The Equal Rights Amendment, Public Opinion, & American Constitutionalism." *Polity* 19: 551–69.

Brilliant, Jon. 1989. "The Modern Day Scarlet Letter: A Critical Analysis of Modern Probation Conditions." *Duke Law Journal* 1989: 1357–85.

Broward County, Florida. 2009. "Final Report: Sexual Offender & Sexual Predator Residence Task Force." https://miamiherald.typepad.com/files/broward-task-force-draft-report.pdf

Burchfield, Keri, Lisa L. Sample, and Robert Lytle. 2014. "Public Interest in Sex Offenders: A Perpetual Panic?" *Criminology, Criminal Justice Law, & Society* 15 (3): 96–117.

Campbell, Michael, and Heather Schoenfeld. 2013. "The Transformation of America's Penal Order: A Historicized Political Sociology of Punishment." *American Journal of Sociology* 118 (5): 1375–1423.

Cassell, Paul. 2017. "Crime Victims' Rights." Academy for Justice: A Report on Scholarship and Criminal Justice Reform. University of Utah College of Law Research Paper No. 224. https://ssrn.com/abstract=3024143 or http://dx.doi.org/10.2139/ssrn.3024143

Ceaser, James. 1986. "In Defense of Separation of Powers." In *The Separation of Powers: Does It Still Work?*, edited by Robert Goldwin and Art Kaufman, 169–93. Washington, DC: American Enterprise Institute.

Ceaser, James. 2006. *Nature and History in American Political Development: A Debate.* Cambridge, MA: Harvard University Press.

Chambers, Simone. 2012. "Deliberation and Mass Democracy." In *Deliberative Systems: Deliberative Democracy at the Large Scale*, edited by John Parkinson and Jane Mansbridge, 52–71. Cambridge: Cambridge University Press.

Chan, Eric, Dale McNiel, and Renee Binder. 2016. "Sex Offenders in the Digital Age." *Journal of the American Academy of Psychiatry and the Law* 44 (3): 368–75.

Clor, Harry. 1969. *Obscenity and Public Morality: Censorship in a Liberal Society.* Chicago: University of Chicago Press.

Cohen, Joshua. 1997. "Deliberation and Democratic Legitimacy." In *Deliberative Democracy: Essays on Reason and Politics*, edited by James Bowman and William Rehg, 67–91. Cambridge, MA: MIT Press.

Cohen, Stanley. 2011. *Folk Devils and Moral Panics: The Creation of the Mods and the Rockers.* London: Routledge.

Cohen, Thomas, and Michelle Spidell. 2016. "How Dangerous Are They: An Analysis of Sex Offenders under Federal Post-Conviction Supervision." *Federal Probation* 80 (2): 21–32.

Collateral Consequences Resource Center. 2019. Reducing Barriers to Reintegration Fair Chance and Expungement Reforms in 2018. http://ccresourcecenter.org/wp-content/uploads/2019/01/Fair-chance-and-expungement-reforms-in-2018-CCRC-Jan-2019.pdf

Copp, David, Jean Hampton, and John Roemer, eds. 1993. *The Idea of Democracy.* Cambridge: Cambridge University Press.

Daugherty, Nicholas. 2013. "Let the Punishment Fit the Crime (Unless It's a Sex Crime): A Critique of the Kansas Supreme Court's Rubber Stamp of Approval upon Mandatory Lifetime Postrelease Supervision for Sex Offenders." *Washburn Law Journal* 52 (3): 649–84.

Diamond, Martin. 1981. *The Founding of the Democratic Republic.* Itsaca, IL: F. E. Peacock Publishers.

Dryzek, John. 1990. *Discursive Democracy: Politics, Policy, and Political Science.* Cambridge: Cambridge University Press.

Dworkin, Ronald. 1978. *Taking Rights Seriously.* Cambridge, MA: Harvard University Press.

Edelman, Murray. 1985. *The Symbolic Uses of Politics.* 2nd ed. Urbana-Champagne: University of Illinois Press.

Edwards, George. 2008. *The Madisonian Constitution.* Baltimore: The Johns Hopkins University Press.

Elliott, Ward. 1974. *The Rise of Guardian Democracy: The Supreme Court's Role in Voting Rights Disputes, 1845–1969.* Cambridge, MA: Harvard University Press.

Epstein, David. 1984. *The Political Theory of* The Federalist. Chicago: University of Chicago Press.

Erlinder, C. Peter. 1993. "Minnesota's Gulag: Involuntary Treatment for the 'Politically Ill.'" *William Mitchell Law Review* 19 (1): 99–159.

Fabian, John. 2003. "Kansas v. Hendricks and Beyond: 'Mental Abnormality,' 'Volition,' 'Dangerousness,' and the Debate between Community Safety and Civil Liberty." *University of West Los Angeles Law Review* 35: 389–439.

Faulkner, Robert. 1989. "Difficulties of Equal Dignity: The Court and the Family." In *The Constitution, the Courts, and the Quest for Justice*, edited by Robert A. Goldwin and William A. Schambra, 93–114. Washington, DC: American Enterprise Institute.

The Federalist. 2001. Ed. Robert Scigliano. New York: Modern American Library.

Feeley, Malcolm, and Jonathan Simon. 1992. "The New Penology: Notes on the Emerging Strategy of Corrections and its Implications." *Criminology* 30 (4): 449–74.

Fenno, Richard. 1978. *Home Style: House Members in Their Districts.* Boston: Little, Brown and Company.

Ferejohn, John. 2000. "Instituting Deliberative Democracy." In *Designing Democratic Institutions* (NOMOS XLII), edited by Ian Shapiro and Stephen Macedo, 75–104. New York: New York University Press.

Filler, Daniel. 2001. "Making the Case for Megan's Law: A Study in Legislative Rhetoric." *Indiana Law Journal* 76 (2): 315–65.

Fishkin, James, and Peter Laslett, eds. 2003. *Debating Deliberative Democracy.* London: Blackwell.

Fortney, Timothy, Jill Levenson, Yolanda Brannon, and Juanita Baker. 2007. "Myths and Facts about Sexual Offenders: Implications for Treatment and Public Policy." *Sexual Offender Treatment* 2 (1): 1–17.

Frankfurter, Felix. 1955. "John Marshall and the Judicial Function." *Harvard Law Review,* 69 (2): 217–38.

Garland, David. 2001. *The Culture of Control: Crime and Social Order in Contemporary Society.* Oxford: Oxford University Press.

General Accounting Office. 2013. Sex Offender Registration and Registration and Notification Act: Jurisdictions Face Challenges to Implementing the Act, and Stakeholders Report Positive and Negative Effects. Report to the Subcommittee on Crime, Terrorism, and Homeland Security, Committee on the Judiciary, House of Representatives. https://www.gao.gov/assets/660/652032.pdf

Geraghty, Sarah. 2007. "Challenging the Banishment of Registered Sex Offenders from the State of Georgia: A Practitioner's Perspective." *Harvard Civil Rights-Civil Liberties Law Review* 42 (2): 513–29.

Gleb, Gary. 1991. "Washington's Sexually Violent Predator Law: The Need to Bar Unreliable Psychiatric Predictions of Dangerousness from Civil Commitment Proceedings." *U.C.L.A. Law Review* 39 (1): 213–50.

Glendon, Mary Ann. 1991. *Rights Talk: The Impoverishment of Political Discourse.* New York: Free Press.

Gould, Jon. 2005. *Speak No Evil: The Triump of Hate Speech Regulation.* Chicago: University of Chicago Press.

Gregg, Gary. 1997. *The Presidential Republic: Executive Representation and Deliberative Democracy.* Lanham, MD: Rowman & Littlefield.

Gutmann, Amy, and Dennis Thompson. 1996. *Democracy and Disagreement.* Cambridge, MA: Harvard University Press.

Gutmann, Amy, and Dennis Thompson. 2004. *Why Deliberative Democracy?* Princeton: Princeton University Press.

Hand, Learned. 1958. *The Bill of Rights.* Cambridge, MA: Harvard University Press.

Harcourt, Bernard. 2010. "Neoliberal Penality: A Brief Genealogy." *Theoretical Criminology* 14 (1): 74–92.

Horowitz, Emily. 2015. *Protecting Our Kids? How Sex Offender Laws are Failing Us.* Santa Barbara, CA: Praeger.

Howarth, David. 2000. *Discourse.* Buckingham, UK: Open University Press.

Human Rights Watch. 2007. No Easy Answers: Sex Offender Laws in the US. https://www.hrw.org/sites/default/files/reports/us0907webwcover.pdf

Human Rights Watch. 2013. Raised on the Registry: The Irreparable Harm of Placing Children on Sex Offender Registries in the US. https://www.hrw.org/report/2013/05/01/raised-registry/irreparable-harm-placing-children-sex-offender-registries-us

Jacobsohn, Gary. 1977. *Pragmatism, Statesmanship, and the Supreme Court.* Ithaca: Cornell University Press.

Janus, Eric, and Wayne Logan. 2003. "Substantive Due Process and the Involuntary Confinement of Sexually Violent Predators." *Connecticut Law Review* 35 (2): 319–84.

Jenkins, Philip. 1998. *Moral Panic: Changing Concepts of the Child Molester in Modern America.* New Haven: Yale University Press.

Kendall, Willmoore. 1971. "American Conservatism and the 'Prayer' Decisions." In *Willmoore Kendall Contra Mundum*, edited by Nellie Kendall, 326–46. New Rochelle, NY: Arlington House.

Kendall, Willmoore. 1971. "Bipartisanship and Majority-Rule Democracy." In *Willmoore Kendall Contra Mundum*, edited by Nellie Kendall, 118–28. New Rochelle, NY: Arlington House.

Kendall, Willmoore. 1971. "The Two Majorities." In *Willmoore Kendall Contra Mundum*, edited by Nellie Kendall, 202–27. New Rochelle, NY: Arlington House.

Kingston, Drew. 2016. "Hypersexuality Disorders and Sexual Offending." In *Sexual Offending: Predisposing Antecedents, Assessments and Management*, edited by Amy Phenix and Harry Hoberman, 103–118. London: Springer.

Kirwin, John. 2003. "One Arrow in the Quiver—Using Civil Commitment as One Component of a State's Response to Sexual Violence." *William Mitchell Law Review* 29 (4): 1135–1220.

Kruttschnitt, Candace, Christopher Uggen, and Kelly Shelton. 2000. "Predictors of Desistance Among Sex Offenders: The Interaction of Formal and Informal Social Controls." *Justice Quarterly* 17 (1): 61–87.

La Fond, John. 1992. "Washington's Sexually Violent Predator Law: A Deliberate Misuse of the Therapeutic State for Social Control." *University of Puget Sound Law Review* 15 (3): 655–708.

Lancaster, Roger. 2011. *Sex Panic and the Punitive State.* Berkeley: University of California Press.

Lave, Tamara Rice, and Franklin Zimring. 2018. "Assessing the Real Risk of Sexually Violent Predators: Doctor Padilla's Dangerous Data." *American Criminal Law Review* 55 (3): 705–88.

Lavi, Shai. 2011. "Turning the Tables on 'Law and . . .': A Jurisprudential Inquiry into Contemporary Legal Theory." *Cornell Law Review* 96 (4): 811–38.

Leff, Arthur. 1978. "Law And." *Yale Law Journal* 87 (5): 989–1011.

Levenson, Jill. 2004. "Reliability of Sexually Violent Predator Civil Commitment Criteria in Florida." *Law and Human Behavior* 28 (4): 357–68.

Lieb, Roxanne. 1996. Washington's Sexually Violent Predator Law. Washington State Institute for Public Policy. http://www.wsipp.wa.gov/ReportFile/1244/Wsipp_Washingtons-Sexually-Violent-Predator-Law-Legislative-History-and-Comparisons-With-Other-States_Full-Report.pdf

Lieb, Roxanne, Vernon Quinsey, and Lucy Berliner. 1998. "Sexual Predators and Social Policy." *Crime and Justice* 23: 43–114.

Lynch, Mona. 2002. "Pedophiles and Cyber-Predators as Contaminating Forces: The Language of Disgust, Pollution, and Boundary Invasions in Federal Debates on Sex Offender Legislation." *Law & Social Inquiry* 27 (3): 529–66.

Mancini, Christina, and Daniel Mears. 2013. "U.S. Supreme Court Decisions and Sex Offender Legislation: Evidence of Evidence Based Policy?" *Journal of Criminal Law & Criminology* 103 (4): 1115–53.

Mansbridge, Jane. 1980. *Beyond Adversary Democracy.* New York: Basic Books.

Marteache, Nerea. 2012. "Deliberative Processes and Attitudes Toward Sex Offenders in Spain." *European Journal of Criminology* 9 (2): 159–75.

Martin, Robert. 2010. "James Madison and Popular Government: The Neglected Case of the 'Memorial.'" *Polity* 42 (2): 185–209.

Mason, Alpheus. 1956. "The Core of Free Government, 1938–40: Mr. Justice Stone and 'Preferred Freedoms.'" *Yale Law Journal* 65 (5): 597–628.

Mayhew, David. 1974. *Congress: The Electoral Connection.* New Haven: Yale University Press.

McAllister, Stephen. 1997. "The Constitutionality of Kansas Laws Targeting Sex Offenders." *Washburn Law Journal* 36 (3): 419–67.

McLeod, Allegra. 2014. "Regulating Sexual Harm: Strangers, Intimates, and Social Institutional Reform." *California Law Review* 102 (6): 1553–1621.

Moghaddam, Amanda. 2010. "Popular Politics and Unintended Consequences: The Punitive Effect of Sex Offender Residency Statutes from an Empirical Perspective." *Southwest Law Review* 40 (1): 223–45.

Morse, Stephen. 1982. "A Preference for Liberty: The Case Against Involuntary Commitment of the Mentally Disordered." *California Law Review* 70 (1): 54–106.

Morse, Stephen. 1996. "Blame and Danger: An Essay on Preventive Detention." *Boston University Law Review* 76 (1 and 2): 113–56.

Nathan, Debbie. 2016. "Listening to Sex Offenders." *Reason* (Book review). http://reason.com/archives/2016/11/17/listening-to-sex-offenders

NJ.Com. 2019. "16 Child Predators, including a Cop and a Minister, used Apps such as Kik and Skout to Lure N.J. Teens, AG says" (April 24). https://www.nj.com/politics/2019/04/a-cop-a-teacher-a-minister-operation-home-alone-nets-16-accused-child-predators-ag-says.html

Parkinson, John, and Jane Mansbridge, eds. 2012. *Deliberative Systems: Deliberative Democracy at the Large Scale.* Cambridge: Cambridge University Press.

Pearce, Marc. 2007. "Civilly Committing Criminals: An Analysis of the Expressive Function of Nebraska's Dangerous Sex Offender Commitment Procedure." *Nebraska Law Review* 85 (3): 575–642.

Peters-Baker, Jean. 1998. "Challenging Traditional Notions of Managing Sex Offenders: Prognosis is Lifetime Management." *University of Missouri-Kansas City Law Review* 66 (3): 629–79.

Petersilia, Joan. 2003. *When Prisoners Come Home: Parole and Prisoner Reentry.* Oxford: Oxford University Press.

PEW Research Center. 2013. Teens, Social Media, and Privacy. https://www.pewresearch.org/wp-content/uploads/sites/9/2013/05/PIP_TeensSocialMediaandPrivacy_PDF.pdf

Post, David. 2016. "The Yellow Star, the Scarlet Letter, and 'International Megan's Law.'" *Washington Post* (January 6). The Volokh Conspiracy blog. https://www.washingtonpost.com/news/volokh-conspiracy/wp/2016/01/06/the-yellow-star-the-scarlet-letter-and-international-megans-law/?noredirect=on&utm_term=.734c3ab5a11b

Prentky, Robert, Raymond Knight, and Austin F. S. Lee. 1997. National Institute of Justice. Research Report, Child Sexual Molestation: Research Issues. https://www.ncjrs.gov/pdffiles/163390.pdf

Quayle, Ethel, Mary Vaughan, and Max Taylor. 2006. "Sex Offenders, Internet Child Abuse Images and Emotional Avoidance: The Importance of Values." *Aggression and Violent Behavior* 11 (1): 1–11.

Rawls, John. 1971. *A Theory of Justice.* Cambridge, MA: Harvard University Press.

Rawls, John. 1993. *Political Liberalism.* New York: Columbia University Press.

Rickard, Diana. 2016. *Sex Offenders, Stigma, and Social Control.* New Brunswick, NJ: Rutgers University Press.

Roberts, Julian, Loretta Stalans, David Indermaur, and Mike Hough. 2002. *Penal Populism and Public Opinion: Lessons from Five Countries.* Oxford: Oxford University Press.

Rosenblum, Nancy. 2006. "Replacing Foundations with Staging: 'Second-story' Concepts and American Political Development." In *Nature and History in American Political Development: A Debate*, 115–40. Cambridge, MA: Harvard University Press.

Rosenthal, Sandra, and Patrick Bourgeois. 1977. "Pragmatism, Scientific Method, and the Phenomenological Return to Lived Experience." *Philosophy and Phenomenological Research* 38 (1): 56–65.

Scalia, Antonin. 1997. *A Matter of Interpretation: Federal Courts and the Law.* Ed. Amy Gutmann. Princeton: Princeton University Press.

Scheingold, Stuart, Toska Olson, and Jana Pershing. 1992. "The Politics of Sexual Psychopathy: Washington State's Sexual Predator Legislation." *University of Puget Sound Law Review* 15 (3): 809–20.

Scheingold, Stuart, Toska Olson, and Jana Pershing. 1994. "Sexual Violence, Victim Advocacy, and Republican Criminology: Washington State's Community Protection Act." *Law & Society Review* 28 (4): 729–64.

Simon, Jonathan. 1998. "Managing the Monstrous: Sex Offenders and the New Penology." *Psychology, Public Policy & Law* 4 (1–2): 452–67.

Simon, Jonathan. 2000. "Megan's Law: Crime and Democracy in Late Modern America." *Law & Social Inquiry* 25 (4): 1111–50.

SMART (Office of Sex Offender Sentencing, Monitoring, Apprehending, Registering, and Tracking). https://www.smart.gov/SOMAPI/pfv.html

Smith, Steven. 2007. *Party Influence in Congress.* Cambridge: Cambridge University Press.

Stivers, Camilla. 1993. "Reflections on the Role of Personal Narrative in Social Science." *Signs* 18 (2): 408–25.

Storing, Herbert. 1995. "The Constitution and the Bill of Rights." In *Toward a More*

Perfect Union: Writings of Herbert J. Storing, edited by Joseph Bessette, 108–28. Washington, DC: American Enterprise Institute.

Sunstein, Cass. 1999. *One Case at a Time: Judicial Minimalism on the Supreme Court.* Cambridge, MA: Harvard University Press.

Tewksbury, Richard. 2007. "Exile at Home: The Unintended Consequences of Sex Offender Residency Restrictions." *Harvard Civil Rights-Civil Liberties Law Review* 42: 531–40.

Thayer, James. 1893. "The Origin and Scope of the American Doctrine of Constitutional Law." *Harvard Law Review* 7 (3): 129–56.

Tocqueville, Alexis de. 2000. *Democracy in America.* Trans. Harvey Mansfield and Delba Winthrop. Chicago: University of Chicago Press.

Tulis, Jeffrey. 2003. "Deliberation Between Institutions." In *Debating Deliberative Democracy*, edited by James Fishkin and Peter Laslett, 200–11. London: Blackwell.

U.S. Congress. 2006. Sex Offender Registration and Notification Act. Pub. L. No. 109–248. H.R. 4472. https://www.justice.gov/archive/olp/pdf/adam_walsh_act.pdf

U.S. Congress. 2016. International Megan's Law to Prevent Child Exploitation and Other Sexual Crimes through Advanced Notification of Traveling Sex Offenders. 130 Stat. 15. https://www.congress.gov/114/plaws/publ119/PLAW-114publ119.pdf

U.S. Sentencing Commission. 2012. *Report to Congress: Federal Child Pornography Offenders.* Washington, DC: U.S. Sentencing Commission. https://www.ussc.gov/sites/default/files/pdf/news/congressional-testimony-and-reports/sex-offense-topics/201212-federal-child-pornography-offenses/Full_Report_to_Congress.pdf

Weiner, Greg. 2012. *Madison's Metronome: The Constitution, Majority Rule, and the Tempo of American Politics.* Lawrence: University Press of Kansas.

Weiner, Greg. 2019. *The Political Constitution: The Case against Judicial Supremacy.* Lawrence: University Press of Kansas.

Weitzer, Ronald. 2007. "The Social Construction of Sex Trafficking: Ideology and Institutionalization of a Moral Crusade." *Politics & Society* 35 (3): 447–75.

Whittington, Keith. 1999. *Constitutional Construction: Divided Powers and Constitutional Meaning.* Cambridge, MA: Harvard University Press.

Whittington, Keith. 2018. *Speak Freely: Why Universities Must Defend Free Speech.* Princeton: Princeton University Press.

Wolak, Janis, David Finkelhor, and Kimberly Mitchel. 2005. National Center for Missing Children. 2005. Child-Pornography Possessors Arrested in Internet-Related Crimes: Findings from the National Juvenile Online Victimization Study. http://unh.edu/ccrc/pdf/jvq/CV81.pdf

Wolak, Janis, David Finkelhor, and Kimberly Mitchel. 2006. National Center for Missing and Exploited Children. Online Victimization of Youth: Five Years Later. http://unh.edu/ccrc/pdf/CV138.pdf

Young, Iris Marion. 1996. "Communication and the Other: Beyond Deliberative Democracy." In *Democracy and Difference: Contesting the Boundaries of the Political*, edited by Seyla Benhabib, 120–35. Princeton: Princeton University Press.

Zgoba, Kristen, Philip Witt, Melissa Dalessandro, and Bonita Veysey. 2008. "Megan's Law: Assessing the Practical and Monetary Efficacy." National Institute of Justice. Document No.: 225370. https://www.ncjrs.gov/pdffiles1/nij/grants/225370.pdf

CASES

A.F.L. v. American Sash & Door Co., 335 U.S. 538 (1949).

Allen v. Illinois, 478 U.S. 364 (1986).

Artway v. Attorney General of New Jersey, 876 F.Supp. 666 (1995).

Ashcroft v. American Civil Liberties Union, 535 U.S. 564 (2002).

Brown v. Entertainment Merchants Association, 564 U.S. 786 (2011).

Day-Brite Lighting v. Missouri, 342 U.S. 421 (1952).

Doe v. Pataki, 940 F.Supp. 603 (1996).

Griffin v. Wisconsin, 483 U.S. 868 (1987).

Illinois v. Morger, 2018 IL App. (4th) 170285 (2018). (Not yet released).

Iowa v. Oliver, 812 N.W.2d 636 (2012).

J.B. v. New Jersey State Parole Board, 433 N.J. Super. 327 (2013).

J.B. v. New Jersey State Parole Board, 444 N.J. Super. 115 (2016).

Kansas v. Allen, 35 Kan.App.2d 466 (2006).

Kansas v. Allen, 283 Kan. 372 (2007).

Kansas v. Dull, 302 Kan. 32 (2015).

Kansas v. Hendricks, 521 U.S. 346 (1997).

Kansas v. Mossman, 294 Kan. 901 (2012).

Kansas v. Spinden, 30 Kan.App.2d 1014 (2002).

Kingsley International Pictures Corp. v. Regents of the University of the State of New York, 360 U.S. 684 (1959).

Kovacs v. Cooper, 336 U.S. 77 (1949).

Lewis v. City of New Orleans, 415 U.S. 130 (1974).

Marbury v. Madison, 5 U.S. 137 (1803).

McCleskey v. Kemp, 481 U.S. 279 (1987).

Minersville School District v. Gobitis, 310 U.S. 586 (1940).

North Carolina v. Packingham, 229 N.C.App. 293 (2013).
North Carolina v. Packingham, 368 N.C. 380 (2015).
Packingham v. North Carolina.
Packingham v. North Carolina, WL 7451277 (2016).
Palko v. Connecticut, 302 U.S. 319 (1937).
Reno v. American Civil Liberties Union, 521 U.S. 844 (1997).
Seling v. Young, 531 U.S. 250 (2001).
Texas v. Johnson, 491 U.S. 397 (1989).
Trop v. Dulles, 356 U.S. 86 (1958).
U.S. v. Abregana, 574 F.Supp.2d 1123 (2008).
U.S. v. Comstock, 560 U.S. 126 (2010).
U.S. v. Farrell, WL 1035856 (2018) (slip opinion).
U.S. v. Knights, 534 U.S. 112 (2001).
U.S. v. Lovett, 328 U.S. 303 (1946).
U.S. v. O'Brien, 391 U.S. 367 (1968).
U.S. v. Rearden, 349 F.3d 608 (2003).
U.S. v. Rock, 863 F.3d 827 (2017).
U.S. v. Scott, 316 F.3d 733 (2003).
Valenti v. Lawson, 889 F.3d 427 (2018).
Washington v. Glucksberg, 521 U.S. 702 (1997).
West Virginia State Board of Education v. Barnette, 319 U.S. 624 (1943).
Winters v. New York, 333 U.S. 507 (1948).
Wisconsin v. Muldrow, 381 Wis.2d 492 (2018).

CHAPTER 2

Confining the Mentally Ill and Dangerous

In 1984 in Louisiana, Terry Foucha, seventeen years old, and about to become a first-time offender (Foucha v. Louisiana 1991a, 49), entered a house carrying a .357 Magnum revolver. He chased the owners from their home and began to rob it. When the police arrived, a gunfight ensued. The police captured Foucha and the state charged him with "aggravated burglary and illegal discharge of a firearm" (Foucha v. Louisiana 1992, 73). Foucha entered two pleas: not guilty and not guilty by reason of insanity (NGRI). The trial court appointed two psychiatrists to examine Foucha. In lieu of a trial, the trial judge found Foucha not guilty by reason of insanity (Louisiana v. Foucha 1990). Under Louisiana law, "a defendant found not guilty by reason of insanity in a non-capital felony case is committed to a mental institution only if the trial court determines that the defendant cannot be released without danger to others or to himself" (Foucha v. Louisiana 1992, 105). Having made that determination, the trial court ordered Foucha committed to the East Feliciana Forensic Facility, a maximum-security forensic facility, "until such time that the insanity acquittee meets the burden of proof that he can be released without danger to himself or others"[1] (Foucha v. Louisiana 1991b, 10).

The Louisiana law regarding commitment following a NGRI verdict raises important questions implicating the due process and equal protection clauses of the Fourteenth Amendment. These constitutional issues also raise important questions about the constitutionality of postconviction civil commitment for sex offenders. This chapter, then, which examines the holding in *Foucha v. Lou-*

isiana, also looks forward to the chapters that discuss mental illness, insanity, and public safety in greater depth. Although *Foucha* is about a not guilty by reason of insanity plea that leads to commitment to a mental facility, the Supreme Court's opinion contains language about the dangers of unlawful detentions, and it emboldened critics of postconviction civil commitment for sex offenders because it outlined the limits of that process.

According to the Supreme Court (Bolton v. Harris 1968), a state must provide a defendant sentenced under a NGRI verdict with notice and a hearing regarding the full extent of the acquittee's criminal commitment. "The process for admitting insanity acquittees to mental hospitals after their acquittals is referred to as criminal commitment. Involuntary hospitalization for other persons is referred to as civil commitment" (Note 1981, 605, n. 2). Civil and criminal commitments share the same goal. "The primary purpose of both . . . is treatment aimed at recovery" (Polstein 1985, 512). However, treatment within a prison, or postconviction treatment in a mental facility, raises constitutional and ethical red flags, which I discuss in chapter 4. The consensus among state and federal judges is that neither type of commitment is punitive. Because the purpose of the Eighth Amendment is to limit the state's ability to punish, the Eighth Amendment protects neither form of commitment from constitutional challenge.

In a NGRI verdict case, commitment follows a criminal act, though not all states have automatic commitment. Some states require psychiatric review prior to commitment, while others presume the insanity to continue. In any case, automatic commitment does not mean indefinite commitment. To protect the committee's due process rights, states can provide acquittees with the means to petition for release, as Louisiana does (Louisiana v. Foucha 1990, 1140). At the time of Foucha's crime, Louisiana made commitment following a NGRI verdict automatic (Louisiana Criminal Procedure Code). Prior to *Foucha,* the Supreme Court had upheld the use of automatic commitment in cases involving NGRI verdicts (Jones v. U.S. 1983).

It is possible that a defendant in a NGRI case may no longer show signs of mental illness at trial. Temporary insanity does not necessarily mean that the defendant's insanity has been eliminated. An underlying psychosis may reveal itself in stressful situations (New Jersey v. Maik 1972). The presence of normal behavior following a criminal act diminishes the possibility that the defendant will be involuntarily committed, but it does not eliminate that possibility. The defendant assumes the burdens associated with a NGRI plea and verdict (Jones

v. U.S. 1983, 366). This means that the proceedings that follow the verdict are not "involuntary" (Weiner 1980, 1069).

In traditional civil commitment cases, commitment is based on a voluntary admission of one's inability to care for oneself. Involuntary commitment is by court order, provided the committee has been found to have mental illness and be dangerous, either to himself or to others, and by court order based on an emergency situation (Heller v. Doe 1993). States have set a higher bar for due process protections in involuntary commitment cases because the individual in question may spend the rest of his or her life confined in a mental institution without fully comprehending the situation (Jackson v. Indiana 1972).

In criminal commitment cases, however, the burden is usually on the acquittee to prove he is not dangerous to himself or to others. As John Kip Cornwell has argued, "Unlike civil committees, insanity acquittees can be detained without any evidence of present mental illness and can obtain discharge only upon proving their eligibility for release" (1996, 663). Legal insanity does not necessarily imply a lack of *mens rea*—the "mental element of the crime charged (known in legal shorthand as . . . [a] guilty mind)" (Clark v. Arizona 2006, 742). The due process standard for criminal commitment is more relaxed. With a NGRI verdict, there is the understanding that a crime—for which the defendant has been held not responsible—has been knowingly and intentionally committed, although the overt meaning of NGRI is that there is "a reasonable doubt that the defendant was sane at the time of the offense" (Bolton v. Harris 1968, 648). In a trial in which the defendant has offered a NGRI defense, the jury must first determine as a threshold matter whether a crime has been committed. A "not guilty by reason of insanity" verdict "means that the defendant *committed the crime*, but established that he was 'incapable of distinguishing between right and wrong' with respect to his criminal conduct" (Foucha v. Louisiana 1992, 103; italics in original). A NGRI verdict does not necessarily mean that the defendant has a terminal or serious mental illness (Krash 1961, 930). An insanity defendant may be fully capable of conducting his or her life on a daily basis, and may not suffer from delusions or neurological disorders that affect cognition or volition. Insanity does not mean the presence of a mental disorder in a neurological or psychological sense. Insanity is a legal designation, which means that concerns about safety shape the contours of the label as much as medical or psychological evidence. A successful insanity plea means that the defendant "lacked the capacity to appreciate the criminality of his conduct or to conform his conduct to the requirements of the law" (Arkansas v. Bailey 2007, 526).

Mental Disorders

Foucha's criminal commitment began in April of 1985. In 1987, Foucha asked for a review of his status, for purpose of release. Louisiana law provides for periodic review of an acquittee's status (Foucha v. Louisiana 1992, 105–6). In March of 1988, a panel of three doctors recommended that Foucha be "conditionally discharged." The panel recommend that Foucha:

> (1) be placed on probation, the length to be determined by the court; (2) remain free from intoxicating and mind-altering substances; (3) attend a Substance Abuse Clinic on a regular basis; (4) submit to regular and random urine drug screens at the local mental health center; and (5) be actively employed or seeking employment. (Louisiana v. Foucha 1990, 1140)

Six months later, after a contradictory hearing,[2] "the court found that defendant was a danger to others and ordered him recommitted." The burden of proving dangerousness falls upon the committee seeking release.

> "Dangerous to others" means the condition of a person whose behavior or significant threats support a reasonable expectation that there is a substantial risk that he will inflict physical harm upon another person in the near future. "Dangerous to self" means the condition of a person whose behavior, significant threats or inaction supports a reasonable expectation that there is a substantial risk that he will inflict physical or severe emotional harm upon his own person. (Louisiana v. Foucha 1990, 1140)

The state court of appeal upheld the trial court's decision to continue Foucha's commitment, as did the state supreme court. Foucha then appealed to the United States Supreme Court. According to Foucha, Louisiana was in violation of both the due process clause of the Fourteenth Amendment—because the state was holding someone who was neither guilty of a crime nor mentally ill—and the equal protection clause of the Fourteenth Amendment—because the state's procedures regarding the civil commitment of insane defendants were different from ordinary committees.

Before turning to the Supreme Court's analysis of Foucha's claims, it is useful to state what Foucha's medical or psychological claims are and to understand the meaning of NGRI and other juridical-medical terms related to mental disorders and criminal behavior. Within two years of his incarceration, Foucha petitioned for release, claiming he was no longer insane and neither dangerous to himself nor to others. He based his sanity claim on a diagnosis he received from three psychiatrists. The doctors attributed Foucha's insanity at the time of his crime to a "drug-induced psychosis" (Louisiana v. Foucha 1990, 1141; DSM 2000, 338–39, 191), which ceased to be an issue during his commitment. Each physician believed that Foucha suffered from Antisocial Personality Disorder (ASPD, sometimes abbreviated APD), and not from any organic mental disease, though one psychiatrist noted that he "would not 'feel comfortable in certifying that [Foucha] would not be a danger to himself or to other people'" (Foucha v. Louisiana 1992, 75). In a prior psychological examination, one doctor said that Foucha suffered from an antisocial personality (but not the disorder), and the other doctor agreed (Foucha v. Louisiana 1992, 75).[3]

The *Diagnostic and Statistical Manual* (*DSM*) "contains a standard set of definitions and criteria for mental disorders, and it is used for diagnostic purposes by virtually all psychiatrists and psychologists in the United States" (U.S. v. Graham 2010, 134). The *DSM*-IV specifically calls attention to the difference between a psychological assessment of behavior and the legal or political judgments that are necessary to determine a person's risk to public safety (DSM 2000, xxxii-xxxiii; Francis and Halon 2013).

The *DSM* regards a personality disorder as

> an enduring pattern of inner experience and behavior that deviates markedly from the expectations of the individual's culture, is pervasive and inflexible, has an onset in adolescence or early adulthood, is stable over time, and leads to distress or impairment. (DSM 2013, 645)

According to Donald Black et al., "Antisocial Personality Disorder (ASPD) is characterized by a pervasive pattern of socially irresponsible, exploitative, and guiltless behavior" (2010, 114). Those with ASPD have impairments in self- and interpersonal-functioning. That is, they are egocentric and manipulative and they lack remorse. "Offenders with ASPD," Black et al. write, "are more likely to report poorer mental health and social functioning, to have substantial psychiatric comorbidity, and to report higher suicide risk" (2010, 119).

The criteria used to diagnose ASPD "overlap greatly with those for criminality and substance abuse, leading to possible overdiagnosis . . . in prisoners and drug addicts" (Moran 1999, 239). Partly for this reason, the treatment for ASPD is "a source of great controversy" (Gatzke and Raine 2000, 51). The disorder is the product of neurological, genetic, and environmental causes, which makes treatment difficult.[4] Also, historically, the diagnosis has been beset with nosological difficulties relating to the terms "antisocial" and "personality" (Pickersgill 2013, 34). The disorder and the controversy over its etiology go back to the late eighteenth century, to another elusive medical concept called *manie sans delire,* or mania without delirium, and is related to other vague nineteenth- and twentieth-century medical appellations, such as "moral insanity," "sociopathy," and "psychopathy." Gatzke and Raine argue that treatment should be directed toward those who show signs of antisocial behavior during childhood and adolescence (2000, 53) because adults with ASPD are difficult to treat. Indeed, the *DSM* states that ASPD must be present in childhood and adolescence, though a clinician cannot make a diagnosis of ASPD until the subject reaches eighteen years of age (2013, 662). In *Foucha,* the justices referred to Foucha's antisocial personality as part of a disorder "for which there is no effective treatment" (Foucha v. Louisiana 1992, 82), which is not incorrect. I am unaware of any court record that mentions Foucha's childhood and adolescent behavior.

In cases of regulatory detention, the state can rely on any one of the following three governmental objectives to justify detention: "(1) protection of the acquittee from danger to self; (2) protection of society from the acquittee's dangerousness to others; and (3) the need for treatment or training to foster a healthy society" (Rowan 1993, 741). The state supreme court, in upholding Foucha's commitment, reasoned as follows. During Foucha's time at Feliciana, Foucha had multiple run-ins with other inmates and was generally disruptive. One psychiatrist wrote that Foucha "remains combative, agitated, and psychotic." Another noted that Foucha "continues to be a menace to society." In 1988, while in Feliciana, Foucha was diagnosed with ASPD, but there was "never any evidence of mental illness or disease since admission," and the defendant was "'in good shape' mentally." Foucha, however, had exhibited "suspicious and paranoid" behavior during his time at Feliciana and one doctor feared that Foucha could relapse if released. Paranoid Personality Disorder is part of the complex of behaviors that constitute ASPD, but the examining psychiatrists believed that Foucha's paranoia was not "related to the diagnosis of Antisocial Personality Disorder." They thought Foucha lacked "insight into his responsibilities for his behavior," a condition which "probably reflects an additional Axis II diagnosis of Paranoid Personality" (Louisiana v. Foucha 1990, 1141; DSM 2000, 690).

The current *DSM*, the fifth edition, distinguishes five axes of assessment. Previous editions, the one Foucha was subject to, identified two. The *DSM* used to separate mental illnesses that are neurological and genetic in nature (Axis I disorders) from personality and developmental disorders (Axis II disorders) that are historical and environmental. Though they differ, they are not, necessarily, distinct. "Axis I disorders and Axis II personality disorders are frequently comorbid" (Stork 2013, 947).

Nevertheless, some distinctions exist. Axis I disorders refer to clinical syndromes such as bipolar, major depression, dissociative identity disorder, and schizophrenia. Axis II disorders refer to developmental disorders, such as "personality disorders and intellectual disabilities" (DSM 1987, 16, 401). Mental health professionals consider Axis I patients to suffer from the most serious of mental disorders, in part because Axis I disorders are incurable, though they may be manageable. Federal courts are divided over the question whether Axis II disorders constitute mental disease in the Axis I sense (Guinon v. Armontrout 1990; Millhouse v. Sage 2014). The *DSM*-III classified ASPD an Axis II disorder because ASPD is a clinical diagnosis of behavioral abnormalities (Black 1999, xii). That is, although there may be neurological and genetic components to the disorder, this definition implies that the disorder contains willful elements that the person refuses to correct.

From a criminological or jurisprudential perspective, Foucha's problem is that paranoid personality disorder (PPD) is a far worse diagnosis than ASPD, although neither is particularly well understood.

> Antisocial personality disorder (ASPD) consists of a characteristic pattern of violations of others' rights, repetitive lying, impulsivity, irritable or aggressive behavior, lack of responsibility, and a general lack of guilt or remorse for one's actions. Because this disorder has a severe impact not only on the diagnosed, but on the community as well, it is of great concern to psychiatric practitioners. However, treatment of ASPD is a source of great controversy. The danger to society that these individuals represent, and the indication that treatment is often unsuccessful, leaves the removal of these persons from society through prison as the most common solution. Consequently, the most recent trend in

> the research of this disorder is to focus on its developmental nature, and design interventions to reach children before they become antisocial adults. (Gatze and Raine 2000, 51)

PPD, however, points to an underlying condition, in which case, if applicable, Foucha was in no way free from mental disease when he petitioned for his release. Some psychiatrists and neurologists believe that PPD is part of a larger, and more serious, set of mental disorders associated with schizophrenia. According to Søren Birkeland (2014, 220):

> the study of behavioral and psychopathological features associated with PPD entails the question if PPD really constitutes a distinct nosological entity or rather signifies, e.g., a mild variant of delusional disorder or schizophrenia. Genetic studies point towards a heritability of PPD itself as well as a link to delusional disorder, schizophrenia, and depressive illness. Correspondingly, it could be hypothesized that PPD is sometimes complicated by full-blown delusional psychosis and that depression sometimes occur. Again, however, there is limited research available to support any role of delusional psychotic episodes and depressive symptoms in individuals with PPD.

The American Psychological Association considers PPD to be part of a "cluster" of personality disorders. According to Michelle Esterberg, Sandra Goulding, and Elaine Walker (2010, 515):

> Those diagnosed with schizotypal, schizoid, and paranoid personality disorders are grouped together in Cluster A, and are classified by the DSM-IV-TR as representing "odd and eccentric behaviors." Considered as the more severe personality disorders, Cluster A personality disorders are assumed by many to be resistant to treatment.

The authors note that "individuals with PPD are at risk of experiencing brief psychotic episodes, as evidenced by delusional ideas or distorted perceptions that are manifested from extreme suspiciousness or paranoia. These can be difficult to differentiate from delusions and may result in misdiagnosis as a schizophrenia-spectrum disorder" (2010, 517).

If Foucha suffered from PPD (and was misdiagnosed as being paranoid without the disorder), it would mean that Foucha's mental problems had not left him. He had not become sane after a couple of years in Feliciana. Rather, his mental disorder was in remission, which suggests that releasing him was inappropriate, given the possibility that Foucha had a more substantive underlying disorder. Insofar as his dangerousness was related to an underlying mental illness (Foucha v. Louisiana 1991a, 23–25, 31), Foucha was never sane during his incarceration.

Not Guilty by Reason of Insanity

In *Jones v. United States* (1983), the Supreme Court held that states could treat NGRI committees differently than civil committees without violating the equal protection clause. *Jones* held that states do not have to release NGRI committees after the end of what would have been their criminal sentence. The Court's decision in *Foucha* altered the meaning of equal protection in commitment cases and clarified the distinction between kinds of committees, though it affected only the six "states that mandate continued retention of the acquittee solely on the grounds of dangerousness" (Halpern 1993, 1155–56).

How does the Supreme Court understand a NGRI verdict? Most crimes require two elements, an objective act and a subjective mind. The Court refers to these elements as *actus reus* and *mens rea. Actus reus* means: "'an act toward the commission of' some offense" (U.S. v. Resendiz-Ponce 2007, 113). *Mens rea* means: "'state of mind,' 'mental state,' 'general intent,' and 'intent'" (Kendrick 2014, 1257, n. 2). Although the Supreme Court has "never articulated a general constitutional doctrine of *mens rea*" (Powell v. Texas 1968, 535), *mens rea* is the ground upon which lawyers and judges determine the culpability of those who commit criminal acts.

Mens rea is not required for proof of all crimes (Comment 2001; U.S. v. Hinckley 1982, 117 nn. 1–2). The Supreme Court, however, generally disfavors criminal laws that require strict liability, that is, no *mens rea* (Staples v. U.S. 1994, 606). Lawyers take mental states into consideration in criminal cases because the Anglo-American legal tradition has long emphasized the value of the "faculties of reason, memory and understanding" (Yannoulidis 2012, 12) in determining the underlying meaning of behavior. The notion of intentionality "is central to the criminal law" (Reznek 1997, 12).

In the American legal tradition, a finding of mental illness, by itself, is not sufficient to negate a trial or a judgment of guilt (U.S. v. Childress 1995, 728–

29). Mental illness is not proof of incompetency and a jury can declare a mentally ill person who commits a crime guilty, including of a capital offense (Ford v. Wainwright 1986; Penry v. Lynaugh 1989). A mentally ill or disturbed individual may still comprehend the meaning of right and wrong in its most basic, functional sense. Psychological and psychiatric experts play a role in informing the meaning of criminal events at trial, but they do not have final say over what determines a defendant's intentions or the meaning of the crime, or how juries understand the status of the victim (Beecher-Monas 2003; U.S. v. Guiteau 1882). "What psychiatrists may consider a 'mental disease or defect' for clinical purposes, where their concern is treatment, may or may not be the same for the jury's purpose in determining criminal responsibility" (McDonald v. United States 1962, 851).

The procedures that govern insanity in the United States largely follow rules first articulated by the House of Lords in 1843. In that year, Daniel McNaughtan, acting on a delusion that the Tory party was persecuting him, attempted to kill the Tory prime minister, Robert Peel. Inadvertently, he shot and killed Peel's secretary, Edward Drummond, who had just walked out of the prime minister's residence. The jury found McNaughtan not guilty by reason of insanity and committed him to a mental hospital. At the Queen's request, the House of Lords drafted a set of rules governing the trials of those who seek to negate or diminish their responsibility by citing mental disease as a defense. According to the McNaughtan rules:

> If the accused was conscious that the act was one which he ought not to do; and if the act was at the same time contrary to law, he is punishable; and the usual course, therefore, has been to leave the question to the jury, whether the party accused had a sufficient degree of reason to know that he was doing an act that was wrong. (Barclay 1855, 589)

The Constitution does not require an insanity defense, and four states do not provide for it (Foucha v. Louisiana 1992, 88–89). Because the Supreme Court has never regarded the McNaughtan rules as a "fundamental principle" (Clark v. Arizona 2006, 736) of constitutional law, states that either forbid an insanity defense or alter it are not violating the due process clause of the Fourteenth Amendment.

Louisiana follows the McNaughtan rules. Louisiana law, like the law in other states with mental defenses, also assumes that all persons are sane until proven otherwise (Louisiana v. Peters 1994). In Louisiana, a defendant can demonstrate insanity by a preponderance of evidence (Louisiana v. Silman 1995, 32). Insanity is an affirmative defense, which means that the burden of proof rests with the defendant.

> An affirmative defense is distinct from other defenses in part because it typically assumes the truth of other elements of the crime. Thus, instead of "I didn't shoot him," it is "I shot him but in self-defense" or "I shot him but I was insane at the time." It is clear that proof beyond a reasonable doubt is required for defenses such as "I didn't shoot him" or "I wasn't there"—in order to get a conviction, the prosecution must prove beyond a reasonable doubt that the defendant was there and did shoot the victim. Like the defendant asserting an alibi, the defendant asserting an affirmative defense claims he did not commit the crime he is charged with. Saying "I shot him in self-defense" is a specific way of contending, "I did not commit murder." But while the prosecution must prove the absence of an alibi beyond a reasonable doubt, states may relieve the prosecution of that burden and shift it to the defendant while lowering the standard of proof for affirmative defenses. (Levy 2013, 281–82)

After the state charges a defendant with a crime and the defendant offers a defense of NGRI, the trial court must order a competency hearing to determine the defendant's mental fitness to stand trial (Demakis 2013). Competence to stand trial is a factual issue that any court can decide (U.S. v. Horowitz 1973; Wood v. Zahradnick 1979). Competence is a legal concept, not a medical one (Krash 1961, 914). Competency is governed by concerns about the administration of justice and is not strictly concerned with the defendant's mental capacity (Dusky v. U.S. 1960; Godinez v. Moran 1993; Riggins v. Nevada 1992). An individual psychiatric examination may precede the competency hearing (Note 2013, 472, n. 1457).

An inquiry into competency refers to the defendant's ability to stand trial and to aid in the preparation for his or her own defense (Cooper v. Oklahoma 1996; Note 2013). Neither a history of mental illness, the presence of mental retardation, nor a low IQ are sufficient to demonstrate incompetency. A defendant claiming diminished responsibility may still understand the charges against him or her and the general tenor of the courtroom (Penry v. Lynaugh 1989, 333–34). A state that fails to order a psychiatric examination for incompetency, however, is in violation of the defendant's due process rights (Drope v. Missouri 1975, 172). States may place the burden of proof of incompetency on the defendant. But a state may not make the test for competence "clear and convincing proof"—the high standard applied against states regarding the commitment of the mentally ill, established in *Addington v. Texas* (1979)—because each case addresses "different substantive issues" (Cooper v. Oklahoma 1996, 368). In setting a lower standard, the Supreme Court "safeguards the fundamental right not to stand trial while incompetent" (Cooper v. Oklahoma 1996, 369).

All defendants have the right to consult with an attorney prior to an examination for competency, but there is no right to have an attorney present during the examination (Buchanan v. Kentucky 1987, 424–25). If a defendant is found to be incompetent to stand trial, a court can do one of two things: it can either dismiss the charges "without prejudice" (Zapf and Roesch 2000, 29) and commit the defendant to a mental facility (the state will then undertake civil commitment proceedings), or it can order the defendant to be placed in a mental hospital until such time as the defendant is rendered competent to stand trial (Halpern 1993).

Dangerous incompetents may be detained longer than nondangerous incompetents; neither can be detained indefinitely. At the time the Court decided *Foucha*, state laws varied regarding detaining mental incompetents. The length of time extends from ninety days to the equivalent of the maximum criminal sentence (Morris and Meloy 1993, 79). Some states do not specify a maximum length at all. States will offer probation in noncapital cases and to those deemed not dangerous; supervision is supposed to be long-term. A detainee also maintains the right to petition a court for release through the writ of habeas corpus (Hess 1980, 586, n. 31).

The Supreme Court has not established a constitutional timeline for the detention of dangerous and nondangerous incompetents (Foucha v. Louisiana 1992, 88). The general rule in the states is between twelve to eighteen months, although any length of time longer than that is not inherently unconstitutional (Morris and Meloy 1993, 12–15; Hur 2014). What is unconstitutional is holding a NGRI defendant indefinitely. Tying detention to the length of the criminal sentence is probably unconstitutional, because it violates the Court's ruling in *Jackson v. Indiana* (1972), though, as Grant Morris and J. Reid Meloy point out, a number of states still permit detention according to the criminal sentence (1993, 17–18 and appendix). In *Jackson*, the Court defined the goal of detention following a finding of incompetence to be restoration to competence, not permanent incapacitation:

> a person charged by a State with a criminal offense who is committed solely on account of his incapacity to proceed to trial cannot be held more than the reasonable period of time necessary to determine whether there is a substantial probability that he will attain that capacity in the foreseeable future. (Jackson v. Indiana 1972, 738)

If there is no possibility that the defendant will become competent, then the state "must resort to civil commitment" (Riggins v. Nevada 1992, 145). This would be an involuntary civil commitment, and the state must prove that the individual is mentally ill and dangerous either to himself or to others (Baxstrom v. Herold 1966; Vitek v. Jones 1980).

If a defendant is declared competent to stand trial, a plea agreement is possible, and can result in prison time. If a trial takes place either with a jury or as a bench trial, and a NGRI verdict is announced, then (as in Louisiana) the defendant can be immediately confined to a jail, prison, or mental institution until a hearing is held to determine whether the defendant "can be discharged or can be released on probation, without danger to others or to himself" (Louisiana Code of Criminal Procedure, art. 654; Ingber 1982). The process of placing an insanity acquittee immediately in a forensic facility is known as automatic commitment.

Automatic commitment following a verdict of not guilty by reason of insanity comes from the British legal tradition (Walker 1968, 42–44). In the wake of an assassination attempt of King George III by James Hadfield, in 1800, Parliament passed a law, the Criminal Lunatics Act, that required insanity acquittees to be confined to a hospital for the insane.

> If [the jury] shall find that such person was insane at the time of the committing such offence, the court before whom such trial shall be had, shall order such person to be kept in strict custody, in such place and in such manner as to the court shall seem fit, until His Majesty's pleasure shall be known. (The Statutes 1872, 598)

As Nigel Walker has written, the verdict in Hadfield's case was an "acquittal in name only, for it tacitly admitted that the doctrine of *mens rea* could not safely be applied to the insane. A criminal lunatic might be as morally innocent as a man who had done harm by accident or in self-defence, but the danger of *treating* him as innocent was too great" (1968, 81; italics in original).

The American states adopted automatic confinement following a NGRI verdict in various stages throughout the nineteenth century, and for various offenses. The ostensible reason was the same as Britain's: a ruling of NGRI proved that the defendant committed a criminal act, requiring confining insanity acquittees to protect public safety (Dershowitz 1974, 822, 830). Automatic confinement laws persisted throughout the twentieth century. Beginning in the 1960s, however, states began altering their automatic commitment statutes, providing defendants with greater due process protections, and making commitment following a NGRI verdict closer to the procedures required for traditional civil commitment (LaFond and Durham 1994). The movement in civil commitment was away from a custodial model and toward care, which involved greater due process protections for inmates (Rothman 1971, 144). One reason for the change was the rise of interest groups calling for deinstitutionalization of the mentally ill. Another was Supreme Court decisions that accorded individuals greater Fourteenth Amendment protections in NGRI situations (Baxstrom v. Herold 1966, 114–15; Vitek v. Jones 1980; Humphrey v. Cady 1972, 510–12; Specht v. Patterson 1967, 608). In light of Supreme Court opinions from the late 1960s and early 1970s that expanded equal protection and due process, John Kip Cornwell has written that federal courts began striking "down provisions relating to the automatic and indefinite commitment of insanity acquittees" (1996, 655). Until that point, there was widespread acceptance of automatic commitment laws. As Justice Tom Clark noted in 1962:

> statutes provide for mandatory commitment of persons acquitted by reason of insanity in 12 States and the Virgin Islands as well as in England and the District of Columbia. Six States permit commitment in the discretion of the trial judge. Eighteen more provide for mandatory or discretionary commitment if the trial judge finds that the defendant's insanity continues or that his discharge would be dangerous to the public peace. In 10 States and in Puerto Rico, mandatory commitment follows a like finding by the trial jury or by a second jury. (Lynch v. Overholser 1962, 727)

In 1954, Judge David Bazelon, of the court of appeals for the District of Columbia circuit, held that courts in the D.C. circuit should give priority to psychiatric experts in determining whether a criminal act was the product of mental disease or defect (Durham v. U.S. 1954, 874–75). The decision as to whether the defendant is insane and criminally irresponsible remained with the jury. *Durham v. U.S.* (1954) altered a history of judging insanity on the McNaughtan rule of right and wrong, which emphasized cognition as the basis for demonstrating insanity, and the irresistible impulse test, which emphasized volition, and which dates to the late nineteenth century (U.S. v. Lee 1886; Smith v. U.S. 1929). *Durham*, in essence, added a volitional prong to the McNaughtan rule. "*Durham* adopted the 'product rule,' pioneered in *State v. Pike*, and exculpated from criminal responsibility those whose forbidden acts were the product of a mental disease or defect" (U.S. v. Brawner 1972, 976). The ruling medicalized the assessment of insanity and reduced "the community's sense of when it is just to hold a man responsible for his act" (U.S. v. Brawner 1972, 1023). In 1957, the same court found that the product test was imprecise and urged this language be used: "But for this disease the act would not have been committed" (Carter v. U.S. 1957, 617). One significant problem with "but for" and "product of" is that courts can take these terms to mean that the presence of mental disorder is the "sole cause" (U.S. v. Lauzon 1991, 331) of the behavior, thereby putting an end to criminal responsibility, while abdicating judicial oversight over the criminal law.

Prior to the *Durham* ruling, the practice regarding insanity acquittees in the District of Columbia was to give federal judges discretion to commit defendants, though the custom in the District was to order commitment. This was not the rule in all federal jurisdictions, where "defendants found not guilty by reason of insanity [were] customarily set free." In some federal cases, however, "a defendant found not guilty by reason of insanity . . . could be committed to a state mental institution in a civil commitment proceedings [sic] in a state court pursuant to applicable state law" (Krash 1961, 942, n. 188). Congress was concerned that the *Durham* ruling made commitment "discretionary, and so by an amendment passed on August 9, 1955, commitment was made mandatory" (Sauer v. U.S. 1957, 651) in every NGRI case in the District of Columbia. In a separate ruling by the D.C. court of appeals the year after *Durham*, *Taylor v. United States*, the court held that in trials involving pleas of NGRI, "counsel may and the judge should inform the jury that if [the defendant] is acquitted by reason of insanity he will be presumed to be insane and may be confined in a 'hospital for the insane' as long as 'the public safety and . . . (his) welfare' require" (Taylor v. U.S. 1955, 404).

The laws regarding insanity acquittees changed again following the NGRI verdict in John Hinckley's case. In 1981, Hinckley attempted to kill President Ronald Reagan in Washington, D.C. Hinckley won a NGRI plea. The federal district court confined Hinckley to St. Elizabeths Hospital, in Washington, D.C., until such time as the court "finds by a preponderance of the evidence that he is not likely to injure himself or other persons due to a mental disease" (Bonnie, Jeffries, and Low 2000, 119; U.S. v. Hinckley 1981).

Many state legislators did not view the *Hinckley* decision favorably, and the result was that "thirty-four states subsequently amended their insanity defense laws" (La Fond and Durham 1994, 83). Congress altered the federal insanity law as well, excusing only the "severely" mentally ill who are "unable" to appreciate the wrongfulness of their conduct (Congress 1984). "Guilty but Mentally Ill" laws began to appear as early as 1975, more so after the *Hinckley* verdict. The purpose of these laws is to ensure that those who argue successfully for mental illness as a mitigating factor in determining criminal responsibility will serve time in prison for their crime (La Fond and Durham 1994, 84).

In the late 1960s, federal courts began to split over whether to treat insanity acquittees the same as civil committees.

> The justifications for according insanity acquittees fewer safeguards include the presumption of the acquittee's continuing insanity, the availability of alternative release procedures, the belief that insanity acquittees pose more danger to society than do civilly committed persons and the intent of legislatures to discourage false pleas of insanity. Underlying these rationales is the perception that insanity acquittees are an exceptional class warranting special treatment. (Polstein 1985, 486–87)

The Supreme Court thought otherwise. According to Justice Lewis Powell, writing for the majority in *Jones v. United States* (1983), there is no reason to conflate the commitment issues of civil committees and insanity acquittees:

> We hold that when a criminal defendant establishes by a preponderance of the evidence that he is not guilty of a crime by reason of insanity, the Constitution permits the Government, on the basis of the insanity judgment, to confine him to a mental institution until such time as he has regained his sanity or is no longer a danger to himself or society. This holding accords with the widely and reasonably held view that insanity acquittees constitute a special class that should be treated differently from other candidates for commitment. (Jones v. U.S. 1983, 370)

The ruling in *Jones v. U.S.* should have adversely affected Foucha's equal protection claim, but it did not. Before turning to that issue, I want to discuss levels of scrutiny in these cases.

The question regarding the length and kind of confinement one undergoes based on the type of commitment law invoked raises the question about the level of scrutiny courts must engage in to assess a commitment scheme's constitutionality. In the section that follows, I will examine the problem of scrutiny levels against the claims that NGRI verdicts create liberty interests that supersede the state's interest in preventing dangerous persons from being set free. According to the Supreme Court, a liberty interest "may 'originate in the Constitution,' or it may have 'its roots in state law'" (Meachum v. Fano 1976, 230). One can also claim a liberty interest from a state or federal statute or regulation (Hewitt v. Helms 1983). If the liberty claim originates in the Constitution, it must be based upon the Fifth or Fourteenth Amendments or from the Constitution by implication. If it is derived from the amendments, then the liberty interest is subject to the test in *Washington v. Glucksberg* (1997): it must be "deeply rooted in this Nation's history and tradition, and implicit in the concept of ordered liberty" (1997, 703).

Judicial Scrutiny of Insanity Claims

The three types of scrutiny the Supreme Court resorts to (strict, intermediate, and rational basis) are not always applied consistently in all types of cases (Linder 1991; Buchanan 1993), and they can be applied differently when the legislation is from Congress or the states. To confuse matters, there are in-between categories within levels of scrutiny, such as "super-heightened scrutiny standard of review" and "enhanced intermediate standard of review" (Smith 1997, 504, 500), which the Court created in *United States v. Virginia* (1996) and *Craig v. Boren* (1976), respectively. There is also an enhanced rational basis test (Romer v. Evans 1996; City of Cleburne v. Cleburne Living Center, Inc. 1985). Enhanced intermediate analyses require an "exceedingly persuasive justification" (Smith 1997, 482) by the state regarding a law for the Court to agree to its constitutionality. In *Doe v. Reed* (2010), the Court created another level of intermediate review, though this level comes closest to strict scrutiny. It is called "exacting scrutiny," and it "requires the challenged law to have 'a substantial relation' to 'a sufficiently important governmental interest,' which 'must reflect the seriousness of the . . . burden' on the exercise of a constitutional right" (Hardy 2014, 1438; Doe v. Reed 2010).

Eric Janus and Wayne Logan have noted that "the Court's civil confinement rhetoric has invoked a range of standards without actually naming them" (Janus and Logan 2003, 366). Such imprecision says more about the Court's problems in fine-tuning the right involved and in defining mental illness, mental abnormality, personality disorder, and dangerousness with precision than it does about the Court's confused standards of review (U.S. v. Virginia 1996, 567–68). Janus and Logan point to elements of heightened scrutiny in *Foucha* and the Court's two key postconviction commitment cases, *Kansas v. Hendricks* (1997) and *Kansas v. Crane* (2002), but this is more an inference than the Court's stated position.

The Supreme Court has never claimed that the postconviction civil commitment of sex offenders interferes with a fundamental right not to be detained (Alschuler 1986, 527–29). To be sure, restrictions on sex offenders are burdensome. The question is whether certain kinds of confinement impose an unnecessary or unjust burden on a minority by an overbearing majority, thereby violating due process in its fundamental sense. What concerns should the Court balance in confinement cases?

As the Court noted in *Addington v. Texas* (1979, 429), "beyond a reasonable doubt" may not be the proper standard in civil commitment. "Given the lack of certainty and the fallibility of psychiatric diagnosis, there is a serious question as to whether a state could ever prove beyond a reasonable doubt that an individual is both mentally ill and likely to be dangerous." In *Foucha*, the dissent brought up the issue of level of review. Justice Anthony Kennedy wrote: "We have often subjected to heightened due process scrutiny, with regard to both purpose and duration, deprivations of physical liberty imposed before a judgment is rendered under this standard" (Foucha v. Louisiana 1992, 93). The criminal character of Foucha's case means that the Court should not analyze Foucha's case at the heightened scrutiny level. As Louisiana had not violated a fundamental right, the Court's scrutiny of the law in question need not be "exacting" (Foucha v. Louisiana 1992, 116). Justice Clarence Thomas, in dissent, suggested that the level of scrutiny in *Foucha* is rational basis. He noted that "We need not decide in this case which precise standard is applicable, since the laws under attack here are at the very least reasonable" (Foucha v. Louisiana 1992, 121).

The most rigorous form of judicial scrutiny is strict scrutiny. The Supreme Court requires strict scrutiny in cases involving "race, national origin, alienage, sex, and nonmarital parentage" (Yoshino 2011, 756). The test places the burden upon "the State to show there is a compelling state interest in the statute, ordinance, or regulation" (Kansas v. Risjord 1991, 501). Although a difficult standard to overcome, strict scrutiny is not always fatal to legislation. For a law to pass strict scrutiny review, the Supreme Court requires that the law in question be "supported by a compelling state purpose and whether the means chosen to accomplish that purpose are narrowly tailored" (Wygant v. Jackson Board of Education 1986, 274). The law must also be the "least restrictive means of serving a compelling government interest" (Burwell v. Hobby Lobby Stores 2014, 2759).

Below strict scrutiny is intermediate scrutiny. Until the Burger Court, the Supreme Court had two tiers of review, strict and rational basis (Buchanan 1993, 1513–18). Finding the rational basis test not sufficiently protective of individual and group rights, the Burger Court added intermediate level to cases involving religion, speech, substantive due process, and equal protection. In *Clark v. Jeter* (1988), the Supreme Court held that to "withstand intermediate scrutiny, a statutory classification must be substantially related to an important governmental objective" (1988, 461). To pass intermediate level review, equal protection cases have to involve "'quasi-suspect' traits like gender or illegitimacy" (Smith 1997, 478). The Court requires that "the classification be 'narrowly drawn'—that is, not substantially more burdensome than is necessary to accomplish the state's objectives" (Cornwell 1996, 678). The burden of proof rests with the government.

Below intermediate scrutiny are rational basis considerations. This level of review is most deferential to legislatures (Williamson v. Lee Optical 1955).

> Under rational basis review, the Court undertakes a two step analysis. First, the Court examines the end or goal that government is pursuing and second, the Court examines the relationship between the government's goal and the particular means employed by government to achieve the goal. (Buchanan 1993, 1518–19)

The rational basis standard is "not a license for courts to judge the wisdom, fairness, or logic of legislative choices"; rather, it is the "paradigm of judicial restraint" (Federal Communications Commission. v. Beach Communications

1993, 313–14). In these cases, courts require that "there is some rational relationship between disparity of treatment and some legitimate governmental purpose" (Central State University v. American Association of University Professors 1999, 128).

The Court determines the level of scrutiny by the right challenged or asserted. The right can be one the Constitution mentions or implies or it can be one affected by the political process (U.S. v. Carolene Products 1938, 152 n. 4; NAACP v. Alabama 1958). There are two issues in civil commitment cases to determine scrutiny levels (but not necessarily in NGRI cases, because a NGRI verdict is based in part on a criminal act, and criminal acts imply dangerousness). One is that involuntary civil commitment involves an important liberty interest (Foucha v. Louisiana 1992, 116). The second is that mental illness is a stigmatizing disorder (Jones v. U.S. 1983, 367). It has, therefore, been suggested (Cornwell 1996, 677–89) that the mentally ill who are civilly committed should be protected at the same level of scrutiny as women and illegitimate children, that is, at the intermediate level. Three issues, however, have kept the Court from raising commitment cases from rational basis to an intermediate level (or higher). One is the status of the right involved (is it fundamental?); the second is the problem of dangerousness that lies at the heart of both NGRI cases and in civil commitment cases involving sexually violent predators. The Court's ruling in *Addington v. Texas* suggests that the Fourteenth Amendment's due process clause requires that states prove dangerousness in civil commitment cases by clear and convincing evidence, a higher standard than rational basis. The third is the question of a committee's mental illness. Heightened scrutiny can be applied to cases of the mentally ill. However, state postconviction commitment laws require a finding of mental abnormality, which because it is a legislative designation is not the same as mental illness (Kansas v. Hendricks 1997, 350; Young v. Weston 1995, 746). If mental illness is not implicated in a commitment, then standards of review can be lower. Any stigma attached to being a sex offender is the consequence of the offender's actions.

Justice Sandra Day O'Connor, in her concurrence in *Foucha*, raised the idea that insanity acquittees have a "strong interest in liberty" (Foucha v. Louisiana 1992, 88) when they become sane during their commitment. O'Connor does not suggest that all involuntary civil commitments be assessed at the intermediate level. Nor does she suggest that the intermediate level is fatal to the state's case to continue the commitment of one considered dangerous. According to O'Connor, but not the majority opinion, a state can continue holding an insanity acquittee who is no longer insane, provided there is a heightened level of judicial scrutiny. For O'Connor, Foucha's return to sanity required that higher level of scrutiny. Nevertheless, O'Connor wrote separately to maintain a distinction between insanity acquittees and civil committees, a point the majority disagreed with. O'Connor wrote: "where the only evidence of dangerousness is that the acquittee committed a nonviolent or relatively minor crime" (Foucha v. Louisiana 1992, 88), the burden shifts to the government to convince a court why the detainee should remain confined. O'Connor did not "understand the Court to hold that Louisiana may never confine dangerous insanity acquittees after they regain mental health" (Foucha v. Louisiana 1992, 87).

Intermediate review has become a substitute for strict scrutiny in cases not involving race but among those who claim to be marginalized by the political process (Dandridge v. Williams 1970; San Antonio Independent School District v. Rodriguez 1973). In *Humphrey v. Cady* (1972, 506), in which Wisconsin automatically committed a sex offender under a sex deviate law rather than by trial, the Court noted that an evidentiary hearing on the petitioner's claims was required, given the potentially indefinite confinement Donald Humphrey was about to experience. In *Jackson v. Indiana* (1972, 729), a case about a defendant's competence to stand trial, the Court relied on a "reasonable justification" standard to review the legislation. The Court noted that the state had not proven that Jackson was dangerous. In both cases, the Court increased the level of review. In *Jackson*, reasonable justification is clearly a higher standard than rational basis, as a rational basis standard would not require the state to prove dangerousness. As John Kip Cornwell has noted, "the Court's continuing sensitivity to the seriousness of restrictions on bodily freedom, coupled with sympathy for the stigmatic effect of involuntary commitment, points to a stricter standard of review, even where conducted under the rational basis label" (1996, 673–74).

The decision in *Foucha* did not settle the matter of levels of scrutiny in NGRI or commitment cases, but it did shine a light on this problem. The final piece of the puzzle is to examine the standard of proof for commitment.

The Standard of Proof for Commitment

The problem facing the Supreme Court in *Foucha* was this: was the Louisiana law governing NGRI, which required detention until such time as the acquittee could convince a court that he was no longer a "'danger to others or himself' regardless of whether the individual remains mentally ill" (Foucha v. Louisiana 1993, 4), a violation of the due process and equal protection clauses of the Fourteenth Amendment? The fifth circuit court of appeals had upheld this law in *Jackson v. Foti* (1982), on the ground that the law in question required a hearing before commitment, and that that standard satisfied both the due process and equal protection clauses of the Fourteenth Amendment.

In upholding the order to retain Foucha on dangerous grounds, the Louisiana supreme court cited federal cases (in circuits other than the fifth, which governs Louisiana) that had upheld state decisions to continue detention, following an insanity acquittal, based on dangerousness alone. The Louisiana supreme court dismissed as *dicta* two federal cases from the fifth circuit that had required "identical standards to civil and criminal commitment decisions" (Louisiana v. Foucha 1990, 1142). In *Hopkins v. Lynn* (1989), which the Supreme Court in *Foucha* ignored, the fifth circuit court of appeals rejected a state court decision that had upheld the continued confinement of an insanity acquittee on dangerousness alone. The court in *Hopkins* did not say that dangerousness could not be used as a basis for continued confinement, only that the state did not prove the defendant's dangerousness. The majority opinion in *Hopkins* relied on *Francois v. Henderson* (1988), another fifth circuit case, in which the court found no "evidence to support a finding that the insanity acquittee was either mentally ill or dangerous. The court held that it was unconstitutional for the state to detain Francois and granted his petition for habeas corpus" (Hopkins v. Lynn 1989, 37).

One fifth circuit case supports the Louisiana supreme court's decision in *Foucha*. In *Powell v. Florida* (1978, 326), the court of appeals held that a state "may treat insanity acquittees differently to the extent that the distinction has some relevance to a legitimate state interest." Protecting society against dangerous persons is a legitimate state interest. The *Powell* decision, however, was suspect by the time of Foucha's case (Congress had also moved Florida into the eleventh circuit in 1981), in light of *Hopkins* and *Francois*, as well as the Supreme Court's decisions in *Baxstrom v. Herold*, *Humphrey v. Cady*, *Jackson v. Indiana*, and *Addington v. Texas* (which I discuss in the next chapter).

Finding conflict within the fifth circuit, the state supreme court in *Foucha* turned to two Supreme Court decisions, *Addington v. Texas* and *Jones v. U.S.* One problem with these two cases is that they are civil not criminal, and thus lead to conclusions that may not be properly within the constitutional parameters required to determine Foucha's future. We should not forget that Foucha is a criminal case. The *Addington* decision held that the civil commitment of those with mental illnesses who cannot take care of themselves "requires the state to justify confinement by proof more substantial than a mere preponderance of the evidence" (Addington v. Texas 1979, 427). This requirement became the basis for the Court's decision in *Foucha. Addington* was a civil commitment case of a mentally ill person whose mother sought indefinite confinement of her son, Frank Addington, given his history of mental problems. It did not involve a sexual offender or any criminal matter. Nor does the holding have any relationship to verdicts of NGRI. It is, however, important because it establishes guidelines for committing the mentally ill, guidelines that have increasingly become the focus of insanity acquittees.

In 1975, Michael Jones was arrested in Washington, D.C., following the attempted theft of a coat from a department store. Had Jones pleaded guilty, or had a jury found him guilty, his maximum sentence would have been one year in jail. Instead Jones pleaded not guilty by reason of insanity. He stood trial, won a NGRI verdict, and was committed to St. Elizabeths Hospital. A hospital psychologist diagnosed Jones with "schizophrenia, paranoid type" (Jones v. U.S. 1983, 359–60). The question before the Supreme Court was "whether petitioner . . . must be released because he has been hospitalized for a period longer than he might have served in prison had he been convicted" (Jones v. U.S. 1983, 356). The Court held that it was constitutional to hold Jones in a mental institution until such time as he had regained his sanity and was no longer a danger to himself or to anyone.

To gain release from a commitment following a NGRI verdict in the District of Columbia, "the confined person must show that he is either no longer mentally ill or no longer dangerous to himself or others" (Jones v. U.S. 1983, 358). The procedure for release from a NGRI verdict follows the same rules that are applied in cases of civil commitment, with one exception. In a civil commitment case, the hospital chief of service can authorize release, whereas with an insanity acquittee, a court must approve the application for release. The difference is required because the release of an insanity acquittee implicates questions of dangerousness. As Ralph Slovenko has noted (1995, 185, 188), hospitals may not be immune to lawsuits regarding the discharge of dangerous persons. State laws make a distinction between the civilly committed and the criminally acquitted on the basis of dangerousness, and not simply on the presence of mental illness. In civil commitment cases, the individual's potential release is based upon medical and psychiatric concerns. But the judgment to commit and maybe release a defendant found NGRI is based on social and legal concerns (Hess 1980, 587).

As required by the law in the District of Columbia, a hearing was held fifty days after the verdict to determine Jones's mental status. Once "some evidence of mental disorder is introduced . . . sanity, like any other fact, must be proved as part of the prosecution's case beyond a reasonable doubt" (Durham v. U.S. 1954, 866; Tatum v. U.S. 1951, 389). If the patient fails to satisfy the standard of proof for sanity, judicial hearings may be held every six months, where, again, the burden of proof rests with the patient to prove "by a preponderance of the evidence" (Jones v. U.S. 1983, 354) that he or she is sane. At the hearing held fifty days after commitment, the staff at St. Elizabeths determined that Jones remained mentally ill. Jones obtained new counsel, and in 1977 another hearing on his mental health was held. "By that date petitioner had been hospitalized for more than one year [i.e., 17 months], the maximum period he could have spent in prison if he had been convicted. On the basis he demanded that he be released unconditionally or re-committed pursuant to the civil-commitment standards" (Jones v. U.S. 1983, 360).

On what constitutional ground did the District of Columbia believe that it had the power to hold Jones indefinitely? According to Justice Lewis Powell, writing for the majority, "A verdict of not guilty by reason of insanity establishes two facts: (1) the defendant committed an act that constitutes a criminal offense, and (2) he committed the act because of mental illness" (Jones v. U.S. 1983, 363). According to the law in the District of Columbia, the first prong, committing a criminal act, indicates dangerousness. It is irrelevant that Jones's act was petty theft. "This Court never has held that 'violence,' however that term might be defined, is a prerequisite for a constitutional commitment" (Jones v. U.S. 1983, 365). To be sure, the opinion cries out for greater clarity regarding the differences between danger and violence. Nevertheless, the Court was satisfied that the required fifty-day hearing and the availability to request hearings satisfied Jones's due process rights.

Jones also raised the claim that the law governing immediate and indefinite detention following a NGRI verdict was unconstitutional. He argued that it violated the due process and equal protection clauses of the Fourteenth Amendment. Jones believed he had an equal protection claim because courts were treating insanity acquittees differently than civil committees. Jones's equal protection claim arose because the Court has generally interpreted the equal protection clause to mean that states cannot treat similarly situated persons or classes differently, without demonstrating an important government objective for doing so (Craig v. Boren 1976).

In *Addington v. Texas*, the Court had held that "proof by clear and convincing evidence" was required for civil commitment, a standard higher than "the preponderance-of-the-evidence standard applicable to other categories of civil cases" (Addington v. Texas 1979, 433). Jones argued that he was unconstitutionally subjected to the lower standard, even though the effect of commitment following a NGRI verdict was functionally the same as if it were a decision in a civil commitment case. Jones's concern was that *Addington*'s more stringent standard prevented courts from confining those who were not mentally ill but exhibited merely "abnormal behavior" (Jones v. U.S. 1983, 367). This is not so. Jones's committal (like Foucha's) was predicated on his claim that he was not guilty by reason of insanity. The Court believed that Congress had acted within its power to assume that a detainee's mental state will continue. Besides, procedures were in place to review the status of detainees over time. Jones's confinement, therefore, was not indefinite, only potentially so. Given the protections afforded NGRI detainees, the Court held that any concern that state governments would start committing anyone and everyone, willy-nilly, was misplaced.

The final question the Court addressed was Jones's claim that he was incarcerated longer than his possible prison term. The reason Congress chose to make NGRI commitment indeterminate is because the duration of mental illness is unknown (Morris and Meloy 1993). Congress was satisfied that indefinite detention did not foreclose the possibility of release, as long as the government provided periodic review. "A particular sentence of incarceration is chosen to reflect society's view of the proper response to commission of a particular criminal offense, based on a variety of considerations such as retribution, deterrence, and rehabilitation" (Jones v. U.S. 1983, 368–69).

Two questions, then: (1) what are the criteria by which a state can commit someone found not guilty by reason of insanity? And (2) Is *Jones v. U.S.* still good law? Although the Court in the early 1970s had muddied the waters regarding due process protections and the meaning of equal protection in civil and criminal cases, the table is set for an analysis of the Supreme Court's *Foucha* decision.

The Supreme Court Decides

The Supreme Court's decision in *Foucha v. Louisiana* was five to four for Parts I and II of a three-part opinion. Part III garnered only a plurality of the justices.

Justice Byron White wrote the majority opinion. Justice Sandra Day O'Connor wrote a separate concurrence, to emphasize that the Court's decision does not "pass judgment on more narrowly drawn laws that provide for detention of insanity acquittees, or on statutes that provide for punishment of persons who commit crimes while mentally ill" (Foucha v. Louisiana 1992, 87). Justice O'Connor separated herself from the part of the opinion that argued that Louisiana had violated Foucha's rights on equal protection grounds. Justice Anthony Kennedy wrote a dissent, which Chief Justice William Rehnquist joined. Justice Clarence Thomas wrote a separate dissent, which Justice Antonin Scalia and the Chief Justice joined.

Part I addresses the facts. In Part II, Justice White noted the controversy between a civil commitment and a NGRI verdict. Civil commitments and NGRI verdicts differ because civil commitments, per the *Addington* decision, require clear and convincing evidence that the person is a danger to himself or to others. States are not under this burden in NGRI verdicts because the verdict is proof that the person is capable of some minimum of violence.

According to Justice White, Louisiana sought to confine Foucha in a mental hospital "on the basis of his antisocial personality" (Foucha v. Louisiana 1992, 78). Justice White found three problems with this: (1) Louisiana could not keep Foucha in a mental hospital "absent a determination in civil commitment proceedings of current mental illness and dangerousness"; (2) if Foucha no longer qualifies as an insanity acquittee, then Louisiana has to justify confining him on "constitutionally adequate procedures"; and (3) on the grounds of substantive due process[5] (Foucha v. Louisiana 1992, 78–80).

Justice White then turned to *Jones v. U.S.*, another NGRI case. According to White, the Court held in *Jones* that "'[t]he committed acquittee is entitled to release when he has recovered his sanity or is no longer dangerous,' *i.e.*, the acquittee may be held as long as he is both mentally ill and dangerous, but no longer" (Foucha v. Louisiana 1992, 77). This is not the holding in *Jones.* The quoted sentence ends with Justice Powell writing that "Congress has chosen . . . to leave the length of commitment indeterminate, subject to periodic review of the patient's suitability for release" (Jones v. U.S. 1983, 368).

In 1975, the Court held in *O'Connor v. Donaldson* that Kenneth O'Connor was entitled to release because he was not dangerous to himself or to others. The case began as a "right to treatment" case but Justice White in *Foucha* turned it into a civil commitment case. The case is about a man committed to a mental facility for fifteen years on the basis of his delusions. O'Connor was never violent or dangerous. He resisted all treatment while confined and ultimately won his freedom. The case is of limited constitutional value for Foucha, given the brief extent of Foucha's insanity and his history of violence. Nevertheless, on *O'Connor*'s reasoning, Justice White declared that it is "unconstitutional for a State to continue to confine a harmless, mentally ill person" (Foucha v. Louisiana 1992, 77; O'Connor v. Donaldson 1975, 575). As it is unconstitutional to detain someone for being mentally ill (and ASPD is not a mental illness), so, too, dangerousness by itself is an insufficient reason to detain someone indefinitely. To be held indefinitely under a NGRI verdict, Louisiana must prove that a defendant is either dangerous to himself, to others, and is mentally ill. Having ruled out mental illness, Louisiana was content that a ruling of dangerousness satisfied the Court's jurisprudence. It did not. For guidance, the Court turned to *Vitek v. Jones* (1980).

Larry Jones was a prisoner in Nebraska, sentenced to three-to-nine years in prison for robbery. After a series of violent acts, prison authorities placed Jones in solitary confinement, where he set fire to his mattress and severely burned himself. The state transferred him to a mental hospital, which was under a separate jurisdiction than the prison. Jones then alleged that the transfer violated the due process clause of the Fourteenth Amendment, which requires notice, a hearing, and counsel. During ongoing legal procedures, the state paroled Jones, "on condition that he accept psychiatric treatment at a Veterans' Administration Hospital" (Vitek v. Jones 1980, 485). Jones violated his parole by failing to continue treatment at the VA hospital. Jones argued, however, that he was receiving treatment against his will.

According to Justice White, writing for the majority in *Vitek*:

> The loss of liberty produced by an involuntary commitment is more than a loss of freedom from confinement. It is indisputable that commitment to a mental hospital "can engender adverse social consequences to the individual" and that "[w]hether we label this phenomena 'stigma' or choose to call it something else . . . we recognize that it can occur and that it can have a very significant impact on the individual." (1980, 492)

The *Vitek* Court held that when a state creates a liberty interest, the prisoner is entitled to due process protections. In transferring Jones from prison to something other than prison, involving a different kind of treatment, Nebraska denied Jones his liberty interest. The Court's difficulty in *Foucha* was in stating Foucha's liberty interest and then joining *Vitek* to *Foucha*.

Justice White argued in *Foucha* that Louisiana misunderstood two key points from the Court's jurisprudence. One, Foucha was never convicted of any crime. Two, Foucha suffers from no known mental illness. Justice White argued that the case law is clear. Foucha's liberty interest lies in the fact that involuntary commitment imposes a "massive curtailment of liberty" (Humphrey v. Cady 1972, 509) on the confined. Because "[i]n our society liberty is the norm, and detention prior to trial or without trial is the carefully limited exception" (Foucha v. Louisiana 1992, 83), the Court held that Louisiana had to release Foucha.

Justice O'Connor declined to join Part III, so Justice White wrote for a plurality of the Court. In Part III, Justice White held that Louisiana's law governing insanity acquittees violates the Fourteenth Amendment's equal protection clause for two reasons. First, he held that the Louisiana law conflicts with the Court's holding in *Jones v. U.S.*, where the Court held that "insanity acquittees may be treated differently in some respects from those persons subject to civil commitment, but Foucha, who is not now thought to be insane, can no longer be so classified" (Foucha v. Louisiana 1992, 85). White argued that states cannot indefinitely detain anyone thought to be only dangerous. Nor can states detain persons who are about to be released from prison on the suspicion that they will continue to be dangerous. Second, the plurality held that, for the state to detain someone indefinitely, "the State must establish insanity and dangerousness by clear and convincing evidence in order to confine an insane convict beyond his criminal sentence, when the basis for his original confinement no longer exists" (Foucha v. Louisiana 1992, 86). In short, according to Justice White, there is no distinction in law between insanity acquittees—or insanity acquittees who become sane—and civil committees.

Instead of understanding equal protection as equal application of the law, Justice White held that equal protection protects against unequal stigma. Insofar as acquittees and committees share a constitutional stigma, they should be treated equally. This is the meaning of Justice White's opinion in Part III of *Foucha*. But the Court had never before equated the status of insanity acquittees with traditional civil committees, for the simple reason that insanity acquittees are not necessarily mentally ill, not necessarily dangerous to themselves or to others, and have committed crimes. In insanity cases, a jury or a judge has decided only that there is a reasonable doubt about a defendant's sanity.

This is the essence of the Court's decision in *Jones v. U.S.*, which Justice White obfuscated.

It seems clear that Justice White forgot that Terry Foucha willingly sought and accepted an insanity verdict, and that this is a criminal, not a civil, case. Foucha's liberty interest, in other words, does not involve a "massive curtailment of liberty" because the state did not create a new due process situation for Foucha when they moved him to Feliciana following the NGRI verdict. Louisiana has not inflicted upon Foucha a "grievous loss" (Morrisey v. Brewer 1972, 482) of liberty because the decision to commit him to Feliciana was based on Foucha's own claim that he was insane. In *Sandin v. Conner* (1995, 480), the Court held that "The Due Process Clause standing alone confers no liberty interest in freedom from state action." Nor did Louisiana seek to permanently incarcerate Foucha and prevent him from petitioning federal courts for habeas corpus. Foucha's liberty interest appeared once he claimed to be sane, which came upon him after a court sentenced him to an indefinite confinement based on a not guilty by reason of insanity verdict—a verdict he wanted. Liberty interests are supposed to be "so fundamental that a State may not interfere with them" (Doe v. Miller 2005, 709).

Foucha's case "proves only that the defendant could not have distinguished between right and wrong" (Foucha v. Louisiana 1992, 99). It does not prove that mental disease or defect caused the criminal act. Moreover, there is no stigma attached to being housed in a mental institution if one seeks a verdict of NGRI. An insanity acquittal means that the defendant has "unhappily manifested the reality of anti-social conduct" (Foucha v. Louisiana 1992, 110). It was not proper, therefore, for Justice White to equate Foucha's liberty interest with a hypothetical case in which a state might wish to detain indefinitely someone about to be released from prison who is thought to be dangerous. Foucha's insanity verdict suggests more about the limits of assigning "liberty interests" to the confined than Justice White was willing to admit.

Foucha did not begin as a civil commitment case, but it ended up as one. This is largely because an acquittal by reason of insanity returns the defendant to something like civil status (Ingber 1982). The case began with Foucha breaking into someone's home and then claiming irresponsibility on the basis of insanity. The case ended, however, when Foucha said he was sane (or not insane) and should no longer be indefinitely confined. The Supreme Court agreed. But Louisiana's dangerousness prong was not an isolated idea in the jurisprudence of civil commitment. "Provisions like those in Louisiana," Justice

Kennedy wrote, "predicated on dangerousness alone, have been endorsed by the Model Penal Code and adopted by the legislatures of no fewer than 11 other states" (Foucha v. Louisiana 1992, 99). The problem the Court had to confront was not whether Louisiana acted within the boundaries of the Constitution to confine Foucha but whether it could lawfully confine a now-sane insanity acquittee possibly indefinitely.

In dissent, Justice Thomas raised the issue of substantive due process in the application of cases involving NGRI verdicts. The standard for review in substantive due process cases is strict scrutiny, though exceptions exist (Fallon 1993). For the Court to apply strict scrutiny, a right must be connected to the "concept of ordered liberty" (Palko v. Connecticut 1937, 325) or be found within the historical practices of the American people. Legislation, the Court has held, must offend "some principle of justice so rooted in the traditions and conscience of our people as to be ranked as fundamental" (Foucha v. Louisiana 1992, 126). The Supreme Court has never declared that the automatic confinement of insanity acquittees violates a fundamental right or raises a liberty interest. Indeed, at the time of Foucha's incarceration, twelve states had automatic commitment laws following a NGRI verdict (Foucha v. Louisiana 1992, 112). This is not to suggest that counting states is the equivalent of constitutional law or that state laws that have existed for a very long time necessarily trump a fundamental right (Lawrence v. Texas 2003, 593). But such practices suggest that historical experiences have not regarded the automatic committal of insanity acquittees as a violation of a fundamental right or principle for more than two hundred years—which raises the question, not answered by the Court, what changed? As Thomas pointed out, historical practice does not validate the idea that involuntary confinement requires strict scrutiny. To be sure, he noted that, in *Jackson v. Indiana*, the Court resorted to substantive due process because "Indiana's provisions for the indefinite institutionalization of incompetent defendants . . . did not bear any 'reasonable' relation to the purpose for which the defendant was committed." And in *O'Connor v. Donaldson,* the Court held that the "State had *no legitimate interest whatsoever* to justify" O'Connor's confinement (Foucha v. Louisiana 1992, 119; italics in original). The proper criterion is the one the Court used in *Jones v. United States*: that the "Due Process Clause 'requires that the nature and duration of commitment bear some *reasonable* relation to the purpose for which the individual is committed'" (Foucha v. Louisiana 1992, 119–20; italics in original). It is not difficult to find a reasonable relationship between Louisiana's need to keep Foucha confined as a dangerous insanity acquittee and Foucha's desire to be set free as a sane person. The Louisiana statute does not require indefinite confinement of insanity acquittees. It requires periodic review. The inquiry into a fundamental right to be free "from indefinite commitment" (Foucha v. Louisiana 1992, 82) does not apply here.

If there is no fundamental right at issue in *Foucha*, then the nagging question is whether it is either a violation of procedural due process or good public policy to continue to confine a sane insanity acquittee. This question goes to the heart of the problem of democratic theory and modern judicial review.

In Foucha's case, the due process clause of the Fourteenth Amendment provides little to no guidance, and case law provides only minimal assistance. Wise policy may necessitate the removal of "sane insanity acquittees from mental institutions" (Foucha v. Louisiana 1992, 125), Justice Thomas noted. But wise policy is beyond the Court's purview. Insanity acquittees are not a "discrete and insular minority" (U.S. v. Carolene Products 1938, 152 n. 4) deserving special protection from the judiciary because of their permanent and marginalized status in the political process. Moreover, the due process clause cannot clarify the meaning of a mental hospital (what if it is attached to a prison?). Nor can the due process clause be elevated to such an extent that confinement of insanity acquittees be subject to time limits equal to the criminal sentence. Such a "cap" (Foucha v. Louisiana 1992, 123) may make good public policy, but it would be inapplicable to Foucha, as his criminal sentence could have been thirty-two years in prison (he had served eight at the time of the Court's decision). In terms of jurisprudence, the wisest course for the Court was to defer to the history of the confinement of those held not guilty by reason of insanity and to the general principles of democratic and deliberative politics in Louisiana.

In *Snyder v. Massachusetts*, Justice Benjamin Cardozo wrote that state procedures do "not run afoul of the Fourteenth Amendment because another method may seem to our thinking to be fairer or wiser or to give a surer promise of protection" (1934, 105) to prisoners or the accused. The *Snyder* decision poses the right question for *Foucha v. Louisiana:*

> The Constitution and statutes and judicial decisions . . . are the authentic forms through which the sense of justice of the people . . . expresses itself in law. We are not to supersede them on the ground that they deny the essentials of a trial because opinions may differ as to their policy or fairness. Not all the precepts of conduct precious to the hearts of many of us are immutable principles of justice . . . There is danger that the criminal law will be brought into contempt—

that discredit will even touch the great immunities assured by the Fourteenth Amendment—if gossamer possibilities of prejudice to a defendant are to nullify a sentence pronounced by a court of competent jurisdiction in obedience to local law, and set the guilty free. (Snyder v. Massachusetts 1934, 122)

Conclusion

Although *Foucha* was not a civil commitment case, it amounts to one, through a sleight of hand that involved changing the province of due process from protective of the political process to substantive regarding individual rights. Its effect on civil commitment jurisprudence is important because it created a similarity, under the due process and equal protection clauses of the Fourteenth Amendment, between civil commitment and NGRI verdicts. Such similarities may be more apparent than real, but they now have the Court's imprimatur. And therein lies the problem that confronts postconviction civil commitment of sex offenders. At bottom, the problems of civil commitment are legislative. But the courts have collapsed necessary distinctions among classes of committees in the name of liberty interests protected by substantive due process. The issue, then, that confronts the remainder of this book is how will the Court respond to these judicial innovations when confronted with legislation that requires sexual offenders who have served prison time to then be transferred to psychiatric hospitals, seemingly indefinitely?

NOTES

1. In 1987, Louisiana amended its law regarding insanity acquittees. The new law provides "for confinement of insanity acquittees solely on a finding of dangerousness" (Francois v. Henderson 1988, 236).

2. In Louisiana, a contradictory hearing is held to allow the state or the defendant to present contradictory evidence in cases involving mental status. Foucha, for example, "requested a contradictory hearing to obtain periodic passes with family supervision" (Louisiana v. Foucha 1990, 1139). Louisiana used it following the judgment that Foucha should be released (Louisiana v. Foucha 1990, 1143).

3. It is possible these physicians refrained from using the word "disorder" because they could not determine if Foucha suffered from ASPD or they wanted to

preserve the idea that Foucha was sane and therefore responsible for his crimes. On the nosology of mental disorders, see Anckarsäter et al. (2009).

4. The placement of sex offenders in mental facilities following the completion of their sentences is not dependent upon their treatability (Kansas v. Hendricks 1997). Also, the presence of an antisocial personality disorder does not include, though it does not exclude, the presence of sexual paraphilias (Vognsen and Phenix 2004, 442).

5. Substantive due process "bars certain arbitrary, wrongful actions 'regardless of the fairness of the procedures used to implement them'" (Foucha v. Louisiana 1992, 80).

REFERENCES

Alschuler, Albert. 1986. "Preventive Pretrial Detention and the Failure of Interest-Balancing Approaches to Due Process." *Michigan Law Review* 85 (3): 510–69.

Anckarsäter, Henrik, Susanna Radovic, Christer Svennerlind, Pontus Höglund, and Filip Radovic. 2009. "Mental Disorder is a Cause of Crime: The Cornerstone of Forensic Psychiatry." *International Journal of Law and Psychiatry* 32: 342–47.

Barclay, Hugh. 1855. *A Digest of the Law of Scotland*, 2nd ed., rev. and enlarged. Edinburgh: T & T Clark.

Beecher-Monas, Erica. 2003. "The Epistemology of Prediction: Future Dangerousness Testimony and Intellectual Due Process." *Washington & Lee Law Review* 60 (2): 353–416.

Birkeland, Søren Fryd. 2014. "Delusional Psychosis in Individuals Diagnosed with Paranoid Personality Disorder: A Qualitative Study." *Current Psychology* 33 (2): 219–28.

Black, Donald. 1999. *Confronting Antisocial Personality Disorder.* Oxford: Oxford University Press.

Black, Donald, Tracy Gunter, Peggy Loveless, Jeff Allen, and Bruce Sieleni. 2010. "Antisocial Personality Disorder in Incarcerated Offenders: Psychiatric Comorbidity and Quality of Life." *Annals of Clinical Psychiatry* 22 (2): 113–20.

Bonnie, Richard, John Jeffries, and Peter Low. 2000. *A Case Study in the Insanity Defense: The Trial of John W. Hinckley, Jr.*, 2nd ed. New York: Foundation Press.

Buchanan, G. Sidney. 1993. "A Very Rational Court." *Houston Law Review* 30 (4): 1509–93.

Comment. 2001. "People v. Lloyd: Michigan's Guilty But Mentally Ill Verdict Created with Intention to Help is Not Really a Benefit at all." *University of Detroit-Mercy Law Review* 79: 75–95.

Cornwell, John Kip. 1996. "Confining Mentally Disordered 'Super Criminals': A Realignment of Rights in the Nineties." *Houston Law Review* 33 (3): 651–730.

Demakis, George. 2013. "State Statutory Definitions of Civil Incompetency/Incapacity: Issues for Psychologists." *Psychology, Public Policy & Law* 19 (3): 331–42.

Dershowitz, Alan. 1974. "The Origins of Preventive Confinement in Anglo-American Law—Part II: The American Experience." *University of Cincinnati Law Review* 43 (4): 781–846.

Diagnostic and Statistical Manual. 1987. III-R. Washington, DC: American Psychiatric Association.

Diagnostic and Statistical Manual. 2000. 4th ed. Washington, DC: American Psychiatric Association.

Diagnostic and Statistical Manual. 2013. 5th ed. Washington, DC: American Psychiatric Association.

Esterberg, Michelle, Sandra Goulding, and Elaine Walker. 2010. "Cluster A Personality Disorders: Schizotypal, Schizoid and Paranoid Personality Disorders in Childhood and Adolescence." *Journal of Psychopathology and Behavioral Assessment* 32 (4): 515–28.

Fallon, Richard. 1993. "Some Confusions about Due Process, Judicial Review, and Constitutional Remedies." *Columbia Law Review* 93 (2): 309–73.

Francis, Allen, and Robert Halon. 2013. "The Uses and Misuses of the DSM in Forensic Settings." *Psychological Injury and Law* 6 (4): 336–44.

Gatzke, Lisa, and Adrian Raine. 2000. "Treatment and Prevention Implications of Antisocial Personality Disorder." *Current Psychiatry Reports* 2 (1): 51–55.

Halpern, Abraham. 1993. "The Insanity Verdict, the Psychopath, and Post-Acquittal Confinement." *Pacific Law Journal* 24 (4): 1125–64.

Hardy, David. 2014. "The Right to Arms and Standards of Review: A Tale of Three Circuits." *Connecticut Law Review* 46 (4): 1435–61.

Hess, Caryl. 1980. "Release from Confinement of Persons Acquitted by Reason of Insanity in Ohio." *Akron Law Review* 13 (3): 582–92.

Hur, Sarah. 2014. "An Attorney's Dilemma: Representing a Mentally Incompetent Client Who Does Not Wish to Raise Mental Illness Issues in Court." *Georgetown Journal of Legal Ethics* 27 (3): 555–68.

Ingber, Warren. 1982. "Rules for an Exceptional Class: The Commitment and Release of Persons Acquitted of Violent Offenses by Reason of Insanity." *New York University Law Review* 57 (2): 281–329.

Janus, Eric, and Wayne Logan. 2003. "Substantive Due Process and the Involuntary Confinement of Sexually Violent Predators." *Connecticut Law Review* 35 (2): 319–84.

Kendrick, Leslie. 2014. "Free Speech and Guilty Minds." *Columbia Law Review* 114 (5): 1255–96.

Krash, Abe. 1961. "The Durham Rule and Judicial Administration of the Insanity Defense in the District of Columbia." *Yale Law Journal* 70 (6): 905–52.

La Fond, John, and Mary Durham. 1994. "Cognitive Dissonance: Have Insanity Defense and Civil Reforms Made a Difference?" *Villanova Law Review* 39 (1): 71–122.

Levy, Jonathan. 2013. "A Principled Approach to the Standard of Proof for Affirmative Defenses in Criminal Trials." *American Journal of Criminal Law* 40 (3): 281–99.

Linder, Douglas. 1991. "Review of Affirmative Action After Metro Broadcasting v. FCC: The Solution Almost Nobody Wanted." *University of Missouri-Kansas City Law Review* 59 (2): 293–319.

Louisiana Code of Criminal Procedure, LSA-C.Cr.P. Art. 654.

Moran, Paul. 1999. "The Epidemiology of Antisocial Personality Disorder." *Social Psychiatry and Psychiatric Epidemiology* 34 (5): 231–42.

Morris, Grant, and J. Reid Meloy. 1993. "Out of Mind? Out of Sight: The Uncivil Commitment of Permanently Incompetent Criminal Defendants." *University of California-Davis Law Review* 27 (1): 1–78.

Note. 1981. "Commitment Following an Insanity Acquittal." *Harvard Law Review* 94 (3): 605–25.

Note. 2013. "Competency to Stand Trial." *Georgetown Law Journal Annual Review of Criminal Procedure* 42: 470–83.

Pickersgill, Martyn. 2013. "How Personality Became Treatable: The Mutual Constitution of Clinical Knowledge and Mental Health Law." *Social Studies of Science* 43 (1): 30–53.

Polstein, Janet. 1985. "Throwing Away the Key: Due Process Rights of Insanity Acquittees in Jones v. United States." *American University Law Review* 34 (2): 479–521.

Reznek, Lawrie. 1997. *Evil or Ill? Justifying the Insanity Defence.* London: Routledge.

Rothman, David. 1971. *The Discovery of the Asylum: Social Order and Disorder in the New Republic.* Boston: Little, Brown and Company.

Rowan, Gretchen. 1993. "Foucha v. Louisiana: Confinement Based on Dangerousness Alone." *Saint Louis University Law Journal* 37 (3): 731–52.

Slovenko, Ralph. 1995. *Psychiatry and Criminal Culpability.* New York: John Wiley & Sons.

Smith, Peter. 1997. "The Demise of Three-Tier Review: Has the United States Supreme Court Adopted a 'Sliding Scale' Approach Toward Equal Protection Jurisprudence?" *Journal of Contemporary Law* 23 (2): 475–513.

The Statutes: Revised Edition. 1872. Vol. III. London: George Edward Eyre and William Spottiswoode.

Stork, Emily. 2013. "A Competent Competency Standard: Should it Require a Mental Disease or Defect?" *Columbia Human Rights Law Review* 44 (3): 927–69.

U.S. Congress. 1984. Insanity Defense Reform Act. 98 Stat. 2057.

Vognsen, Jack, and Amy Phenix. 2004. "Antisocial Personality Disorder is not Enough: A Reply to Sreenivasan, Weinberger, and Garrick." *Journal of the American Academy of Psychiatry and the Law* 32 (4): 440–42.

Walker, Nigel. 1968. *Crime and Insanity in England. Vol. 1: The Historical Perspective.* Edinburgh: University of Edinburgh Press.

Weiner, Barbara. 1980. "Not Guilty by Reason of Insanity: A Sane Approach." *Chicago-Kent Law Review* 56 (4): 1057–85.

Yannoulidis, Steven. 2012. *Mental State Defences in Criminal Law.* Surrey, England: Ashgate.

Yoshino, Kenji. 2011. "The New Equal Protection." *Harvard Law Review* 124 (3): 747–803.

Zapf, Patricia, and Ronald Roesch. 2000. "Mental Competency Evaluations: Guidelines for Judges and Attorneys." *Court Review*: 28–35. http://aja.ncsc.dni.us/courtrv/cr37/cr37-2/CR37-2ZapfRoesch.pdf

CASES

Addington v. Texas, 441 U.S. 418 (1979).

Arkansas v. Bailey, 368 Ark. 518 (2007).

Baxstrom v. Herold, 383 U.S. 107 (1966).

Bolton v. Harris, 395 F.2d 642 (1968).

Buchanan v. Kentucky, 483 U.S. 402 (1987).

Burwell v. Hobby Lobby Stores, 134 S.Ct. 2751 (2014).

Carter v. U.S., 252 F.2d 608 (1957).

Central State University v. American Association of University Professors, 526 U.S. 124 (1999).

City of Cleburne v. Cleburne Living Center, 473 U.S. 432 (1985).

Clark v. Arizona, 548 U.S. 735 (2006).

Clark v. Jeter, 486 U.S. 456 (1988).

Cooper v. Oklahoma, 517 U.S. 348 (1996).

Craig v. Boren, 429 U.S. 190 (1976).

Dandridge v. Williams, 397 U.S. 471 (1970).

Doe v. Miller, 405 F.3d 700 (2005).

Doe v. Reed, 561 U.S. 186 (2010).

Drope v Missouri, 420 U.S. 162 (1975).

Durham v. U.S., 214 F.2d 862 (1954).

Dusky v. United States, 362 U.S. 402 (1960).

Federal Communications Comm. v. Beach Communications, 508 U.S. 307 (1993).
Ford v. Wainwright, 477 U.S. 399 (1986).
Foucha v. Louisiana, WL 636278 (1991a).
Foucha v. Louisiana, WL 527591 (1991b).
Foucha v. Louisiana, 504 U.S. 71 (1992).
Foucha v. Louisiana, WL 344337 (1993).
Francois v. Henderson, 850 F.2d 231 (1988).
Godinez v. Moran, 509 U.S. 389 (1993).
Guinon v. Armontrout, 909 F.2d 1224 (1990).
Heller v. Doe, 509 U.S. 312 (1993).
Hewitt v. Helms, 459 U.S. 460 (1983)
Hopkins v. Lynn, 888 F.2d 35 (1989).
Humphrey v. Cady, 405 U.S. 504 (1972).
Jackson v. Foti, 670 F.2d 516 (1982).
Jackson v. Indiana, 406 U.S. 715 (1972).
Jones v. U.S., 463 U.S. 354 (1983).
Kansas v. Crane, 534 U.S. 407 (2002).
Kansas v. Hendricks, WL 471020 (1996).
Kansas v. Hendricks, 521 U.S. 346 (1997).
Kansas v. Risjord 249 Kan. 497 (1991).
Lawrence v. Texas, 539 U.S. 558 (2003).
Louisiana v. Foucha, 563 So.2d 1138 (1990).
Louisiana v. Peters, 643 So.2d 1222 (1994).
Louisiana v. Silman, 663 So.2d 27 (1995).
Lynch v. Overholser, 369 U.S. 705 (1962).
McDonald v. U.S., 312 F.2d 847 (1962).
Meachum v. Fano, 427 U.S. 215 (1976).
Millhouse v. Sage, WL 4092837 (2014).
Morrissey v. Brewer, 408 U.S. 471 (1972).
NAACP v. Alabama, 357 U.S. 449 (1958).
New Jersey v. Maik, 287 A.2d 715 (N.J. 1972).
O'Connor v. Donaldson, 422 U.S. 563 (1975).
Palko v. Connecticut, 302 U.S. 319 (1937).
Penry v. Lynaugh, 492 U.S. 302 (1989).
Powell v. Florida, 579 F.2d 324 (1978).
Powell v. Texas, 392 U. S. 535 (1968).
Riggins v. Nevada, 504 U.S. 127 (1992).
Romer v. Evans, 517 U.S. 620 (1996).
San Antonio Independent School District v. Rodriguez, 411 U.S. 1 (1973).

Sandin v. Connor, 515 U.S. 472 (1995).
Sauer v. U.S., 241 F.2d 640 (1957).
Smith v. U.S., 36 F.2d 548 (1929).
Snyder v Massachusetts, 291 U.S. 97 (1934).
Specht v. Patterson, 386 U.S. 605 (1967).
Staples v. U.S., 511 U.S. 600 (1994).
Tatum v. U.S., 88 U.S.App.D.C. 386 (1951).
Taylor v. U.S., 222 F.2d 398 (1955).
U.S. v. Brawner, 471 F.2d 969 (1972).
U.S. v. Carolene Products 304 U.S. 144 (1938).
U.S. v. Childress, 58 F 3d 693 (1995).
U.S. v. Graham, 683 F.Supp.2d 129 (2010).
U.S. v. Guiteau, 1 Mackey 498 (1882).
U.S. v. Hinckley, 525 F.Supp. 1342 (1981).
U.S. v. Hinckley, 672 F.2d 115 (1982).
U.S. v. Horowitz, 360 F.Supp. 772 (1973).
U.S. v. Lauzon, 938 F.2d 326 (1991).
U.S. v. Lee, 4 Mackey 489 (1886).
U.S. v. Resendiz-Ponce, 549 U.S. 102 (2007).
U.S. v. Virginia, 518 U.S. 515 (1996).
Vitek v. Jones, 445 U.S. 480 (1980).
Washington v. Glucksberg, 521 U.S. 702 (1997).
Williamson v. Lee Optical, 348 U.S. 483 (1955).
Wood v. Zahradnick, 475 F.Supp. 556 (1979).
Wygant v. Jackson Board of Education, 476 U.S. 267 (1986).
Young v Weston, 898 F.Supp. 744 (1995).

CHAPTER 3

The Psychopathic Offender and Civil Commitment

There are two aims to this chapter. One is to chart the movement of the equal protection clause from its limited understanding of equal application of the law to its more robust understanding as a substantive vehicle for the implementation of criminal protections in a series of civil commitment cases in the 1960s and 1970s. The second is to highlight the interplay that exists between the psychological and social scientific understanding of risk and dangerousness and the legislative and juridical understanding of the importance of public safety in commitment cases. These two ideas are linked: the more the Supreme Court extended the equal protection and due process clauses to civil committees, the more state and federal courts relied upon social scientific studies of risk to overturn the states' civil commitment schemes.

In the 1930s, the creation of a class of dangerous individuals known as sexual psychopaths created a stark dichotomy between legislators, who focused on danger and public safety, and social scientists, who focused on risk, treatment, and prevention. After going dormant for a couple of decades, the rift resurfaced in the 1990s. On one side was disinterested scientific inquiry into the determined reasons for behavior; on the other was a legal and philosophical commitment to the idea that individuals make choices that affect public safety. How would courts reconcile these two opposing views?

The emancipation of equal protection from historical and institutional constraints during the Warren Court era (1953–1969) is not unrelated to the judiciary's greater reliance, during the same period, on the psychological and social sciences in determining the constitutional boundaries of law. When the Warren Court turned to equal protection to extend criminal protections for the civilly confined criminally insane, it abandoned doctrinal principles in use for one hundred years, such as deference to state law regarding civil confinement and the civil-criminal distinction.[1] In treating those with behavioral instabilities as if they were so mentally disturbed as to need greater state care and protection, the Warren Court transferred power from the representative branches of government to the judiciary and to social scientists. The Warren Court took upon itself the role of guardian of democratic practices. In that role, as Ward Elliott wrote in his book on the Warren Court and reapportionment, the Court "was keenly sensitive to the most minute transgression of formal equality but blind alike to considerations of practical equality and to freedom of political choice for individual citizens and their representatives" (1974, viii). Elliott called the Court's democratic stress on equality and its undemocratic focus on administration the "Guardian Ethic." By investing equal protection with notions of fairness and equality derived from philosophical texts and scientific studies, rather than from "our civil and political institutions" and a "community's sense of fair play and decency" (Dowling v. U.S. 1990, 353), the Court has not only introduced alien substantive considerations into Fourteenth Amendment jurisprudence, it has subordinated foundational legal principles, such as the separation of powers and limited government, to psychological and structural explanations of criminal behavior. In abandoning the central meaning of the Constitution's key ideas and concepts—the separation of powers, majority rule, and legislative deliberation—the Warren Court made it acceptable for state and federal courts to make constitutional law truly scientific: risk analyses would decide the legality of civil commitment requests, and all civil commitments would now appear to be criminal punishment. The Warren Court made constitutional law truly progressive. The Court created an understanding of equal protection based on evolving standards of fairness, dignity, and autonomy for the individual, each of which, in its own way, undermined the role of legislative deliberation and weakened federalism, the separation of powers, and the political process jurisprudence of the New Deal Court.

To sort out these issues, after briefly discussing the first and second eras of civil commitment laws, I will focus on a number of cases from the third and fourth eras. The problem that confronts the third and fourth eras of commitment laws is the problem of diagnosis. How should courts regard those convicted of sexual offenses who remain potentially dangerous? If as ill, then the dominant form of understanding must come from medical science, and courts must subject legal judgment to forensic analysis. If as willful criminals, then the political branches, juries, and the judiciary should assess their dangerousness.

According to Samuel Brakel and James Cavanaugh (2000), the history of the civil commitment of sex offenders can be broken into four periods. The first, which did not concern sex offenders, occurred from the founding to the early 1930s, when the states undertook the commitment of those who could not care for themselves. Commitment was done under the states' *parens patriae* powers.[2] Courts understood commitment laws to be extensions of the states' right to commit those who could not care for themselves. Commitments were largely unsupervised by legal authorities, care was arbitrary, and treatment was largely ineffectual (Rothman 1971; Appelbaum and Kemp 1982).

The second era was explicitly concerned with sex offenses, public safety, and rehabilitation (Brakel and Cavanaugh 2000, 71–72). The states relied upon a mixture of their *parens patriae* powers and police powers.[3] This era extends from the passage of sexual psychopath statutes in Minnesota and Michigan in the late 1930s to the beginning of the Warren Court's intervention in civil commitment laws in the 1960s. In the one case the Supreme Court decided on this issue, *Minnesota ex rel. Pearson v. Probate Court of Ramsey County* (1940a), it upheld the law, which the Minnesota supreme court had altered but nevertheless sustained.

The third era begins with the Warren and Burger Courts' expansion of the equal protection clause to civil committees. This era covers the end of the Warren Court to the end of the Burger Court (1986). Here I survey *Baxstrom v. Herold* (1966a), *Specht v. Patterson* (1967), and two Burger Court cases, *Humphrey v. Cady* (1972) and *Vitek v. Jones* (1980). By expanding the meaning of equal protection and due process in each case, the Warren and Burger Courts introduced substantive concerns about equality into the equal protection and due process clauses.

The fourth era begins under Chief Justice William Rehnquist, in 1986, and continues to this day. This era focuses on postconviction civil commitment and the implementation of risk analysis in the determination of dangerousness. I first examine two Minnesota cases, *In re Blodgett* (1994) and *In re Linehan* (1993; 1994; 1996a; 1996b). Then I critically examine the problem of risk analysis and mental illness designations. To assist this analysis, I examine three cases, *U.S. v. Hall* (2012), *U.S. v. Caporale* (2012), and *Iowa v. Barnes* (2004). Each of these cases involves either a designation of psychopathic personality disorder or antisocial personality disorder or both. Each of these cases required the courts to balance the claims of science and the demands of public safety.

The Psychopathic Personality in the First and Second Eras of Commitment

Throughout the nineteenth century, and well into the first half of the twentieth, the commitment of individuals who could not care for themselves was a relatively uncomplicated process, done without judicial oversight. No court held that the due process clauses of the Fifth or Fourteenth Amendments embodied protections for those thought to be incapable of governing themselves. The states exercised their commitment power over individuals through a doctrine known as *parens patriae*. Under English law at the time of the settling of the American colonies, the "sovereign, as father of the country, was responsible for the care and custody of 'all persons who had lost their intellects and become . . . incompetent to take care of themselves'" (Note 1974, 1207–8). This idea passed, with necessary changes, into the American system of civil commitment. The classic *parens patriae* case in American law is *In the Matter of Oakes* (1845), which held that "The right to restrain an insane person of his liberty is found in that great law of humanity, which makes it necessary to confine those whose going at large would be dangerous to themselves or others" (In the matter of Oakes 1845, 125).

Commitment in the second era gets more complicated. A decade or so prior to World War II and extending past it, psychopathy develops as a descriptive term for sexual predators. According to Laura Barnickol (2000, 324):

> Sexual psychopath statutes were based on four presumptions: (1) sexual psychopaths are distinguishable from generic sex offenders; (2) individuals commit sexual offenses because of a mental disease; (3) mental diseases are treatable and curable; and (4) mental health professionals can successfully predict which sex offenders are likely to reoffend in the future.

Mid-century psychologists believed that psychopathic problems stemmed from early childhood experiences (Lipton 1950; Sutherland 1950; Levy 1942). The psychopath's problem was no longer anatomical and hereditarian, as it was in the late nineteenth century and early twentieth century; it is social and psychological. The psychopath lacks the repressive qualities necessary to behave properly. Consequently, states committed sexual psychopaths to hospitals, often indefinitely, and without the possibility of plea bargaining (Freedman 1987, 83). If resident aliens, they could be deported (Boutilier v. Immigration and Naturalization Service 1966). By 1960, twenty-six states and the District of Columbia had passed legislation dealing with "the commitment of 'psychopathic sex offenders'" (Swanson 1960, 215).

Psychopathy has been called "the most dangerous of the personality disorders" (Babiak et al. 2012, 3). The legal understanding of "personality disorder" is a demonstration of a persistent "disregard for and violation of the rights of others" (McGee v. Bartow 2010, 560). To assess psychopathy, researchers rely on the Psychopathy Checklist (now called the Psychopathy Checklist-Revised [PCL-R]), which is a rating scale of twenty items to assess a subject's proclivity for psychopathy. The highest score a subject can receive is forty; thirty establishes a baseline judgment of psychopathy. The checklist is a classification of personality traits or behaviors. The difference between traits and behavior is fundamental to psychopathy's meaning. If psychopathy is a behavioral disorder, then it is susceptible to correction. The *Diagnostic and Statistical Manual* (*DSM*) rejects the term psychopathy in favor of Antisocial Personality Disorder (ASPD), as we saw in the last chapter. A disorder is something that is "clinically significant." The meaning of disorder is derived from a "judgment that the condition is distressing" (Stein et al. 2010, 1761). According to the *DSM*, those with ASPD:

> fail to conform to social norms with respect to lawful behavior. They may repeatedly perform acts that are gounds for arrest. . . . Persons with this disorder disregard the wishes, rights, or feelings of others. (DSM 2013, 660)

If, however, psychopathy is a personality trait,[4] then it is less easily corrected, and psychopaths represent an evil force in society. Those who prefer this understanding regard the condition as untreatable. Robert Hare, a prominent advocate of this view, believes that psychopathy is a "*choice*, freely exercised" (Hare 1999, 22; italics in original) by an individual. For Hare, psychopathy is the science of traits. Examination under the checklist reveals the latent trait and exposes it to the presuppositions that govern the meaning of psychopathy. The latency of a trait should not be confused with its potentiality; the trait exists as potential behavior. Traits are internal mental thoughts that are not products of structural, historical, or cultural factors. The personality traits of psychopaths are "guiltlessness, callousness, egocentricity, manipulativeness, fearlessness, and incapacity to form deep emotional attachments" (Douglas et al. 2008, 512). The more practical distinction between traits and behavior is the predictability of traits over behavior (Wilson and Herrnstein 1985, 208). This is why, just after World War II, the psychopath's potential dangerousness replaced actual guilt as the operative criterion for psychopathy, and why psychopathy will always remain on the border between "the science of medicine" and the "welfare of society" (Cleckley 1964, 470; Skeem and Cooke 2010).[5]

California had a sex registry in place in 1937. Michigan was the first state to pass a sexual psychopath law, also in 1937.[6] The Michigan law replaced conviction in prison with commitment to a hospital. The law prohibited the prosecution of the subject once commitment proceedings began. The Michigan law defined a sexual psychopath as someone who suffers "from a mental disorder" but who is "not insane or feeble-minded" (Michigan v. Chapman 1942, 590). The Michigan supreme court upheld this law on general police powers, despite due process, equal protection, and ex post facto challenges (Michigan v. Frontczak 1938).

The 1939 Minnesota law governing civil commitment applied to "any person of such conditions of emotional instability, or impulsiveness of behavior, or lack of customary standards of good judgment, or failure to appreciate the consequences of his acts, or a combination of any such conditions, as to render such person irresponsible for his conduct with respect to sexual matters and thereby dangerous to other persons" (Minnesota ex rel. Pearson v. Probate Court of Ramsey County 1939, 546). In the seminal court case of the second era that challenged this law, *Minnesota ex rel. Pearson v. Probate Court of Ramsey County* (1939), the Minnesota supreme court upheld the commitment law on public safety grounds and found the act to be a civil regulation and not criminal punishment. The court also narrowed the type of person the state could commit. The court created a three-part test, and ruled that the act was intended for those

> who, [1] by a habitual course of misconduct in sexual matters, have [2] evidenced an utter lack of power to control their sexual impulses and who, as a result, are [3] likely to attack or otherwise inflict injury, loss, pain or other evil on the objects of their uncontrolled and uncontrollable desire. (Minnesota ex rel. Pearson v. Probate Court of Ramsey County 1939, 555)

The Minnesota law allowed the committee a number of due process protections, including the calling of witnesses and the right to an attorney. In 1940, the Supreme Court unanimously upheld the Minnesota supreme court's ruling.

Pearson's equal protection claim proceeded "on the view that the statute has selected a group which is a part of a larger class" (Minnesota ex rel. Pearson v. Probate Court of Ramsey County 1940a, 274). He argued that the act treated one group, "psychopathic personalities," differently than other insane persons (Minnesota ex rel. Pearson v. Probate Court of Ramsey County 1939, 546).[7] Pearson claimed underinclusion, not overinclusion, and exclusion from the political process, and that the law conferred special privileges on one group but not others.[8] The Court under Chief Justice Charles Evans Hughes was willing to tolerate, in the name of deference to deliberative bodies, underinclusive classifications, because "the equal protection clause is not 'a pedagogic requirement of the impracticable'" (Tussman and tenBroek 1949, 348).

In his brief, Pearson argued that "The Minnesota decisions are unanimous in holding that all members of a class embraced in any act of the legislature must be treated alike or the act is void" (Minnesota ex rel. Pearson v. Probate Court of Ramsey County 1940b, 23). Under the pre-Warren Court understanding of the equal protection clause, the question before the Court was whether the legislation singled out a group for favor and excluded others. The Hughes Court said no. But under the Warren Court, the question will involve determining the fundamental nature of the claim, in particular, whether the person is being held indefinitely and whether sexual offenders are being treated differently than other possible committees, then subjecting the state law to heightened scrutiny analysis, and finally, assessing how the political process affected the asserted rights claim. The legislative aim of a particular law has to be "compelling" (Gunther 1972, 21) and not merely rational.

By the time *Pearson* was decided, an impermissible classification would have included race (Yick Wo v. Hopkins 1886; Pace v. Alabama 1883) but not mental disorders. This was so, in part, because courts did not consider the care of the mentally ill a civil right or liberty interest found within the Fourteenth Amendment's jurisdiction. In cases involving equal protection prior to *Pearson*—mostly cases involving business and administrative regulations—the Court's stance was deferential toward police powers (Powell v. Pennsylvania 1888, 687; In re Heff 1905). Given that committees were criminals but neither insane nor feeble-minded, the states had reasonable and justifiable grounds for considering them dangerous. "Prior to 1937, the Equal Protection Clause

[was] construed solely as a rationality test" (Klarman 1991, 216). This was done to protect state policy innovation. The "Equal Protection Clause," Justice Felix Frankfurter wrote, "did not write an empty formalism into the Constitution. Deeply embedded traditional ways of carrying out state policy . . . are often tougher and truer law than the dead words of the written text" (Nashville, Chattanooga, and St. Louis Railway v. Browning 1940, 369). The equal protection clause was designed "to prevent hostile and discriminating State legislation against any person or class of persons" (Pace v. Alabama 1882, 584) and not to disallow distinctions with a rational purpose.

The only question for the Court in *Pearson* was whether Minnesota's selection of a particular class of offenders suitable for commitment was based on a "rational basis for such a selection" (Minnesota ex rel. Pearson v. Probate Court of Ramsey County 1940a, 274). The *Pearson* Court understood the Fourteenth Amendment as not interfering with "the power of the state, sometimes termed its police power, to prescribe regulations to promote the health, peace, morals, education, and good order of the people" (Barbier v. Connolly 1885, 31; Nebbia v. New York 1934, 537). Moreover, the Court did not regard Pearson, a sex offender, as belonging to a group with "immutable characteristics" that the Fourteenth Amendment protects (Regents of the University of California v. Bakke 1978, 361). The Court did not even consider the possibility that Pearson belonged to a group covered under *U.S. v. Carolene Products*' footnote 4 (1938)—a decision rendered just two years prior to *Pearson*.

In a footnote to a case dealing with interstate commerce, *United States v. Carolene Products*, Justice Harlan Stone created a model by which a state law's constitutionality could be assessed, free from the "substantive due process" or "natural law" interpretations of the Court's nineteenth-century jurisprudence in economic cases. In footnote four of his opinion, Justice Stone noted that the Court would subject economic regulations to a "rational basis" test and then outlined the Court's understanding of judicial intervention in cases dealing with the civil rights of "discrete and insular minorities":

> [Paragraph 1]: when legislation appears on its face to be within a specific prohibition of the Constitution, such as those of the first ten Amendments, which are deemed equally specific when held to be embraced within the Fourteenth.
>
> [Paragraph 2]: legislation which restricts those political processes which can ordinarily be expected to bring about repeal of undesirable legislation, is to be

> subjected to more exacting judicial scrutiny under the general prohibitions of the Fourteenth Amendment than are most other types of legislation.
>
> [Paragraph 3]: whether prejudice against discrete and insular minorities may be a special condition, which tends seriously to curtail the operation of those political processes ordinarily to be relied upon to protect minorities, and which may call for a correspondingly more searching judicial inquiry. (U.S. v. Carolene Products 1938, 152–53)

Pearson did not belong to a group traditionally harmed by the political process (Reynolds v. Sims 1964, 568). The Court isolated a rational basis by reference to general principles of interpretation in a federal system. The "legislature is free to recognize degrees of harm, and it may confine its restrictions to those classes of cases where the need is deemed to be clearest" (Minnesota ex rel. Pearson v. Probate Court of Ramsey County 1940a, 275).

The Third Era: Substantive Equal Protection

From 1966 to 1986, the Warren and Burger Courts "expanded the definition of 'state action,' introduced the concept of 'suspect' classifications, announced the requirement of discriminatory 'intent' or 'purpose,' and settled into a rigid multi-tiered standard of review" (Saunders 1997, 301–2). The Court subjected the equal protection clause to rigorous scrutiny, abandoning its deferential stance toward legislatures. The Court also downgraded the political process idea, moving away from its deferential stance toward political majorities, and began actively looking for instances when the political process became "infected by discriminatory intent" (McConnell 1995, 993).

Two key jurisprudential ideas constitute the Court's third era of civil commitment jurisprudence. First, the Supreme Court imposed requirements, grounded in the expanded meaning the Warren Court had bestowed on equal protection and due process in other cases, on states that wanted to treat the commitment of sexually violent predators differently than the commitment of the mentally ill. The turn toward the Fourteenth Amendment to protect a class of persons the Court had previously not regarded as within the scope of equal protection signaled that the Warren Court was no longer willing to defer to the states' understanding of what constituted both their *parens patriae* and police powers. Second, the Court began to blur the distinction between civil and criminal case law.

The common understanding is that there is a neat division between the civil and criminal realms. The intent of civil commitment laws is not punishment but treatment (Jones v U.S. 1983, 365 n. 13). As Justice Potter Stewart once noted, "The object of the one [i.e., civil law] is correction of a condition. The object of the other [i.e., criminal law] is conviction and punishment for a criminal act" (In re Gault 1967, 79). Civil commitment laws, particularly those passed after 1990 that seek to incarcerate sexually violent offenders following conviction, presumably violate this distinction because they conceal the criminal nature of the commitment and hide its punitive function (Kansas v. Hendricks 1997, 388–89). States, in other words, now treat civil committees as criminals, but without the protections of the Fourteenth Amendment.

The impetus toward collapsing the civil-criminal distinction was the Warren Court's insistence that certain kinds of civil cases—those involving confinement in mental facilities, but not limited to them—require extensive due process protections (Specht v. Patterson 1967). These were policy choices the Warren Court created, without addressing why dangerous criminals with mental abnormalities should be classified, for constitutional purposes, with those who cannot care for themselves. These decisions were not compelled by the logic of due process or equal protection, as we will see in the four cases discussed below.

In *Baxstrom v. Herrold* (1966), New York State sentenced Johnny Baxstrom to two-and-one-half years to three years in prison for second-degree assault. Two years later, in 1961, a physician certified Baxstrom as insane. New York then transferred Baxstrom from prison to Dannemora State Hospital and altered Baxstrom's designation, from insane criminal to criminally insane. Although Dannemora was under the jurisdiction of the Department of Correction, it was "used for the purpose of confining and caring for male prisoners declared mentally ill while serving a criminal sentence" (Baxstrom v. Herold 1966a, 108). It did not function like a prison. The chief executive officer was a physician, not a warden; no one carried weapons; there were no cells; there were no punishments for infractions; and it had a liberal visitation policy (Baxstrom v. Herold 1965a, 5; Baxstrom v. Herold 1965b, 23–24). In November 1961, the director of Dannemora filed a petition requesting that, as Baxstrom's sentence was about to end, he should be civilly confined. The director believed that Baxstrom was "violent and dangerous," as well as psychotic, a result of epileptic seizures (Baxstrom v. Herold 1965a, 3; Baxstrom v. Herold 1965b, 11). The state court held a hearing with doctors present. Baxstrom had no Sixth Amendment right to an attorney, and so he appeared without counsel, but the state gave him time to ask questions (Baxstrom v. Herold 1965b, 11–20; Baxstrom v. Herold 1965a, 13–16; Baxstrom v. Herold 1966b, 6–7). The hearing was not a criminal inquiry but a "*proceeding solely to elicit facts*" (Baxstrom v. Herold 1965a, 14; italics in original). At that point, there was a request to move Baxstrom to the Department of Mental Hygiene, a civil hospital, where he would stay until he regained his sanity. The judge said he had no jurisdiction to move Baxstrom; only the Department of Mental Hygiene could make that request. In fact, the Department of Mental Hygiene had already declared that Baxstrom was "not suitable for care in a civil hospital" (Baxstrom v. Herold 1966a, 109). On December 18, 1961, Baxstrom's time in prison was over and—for unexplained reasons in the Supreme Court's opinion—New York transferred jurisdiction over Baxstrom to the Department of Mental Hygiene but continued to house him at Dannemora.

In a unanimous opinion, Chief Justice Warren held that Baxstrom "was denied equal protection of the laws by the statutory procedure under which a person may be civilly committed at the expiration of his penal sentence without the jury review available to all other persons civilly committed in New York" (Baxstrom v. Herold 1966a, 110). The Court rejected New York's argument that the law governing transfers satisfied the rational basis test, and that notice and a hearing satisfied due process. Instead the Court required New York to treat those it wants to civilly commit, postconviction (as a result of becoming insane), to be afforded the same rights and protections as those it civilly commits because of their incapacity to govern themselves (Baxstrom v. Herold 1966a, 111). This innovative understanding comes without any reference to the history of equal protection or civil commitment.

The Court's decision in *Specht v. Patterson* (1967) made it clear that the Court would no longer defer to state court judgments regarding the constitutionality of the commitment of sex offenders. Specht was convicted in Colorado of indecent liberties, for which, by law, he could have served no more than ten years in prison. Colorado, however, sentenced Specht under the Sex Offenders Act, which meant that Specht could serve from one day to the end of his life in prison, "without notice and full hearing" (Specht v. Patterson 1967, 607). The Colorado supreme court upheld the lower court's decision; a federal court dismissed Specht's habeas corpus petition, and the tenth circuit federal court of appeals affirmed.

Before Colorado invoked the Sex Offenders Act, the state, as required by law, conducted a full psychiatric report and submitted to a court all facts and findings. Specht argued, however, that these procedures violated due process because the regulations did not allow Specht to "confront and cross-examine adverse witnesses and present evidence of his own by use of compulsory process, if necessary" (Specht v. Patterson 1967, 608). Justice William Douglas, writing for a unanimous court, held that commitment proceedings are subject to the requirements of the equal protection and due process clauses. Because, Justice Douglas wrote, the Sex Offender Act "makes one conviction the basis for commencing another proceeding. . . . That is a new finding of fact" (Specht v. Patterson 1967, 608). Moreover, he held that the Sex Offender Act was criminal, not civil. He likened the law to a habitual recidivist statute, which requires "reasonable notice and an opportunity to be heard" (Specht v. Patterson 1967, 610). *Specht* subjected civil committees to the same level of due process protections afforded criminal defendants and (in the civil realm) to immigrants Congress wanted to deport because of their connection to the Communist Party (Frank v. Mangum 1915; Bridges v. Wixon 1945). Douglas also distinguished *Specht* from *Pearson*, because the law there afforded more protections than the Colorado law, as it allowed for counsel to be present during a determination of a psychopathic personality.

In *Humphrey v. Cady* (1972), Justice Thurgood Marshall, again writing for a unanimous Court, now headed by Chief Justice Warren Burger, held the Wisconsin Sex Crimes Act unconstitutional. The act allowed the state to commit a defendant to the Department of Public Welfare, following conviction for a sex offense, and after the state determined that the defendant was "in need of 'specialized treatment for his mental or physical aberrations'" (Humphrey v. Cady 1972, 510). The law allowed the state to commit a criminal defendant to a prison without the same protections afforded other civil committees, such as providing the right to an attorney and providing for treatment for the disease or disorder. The law provided the individual with due process protections, including a requirement that the state could not hold the person longer than the criminal sentence. The law also allowed the state to detain the individual for five years, with review (Humphrey v. Cady 1972, 507).

Had Wisconsin not invoked the Sex Crimes Act, Donald Humphrey would have served one year in jail. The Court found Wisconsin's procedures in lieu of sentencing to be in violation of the Fourteenth Amendment's equal protection and due process clauses because it denied Humphrey a jury trial, a right not denied to other committees. The Court held that the Sex Crimes Act was a different form of sentencing that created a new liberty interest: "an independent commitment for treatment" (Humphrey v. Cady 1972, 511) requires a jury determination for commitment based on a finding of mental illness.

Finally, *Vitek v. Jones* (1980, 487) concerns "whether the involuntary transfer" of Jones, who became mentally ill during his incarceration in Nebraska for robbery, "to a mental hospital implicates a liberty interest that is protected by the Due Process Clause." The Court's answer was yes, and in doing so it greatly broadened the meaning of equal protection and due process in civil commitment cases.

The Burger Court was concerned that, without strict limits on states' power to transfer prisoners to mental facilities, a state could transfer an unruly prisoner to a psychiatric ward without showing evidence of mental illness. In the language of strict scrutiny, the Nebraska law was not narrowly tailored; it did not apply the least restrictive means to arrive at its goal. The concerns about Soviet psychiatric practices with political prisoners also loom large here (Allen v. Illinois 1986, 383, n. 19; Spencer v. Lee 1989, 1382). These concerns are, to be sure, overblown, given the due process protections in place and the existence of an independent court system. Nevertheless, to lessen that possibility, the Court held: "It is precisely '[t]he subtleties and nuances of psychiatric diagnoses' that justify the requirements of adversary hearings" (Vitek v. Jones 1980, 495).

In these four cases,[9] the Warren and Burger Courts extended the meaning of due process and equal protection to cases involving the commitment of those with mental illnesses or disorders far beyond their established meanings. The Court made no claim that the mentally ill or sex offenders who were mentally ill were a "discrete and insular minority" (paragraph three of *Carolene Products*' footnote 4) or were excluded from the political process by ingrained prejudice (paragraph two of *Carolene Products*' footnote 4). The Court made no mention as to why the political process was so deficient in these instances as to warrant judicial intervention. The upshot of these rulings is that dangerous inmates with mental disorders now constitute a class deserving constitutional protection previously afforded only to those who were incapable of taking care of themselves. Although the reasons for these decisions may appear compelling as a matter of social policy—the possibility of indefinite detention of those with mental and behavioral disabilities raises substantive issues about the meaning of liberty—they fail to make the legal case why state procedures governing the commitment of criminally insane persons were inadequate from the standpoint of equal protection or due process; why *Pearson*'s rational basis test was ignored; why the equal protection clause was used in ways that were clearly contrary to its historical focus (Saunders 1997, 268; Bickel 1955); and why heightened forms of scrutiny were required in cases that were not considered to be part of the "concept of ordered liberty" (Palko v. Connecticut 1937, 325). Instead the Warren and Burger Courts conflated the differences between the rights of those who could not govern themselves and convicted criminals, or those accused of serious criminal activity, who have mental abnormalities or illnesses—and asserted that equal protection requires collapsing such distinctions. Despite advances in our society's understanding of equality and equal protection, the equal protection clause has allowed for "discriminations when founded on an important public policy" (Eskridge 2015, 1090). The justices made these changes without acknowledging the innovation they were creating and without considering the effects of this innovation on other areas of law and politics.

In the section that follows, the concerns of both defendants and the courts turn toward risk assessment and definitions of mental illnesses. The Court's "Guardian Ethic" regarding civil committees' equality claims expands to include social scientific evidence of discrimination. In fact, scientific language about risk and danger replaces jurisprudential and political ideas about judicial restraint, the separation of powers, and public safety.

Between the Third and Fourth Eras: The Minnesota Cases

In 1982, Wisconsin declared Phillip Jay Blodgett, age sixteen, a sexual offender. In 1985, Blodgett was in a Minnesota jail "for burglary and obstructing the legal process." Three hours after being released, he sexually assaulted his ex-girlfriend and was sent to prison. In 1987, Blodgett, enrolled in a release program, sexually assaulted a woman in a parking lot. Five weeks later, Blodgett, on "supervised release to a half-way house and enrolled in a treatment program," raped a sixteen-year-old girl. "As a result of these incidents, Blodgett pled guilty to two counts of criminal sexual conduct in the second degree and was returned to prison" (In re Blodgett 1994, 911).

Just prior to Blodgett's scheduled release from prison, in 1991, the Minnesota Department of Corrections had him evaluated to assess his danger risk and the state of his rehabilitation. The Minnesota law applied to Blodgett was the same as the one applied to Pearson, and under the same revision adopted by the state supreme court.

The Department of Corrections ordered Blodgett committed indefinitely to the Minnesota Security Hospital (MSH) with a diagnosis of ASPD. The staff at MSH agreed with the findings but opposed Blodgett's commitment, finding that he suffered from no known mental illness (In re Blodgett 1994, 912). The court of appeals upheld the lower court's decision to have Blodgett committed, and Blodgett appealed to the Minnesota supreme court, in a case called *In Re Phillip Jay Blodgett, Alleged Psychopathic Personality.*

To narrow the focus of the legislation and prevent arbitrary confinements, the *Blodgett* decision excluded from the meaning of ASPD "forms of social delinquency" (In re Blodgett 1994, 915). Nevertheless, Blodgett argued that Minnesota's commitment law violated both substantive due process and the equal protection clauses of the Minnesota and federal constitutions. The 1939 Minnesota law had isolated the psychopathic personality as the ground for commitment, and used it in lieu of prosecution. Minnesota now applied the law postconviction. Blodgett argued that the Supreme Court's decision in *Foucha v. Louisiana*, which restricts a state's power to indefinitely commit individuals who are not mentally ill, following a NGRI verdict, had overruled *Pearson*. Like Foucha, Blodgett argued that ASPD is not a mental illness. Not being ill, the state could not civilly confine him on danger alone (In re Blodgett 1994, 914).

Because Blodgett was never insane, *Foucha* should not apply. But the state supreme court held, in accordance with *Foucha*'s meaning, that should Blodgett's illness be "brought under control" (In re Blodgett 1994, 916), the state must release him. Minnesota had to justify Blodgett's commitment on two grounds: (1) that Blodgett was mentally disordered or that he suffered from a personality disorder; and (2) that he was dangerous.

To pass strict scrutiny analysis in cases involving fundamental rights, the law in question has to be narrowly tailored. The Minnesota supreme court argued that the law in question was "limited to sexual assaultive behavior and excludes mere sexual promiscuity" (In re Blodgett 1994, 915 and n. 10). The court also dismissed Blodgett's equal protection argument as a variation of his substantive due process argument. Blodgett argued that "it is a denial of equal protection to deny sexual predators their liberty when others who may be dangerous but not recognized medically as mentally ill retain their personal freedom" (In re Blodgett 1994, 917, 916). The state supreme court held that there is no violation of equal protection when legislatures treat certain crimes harsher than others.

This was not, in other words, a case in which the legislature had singled out, arbitrarily, one group for censure, punishment, or extra-long imprisonment. The Minnesota supreme court's decision in *Pearson*, the same court noted, had outlined "genuine and substantial distinctions" in defining classes of offenders, a decision the Supreme Court had upheld. And that decision, the state supreme court declared, should be followed "until the Supreme Court says otherwise" (In re Blodgett 1994, 917–18).

The Minnesota supreme court's *Blodgett* decision did not last long. In *In re Linehan*, the state supreme court reviewed *Pearson*'s three-part test and its application in the case of Dennis Darol Linehan and ordered Linehan released. In fact, the state supreme court reviewed Linehan's case six times (issuing two decisions on the same day and four times on the question of his civil confinement), once finding for him.

Linehan's story began in 1965, when a grand jury indicted him for kidnapping and murder in the first- and second-degrees. Linehan pleaded guilty to kidnapping; the state dropped the murder charges (Minnesota v. Linehan 1967, 349). In 1967, the Minnesota supreme court remanded Linehan's case to the district court to consider a claim of unlawful confession. The district court denied the motion to vacate Linehan's sentence and he appealed to the state supreme court (Minnesota v. Linehan 1969), which also rejected his argument.

On December 30, 1992, in the twentieth year of Linehan's forty-year sentence for kidnapping, Minnesota began the process of civilly committing Linehan as a "psychopathic personality," or, more precisely, as one who has an antisocial personality disorder and is "chemically dependent" (In re Linehan 1994, 610). The legislation does not address the differences between ASPD and psychopathy.

While incarcerated in Minnesota and in Michigan (for sexual assault, where he escaped), Linehan began treatment programs. Two Minnesota physicians had declared his treatment unsuccessful and two thought it was successful. The trial court admitted that some of the treatment was successful, but that Linehan "had not even completed the first step of admitting his past behavior and its effect on the victims" (In re Linehan 1993, 145). In all, four doctors examined Linehan prior to his release date: two believed Linehan was a psychopathic personality and two did not. The trial court sided with the two physicians who believed Linehan had a psychopathic personality and paraphilia (not otherwise specified)[10] and had him committed for sixty days (Prentky et al. 1996, 366–67). During a hearing to determine Linehan's future status, the trial court concluded that Linehan's "conduct shows an utter lack of power and ability to control his sexual impulses." The trial court then committed Linehan for "an indeterminate period to the Minnesota Security Hospital as a psychopathic personality" (In re Linehan 1993, 146).

The first *Linehan* state supreme court case, decided the same year as *Blodgett*, turned on an interesting problem not addressed in *Blodgett*. Neither of the two physicians who found Linehan to suffer from ASPD had read *Pearson*. In *Blodgett*, the Minnesota supreme court held that the court would "reverse cases that misapplied the statute as narrowed by that case" (In re Linehan 1994, 610; In re Blodgett 1994, 915).

In assessing Linehan's mental state, the examining physicians had relied on their own clinical impressions and the statutory language to support their claims that Linehan was a psychopath. The legal rule to commit a criminal defendant following conviction places the burden on the state to find, by "clear and convincing evidence, each of the three elements set out in *Pearson*" (In re Linehan 1994, 610; Addington v. Texas 1979, 433). Yet, when Dr. Richard Friberg testified that Linehan had a psychopathic personality, his answers reflected the "definition of the Minnesota statute," using such statutory language as "'impulsiveness of behavior,' 'irresponsible,' 'dangerous,' and 'appreciates the consequences of his acts'" (In re Linehan 1994, 612). Dr. Hector Zeller, the other physician who supported Dr. Friberg's opinion, also relied on the statutory language and his own clinical impressions (In re Linehan 1994, 613).

The supreme court, however, noted that the two physicians' clinical assessment of what constitutes a psychopathic personality failed to consider *Pearson*'s utter lack of control element. Consequently, the court ruled that there is "no clear and convincing evidence that appellant has an utter lack of power to control his sexual impulses" (In re Linehan 1994, 614). The test for utter lack of control is related, the court held, to the criteria that establish dangerousness:

> (a) the person's relevant demographic characteristics (e.g., age, education, etc.); (b) the person's history of violent behavior (paying particular attention to recency, severity, and frequency of violent acts); (c) the base rate statistics for violent behavior among individuals of this person's background (e.g., data showing the rate at which rapists recidivate, the correlation between age and criminal sexual activity, etc.); (d) the sources of stress in the environment (cognitive and affective factors which indicate that the person may be predisposed to cope with stress in a violent or nonviolent manner); (e) the similarity of the

> present or future context to those contexts in which the person has used violence in the past; and (f) the person's record with respect to sex therapy programs. (In re Linehan 1994, 614)

According to the Minnesota supreme court, the basis for a commitment evaluation must, first, come from *Pearson* and not from any clinical source, and second, include an assessment of the subject's utter lack of control. Because the state did not properly prove Linehan's "utter lack of power to control" from *Pearson*, the court ordered Linehan released on parole and vacated his commitment. The conditions of his parole were extensive. He had to live on the grounds of Stillwater Correctional Facility; his communications were subject to monitoring; and he was under twenty-four-hour surveillance, which included having the premises monitored by four hidden cameras (In re Linehan 1996a, 311).

In August 1994, while Linehan was on parole, Minnesota passed a sexually dangerous persons act (SDPA) that incorporated the *Pearson* holding, but abandoned the utter lack of control element. The law was directed at the Minnesota supreme court's holding releasing Linehan. The new law replaced part of *Pearson* with the following findings: That the state find, by clear and convincing evidence, that a potential committee has: (1) "engaged in a course of harmful sexual conduct as defined in subdivision 7a"; (2) "manifested a sexual, personality, or other mental disorder or dysfunction"; and (3) "as a result, [is] likely to engage in acts of harmful sexual conduct as defined in subdivision 7a" (In re Linehan 1996a, 316). The statute defines "harmful sexual conduct" as "sexual conduct that 'creates a substantial likelihood of serious physical or emotional harm to another'" (In re Linehan 1996a, 312).

One month after the passage of the act, Minnesota filed charges to commit Linehan to a mental hospital, and on July 27, 1995, Minnesota committed Linehan under the SDPA. Linehan was then fifty-four years old, having spent "most of his life in the criminal justice system for sex-related crimes" (In re Linehan 1996b, 174). A court-appointed examiner "testified Linehan does not presently exhibit a personality disorder, a sexual disorder, or a mental disorder, even though that expert had diagnosed Linehan with an antisocial personality disorder in 1992." The court of appeals, however, which was hearing Linehan's appeal to reject the state's pursuit of his commitment, noted that "Linehan has an alcohol dependence (in remission), impulse control disorder, and an antisocial personality disorder and supported his commitment as a sexually dangerous person" (In re Linehan 1996a, 323). The state supreme court upheld Linehan's commitment.

The trial court had found that Linehan had engaged in "harmful sexual conduct" by, over the course of his life, taking "indecent liberties with a four-year-old girl," raping two women, committing "criminal sexual misconduct with four different females," and killing "a 14-year-old girl while attempting to sexually assault her" (In re Linehan 1996a, 312). Linehan argued that those acts all occurred in the past and thus could not constitute a judgment of dangerousness regarding his future. The appellate court, however, held that the law was not offended by judgments about potential dangerousness based on past actions, a point the state supreme court agreed with. As the Supreme Court held in *Jones v. U.S.* (1983), "The fact that a person has been found, beyond a reasonable doubt, to have committed a criminal act certainly indicates [future] dangerousness" (1983, 364).

On appeal, Linehan asked for strict scrutiny analysis, given that Minnesota was holding him on an indeterminate sentence and without diagnosing him with an identifiable mental illness. Linehan argued that a substantive interpretation of the due process clause from *Foucha v. Louisiana* would win him his freedom (In re Linehan 1996b, 180). Three questions can be raised about Linehan's appeal: One, has Minnesota denied Linehan a right implicating the due process and equal protection clauses in their substantive meaning? Two, can Minnesota commit Linehan for what he has done and may (only possibly) continue to do? And three, can Minnesota commit Linehan under a law that requires a diagnosis of ASPD, if, under *Foucha*, the state may not civilly commit an individual, following a NGRI verdict, who is sane or who does not suffer from "a true mental illness"? (In re Linehan 1996a, 312). If this is the situation in Minnesota, then two things follow: (1) the proper judicial standard to review civil commitment is the highest one, strict scrutiny, not rational basis; and (2) the proper standard for confinement must be criminal, not civil. In fact, Linehan's argument cannot stand because both the Minnesota district court and the court of appeals "concluded that APD is a mental disorder that the state may use to trigger civil commitment of dangerous persons" (In re Linehan 1996b, 180).[11]

At the same time the Minnesota courts were deciding Blodgett's and Linehan's cases, they also decided three other cases involving sex offenders. In one case, Minnesota committed Barry Bieganowski following his conviction for a number of sexual assaults. In 1979, when Bieganowski was twenty and his sister-in-law was sixteen, he "beat her with his fists, causing bruising around her eyes, face and throat, disrobed her, and forced her to engage in sexual intercourse" (In re Bieganowski 1994, 525). Minnesota paroled him in 1983, but from "December 1983 until his arrest in January 1985," Bieganowski "engaged in multiple acts of oral sex with his seven-year-old son and six-year-old stepdaughter, and in anal intercourse on at least one occasion with his seven-year-old son" (In re Bieganowski 1994, 526). In 1992, Minnesota committed Bieganowski to the Minnesota Security Hospital, as a psychopathic personality, which he challenged and lost.

In 1993, Minnesota committed Raymond Irwin to the Minnesota Security Hospital as a psychopathic personality. In 1965, Irwin "fondled his 15-year-old half-sister in bed. She testified that appellant thought it was acceptable for him to have sex with her because she was only his half-sister." In 1967, Irwin "was convicted of forced sexual contact with a 17-year-old girl in Los Angeles" (In re Irwin 1995, 368). Irwin also confessed to engaging in "seven to eight separate criminal sexual incidents with his stepdaughter" (In re Irwin 1995, 369). In 1984, he was convicted of rape of a fourteen-year-old girl. Despite Irwin's substantive claims of denial of liberty, the court of appeals upheld his indeterminate detention.

Finally, Minnesota committed Michael Pirkl to the Minnesota Security Hospital as a psychopathic personality. "Pirkl's lengthy history of sexual assaults against women and other crimes began when he was a juvenile, when he was convicted of burglary in 1969, illegal entry of a bus, theft, illegal entry of a building, and attempted aggravated rape in 1971, and theft, aggravated assault, and attempted aggravated rape in 1972" (In re Pirkl 1995). Pirkl continued sexually assaulting women as an adult. The court of appeals upheld Pirkl's commitment to a security hospital.

As in *Blodgett* and *Linehan*, the petitioners' in these three cases asked the courts to rely upon scientific diagnoses of mental illnesses and disregard the public safety component of the laws in question. In all three cases, the Minnesota court of appeals upheld the state's argument for commitment. I bring up these sordid stories to highlight the very real problems states confront with sex offenders who have been paroled and yet remain dangerous. (Irwin was not on parole.) Deliberation is not an idealized notion of legislation. It is the product of facts that arise in cases such as these. In each case, the Minnesota courts spent time going over the conflicting psychiatric and psychological claims alleged. They paid attention to the constitutional claims asserted. And they noted that the three petitioners had harmed people and destroyed the sense of safety of those around them. Either sexual violent predator (SVP) laws are examples of the "deliberative sense of the community" or sex offenders constitute a group that courts need to protect. If the latter, then judges have to explain why the political process fails convicted sex offenders, an argument I have yet to see. We should not lose sight of the fact that psychopathy's primary marker is antisocial behavior, not a lesion on the brain. There must be legal judgments about psychopaths that accept the scientific evidence but do not succumb to it, given the gray zone the concept occupies scientifically (Shaw 1913, 152; Jalava, Griffiths, and Maraun 2015).

In the remaining part of this chapter, I will examine a number of cases that highlight the conflict over statistical risk and reasoned judgment. The many decisions regarding Linehan did not resolve these issues and there is no Supreme Court decision to guide us. At its core, the problem of the "mad" and the "bad" caught up in one individual is a challenge to the deliberative aspects of our political system.

Risk and the Nomenclature of Mental Disorders

Clyde Hall is a sex offender with a diagnosed case of ASPD and pedophilia. While in federal prison for possession of child pornography, he attended a treatment program. Upon his release from treatment, the state continued to regard him as "high risk" for reoffending. The government released him in 2004 but revoked his supervised release in 2006.

In 2007, "the United States Probation Office was notified that Hall had viewed pornography and engaged in sex with an adult [Alcoholics Anonymous] participant." He fled but was caught. At that point, "Hall's supervision was again revoked, and he was additionally charged and convicted for failure to register as a sex offender. . . . In April of 2008, was sentenced to 25 months' imprisonment and 25 years' supervised release" (U.S. v. Hall 2012, 460). In 2009, the government transferred Hall to FCI Butner, a medium-security prison in North Carolina, readying him for a postconviction civil commitment hearing. The federal Bureau of Prisons determined that Hall was a "sexually dangerous person" because he was "in possession of sexually inappropriate materials at FCI Butner, including pictures of prepubescent children and traced drawings of prepubescent girls with their clothing removed and their genitals drawn" (U.S.

v. Hall 2012, 461). At an evidentiary hearing in 2011, the federal district court held that the government had not proven that Hall was a sexually dangerous person. Hall's case then went to the court of appeals.

Under the Adam Walsh Act, which governs federal postconviction civil commitment regulations, the government has to prove that Hall:

> (1) "has engaged or attempted to engage in . . . child molestation" in the past; (2) currently "suffers from a serious mental illness, abnormality, or disorder"; and (3) as a result of the illness, abnormality, or disorder, "would have serious difficulty in refraining from . . . child molestation if released." (U.S. v. Hall 2012, 461)

The government has the burden of proving each of these elements by clear and convincing evidence. The government proved the first prong by citing as evidence Hall's past crimes. The government proved the second prong by the presentation of expert witnesses who diagnosed Hall with pedophilia and ASPD, diagnoses Hall did not dispute. Hall disputed the third prong.

The three experts who testified in court (two for the state, one for Hall) used "actuarial tests, psychological tests, and their clinical judgment" to decide Hall's level of danger. Two physicians, Dale Arnold and Lela Demby, argued that Hall would have "serious difficulty refraining from child molestation if released" (U.S. v. Hall 2012, 463), but Dr. Luis B. Rosell testified that Hall would not experience this difficulty.

Clinicians rely upon a number of analytic tools for static evaluations. The Dangerous Behavior Rating Scheme (DBRS), the Violent Risk Appraisal Guide (VRAG), HCR-20, RRASOR, the Structured Anchored Clinical Judgment (SACJ), the Sexual Offender Risk Appraisal Guide (SORAG), the California Actuarial Risk Assessment Tables (CARAT), the New York State Risk Assessment Instrument (RAI), the Adult Sex Offender Risk Assessment Schedule (ASORAS), the New Jersey Registrant Risk Assessment Scale (RRAS), and the Psychopathy Checklist-Revised (PCL-R) (which is not an actuarial prediction instrument; it is used to assess levels of antisocial behavior; see New York v. Michael R. 2014, 6). For juveniles, there are the Juvenile Sex Offender Assessment Protocol-II (JSOAP-II) and the Estimate of Risk of Adolescent Sexual Offense Recidivism (ERASOR).

Dr. Arnold relied on an actuarial tool called Static-99R and Static-2002R, as well as the Minnesota Sex Offender Screening Tool-Revised (MnSOST-R).

Static-99 is a tool used "for adult males who have already been charged with or convicted of at least one contact sexual offense against a child or non-consenting adult" (Cohen and Spindell 2016, 23). "VRAG and Static-99 remain the favored vehicles for statistics-derived predictions for violent and sexual reoffending" (Hamilton 2015, 17). Dr. Demby used Static-99R and Static-99. The highest score on Static-99R is 12; a score of six or higher is considered to be high risk. According to one research finding, "90 percent of those with a score of six on the Static-99 scale committed another sexual offense within 14 years, and all of those with a score of seven or higher committed another sexual offense within that period" (California v. Allen 2008, 854). Dr. Rosell, who came to a different conclusion regarding Hall's dangerousness, used Static-99R, Static-2002R, and the Multisample Age Stratified Table of Sexual Recidivism Rate ("MATS"). Each doctor also relied on his or her own clinical assessment of Hall's psychological makeup and overall behavior.

The district court found Dr. Rosell's analysis to be the compelling one. The court did not weigh the value of each statistical assessment or express concern that three scientists arrived at three different conclusions about one person's mental health and behavioral capabilities. Rather, the court relied on Dr. Rosell's conclusions that Hall, when under supervised release, did not commit any sexual offenses against minors and that a twenty-five-year supervision of Hall would be a successful deterrent to any future desires he may have to recidivate (U.S. v. Hall 2012, 465). The court of appeals did not find the district court's ruling "clearly erroneous" and upheld the order to dismiss the government's case against Hall.

Actuarial risk tools are not without their faults. Some mental health professionals claim that "there are no actuarial measures of risk that can be used" on those "whose offenses occurred prior to age 14" (In the Matter of the Civil Commitment of Eischens 2014, 3). Also, insofar as these tools rely on captive populations, they may skew toward dangerousness. And because sex offenses are underreported, it is equally possible that static evaluations underestimate the possibility of recidivism. Because they rely on general samples from a population and "then identify the traits or risk factors shared by those offenders," they also do not take into consideration the individual offender on trial. It is important to note that assessment is not prediction.

> The Static 99, or indeed any ARA [Actuarial Risk Assessments] cannot predict the risk that any particular sex offender will reoffend. It merely describes how

> an individual's characteristics compare with those of offenders who have reoffended at a given rate over a given period of time. (New York v. Santos 2009, 4)

In general, mental health professionals favor the use of static models over clinical judgments, which are deemed "highly subjective in nature" and "less than adequate" (Kondo 2003, 203), because they can be compared to the predictions of an educated person. Indeed, clinicians prefer to rely on statistical analyses because those mental health professionals who do not resort to statistical analyses in evaluating dangerousness are considered "nonscientifically minded," and their "professional judgments are not to be trusted" (Browne and Harrison-Spoerl 2008, 1205; Skeem and Monahan 2011). Yet static factors are not as good predictors of dangerousness as dynamic factors, which focus on behaviors that "may be changeable with treatment" (Kondo 2003, 202). Judges find both static and dynamic assessments problematic because their burden is to evaluate the entirety of the offender's life-history, including statements from the offender regarding remorse and knowledge of his actions. "Neither low actuarial scores nor any other single factor is determinative of whether someone is highly likely to reoffend" (In the Matter of the Civil Commitment of Eischens 2014, 4). In *McGee v. Bartow* (2010), the court of appeals for the seventh circuit declared that the limits of modern psychiatry do not impose the same limits on the law.

> The clinical and scientific considerations involved in categorization of these conditions may not be wholly relevant to legal judgments, for example, that take into account such issues as individual responsibility, disability determination, and competency. (2010, 575–76)

The basic claim behind the use of assessment tools in civil commitment cases is that, without them, courts would have an easier time incarcerating seemingly dangerous individuals. Decisions to incarcerate, in other words, would be based on nonscientific criteria, i.e., the prejudices or passions of communities, legislators, or judges. Examining civil commitment cases, however, does not lead to that conclusion. In *Hall*, the federal district court denied the government's claim that Hall posed a future danger, despite the fact that the government had two psychiatrists testify that Hall was dangerous. The court of appeals found no legal reason to overturn that decision. Whatever the merits of the decision, the majority opinion was deliberative and reasonable. So, too, was the decision in *U.S. v. Francis* (2012) where, despite Sean Francis's compulsion to make obscene phone calls—a condition called telephone scatalogia, which falls within the definition of paraphilia in the *DSM*—the district court ruled against the government's motion to civilly commit and the court of appeals upheld that motion. States and the federal government also lost in the following cases, all involving sex offenders with mental disorders: *U.S. v. Begay* (2012), *U.S. v. Graham* (2010), *New York v. Donald DD* (2014), and *Thomas v. Missouri* (2002).

One of the most perplexing sex offender cases is *U.S. v. Caporale* (2012). The United States sought to civilly commit Patrick Caporale, age fifty-nine, under the terms of the Adam Walsh Act, following the completion of his term in a federal prison. In his twenties, Caporale had had sex with male and female minors in two states and was caught in possession of pornography. He committed more sexual offenses after twice being released. The fourth circuit federal district court directed the government to release Caporale, finding that he did not suffer from a "serious mental illness, abnormality, or disorder." And, while the court of appeals found that Caporale did suffer from a "qualifying mental impairment" (U.S. v. Caporale 2012, 130), it upheld the district court's opinion that the government failed to prove that Caporale will reoffend.

Three psychologists interviewed Caporale. The government's witnesses were Drs. Gary Zinik and Lela Demby. Caporale's expert witness was Dr. Joseph Plaud. According to Dr. Plaud, "Caporale is sexually interested in pubescent to post-pubescent males, '12, 13 up to 16, 17 years old.'" Dr. Zinik was more exact, noting that "Caporale is attracted to [p]ubescent boys, approximately 11 to 14." According to Dr. Demby, however, "Caporale prefers 'pre-pubescent boys . . . who ha[ve] not yet developed the majority of their secondary sexual characteristics . . . as young as 11 and 12'" (U.S. v. Caporale 2012, 132). It matters a whole lot to this case whether Caporale is a pedophile. Treatment, risk assessment, and civil commitment are at stake. The experts also differed on what kind of risk Caporale posed if released. The government's experts believed that Caporale was a continuing threat because Caporale had scored "high risk" and "moderate high risk" on two of three risk analyses (U.S. v. Caporale 2012, 134). But Dr. Plaud, Caporale's doctor, noted that "since 1992, Caporale had committed only noncontact offenses." He also objected to the government's use of risk analysis. Dr. Plaud argued that "the actuarial risk decreases to less than ten percent for men sixty and over, an age that Caporale has nearly attained" (U.S. v. Caporale 2012, 135). The matter was joined not on the question of risk as such but on what psychological illness Caporale actually suffers from.

The *Diagnostic and Statistical Manual*-III (*DSM*-III) replaced "sexual deviation" with "paraphilia" because the latter term "correctly emphasizes that the deviation (para-) lies in that to which the person is attracted (philia)" (1987, 279). The *DSM*-V lists eight types of paraphilias, though the list is not exhaustive: "voyeuristic, exhibitionistic, frotteuristic, sexual masochism, sexual sadism, pedophilic, fetishistic, and transvestic" (First 2014, 192, 198; DSM 2013, 685). For thirty-four years, the *DSM* had defined paraphilia as a "nonpathological, atypical sexual interest." The *DSM*-V, however, redefined "the term paraphilia so that it now refers to a persistent, intense, atypical sexual arousal pattern, independent of whether it causes any distress or impairment, which, by itself, would not be considered disordered" (First 2014, 192; DSM 2013, 685). As not everyone with a paraphilic interest has a paraphilic disorder, the *DSM*-V makes clear that only those whose intense interests cause distress suffer from the disorder.

The *DSM*-V defines pedophilic disorder as follows:

> A. Over a period of at least 6 months, recurrent, intense sexually arousing fantasies, sexual urges, or behaviors involving sexual activity with a prepubescent child or children (generally age 13 years or younger).
> B. The individual has acted on these sexual urges, or the sexual urges or fantasies cause marked distress or interpersonal difficulty.
> C. The individual is at least age 16 years and at least 5 years older than the child or children in Criterion A. Note: do not include an individual in late adolescence involved in an ongoing sexual relationship with a 12- or 13-year-old. (DSM 2013, 697)

A pedophile is one who has an "erotic preference for prepubescent children" (Blanchard et al. 2009, 335; DSM-V 2013, 698). Pedophilia is "the most commonly diagnosed paraphilia among men convicted of sexual offenses" (First and Halon 2008, 451). Its origins are uncertain (Stephens and Seto 2015). Hebephilia is the "erotic preference for pubescent children" (Demazeux and Singy, eds. 2015, xx), by which is meant those between the ages of eleven and fourteen. An ephebophile is someone with an erotic preference for adolescents, i.e., those fifteen years old to nineteen years old. The latter two terms are not widely used in nosological descriptions of sexual disorders (Blanchard et al. 2009, 336; U.S. v. Carta 2009, noting that Carta is a pedophile, a hebephile, and an ephebophile; New York v. Donald DD 2014, 242, U.S. v. Shields [2007], and

U.S. v. Abregana [2008] reject hebephilia as a mental disorder). Hebephilia is not to be confused with hebephrenia.[12] The *DSM*-V does not recognize ephebephilia as a category of paraphilia because the sexual desire for those who can reproduce is not thought to be statistically abnormal. After much debate, the *DSM*-V added "paraphilic coercive disorder and hypersexual disorder" (First 2014, 192) but rejected adding hebephilia to the broader term paraphilia.

The case of Allen Albert Barnes highlights the borderland of scientific diagnosis and reasoned judicial judgment.

> Barnes has a long history of sexual misconduct. When he was thirteen, he sexually molested his nephew. In 1981, while on work release from a conviction for forgery, he committed voyeurism. In 1985, he was convicted of three counts of third-degree sexual abuse. He raped three different women at knifepoint. He was also convicted of one count of assault with intent to commit sexual abuse for attempting to rape a fourth woman. He was imprisoned until 1990. In 1996, he was again convicted of third-degree sexual abuse. He forced his way into a woman's house and raped her. He was imprisoned until 2001. While in prison, Barnes was terminated from the sex offender treatment program four times for sexual misconduct and for engaging in inappropriate behavior towards female staff. (Iowa v. Barnes 2004, 456–57)

Dr. Caton Roberts diagnosed Barnes with ASPD and argued that he met the criteria for psychopathy.

Though separate disorders, one can have both psychopathic tendencies and ASPD. ASPD is not highly correlated with sexually violent offenses or disorders. ASPD is not a paraphilia. Nor is ASPD an involitional disorder. It "is not a mental incapacity. It is descriptive of a way people act in society" (In the Matter of the Commitment of W.Z. 2001, 561). However, legislatures and courts can (and do) consider it a "mental abnormality" (New York v. Donald DD 2014, 177), which is a legal category, not a medical classification. State courts are divided on the question of whether someone diagnosed with ASPD plus dangerousness qualifies as "mentally abnormal" and thus qualifies for postconviction civil commitment. The argument against relying solely on ASPD as a basis for commitment is that it could be applied to robbers, rapists, and murderers.

> The reason that ASPD strikes us as a potentially invalid predicate for civil management is because once we accept such a notion, in an important sense, we lift

> the veil on the sex offender civil management systems we have created and are forced to acknowledge that we are not confining and supervising sex offenders because they are subject to uniquely uncontrollable urges or incomprehensible compulsions. We are subjecting them to potential lifetime confinement because we hate what they are at risk to do. (New York v. Michael R. 2014, 20)

Lynn Maskel, Barnes's forensic psychiatric expert witness, testified that "antisocial personality disorder is common among criminals in general and that forensic psychiatrists do not consider it to predispose a person to commit sexually violent offenses." Dr. Caton Roberts, the state's expert witness, testified that ASPD "is a condition that is either congenital, acquired, or both," and he stated that Barnes's ASPD affected his "emotional and volitional capacity" (Iowa v. Barnes 2004, 457–58). Dr. Maskel said it did not. The district court ruled in favor of the state's petition to commit Barnes, but not because the scientific evidence was better in one instance and not the other. The Iowa district court deferred to the lower court's opinion of Barnes's dangerousness.

Barnes appealed, contending that a diagnosis of ASPD is "overly broad and violates due process" because that diagnosis is "not correlated with sex-offending and that forty to sixty percent of the prison population has this designation" (Iowa v. Barnes 2004, 457–58). If Barnes does not suffer from a "mental disorder or abnormality" that leads to sexual offending, then he cannot be committed.

The Iowa law requires the state to prove that the potential committee is sexually dangerous, not that the potential committee suffers from ASPD or psychopathy. Indeed, Barnes's expert witness, Dr. Maskel, had correctly established that there is no necessary correlation between ASPD and sexual offending. Maskel based her argument on the idea that ASPD does not limit one's will. The net effect of her argument, not mentioned by the Iowa supreme court, was that, insofar as Barnes has ASPD, he is willfully dangerous. Contrary to her client's interest, Maskel's diagnosis argues for Barnes's commitment. Roberts's diagnosis argues for Barnes's lack of freedom, because he connected ASPD to sexual offending, as if Barnes lacked the freedom to choose. There is nothing in this case to suggest that the Iowa supreme court believed Roberts's understanding of determinism over Maskel's understanding of free will. What the Iowa supreme court did was to side with the lower court—out of deference, not substance, which sided with Roberts's version of ASPD and sexual offending.

The *Barnes* and *Caporale* cases reveal the problem of civil commitment and mental illnesses, which I discuss more in depth in the next chapter. The problem, briefly, is not one of "justice" in some abstract, discursive, or narrative sense. No interest group pressured these courts to rule as they did. Neither Barnes's nor Caporale's civil commitment was the result of a tyrannical majority putting the screws to members of a discrete and insular minority. Both were provided with due process and pursued appeals. Both called their own psychiatric witnesses. Indeed, the Iowa court in Barnes's case treated him as if he were a patient, not a criminal, which tells us a lot about the interdisciplinary state of the law these days. The courts that heard Barnes's case (and the others mentioned in this chapter) relied far more on psychiatric testimony than they did on constitutional analyses and republican principles. The court of appeals' decision in *Caporale* is a seminar on mental disorders.

Barnes reveals the paradox that lies at the heart of the scientific evidence that purports to determine the law's outcome. What *Iowa v. Barnes* did not solve, which *Kansas v. Hendricks* attempts to solve but also does not, as no court has, is the problem of the relationship between mental abnormality and control, for here is the real problem with the application of psychiatric categories in legal analysis, particularly in civil commitment cases, a problem which drags the Supreme Court unnecessarily into the debate over free will and determinism.

Conclusion

As long as medical diagnoses of mental processes and behavior remain "fraught with . . . scientific uncertainties" (In re Linehan 1996b, 184), the case for judicial minimalism remains heightened. "Our duty to abstain from confounding policy with constitutionality," Justice Frankfurter wrote, "demands perceptive humility as well as self-restraint in not declaring unconstitutional what in a judge's private judgment is deemed unwise and even dangerous" (Dennis v. U.S. 1951, 552). Deference to the opinions of judges, in cases involving evidence, and deference to the judgment of legislators, in cases involving psychological and psychiatric testimony, go hand-in-hand.[13] For courts to substitute their judgment for that of legislators, or for courts to defer to psychological or psychiatric experts, whose understanding of mental diseases and disorders remains specific to the discipline of medicine, is to abdicate the role the Constitution has assigned to courts to say what the law is.

There is no doubt that the more the Supreme Court has focused on equality as outcome, the more it and the state and federal courts have resorted to scientific studies and statistical analyses to achieve that outcome. One only has to consider reapportionment cases, which are mired in statistical analyses of voters in counties down to the last digit (Goldberg 1962). In terms of sex offender legislation, the question the advocates for science raise is: shouldn't experts on risk make decisions about risk and danger in a democracy and not legislators beholden to public opinion or judges relying on formal principles of law? But isn't the operative term regarding civil commitment "democracy" and not "experts"? Don't the scientists evince a hostility toward democracy in their focus on psychological determinism and their dismissal of the public's opinion about safety? Isn't there a place in constitutional law for community sentiment that avoids comparison to the Salem Witch Trials? As Greg Weiner writes, "just as individuals have claims against the community, so does the community have claims on individuals" (2019, 15). Doesn't the civil commitment of persons properly belong, first with legislatures, then with courts, but not first to psychologists or statisticians, for the simple reason that legislatures and courts are public bodies responsible for making, implementing, and deciding public policy? As I have shown, the judgment to commit an ill and dangerous individual relies upon more factors than the scientific evidence admits. Courts need to decide cases "from the totality of expert testimony and the other record evidence" (U.S. v. Graham 2010, 143).

If all behavior is the product of psychological determinism, then no rational judgments are possible, and democratic government is a mirage. By all means, then, let the judgment of treatment success or failure fall on psychologists. But let courts decide risks to society on constitutional grounds, for that is their constitutional obligation. The alternative to the positivism of the scientists must be constitutional, deliberative politics. What Edward Banfield and James Q. Wilson wrote about city politics applies to politics in general: that the "day-to-day workings of city government in the United States are best understood by looking at the differences of opinion and interest that exist . . . and the ways institutions function to resolve (or fail to resolve) them" (1967, 1). When the democratic nature of politics gets obscured by scientific or social scientific analyses, the solution, as in *Hall*, is risk analysis. But that decision was beset by contradictions from within the psychiatric community about Hall's dangerousness. It is impossible to say, in a scientific sense, who was right. It is doubtful even more scientific inquiry can solve this problem.

NOTES

1. The key distinction between criminal and civil law is that a criminal law involves punishment and a civil law is regulatory. In a case about the electronic monitoring of a sex offender, the South Carolina supreme court held "that 'electronic monitoring is *not a punishment*,' but a civil requirement" (South Carolina v. Nation 2014, 481; italics in original). But as Alexander Brooks (1992, 718) has noted, "a 'civil' designation need not be taken at face value if that term conceals actual punishment."

2. "This term, meaning literally 'parent of the country,' refers traditionally to [the] role of [the] state as sovereign and guardian of persons under legal disability, such as juveniles" (Stickler 1997, 377 n. 4).

3. The states' police power is the "acknowledged power of a State to regulate its police, its domestic trade, and to govern its own citizens" (Gibbons v. Ogden 1824, 80). The classic police power case is *Jacobson v. Massachusetts* (1905), concerning compulsory vaccination.

4. A personality trait is an enduring pattern of "perceiving, relating to, and thinking about the environment and oneself that are exhibited in a wide range of social and personal contexts." Personal traits can rise to the level of a personality disorder "only when . . . [they become] inflexible and maladaptive and cause significant functional impairment or objective distress" (DSM 2013, 647).

5. On the neurological sources of psychopathy, see Cima, Tonnaer, and Hauser 2010, 59; Boccardi et al. 2011, 86; Anckarsäter 2006.

6. Michigan and Illinois preceded Minnesota by two years. Ohio, Wisconsin, California, and Massachusetts followed Minnesota (Brakel and Cavenaugh 2000, 71; Kirwin 2003, 1138–39).

7. Given that Minnesota law prohibited the insane from a number of daily tasks, e.g., engaging in contracts, providing a spouse with grounds for divorce, the implications of a psychopathic personality being considered insane—or even being "alleged" insane, as was the case here—was profound (Minnesota ex rel. Pearson v. Probate Court of Ramsey County 1940b, 58).

8. Overinclusive classifications, though not presumptively unconstitutional, can easily run afoul of the equal protection clause (Korematsu v. U.S. 1944).

9. We can add *Jackson v. Indiana* (1972), which relied on *Baxstrom*, and expanded the equal protection clause to the pretrial commitment of incompetent defendants.

10. The DSM classifies exhibitionism, fetishism, frotteurism, pedophilia, sexual sadism, sexual masochism, transvestic fetishism, and voyeurism as paraphilias. "Every category of diagnosis in the *DSM*-IV-TR contains an 'NOS' diagnosis" (U.S.

v. Graham 2010, 136), because not every paraphilic category can encompass every possible outcome. In *DSM*-V, paraphilia NOS is now called "Other Specified Paraphilic Disorder." Examples listed by the *DSM*-5 (2013, 705) of ASPD are telephone scatologia, necrophilia, zoophilia, coprophilia, klismaphilia, and urophilia—there is no evidence that Linehan engaged in any of these paraphilias.

11. This is a controversial area of law and psychiatry. As Sreenivasan, Weinberger, and Garrick have noted (2003), ASPD is a sufficient condition to merit civil commitment. Whether it is "clinically appropriate" (Vognsen and Phenix 2004, 440) is a separate matter. Moreover, to be civilly committed under a statute with a "mental abnormality" criterion probably requires that the committee have both ASPD and be a sexually violent offender.

12. Hebephrenia has been a psychological diagnosis since 1870. Nineteenth-century physicians described hebephrenia as a "second form of the insanity of pubescence" (Christian 1901, 214–16). Hebephrenia is a form of insanity that develops around the age of postpuberty, which in the late nineteenth century was eighteen to twenty-two years old, though asylum physicians had diagnosed hebephrenia in children as young as fourteen. Hebephrenia manifests itself in "mania, melancholia, and craziness," which includes auditory and visual hallucinations, impudence, sexual crimes, and masturbation; it culminates in "mental weakness" and "dementia" (Lane 1895, 311).

13. In *Daubert v. Merrell Dow Pharmaceuticals,* the Supreme Court declared that in cases involving scientific testimony and the submission of scientific evidence, judges should consult four factors regarding admissibility:

> Has the theory or technique been (or can it be) tested? (2) Has the theory or technique been subjected to peer review and publication? (3) What is the technique's known or potential rate of error? (4) Has it been generally accepted in the relevant scientific community? (Regnier 2004, 494; Daubert v. Merrell Dow Pharmaceuticals 1993, 593–94)

Daubert is a federal civil case; it does not apply to sentencing hearings or state criminal cases. But *Daubert* points to a regard for deference to legislative enactments because the meaning of scientific evidence in cases concerning mental illness is not always certain to scientists and nonscientists, and the importance of the evidence may be at odds with good public policy.

REFERENCES

Anckarsäter, Henrik. 2006. "Central Nervous Changes in Social Dysfunction: Autism, Aggression, and Psychopathy." *Brain Research Bulletin* 69 (3): 259–65.

Appelbaum, Paul, and Kathleen Kemp. 1982. "The Evolution of Commitment Law in the Nineteenth Century: A Reinterpretation." *Law and Human Behavior* 6 (3/4): 343–54.

Babiak, Paul, Jorge Folino, Jeffrey Hancock, Robert Hare, Matthew Logan, Elizabeth Leon Mayer, J. Reid Meloy, Helina Hakkanen-Nyholm, Mary Ellen O'Toole, Anthony Pinizzotto, Stephen Porter, Sharon Smith, and Michael Woodworth. 2012. "Psychopathy: An Important Forensic Concept for the 21st Century." *FBI Law Enforcement Bulletin: Psychopathy* 81: 3–8.

Banfield, Edward, and James Q. Wilson. 1967. *City Politics.* Cambridge, MA: Harvard University Press.

Barnickol, Laura. 2000. "Missouri's Sexually Violent Predator Law: Treatment or Punishment?" *Washington University Journal of Law and Policy* 4: 321–39.

Bickel, Alexander. 1955. "The Original Understanding and the Segregation Decision." *Harvard Law Review* 69 (1): 1–65.

Blanchard, Ray, Amy Lykins, Diane Wherrett, Michael E. Kuban, James M. Cantor, Thomas Blak, Robert Dickey, and Philip Klassen. 2009. "Pedophilia, Hebephilia, and the DSM-V." *Archive of Sexual Behavior* 38 (3): 335–50.

Boccardi, Marina, Giovanni Frisoni, Robert Hare, Enrica Cavedo, Pablo Najt, Michela Peivani, Paul Rasser, Mikko Laakso, Hannu Sronen, Eila Repo-Tiihonen, Olli Vaurio, Paul Thompson, and Jari Tiihonen. 2011. "Cortex and Amygdala Morphology in Psychopathy." *Psychiatry Research: Neuroimaging* 193 (2): 85–92.

Brakel, Samuel Jan, and James Cavanaugh. 2000. "Of Psychopaths and Pendulums: Legal and Psychiatric Treatment of Sex Offenders in the United States." *New Mexico Law Review* 30 (1): 69–94.

Brooks, Alexander. 1992. "The Constitutionality and Morality of Civilly Committing Violent Sexual Predators." *University of Puget Sound Law Review* 15 (3): 709–54.

Browne, M. Neil, and Ronda Harrison-Spoerl. 2008. "Putting Expert Testimony in its Epistemological Place: What Predictions of Dangerousness in Court Can Teach Us." *Marquette Law Review* 91 (4): 1119–1212.

Christian, J. "Dementia Praecox." 1901. *Journal of Insanity* 58 (2): 215–41.

Cima, Maaike, Franca Tonnaer, and Marc Hauser. 2010. "Psychopaths Know Right from Wrong but don't Care." *Social Cognitive and Affective Neuroscience* 5 (1): 59–67. doi:10.1093/scan/nsp051.

Cleckley, Hervey. 1964. *The Mask of Sanity*, 4th ed. St Louis: C. V. Mosby Company.

Cohen, Thomas, and Spidell, Michelle. 2016. "How Dangerous Are They: An Analysis of Sex Offenders under Federal Post-Conviction Supervision." *Federal Probation* 80 (2): 21–32.

Demazeux, Steeves, and Patrick Singy, eds. 2015. *The DSM-5 in Perspective: Philosophical Reflections on the Psychiatric Babel.* New York: Springer.

Diagnostic and Statistical Manual. 1987. III-R. Washington, DC: American Psychiatric Association.

Diagnostic and Statistical Manual. 2013. 5th ed. Washington, DC: American Psychiatric Association.

Douglas, Kevin, Scott Lilienfeld, Jennifer Skeem, Norman Poythress, John Edens, and Christoper Patrick. 2008. "Relation of Antisocial and Psychopathic Traits to Suicide-related Behavior among Offenders." *Law and Human Behavior* 32 (6): 511–25.

Elliott, Ward. 1974. *The Rise of Guardian Democracy: The Supreme Court's Role in Voting Rights Disputes, 1845–1969.* Cambridge, MA: Harvard University Press.

Eskridge, William. 2015. "Original Meaning and Marriage Equality." *Houston Law Review* 52 (4): 1067–1119.

First, Michael. 2014. "DSM-5 and Paraphilic Disorders." *Journal of the American Academy of Psychiatry and the Law* 42 (2): 191–201.

First, Michael, and Robert Halon. 2008. "Use of DSM Paraphilia Diagnoses in Sexually Violent Predator Commitment Cases." *Journal of the American Academy of Psychiatry and the Law* 36 (4): 443–54.

Freedman, Estelle. 1987. "'Uncontrolled Desires': The Response to the Sexual Psychopath, 1920–1960." *Journal of American History* 74 (1): 83–106.

Goldberg, Arthur. 1962. "The Statistics of Malapportionment." *Yale Law Journal* 72 (1): 90–107.

Gunther, Gerald. 1972. "Foreword: In Search of Evolving Doctrine on a Changing Court: A Model for a Newer Equal Protection." *Harvard Law Review* 86 (1): 1–48.

Hamilton, Melissa. 2015. "Adventures in Risk: Predicting Violent and Sexual Recidivism in Sentencing Law." *Arizona State Law Journal* 47 (1): 1–62.

Hare, Robert. 1999. *Without Conscience: The Disturbing World of the Psychopaths Among Us.* New York: Guilford Press.

Jalava, Jarkko, Stephanie Griffiths, and Michael Maraun. 2015. *The Myth of the Born Criminal: Psychopathy, Neurobiology, and the Creation of the Modern Degenerate.* Toronto: University of Toronto Press.

Kirwin, John. 2003. "One Arrow in the Quiver—Using Civil Commitment as one Component of a State's Response to Sexual Violence." *William Mitchell Law Review* 29 (4): 1135–1219.

Klarman, Michael. 1991. "An Interpretative History of Modern Equal Protection." *Michigan Law Review* 90 (2): 213–318.

Kondo, Leroy. 2003. "The Tangled Web—Complexities, Fallacies and Misconceptions Regarding the Decision to Release Treated Sexual Offenders from Civil Commitment to Society." *Northern Illinois University Law Review* 23 (2): 195–226.

Lane, Edward. 1895. "Observations upon Hebephrenia." *Journal of Insanity,* 51 (3): 310–18.

Levy, David. 1942. "Psychopathic Personality and Crime." *Journal of Educational Sociology* 16 (2): 99–114.

Lipton, Harry. 1950. "The Psychopath." *Journal of Criminal Law and Criminology* 40 (5): 584–96.

McConnell, Michael. 1995. "Originalism and the Desegregation Decisions." *Virginia Law Review* 81 (4): 947–1140.

Note. 1974. "Civil Commitment of the Mentally Ill." *Harvard Law Review* 87 (6): 1190–1406.

Prentky, Robert, Eric Janus, Howard Barbaree, Barbara Schwartz, and Martin Kafka. 2006. "Sexually Violent Predators in the Courtroom." *Psychology, Public Policy, and Law* 12 (4): 357–93.

Regnier, Thomas. 2004. "Barefoot in Quicksand: The Future of Future Dangerousness Predictions in Death Penalty Sentencing in the World of Daubert and Kumho." *Akron Law Review* 37 (3): 469–508.

Rothman, David. 1971. *The Discovery of the Asylum: Social Order and Disorder in the New Republic.* Boston: Little, Brown and Company.

Saunders, Melissa. 1997. "Equal Protection, Class, Legislation, and Colorblindness." *Michigan Law Review* 96 (2): 245–337.

Shaw, John. 1913. *Essentials of Nervous Diseases and Insanity, Their Symptoms and Treatment, 5th ed.* Philadelphia: W.B. Saunders.

Skeem, Jennifer, and David Cooke. 2010. "One Measure Does not a Construct Make: Directions Toward Reinvigorating Psychopathy Research—Reply to Hare and Neumann." *Psychological Assessment* 22 (2): 455–59. doi: 10.1037/a0014862.

Skeem, Jennifer, and John Monahan. 2011. "Current Directions in Violence Risk Assessment." *Current Directions in Psychological Science* 20 (1): 38–43.

Sreenivasan, Shoba, Linda Weinberger, and Thomas Garrick. 2003. "Expert Testimony in Sexually Violent Predator Commitments: Conceptualizing Legal Standards of 'Mental Disorder' and 'Likely to Reoffend.'" *Journal of the American Academy of Psychiatry and Law* 31 (4): 471–85.

Stein, Dan, Katharine Phillips, Derek Bolton, K. W. M Fulford, John Z. Sadler, and Kenneth S. Kendler. 2010. "What Is a Mental/Psychiatric Disorder? From DSM-IV to DSM-V." *Psychological Medicine* 40 (11): 1759–65. doi:10.1017/S0033291709992261.

Stephens, Skye, and Michael Seto. 2015. "Hebephilic Sexual Offending." In *Sexual Offending: Predisposing Antecedents, Assessment and Management*, edited by Amy Phenix and Harry Hoberman, 29–43. New York: Springer. doi: 10.1007/978-1-4939-2416-5.

Stickler, Christine Steib. 1997. "In Re S.G.: Parens Patriae and Wardship Proceedings—Exactly Who in the State Should Determine the Best Interest of the Child." *Widener Journal of Public Law* 7 (2): 377–402.

Sutherland, Edwin. 1950. "The Sexual Psychopath Law." *Journal of Criminal Law and Criminology* 40 (5): 543–54.

Swanson, Alan. 1960. "Sexual Psychopath Statutes: Summary and Analysis." *Journal of Criminal Law, Criminology, and Police Science* 51 (2): 215–35.

Tussman, Joseph, and Jacobus tenBroek. 1949. "The Equal Protection of the Laws." *California Law Review* 37 (3): 341–81.

Vognsen, Jack, and Amy Phenix. 2004. "Antisocial Personality Disorder Is Not Enough: A Reply to Sreenivasan, Weinberger, and Garrick." *Journal of the American Academy of Psychiatry and the Law* 32 (4): 44–42.

Weiner, Greg. 2019. *The Political Constitution: The Case against Judicial Supremacy.* Lawrence: University Press of Kansas.

Wilson, James Q., and Richard Herrnstein. 1985. *Crime & Human Nature.* New York: Simon & Schuster.

CASES

Addington v. Texas, 441 U.S. 418 (1979).
Allen v. Illinois, 478 U.S. 364 (1986).
Barbier v. Connolly, 113 U.S. 27 (1885).
Baxstrom v. Herold, WL 130156 (1965a).
Baxstrom v. Herold, WL 115400 (1965b).
Baxstrom v. Herold, 383 U.S. 107 (1966a).
Baxstrom v. Herold, WL 115388 (1966b).
Boutilier v. Immigration and Naturalization Service, 363 F.2d 488 (1966).
Bridges v. Wixon, 326 U.S. 135 (1945).
California v. Allen, 44 Cal. 4th 843 (2008).
Daubert v. Merrell Dow Pharmaceuticals, 509 U.S. 579 (1993).
Dennis v. U.S., 341 U.S. 494 (1951).
Dowling v. U.S., 493 U.S. 342 (1990).
Frank v. Mangum, 237 U.S. 309 (1915).
Gibbons v. Ogden, 22 U.S. 1 (1824).

Humphrey v. Cady, 405 U.S. 504 (1972).
In re Bieganowski, Alleged Psychopathic Personality, 520 N.W.2d 525 (1994).
In re Blodgett, Alleged Psychopathic Personality, 510 N.W.2d 910 (1994).
In re Gault, 387 U.S. 1 (1967).
In re Heff, 197 U.S. 488 (1905).
In re Irwin, 529 N.W.2d 366 (1995).
In re Linehan, 503 N.W.2d 142 (1993).
In re Linehan, 518 N.W.2d 609 (1994).
In re Linehan, 544 N.W.2d 308 (1996a).
In re Linehan, 557 N.W.2d 171 (1996b).
In re Pirkl, 531 N.W.2d 902 (1995).
In the Matter of Oakes, 8 Law Rep. 123 (1845).
In the Matter of the Civil Commitment of Eischens, WL 2808060 (2014).
In the Matter of the Commitment of W.Z., 339 N.J.Super. 549 (2001).
Iowa v. Barnes, 689 N.W.2d 455 (2004).
Jackson v. Indiana, 406 U.S. 715 (1972).
Jacobson v. Massachusetts, 197 U.S. 11 (1905).
Jones v. U.S., 463 U.S. 354 (1983).
Kansas v. Hendricks, 521 U.S. 346 (1997).
Korematsu v. U.S., 323 U.S. 214 (1944).
McGee v. Bartow, 593 F.3d 556 (2010).
Michigan v. Chapman, 301 Mich. 584 (1942).
Michigan v. Frontczak, 286 Mich. 51 (1938).
Minnesota v. Linehan, 276 Minn. 349 (1967).
Minnesota v. Linehan, 282 Minn. 254 (1969).
Minnesota ex rel. Pearson v. Probate Court of Ramsey County, 205 Minn. 545 (1939).
Minnesota ex rel. Pearson v. Probate Court of Ramsey County, 309 U.S. 270 (1940a).
Minnesota ex rel. Pearson v. Probate Court of Ramsey County, WL 46385 (1940b).
Nashville, Chattanooga & St. Louis Ry. Co. v. Browning, 310 U.S. 362 (1940).
Nebbia v. New York, 291 U.S. 502 (1934).
New York v. Donald DD., 24 N.Y.3d 174 (2014).
New York v. Michael R., 42 Misc.3d 1222(A) (2014).
New York v. Santos, 25 Misc.3d 1212(A) (2009).
Pace v. Alabama, 106 U. S. 583 (1883).
Palko v. Connecticut, 302 U.S. 319 (1937).
Powell v. Pennsylvania, 127 U.S. 678 (1988).
Regents of the University of California v. Bakke, 438 U.S. 265 (1978).
Reynolds v. Sims, 377 U.S. 533 (1964).

South Carolina v. Nation, 408 S.C. 474 (2014).
Specht v. Patterson, 386 U.S. 605 (1967).
Spencer v. Lee, 864 F.2d 1376 (1989).
Thomas v. Missouri, 74 S.W.3d 789 (2002).
U.S. v. Abregana, 574 F.Supp.2d 1123 (2008).
U.S. v. Begay, 880 F.Supp.2d 707 (2012).
U.S. v. Caporale, 701 F.3d 128 (2012).
U.S. v. Carolene Products Company, 304 *U.S.* 144 (1938).
U.S. v. Carta, 620 F.Supp.2d 210 (2009).
U.S. v. Francis, 686 F.3d 265 (2012).
U.S. v. Hall, 664 F.3d 456 (2012).
U.S. v. Graham, 683 F.Supp.2d 129 (2010).
U.S. v. Shields, 522 F.Supp.2d 317 (2007).
Vitek v. Jones, 445 U.S. 480 (1980).
Yick Wo v. Hopkins, 118 U.S. 356 (1886).

CHAPTER 4

The Postconviction Commitment of Sexual Offenders

The third era of civil commitment statutes did not bestow upon the fourth clear criteria for assessing the constitutionality of postconviction civil commitment. This is evident in the Supreme Court's decision in *Kansas v. Hendricks* (1997), which is riddled with puzzles: whether civil commitment after criminal confinement can be considered a civil remedy and therefore not subject to Eighth Amendment scrutiny; whether postconviction sex offender statutes can allow states to confine persons with behavioral-control issues but nothing more by way of mental disease or illness; whether postconviction civil commitment requires states to provide treatment; and whether Kansas's Sexually Violent Predator Act violates the constitutional ban on ex post facto laws and double jeopardy (Collins v. Youngblood 1990, 43; Calder v. Bull 1798). The purpose of this chapter is to address these vexing medical and juridical questions by looking closely at the meaning of mental illnesses and disorders as they pertain to *Kansas v. Hendricks* and the case that followed it, *Kansas v. Crane* (2002).

Law and Psychology: A Primer

In 1994, Kansas passed the Sexually Violent Predator Act (SVPA). The SVPA's purpose is different from Kansas's law regulating the commitment of the mentally ill who are not sex offenders: the SVPA establishes a "procedure for the long-term care and treatment of the sexually violent predator" (Kansas v. Hendricks 1997, 367). The Kansas legislature noted that treatment within a prison setting is not conducive to success, so it required treatment after the prisoner is civilly committed. The law contains three key provisions. The first defines a sexually violent predator:

> [A] "Sexually violent predator" means any person who has been convicted of or charged with a sexually violent offense and who suffers from a mental abnormality or personality disorder which makes the person likely to engage in the predatory acts of sexual violence. (In re Hendricks 1996, 267)

Sexual offenses include "any act which either at the time of sentencing for the offense or subsequently during civil commitment proceedings pursuant to this act, has been determined beyond a reasonable doubt to have been sexually motivated" (In re Hendricks 1996, 268). Robert Teir and Kevin Coy (1997, 417 n. 59) note that the act includes the following criminal behaviors:

> rape, indecent liberties and aggravated indecent liberties with a child, criminal and aggravated criminal sodomy, indecent and aggravated indecent solicitation of a child, sexual exploitation of a child, [and] aggravated sexual battery.

The second provision defines "mental abnormality" as a "congenital or acquired condition affecting the emotional or volitional capacity which predisposes the person to commit sexually violent offenses in a degree constituting such person a menace to the health and safety of others." And the third defines "sexually motivated" to mean that the crime was dependent upon "the defendant's sexual gratification" (In re Hendricks 1996, 267).

The SVPA also includes provisions for the commitment of sexual offenders who are incompetent to stand trial and for those found not guilty by reason of insanity "of a sexually violent offense."

> A "sexually violent offense" is both strictly and expansively defined as (1) rape, (2) indecent liberties with a child, (3) aggravated indecent liberties with a child, (4) criminal sodomy, (5) aggravated criminal sodomy, (6) indecent solicitation of a child, (7) aggravated indecent solicitation of a child, (8) sexual exploitation of a child, (9) aggravated sexual battery, (10) comparable federal or state crimes, (11) attempts, conspiracies, or criminal solicitations of the above crimes, and (12) "any act which either at the time of sentencing for the offense or subse-

> quently during civil commitment proceedings pursuant to this act, has been determined beyond a reasonable doubt to have been sexually motivated." (In re Hendricks 1996, 267)

Finally, the Act requires the "involuntary detention or commitment" of sexually violent offenders following the termination of their prison sentence. It requires that the commitment "conform to constitutional requirements for care and treatment" (Kansas v. Hendricks 1997, 353).

> When it appears that the person presently confined may be a sexually violent predator, the prosecuting attorney of the county where the person was convicted or charged or the attorney general if requested by the prosecuting attorney may file a petition, within 45 days of the date the prosecuting attorney received the written notice . . . alleging that the person is a sexually violent predator and stating sufficient facts to support such allegation. (In re Hendricks 1996, 251)

There is a potential due process problem here because a jury will determine the convict's status as a committee based on their knowledge of his prior act (Bodine 1990, 123–25). The Supreme Court in *Hendricks* did not address this issue.

Next, "a judge determines whether probable cause exists to believe that the person named in the petition is a sexually violent predator. If so, the person is transferred to an appropriate facility for a professional evaluation" (In re Hendricks 1996, 251). Then a court will conduct a trial to determine whether the individual in question is a sexually violent predator. The individual is entitled to counsel and can request a jury or a bench trial. Finally, the determination of the individual's status must be made "beyond a reasonable doubt" (In re Hendricks 1996, 252), the highest standard of proof applied in criminal cases. In civil cases (which a commitment hearing is), the standard of proof is preponderance of the evidence, a lower standard than beyond a reasonable doubt. If the court finds the prisoner to be a sexually violent predator beyond a reasonable doubt, the court then orders the prisoner transferred

> to the custody of the secretary of social and rehabilitation services for control, care and treatment until such time as the person's mental abnormality or personality disorder has so changed that the person is safe to be at large. Such control, care and treatment shall be provided at a facility operated by the department of social and rehabilitation services. (In re Hendricks 1996, 252)

Failure to prove that the individual is a sexually violent offender beyond a reasonable doubt means the prisoner will be free following the completion of his prison term.

It is said of postconviction civil commitment laws that the term of commitment is indefinite and thus in violation of the due process clause of the Fourteenth Amendment because indefinite detention violates a fundamental liberty interest. It is not. The term of commitment is one year, renewable upon a court's determination "beyond a reasonable doubt that that the detainee satisfies the same standards as required for the initial confinement" (Kansas v. Hendricks 1997, 364). If "the person's mental abnormality or personality disorder has so changed that the person is safe to be at large and will not engage in acts of sexual violence if discharged" (In re Hendricks 1996, 252), then a hearing is held and the state bears the burden of proving dangerousness and mental abnormality, subject to the "beyond a reasonable doubt" standard. Moreover, the secretary of the Department of Social and Rehabilitative Services (in Kansas) can, at any time, petition a court regarding the committee's changed mental status. In short, Kansas's SVPA isolates four criteria for determining whether a criminal defendant can be civilly committed:

> (1) a history of sexual violence, (2) a current mental disorder or "abnormality," (3) risk of future sex crimes, and (4) some form of connection between the mental disorder and the danger, such that the mental impairment predisposes the individual to future sexual violence or "makes" it likely that the future harm will occur. (Mercado, Schopp, and Bornstein 2005, 293)

Most states with sexually violent predator (SVP) laws reject over 75 percent of "sexually motivated offenders" for postconviction civil commitment proceedings. As Samuel Brakel and James Cavanaugh have written, the reasons for this are "driven in part by considerations other than purely clinical ones. Such other considerations would include economics (evaluation costs, ultimately treatment and even legal resource limitations) as well as more qualitative policy concerns on the order of what the public will accept in terms of social risk versus the cost of containing it, and even stated legislative estimations or aspirations that the number of ultimately committable offenders be small" (2005, 70–80).

Let us look at why Kansas sought to make Hendricks the first person committed under their new law.

In 1996, Hendricks was sixty years old, but he first "exhibited unlawful sexual behavior" in 1955, at the age of twenty, when he "pled guilty to indecent exposure." In 1957, he was "convicted of lewdness for playing strip poker with a teenage girl." Three years later, he was incarcerated for three years for "molesting two young boys." Paroled in 1963, he was imprisoned that same year for "molesting a 7-year-old girl." In 1967, Hendricks was again imprisoned for having sex with two minors, one male, the other female. In prison, he was diagnosed as a pedophile, refused treatment, and was paroled in 1972 (In re Hendricks 1996, 269–70).

While free, Hendricks entered into a treatment program but stopped attending sessions soon thereafter. Admitting that he molested children when he got "stressed out," he began "molesting his stepdaughter and stepson" for a period of four years. Years later, during an interview with a psychologist, Hendricks would say, "treatment was bullshit" (In re Hendricks 1996, 248, 270). In 1984, as part of a plea agreement, Hendricks was again incarcerated, this time for "indecent liberties."[1] The state set his term of confinement between five and twenty years. His conditional release date was 1994, which is when Kansas brought the commitment action against him.

At one point in Hendricks's evaluation, a clinical social worker with a specialization in sexual offenses "testified [that] Hendricks had a diagnosis of personality trait disturbance, passive-aggressive personality, and pedophilia" (In re Hendricks 1996, 270). Personality trait disturbance is linked with passive-aggressive behavior, compulsive personality, and emotional instability (Graeve 2007, 54). The *DSM* does not classify personality trait disturbances as an organic or neurologically based mental disorder, and thus does not regard it as debilitating. According to the *DSM*-IV-TR, "Only when personality traits are inflexible and maladaptive and cause significant functional impairment or subjective distress do they constitute personality disorders" (DSM 2000, 630). The *DSM*-V defines personality disorder as "an enduring pattern of inner experience and behavior that deviates markedly from the expectations of the individual's culture" (Ahluwalia 2006, 12; DSM 2013, 645). In legal settings, evaluators are free to interpret "personality disorders" in accordance with the *Diagnostic and Statistical Manual* or not. Legislators, too, can interpret these concepts broadly when drafting statutes.

To separate those who have difficulty restraining themselves from criminal behavior, but who still maintain the ability to reason about right and wrong, and those who cannot govern themselves at all, postconviction civil commitment laws rely upon a distinction between personality disorders and mental disorders. This distinction is difficult, though not impossible, to maintain. The *DSM* states that "no definition adequately specifies precise boundaries for the concept of 'mental disorder'" (DSM 2000, xxx). Yet mental disorders can be considered "serious," causing long-term damage to the affected person's overall health and prospects for longevity. Personality disorders are thought to be something less than this, and partly the result of choice. Personality disorders can range from narcissism to forms of schizophrenia, although personality disorders are not usually associated with the more serious mental illnesses associated with neurological and physiological disorders, including schizophrenia. State and federal courts do not consider personality disorders to be on the same level as "substantial psychiatric disorder[s]" (In re El-Rashad 1987, 568), although legislatures and courts are constitutionally permitted to equate them with the term "mental illness or defect" (In re El-Rashad 2987, 570). In terms of the Kansas sexual violent predator law, personality disorder refers to antisocial personality disorder (ASPD) and not (necessarily) to neurologically or physiologically serious mental illnesses. ASPD can serve as a predicate for postconviction civil commitment. It cannot, by itself, serve as the reason for commitment, as it has no causal link with sexual offenses (New York v. Donald DD 2014).

The "World Health Organization and the American Psychiatric Association include personality disorders in their classifications of mental disorders" (Kendell 2002, 113). The World Health Organization (WHO) admits that the word "disorder"

> is not an exact term, but it is used here to imply the existence of a clinically recognizable set of symptoms or behaviour associated in most cases with distress and with interference with personal functions. Social deviance or conflict alone, without personal dysfunction, should not be included in mental disorder as defined here. (WHO n.d., 11)

R. E. Kendell writes that personality and mental disorders belong as much to "socio-political" concerns as they do to "biomedical" concerns. Personality disorders are conceptually heterogeneous," Kendell writes, acknowledging that "information about [personality disorders] is limited," and "existing knowledge is largely derived from unrepresentative clinical populations" (Kendell 2002, 113).

As for the term "mental disorder," it is elastic enough that six states (Arizona, California, Illinois, Minnesota, North Dakota, and Wisconsin) use it in reference to SVP laws, while ten states use "mental abnormality" (Florida, Iowa, Kansas, Massachusetts, Missouri, New Jersey, Pennsylvania, South Carolina, Virginia, and Washington), and one state, Texas, uses "behavioral abnormality." As Thomas Zander points out, "[t]he term 'mental abnormality' is totally foreign to the *DSM*, while the term 'mental disorder' embraces almost *all* diagnostic categories in the *DSM*" (2005, 25–26; italics in original; DSM 2000, xxxi).

Justice Stephen Breyer argued, in dissent, that Hendricks suffered from a mental illness and a "serious mental disorder" (Kansas v. Hendricks 1997, 375). The Kansas law does not require a finding of mental illness, in part because the precise meaning of the term remains elusive within the psychological and medical literature. Mental illness and disorder can suggest legal irresponsibility (McNeil v. Director, Patuxent Institution 1972, 251). The American Psychiatric Association (APA), in a brief filed in *Indiana v. Edwards* (2008), defined severe mental illness as "[d]isorganized thinking, deficits in sustaining attention and concentration, impaired expressive abilities, [and] anxiety" (2008, 176). In its brief in *Delling v. Idaho* (2012), the APA stated that severe mental illness "can seriously impair a sufferer's ability rationally to appreciate the wrongfulness of conduct" (2012, 505). In *Ake v. Oklahoma* (1985), a psychiatrist diagnosed Glen Burton Ake with severe mental illness, noting the "intensities of his rage, his poor control, his delusion" (1985, 71), which points to the comorbid features of personality and mental disorders. And in *Vincent v. Louisiana* (1985), Justices William Brennan and Thurgood Marshall equated severe mental illness with the defendant's inability to "meet the constitutional standard of triability," noting that Harold Vincent could neither understand "the charges against him" nor "assist his attorney" (1985, 928). In other cases, however, the Supreme Court has stated that the relationship between mental illness and competence to stand trial is not direct, meaning that one can be mentally ill or mentally retarded and sane enough for trial purposes (Drope v. Missouri 1975; Indiana v. Edwards 2008). Most important is the fact that no justice has ever said in what way "severe" modifies "mental illness," and whether the distinction between severe and nonsevere mental illness creates a constitutional rule to follow.

Severe mental illness can include prior institutionalization, though it is not required to satisfy the definition (Brown v. Dodd 1987). In *Olmstead v. L.C. ex rel Zimring* (1999), Justice Anthony Kennedy wrote that advances in medical science have demonstrated that "severe mental illness is often treatable," though he cautioned that health professionals and government officials have "yet to grasp the potential for treating mental disorders, especially severe mental illness" (1999, 608). Part of the problem with "severe mental illness" is that it refers to no specific mental disease. In jurisprudence, it does not mean that one has lost the ability to act on one's own. In *Colorado v. Connelly* (1986, 174), for example, the Court acknowledged that "Mr. Connelly suffered from a 'longstanding severe mental disorder,' diagnosed as chronic paranoid schizophrenia." Connelly had confessed to a murder without prompting, and his lawyer sought to suppress the confession. The Supreme Court rejected that argument, holding that absent police coercion, Connelly made the decision to confess freely, and there was no violation of the due process clause. In Eric Clark's murder case, the trial judge, relying on expert psychiatric testimony, held that Clark's "paranoid schizophrenia" "'did not . . . distort his perception of reality so severely that he did not know his actions were wrong'" (Clark v. Arizona 2006, 746), a position the Supreme Court upheld. And in *Kansas v. Hendricks* (1997, 377), Justice Kennedy declared that the "[c]apacity to make an informed decision about treatment is not always or obviously incompatible with severe mental illness."

A further problem with using mental illness in law is that the *DSM*-V defines mental disorder but not mental illness.

> A mental disorder is a syndrome characterized by clinically significant disturbance in an individual's cognition, emotion regulation, or behavior that reflects a dysfunction in the psychological, biological, or developmental processes underlying mental functioning. Mental disorders are usually associated with significant distress in social, occupational, or other important activities. An expectable or culturally approved response to a common stressor or loss, such as the death of a loved one, is not a mental disorder. Socially deviant behavior (e.g., political, religious, or sexual) and conflicts that are primarily between the individual and society are not mental disorders unless the deviance or conflict results from a dysfunction in the individual. (DSM 2013, 20)

The editors of the *DSM*-V add a warning: "This definition of mental disorder was developed for clinical, public health, and research purposes." More is required for "legal judgments."

The most pressing constitutional problem that plagues the decisions in *Hendricks* and *Crane* is whether someone with a personality disorder can control his or her behavior. The Kansas legislature wrote that personality disorders increase the likelihood that the affected person will "engage in predatory acts of sexual violence" (Kansas v. Hendricks 1997, 352). This means that the Kansas law regards sexual predators as responsible for their actions and therefore committable, even as the postconviction commitment law regards predators as having impulse problems, which diminishes the committee's free choice. The constitutional question about personality disorders is whether the subject lacks the "emotional capacity to control" his behavior but maintains "volitional control" over his "sexual impulses" (In the Matter of the Commitment of W.Z. 2001, 555).

The Constitution requires some correlation between mental illness and dangerousness to justify civil confinement (Specht v. Patterson 1967; O'Connor v. Donaldson 1975). In the nineteenth century, the general test for a defendant to establish nonresponsibility was to prove that his will was insufficient "to restrain the impulse" that arose "from a diseased mind" (DeJarnette v. Virginia 1881, 7). From the late nineteenth century and into the twentieth, the borderland of sanity and insanity was occupied by the idea that some persons have an "irresistible impulse" that they cannot control but which is not necessarily a sign of irresponsibility derived from mental disease (Pennsylvania v. Mosler 1846). In fact, many courts did not like the irresistible impulse idea because of the term's uncertainties regarding the source of the impulse. According to the common medical understanding, irresistible impulse has to come from a disease, else it is nothing more than an impulsive criminal act (Wharton 1874, 33; Connecticut v. Johnson 1873). The California supreme court dismissed the concept entirely, wondering whether the impulse was only irresistible in the absence of a police officer (California v. Hubert 1897, 224).

Writing in dissent in *Kansas v. Hendricks,* Justice Breyer claimed that Hendricks suffered from an "unusual inability to control his actions" and that "irresistible impulse" has shaped the juridical understanding of insanity for purposes of confinement (Kansas v. Hendricks 1997, 375–76). Justice Breyer's intention to revive irresistible impulse is odd. If he is suggesting that states are free to set the standard for commitment by a volitional standard, then he has created no constitutional problem (Davis v. U.S. 1895; West Virginia v. Harrison 1892, 987–88). But if he is trying to merge the aims of the criminal law with the methods of science, he has weakened the law and misunderstood the science. As Mercado, Schopp, and Bornstein have written, "Not only is there no clear articulation of what qualifies as inability to control, but also, court opinions often seem contradictory in nature" on this topic. They add, importantly, that "there does not appear to be a consistent notion of volitional impairment or low self-control in the theoretical or empirical literatures, nor in psychological practice guidelines. Instead, there is pervasive vagueness and uncertainty, with a clear definition rarely given" (Mercado, Schopp, and Bornstein 2005, 299, 305).

Neither legislators nor judges understand causation the same way as scientists do. "Causation," write Alec Buchanan and Howard Zonana, "implies a form of explanation based on scientific laws that is more suited to the physical sciences" (2009, 146) than law. Herbert Wechsler once noted that the law does not recognize mental illness as leading to irresponsibility, not because it rejects scientific evidence but because courts are invested in the making of "moral judgments," and not in validating scientific speculations (1955, 371). Courts require more comprehensive tests of responsibility than are provided by science, one "less relaxed than but-for cause but less demanding than complete exclusion of volition" (Wechsler 1955, 371). Breyer's revival of a nineteenth-century concept that had little support among state courts[2] has not resolved how courts and juries should assess the resistibility of an impulse to commit crime; if anything, he has made matters worse (Buchanan and Zonana 2009, 143; Madden v. Collins 1994), a point I return to at the end of the chapter.

Civil Law and Substantive Due Process

The decision in *Hendricks* was 5–4 against the Kansas supreme court's ruling that the Kansas Sexually Violent Predator Act was unconstitutional. But the 5–4 decision hides a general agreement about the content of Kansas's law. All the justices, except Ruth Bader Ginsburg, agreed that "the civil commitment of a 'mentally ill' and 'dangerous' person does not automatically violate the Due Process Clause provided that the commitment takes place pursuant to proper procedures and evidentiary standards" (Kansas v. Hendricks 1997, 374). Regarding procedures for treatment, all the justices, except Ginsburg, agreed that the "Constitution permits a State to follow one reasonable professional view" regarding treatment and the definition of mental illness and disorder "while rejecting another" (Kansas v. Hendricks 1997, 375).

Leroy Hendricks sought to undermine Kansas's chief claim about the post-conviction civil commitment of sex offenders by denying that it is a civil regulation. He argued that the SVPA "violates the prohibition against double jeopardy and ex post facto laws, fails to provide equal protection and procedural or substantive due process, and is void as overly broad and vague" (Kansas v. Hendricks 1997, 253). Hendricks based his double jeopardy complaint on the idea that the civil commitment that followed imprisonment for a criminal offense was punishment for the same offense he was convicted of. A law can only violate double jeopardy if it is criminal not civil, though the Supreme Court has held, in *U.S. v. Halper* (1989), "that a civil sanction that 'qualif[ies] as "punishment" in the plain meaning of the word' is subject to the constraints of the Double Jeopardy Clause" (Porter 1997, 519; U.S. v. Halper 1989, 449). In *U.S. v. Ward* (1980, 248), the Supreme Court outlined a two-part test to determine a law's status:

> First, we have set out to determine whether Congress, in establishing the penalizing mechanism, indicated either expressly or impliedly a preference for one label or the other. Second, where Congress has indicated an intention to establish a civil penalty, we have inquired further whether the statutory scheme was so punitive either in purpose or effect as to negate that intention.

Kansas's SVPA appears under its civil law. Moreover, Kansas considers the SVPA to be civil because: (1) the commitment proceedings are not adversarial; (2) no scienter is required, as it is in criminal cases (scienter is the knowledge one has that one has committed a wrong); (3) the commitment is based on a finding of mental abnormality and not upon criminal intent; and (4) because the determination to commit is made, in part, by physicians, not by anyone associated with the administration of criminal justice. To be sure, if the law is classified as civil but has a criminal effect, then it can qualify as criminal and violate the constitutional prohibition against double jeopardy, the ex post facto clause of the Constitution, and other safeguards of the Bill of Rights. As the Supreme Court held in *Allen v. Illinois* (1986, 369), "the 'civil' label to a proceeding is not always dispositive."

In the separation of powers scheme that informs each branch of government's jurisdiction, the judiciary is under a burden to presume legislation constitutional. "If there is any reasonable way to construe the Act as constitutionally valid," the Kansas supreme court held, "we must do so" (In re Hendricks 1996, 253; Kansas v. Hendricks 1997, 381). Yet the Kansas supreme court declared the law unconstitutional because Kansas committed Hendricks though he was without mental illness. What, then, is the intent and effect of Kansas's SVPA, and how should courts understand it?

In postconviction civil commitment cases involving sexual predators, the proceedings are not adversarial because no criminal act is involved. State legislatures have classified the detention of juveniles who have violated criminal laws not as criminals but as "delinquents," in an effort to "immunize juveniles from 'punishment' for 'crimes'" caused by "youthful indiscretions" (In re Gault 1967, 24, 60). The same holds true for the civil commitment of sexual offenders. The stigma of being a sex offender is removed because the proceedings are civil and premised upon a finding of a mental disorder or abnormality, rather than a criminal offense. What matters most to judges, when deciding whether a law is civil or criminal, is that there are distinct differences in the in-take, administration, release, and postrelease of subjects, rooted in rational policy means and ends. If the law is civil, then what is the appropriate constitutional standard to assess a law's effect on those it seeks to care for but not punish?

The Kansas supreme court held that the SVPA violated the "substantive" component of the Fourteenth Amendment's due process clause because "the State must prove by clear and convincing evidence that the individual is both mentally ill and dangerous" (In re Hendricks 1996, 263). Justice Clarence Thomas, for the majority, wrote: "Kansas argues that the Act's definition of 'mental abnormality' satisfies 'substantive' due process requirements. We agree" (Kansas v. Hendricks 1997, 356). Justice Thomas's "We agree" means that Kansas's use of "mental abnormality" in place of "mental illness" satisfied substantive due process. Justice Thomas mentions substantive due process four times in his *Hendricks* opinion. Each time, he put substantive in quote marks but not due process, demonstrating his distaste for the concept. Justice Kennedy, concurring in the decision, did not use the phrase at all. Only Justice Breyer relied on substantive due process. He wrote in dissent that Kansas's intent "was to punish" (Kansas v. Hendricks 1997, 388) because its treatment of Hendricks was meager. The lack of treatment for civil committees violated substantive due process, he argued, a point the majority rejected. Justice Thomas dismissed the treatment problem because commitment primarily involves "incapacitation," which is a "legitimate end of the civil law" (Kansas v. Hendricks 1997, 365–66; In re Hendricks 1996, 258).

Substantive due process requires more than a finding that the legislation be "merely arbitrary or unreasonable" (In re Hendricks 1996, 263). According to Justice Antonin Scalia, "'[s]ubstantive due process' analysis must begin with a careful description of the asserted right, for '[t]he doctrine of judicial self-restraint requires us to exercise the utmost care whenever we are asked to break new ground in this field'" (Reno v. Flores 1993, 302). It requires a finding that a right must be "deeply rooted in this Nation's history and tradition" (Washington v. Glucksberg 1997, 721). The Court has acknowledged that fundamental rights under the due process clause include, but are not limited to, the following type of cases: "personal decisions relating to marriage, procreation, contraception, family relationships, child rearing, and education" (Washington v. Glucksberg 1997, 726). These cases differ in substance from the kind of claim Hendricks made. The key question in *Hendricks* is whether Kansas created a "hardship so acute and shocking that our polity will not endure it" (Washington v. Glucksberg 1997, 762). But Kansas does not seek to commit Hendricks without legal process. So the answer is no. Hendricks has not created a reasonable ground for a court to consider his claim substantive. Hendricks, then, attempted to do two things. One, he argued that Kansas had denied him due process in the procedural sense, as his commitment followed from a criminal conviction, and thus violated the prohibition against ex post facto laws and double jeopardy. Second, he tried to extract a substantive due process argument from a procedural one, by arguing that Kansas violated substantive due process in the sense that the state has "no substantively adequate justification" (Washington v. Glucksberg 1997, 755) for civilly committing a nonmentally ill person.

Hendricks asked the Court to grant a right that had not hitherto existed. To be sure, Justice Byron White, in *Foucha v. Louisiana*, did write that "Freedom from physical restraint" is "a fundamental right," although he meant it to apply to "insanity acquittees who are no longer mentally ill" (which is the next part of the sentence), and not to those committed under SVP laws, as that was not the issue in *Foucha*. Moreover, White placed the idea of Foucha's fundamental freedom in part III of the decision, which garnered the approval of only three other justices (Foucha v. Louisiana 1992, 86). *Foucha*, in other words, does not establish a substantive due process right to be free from bodily or physical restraint in all instances. In *Youngberg v. Romeo* (1982), the Court resorted to substantive due process and used the phrase "physical restraint" to apply to a situation in which an "institutionalized, mentally retarded patient . . . had been restrained *by shackles placed on his arms* for portions of each day" (Foucha v. Louisiana 1992, 117 n. 12; italics in original). That holding cannot apply to Hendricks, either. Thus Justice Thomas could correctly write, in *Foucha*: "If convicted prisoners could claim such a right [i.e., to be free from physical restraint] . . . we would subject all prison sentences to strict scrutiny. This we have consistently refused to do" (Foucha v. Louisiana 1992, 118).

For Hendricks to prove he is part of a subgroup that requires strict scrutiny analysis, he has to prove that his existence in that group creates suspect classifications equal to those protected because of their "race, ancestry, and alienage" or because the "fundamental rights expressly or implicitly guaranteed by the Constitution" (In re Hendricks 1996, 273) apply to him. Sex offenders do not fall under the "race, ancestry, and alienage" category. Do postconviction civil commitment laws violate what the Court calls "implicit in the concept of ordered liberty"? (Palko v. Connecticut 1937, 325).

The Supreme Court's strict scrutiny analysis in cases involving fundamental rights is not always fatal to legislation (Fisher v. University of Texas 2013). Certainly, Kansas has made a convincing case that the law in question—should it be thought to involve a fundamental right—is "narrowly tailored," a necessary requirement of laws that touch upon fundamental rights. The Kansas law "does not apply to all persons accused of sexually violent offenses, but only those previously charged or convicted." Moreover, the standard for the state to commit someone is high. The law requires the state "to prove beyond a reasonable doubt that a person qualifies for confinement." Finally, the law requires treatment in a facility not within the Department of Corrections (In re Hendricks 1996, 283). The Constitution does not require that states adhere to or apply one standard for treatment (Youngberg v. Romeo 1982).

Kansas's law represents a fundamentally different kind of civil confinement, one following immediately after a prison term has expired and focusing on personality disorders rather than mental illnesses. Such a distinction is constitutionally permissible because the Court has stated that "procedural innovations by the states will be deemed presumptively valid unless they violate some principle" (Kansas v. Hendricks 1996a, 16) found to exist within the concept of ordered liberty. Thus for Hendricks to argue that sex offenders are protected under Justice Benjamin Cardozo's ordered liberty reasoning in *Palko v. Connecticut* (1937) he would have to demonstrate that sex offenders are "saddled with such disabilities, or subjected to such a history of purposeful unequal treatment, or relegated to such a position of political powerlessness as to command extraordinary protection from the majoritarian political process" (San Antonio Independent School District v. Rodriguez 1973, 28). This raises a formidable question: why do sex offender advocates look to the courts to achieve change even though the political process does not exclude sex offenders?

While it is true that elements within American society can discriminate and stigmatize sex offenders, in footnote four of *United States v. Carolene Products*

(1938), Justice Harlan Stone set out to protect those who, in the words of Simeon Schopf, are "burdened by prejudice and diminished political protection" (1995, 124). With sex offenders, it is their crimes that marginalize and stigmatize them from society and the political order. Moreover, the logic of footnote four raises the question of whether judges should be the constitutional officers making decisions about how the political process divides and distributes protections for interests that are not permanently in a minority status (Ely 1980, 151). Sex offenders are understood to be sex offenders by choice, or by choice in combination with some kind of personality disorder that inhibits clear reasoning about choices, but which does not destroy the capacity to choose. In any event, they cannot be put into the same classification that includes racial, ethnic, and religious minorities. The concept of ordered liberty means that elected leaders understand citizens as multifaceted in their interests. By resorting to the concept of ordered liberty, Cardozo in *Palko* created a burden on judges not to turn alterable, process-based interests into intractable existential questions about power. Doing so can only undermine the legitimacy of the democratic and deliberative political process.

Finally, it is worth asking what fundamental right Hendricks thinks Kansas has denied him. He cannot claim any right found within a general privacy right. Nor can he claim a "right to be free from incarceration" (Kansas v. Hendricks 1996a, 17), as no such right exists; nor can such a claimed right be taken seriously, given the long history of the confinement of sex offenders. Hendricks can only claim that it is unconstitutional for Kansas to confine him because he is not mentally ill.

Mental Illness

The Kansas SVPA allows for the commitment of those who suffer from mental abnormalities that "prevents them from exercising adequate control over their behavior" (Kansas v. Hendricks 1997, 362). Hendricks argued that "a 'mental abnormality' is *not* equivalent to a 'mental illness' because it is a term coined by the Kansas Legislature, rather than by the psychiatric community" (Kansas v. Hendricks 1997, 359; italics in original). To demonstrate mental illness could require a finding that the committee is unable to perform everyday skills, and thus more suitable for traditional civil commitment. On the other hand, while mental illness can be linked to behavioral irresponsibility, the term has a more flexible meaning, thanks in part to government-funded studies of the relationship between the mentally ill and violence. The MacArthur Treatment Competence Study, for example, has demonstrated that the mentally ill are a diverse group: "The majority of schizophrenic patients did not manifest deficits in decision-making ability, and the researchers attributed the lower overall score to a minority within that group" (Karasch 2003, 505; Appelbaum and Grisso 1995; Grisso et al. 1995; Grisso and Appelbaum 1995).

Kansas defined mental illness the following way:

> a mentally ill person is any person who: (1) is suffering from a severe mental disorder to the extent that such person is in need of treatment; (2) lacks capacity to make an informed decision concerning treatment; and (3) is likely to cause harm to self or others. (In re Hendricks 1996, 261)

The Kansas sex offender legislation attempted to maintain a balance between the committee's sanity and the committee's abnormal desires and behavior, which may be the result of compulsions outside of the person's will. This is a difficult line to maintain, but not impossible, as the idea that there is a blurring "between ordinary and pathological conditions" has been around since Sigmund Freud and dynamic psychiatry (Horwitz 2002, 1).

The Supreme Court has struggled to define mental illness and its limitations on behavior since the states began adopting, in the 1840s, the essential holdings of the *McNaughtan* rules that govern insanity cases (M'Elroy's Case 1843). Not only has the Court never clarified the meaning of mental illness, it has fomented confusion by using interchangeably the words "mental illness," "mental disorder," "insanity," and other related terms. In *Jones v. U.S.* (1983), for example, the Court used the terms "mental illness" and "insanity" to mean the same thing, despite the fact that insanity has no medical meaning at all (1983, 363; Ray 1838, chap. 4). The Court has stated that insanity is something like the total loss of memory, the inability to understand proceedings, the state of being "mad" (Ford v. Wainwright 1986, 406–7), and "total idiocy" (Penry v. Lynaugh 1989, 331). Yet each term is associated with a different set of behaviors. Since reinstating the death penalty in 1976, the Court has tried to clarify the relationship between mental illness and behavior.

In *Ford v. Wainwright* (1986), a plurality of the Court held unconstitutional the execution of an insane prisoner because insanity interferes with both cognition and volition. It is therefore unconstitutional to execute the insane because it offends humanity, fails to deter others, and serves no retributive function. Perhaps because there was no majority opinion in the case and the plurality did not define insanity, the Court did not create a strong link between insanity and volition, though it accepted as fact that Alvin Ford's cognitive functions were poor, as he "does not know that he is to be executed" (1986, 422). *Ford*, however, provides no guidance regarding insanity and volition. The Supreme Court has upheld laws that involve both cognitive and volitional elements and laws that exclude one element, including allowing states the right not to have an insanity defense. The Court also allows states to set different standards for the determination of insanity. "It is clear that no particular formulation has evolved into a baseline for due process, and that the insanity rule, like the conceptualization of criminal offenses, is substantially open to state choice" (Clark v. Arizona 2006, 737; Ford v. Wainwright 1986, 416–17). As the Court held in *Clark v. Arizona* (2006, 749), "History shows no deference to *M'Naghten* that could elevate its formula to the level of fundamental principle."

The Court's decision in *Penry v. Lynaugh* (1989, 340) holds that the Eighth Amendment does not preclude "the execution of any mentally retarded person of Penry's ability convicted of a capital offense simply by virtue of his or her mental retardation alone." In *Atkins v. Virginia* (2002), the Court, never invoking the term mental illness, held that the execution of a mentally retarded individual is unconstitutional. According to the Court, there are verifiable physiological and mental markers that establish one's mental retardation. The Court has accepted the medical profession's definition of mental retardation.

> [1] subaverage intellectual functioning, but also [2] significant limitations in adaptive skills such as communication, self-care, and self-direction that [3] became manifest before age 18. (2002, 309, 308 n. 3)

No such legal rule or set of legal rules exists for mental illness, severe mental illness, mental disorder, insanity, mental abnormality, or personality disorders (Brewer v. Quarterman 2007, 294; Smith v. Spisak 2010, 153; U.S. v. Comstock 2010, 130). In 2014, the Court struck down a Florida law requiring a baseline IQ as a standard for judging mental incapacity and responsibility (Hall v. Florida 2014).

The Court's clearest statement regarding mental illness occurred in *Indiana v. Edwards* (2008). In a case about mental incompetence and the right to an attorney, the Court held that:

> Mental illness itself is not a unitary concept. It varies in degree. It can vary over time. It interferes with an individual's functioning at different times in different ways. . . . In certain instances an individual may well be able to satisfy *Dusky*'s mental competence standard, for he will be able to work with counsel at trial, yet at the same time he may be unable to carry out the basic tasks needed to present his own defense without the help of counsel. (2008, 175–76)

The Court has consistently refused to accept that the designation "mental illness" always refers to "an 'immutable characteristic determined solely by the accident of birth'" (Schweiker v. Wilson 1981, 229 n. 11). Instead the Court has repeatedly referred to mental illness not as an unalterable condition (like dementia, for example) but rather as "treatable" (Kansas v. Hendricks 1997, 366) and "curable" (Pennhurst State School and Hospital v. Halderman 1981, 7 n. 2), presumably to differentiate it from severe or debilitating mental illness. This is why Justice Thomas wrote, in *Hendricks* (1997, 359), that the term "mental illness" lacks "talismanic significance." The Court's understanding of mental illness suggests that, even when a *DSM*-recognized psychotic disorder is present in a case, the Court will allow states to regard the individual sufferer as maintaining a degree of personal responsibility over his or her actions.

The idea persists in jurisprudence that mental illness has a specific meaning, usually centered around the idea of psychosis (Stewart v. U.S. 1961, 13) and "fixed delusions" (Greenwood v. U.S. 1956, 371). This is untrue. In *Addington v. Texas* (1979, 420, 425–26, 429) the Court conflated "emotional disorders" and "emotional difficulties" with "mental illness" and "mental disorder." In *Atkins* (2002, 340), Justice Scalia pointed out that only Kansas prohibits the execution of the severely mentally retarded, while other states with similar prohibitions do not use the modifier "severely" before "mental retardation." Justice Thomas noted that Hendricks's pedophilia (a subset of paraphilia) is a "serious mental disorder" (Kansas v. Hendricks 1997, 360), although the *DSM* does not refer to paraphilias as serious mental disorders. Indeed, there is no psychiatric consensus on whether paraphilias even meet the criteria for mental illness or serious mental disorders (Krueger 2010, 335). Justice Breyer's dissent in *Hendricks* did not discuss the legal implications of paraphilia at all.

Insofar as the Kansas law requires a finding of mental abnormality, and not mental illness, two points are worth highlighting. First, the Court has not found a due process violation among laws that require mental abnormality as a standard for postconviction civil commitment. In the civil commitment case *Jackson v. Indiana* (1972), Indiana defined psychiatric disorder "to be any mental illness or disease, including any mental deficiency, epilepsy, alcoholism, or drug addiction" (1972, 722), a position the Court did not dispute, but one that raises a host of questions regarding the boundaries of mental illness and personal responsibility. In *U.S. v. Salerno* (1987, 748–49) the Court upheld a requirement for the pretrial detention of "mentally unstable individuals who present a danger to the public," without requiring Congress to use the term "mental illness" as the criterion for pretrial confinement. Mental instability is not a term found in any edition of the *DSM*. In these cases, the Court has equated, for responsibility purposes, epilepsy, which is a neurological disorder, with alcoholism, which may or may not be a genetic disorder. Does the Court mean to say that all "psychiatric disorders" are mental illnesses, including alcoholism? (Fingarette 1970).

Because "psychiatrists disagree widely and frequently on what constitutes mental illness" (Ake v. Oklahoma 1985, 81), it is best to leave such definitions to the states. As Justice Thomas wrote in *Hendricks*: "we have traditionally left to legislators the task of defining terms of a medical nature that have legal significance" (Kansas v. Hendricks 1997, 359). While it is true that the Court could lay down a precise definition of mental illness for all the states to follow, it is not clear what this would accomplish. The meaning of mental illness and disorder continues to evolve, as the different versions of the *DSM* make clear.

The Problem of Deterrence-I

Leroy Hendricks "conceded that, when he becomes 'stressed out,' he cannot 'control the urge' to molest children. This admitted lack of volitional control," Justice Thomas wrote, justifies Kansas's purpose to civilly commit Hendricks. Thomas also noted that the law's addition of "mental illness" and "mental abnormality" "limit involuntary civil confinement to those who suffer from a volitional impairment rendering them dangerous beyond their control" (Kansas v. Hendricks 1997, 358). The act's purpose is to provide treatment and care and "to continue the segregation of sexually violent offenders from the public" (Kansas v. Hendricks 1997, 351, 365). The question *Hendricks* raises is whether the law's requirement, that committees demonstrate "adequate control over their behavior" as a result of a mental abnormality, turns a civil remedy of incapacitation and rehabilitation into a punishment that violates the Eighth Amendment.

Hendricks argued, and Justice Breyer in dissent agreed, that the act was punitive because it failed "to offer any legitimate 'treatment'"[3] to offenders (Kansas v. Hendricks 1997, 365, 388), leaving commitment based on dangerousness alone. Breyer's dissent is an invitation for courts to assess every treatment program to see how effective it is, and to assign every treatment program a constitutional value under the due process clause. The majority in *Hendricks* was reluctant to require treatment in these types of cases because of the lack of success of treatment in such cases. Justice Thomas noted, for example, that to require treatment in cases where the success rate is low could have adverse consequences for civil committees and society. Such a scheme "would obligate a State to release certain confined individuals who were both mentally ill and dangerous simply because they could not be successfully treated for their afflictions" (Kansas v. Hendricks 1997, 366). Thomas was also concerned that if courts favor one type of psychological assessment and behavioral modification plan over others, then by what constitutional calculus would a court decide which treatment conforms to due process and which does not? Judges would become de facto rulers of mental hospitals.

The Supreme Court has declared that some forms of detention are "regulatory, not penal" (U.S. v. Salerno 1987, 746). The consensus among state and federal courts is that postconviction civil commitment is "remedial" not "punitive" (Smith v. Doe I 2002, 94). The Supreme Court has upheld pretrial detention as a way to prevent flight (Bell v. Wolfish 1979) and the "detention of potentially dangerous resident aliens pending deportation proceedings" (U.S. v. Salerno 1987, 748). The Court has allowed states to "detain mentally unstable individuals who present a danger to the public," and has upheld a law allowing for the detention of "dangerous defendants who become incompetent to stand trial." The Court has also "approved of postarrest regulatory detention of juveniles when they present a continuing danger to the community." And the Court has allowed the police to detain an individual, suspected of a crime, "until a neutral magistrate determines whether probable cause exists" to continue the detention and proceed with charges (U.S. v. Salerno 1987, 748–49; Schall v. Martin 1984). In *Bennis v. Michigan* (1996) and *United States v. Ursery* (1996), the Rehnquist Court broke with the idea "that a deterrent purpose marks a statute as punitive" by asking whether Congress intended to "establish a civil remedial mechanism" and whether there is the "clearest proof" that the law is "so punitive" as to "negate" the legislature's intent (Klein 1999, 699–700). The same logic applies to state cases (Kansas v. Hendricks 1997, 361).

Retribution presumes that offenders commit crimes willfully and therefore deserve the punishment they receive. Deterrence seeks, through punishment, to deter others from committing crimes. According to Justice Thomas, Kansas's SVP Act is not "retributive because it does not affix culpability for prior criminal conduct" (Kansas v. Hendricks 1997, 362).

> Nor can it be said that the legislature intended the Act to function as a deterrent. Those persons committed under the Act are, by definition, suffering from a "mental abnormality" or a "personality disorder" that prevents them from exercising adequate control over their behavior. Such persons are therefore unlikely to be deterred by the threat of confinement. (Kansas v. Hendricks 1997, 362–63)

It must be conceded that such a law must have a deterrent effect. Why wouldn't a person still in possession of his faculties, although with a heightened desire to commit crimes that perhaps could be a sign of a mental disorder, be unlikely to be deterred by a commitment law that could last a lifetime? Deterrence acts on those who can calculate pain and pleasure or costs and benefits. As one dissenting judge in *In re Linehan* wrote, between Darol Linehan's irresponsible but sane conduct that got him sent to prison and his diagnosis of psychopathic personality, which put him in a mental hospital, did his ability to think about guilt disappear "into a void"? (In re Linehan 1996, 312). No medical professional ever said that Leroy Hendricks is incapable of understanding right and wrong.

"If there is nothing to treat . . . there is no mental illness" (In re Hendricks 1996, 258), the Kansas supreme court declared in Hendricks's case. The Washington State SVPA, the first in the nation, states that "sexually violent predators generally have antisocial personality features which are unamenable to existing mental illness treatment modalities . . . the prognosis for curing sexually violent offenders is poor" (Bodine 1990, 120 n. 99). One study in California showed small differences in the recidivism rates of sex offenders given treatment and those who did not undergo treatment. Another showed greater success in outpatient treatment over inpatient treatment. Overall, as Rudolph Alexander has written, "evidence of the effectiveness of sex offender treatment [is] lacking" (2004, 363–64). There is no doubt that "unlikely to be deterred" suggests difficulty in treatment—a paradoxical state that includes both a lack of free agency and a determined will to inflict harm (Bannister 1894). But the Kansas supreme court misses the point about criminal responsibility: with sex offenders, there is not nothing to treat; rather, what plagues sex offenders—the urge to molest, as Hendricks admitted—is untreatable, or untreatable under certain conditions, such as age or mental capacity, or the treatment's effects are not immediately apparent to researchers. Justice Thomas suggests that Hendricks has sufficient difficulty restraining his urges to incapacitate him, but not so much as to render him incapable of governing himself. Justice Thomas clearly meant that "unlikely to be deterred" is not identical to being incapable of being deterred, although the problem is why committees are unlikely to be deterred.

In *Kansas v. Crane*, Justice Scalia attempted to clarify Thomas's point about deterrence:

> What the opinion [*Hendricks*] was obviously saying was that the SVPA's required finding of a *causal connection* between the likelihood of repeat acts of sexual violence and the existence of a "mental abnormality" or "personality disorder" *necessarily* establishes "difficulty if not impossibility" in controlling behavior. (Kansas v. Crane 2002, 419; italics in original)

The inability of mental health professionals to draw a distinct line between behavior and disorder raises the question: why not sentence Hendricks to a longer prison term, abandoning postconviction commitment and the ethical and medical issues that buttress the argument? Governments commit sex offenders postconviction because they remain unable to control their behavior after serving time in prison; but treatment—whose goal is to teach "impulse control" (Bodine 1990, 120, n. 99)—is largely ineffective. Effectively, civil commitment incapacitates sex offenders after a prison sentence, functioning as a double sentence and a harsh deterrent. But the Supreme Court requires a finding of mental abnormality to ensure that states are not circumventing short criminal sentences or putting just anyone in mental facilities. The judgment to commit someone, moreover, belongs to the jury, not mental health professionals. What does this mean for the psychological language that is necessary for jurors to consider when considering civil commitment? It might be best to drop the language of "inability to control" and assess, instead, what Stephen Morse calls "the lack of capacity for rationality" (2002, 1039). For Morse, that sex offenders usually do not suffer from serious mental illnesses means that "[m]ost sexually violent agents are firmly in touch with reality, instrumentally rational, and fully aware of the applicable moral and legal rules. . . . although predators' sexual desires and behavior may be statistically abnormal and morally objectionable, predators are instrumentally rational when they satisfy those desires" (2002, 1068–69). Such a view, at the least, shines a light on the deliberations of jurors considering public safety and rationality as the tests for commitment.

Thomas's point about deterrence highlights the problem when one discipline, law, tries to merge with another, psychiatry, which has a completely different methodology and aim. The law assumes free agency, the "psy disciplines" do not. But consider Justice Scalia's interpretation of *Hendricks*'s ruling in *Crane*: "because their mental illness is an affliction and not a choice, [sex offenders] are unlikely to be deterred" (Kansas v. Crane 2002, 420). Scalia is arguing that Kansas cannot commit just any criminal following conviction. There must be a finding of "mental illness"—a mental abnormality—to distinguish criminals from committees. And yet, according to Scalia, Hendricks is not fully free to choose his crimes. Hendricks has an "affliction." If Hendricks is rational in a legal sense, then he understands the consequences of his behavior, and he (and others similarly situated) are likely to be deterred from committing such crimes. If the test is rationality and not the ability to control urges, then commitment functions, in part, as a deterrent, contra Thomas's argument. Deterrent effects, however, do not make a civil law criminal. To "hold that the mere presence of a deterrent purpose renders a statute criminal would severely undermine the government's ability to engage in effective regulation" (Illinois v. Leroy 2005, 541). In trying to separate the aims of punishment[4] from the aims of commitment, Thomas has confused the very justification for commitment that the Court upheld.

A careful reading of *Hendricks* supports the idea that a committee is not sufficiently mentally disturbed as to be incapable of governing himself. The perplexing question is: how determined by mental abnormality does a person have to be to have the state treat the committee as free enough to be suitable for postconviction civil commitment and not as a committee who cannot govern himself? Antisocial behavior is usually a "combination of willful and uncontrollable behavior" (Kansas v. Crane 2002, 417). We do know that treatment for antisocial personality disorders is complicated by the fact that "[i]ndividuals with [ASPD] . . . tend to be consistently and extremely irresponsible" (DSM 2013, 660), which means that they act on impulses and urges, without thinking about consequences. The *DSM*-V admits that paraphilias are difficult to treat, and that "pedophilia," which Hendricks suffers from, "appears to be a lifelong condition" (2013, 699). But the *DSM* makes no claim about deterrability or the intensity of the desires. This is a question for juries.

Most likely, Thomas failed to address the complexity of undeterrability because he did not seek to alter the traditional legal understanding of volitional control that undergirds legal reasoning about intentions. But he seems not to have noticed the problem of volition and deterrence that is at the heart of his opinion regarding deterrence. Justice Scalia once noted, importantly, that the Court has never established a "correlation between mental acuity and the ability to conform one's conduct to the law" (Atkins v. Virginia 2002, 350). And the Court has held that, while a person's reduced mental capacity defense can mitigate a criminal sentence, it does not, of itself, negate a criminal act (Penry v. Lynaugh 1989, 312). Nevertheless, the Court has drawn conflicting inferences about mental acuity and conduct or deterrability, and the Court in *Hendricks* was wise to stay away from such inferences. In *Zinermon v. Burch* (1990, 115), the Court noted that mental illness could interfere with a person's ability to make informed consent, which raises the question of whether the Court believes that mental illness, by itself, interferes with rational thought about means and ends. In *Atkins v. Virginia* (2002, 318), the Court held that the "cognitive and behavioral impairments" associated with mental retardation diminish the defendant's "ability to understand and process information." In making a connection between deterrence and mental disability, the Supreme Court held, in *Hall v. Florida* (2014, 1993), that "those with intellectual disability are, by reason of their condition, likely unable to make the calculated judgments that are the premise for the deterrence rationale." In one case, mental illness *could* interfere with rational thought; in another, mental retardation *does* interfere with rational thought; and in another, mental disability makes sound judgment unlikely.

Lacking a clear legal definition of insanity and mental illness, and a clear connection between mental disorder and behavior, the general legal principle regarding a demonstration of responsibility is sanity, that is, rational behavior, the anticipation of outcomes, and knowledge of right and wrong. New Jersey offers a good example of a law that takes into consideration behavior and disease. It requires proof of a "'substantial disturbance' of perception or orientation" to demonstrate an "impaired capacity to control behavior" (Cornwell 1996, 1302; Hughes 1959, 526). New York's civil commitment law, written after *Kansas v. Crane,* states:

> A sex offender qualifies for civil management in New York when he is found to have a "mental abnormality," which is some congenital or acquired condition that impacts the individual's emotional, cognitive, or volitional capacity so as to

> predispose the individual to committing sex offenses, and causes him to have "serious difficulty" controlling his sexual conduct. (Maizel 2015, 716)

These are two good ways to judge behavior and maintain a commitment to individual responsibility in sex offender cases. But because I am skeptical of the judiciary's ability to assess psychological categories, I would prefer that courts focus on the responsibility of the sex offender, as Stephen Morse has argued.

The Problem of Deterrence-II

Following the unsuccessful challenge by Leroy Hendricks, Kansas sought to commit Michael Crane, who "suffers from both exhibitionism and antisocial personality disorder" (Kansas v. Crane 2002, 411). In 1987, Crane "received probation for attempted forcible rape and two counts of sexual abuse in Missouri" (New York Times 2003). In 1993, Crane engaged in two separate acts of sexual assault on the same day. In 1994, a trial court in Kansas convicted Crane of "lewd and lascivious behavior" for his attack against a female store clerk, where he threatened her with rape. The state supreme court upheld that conviction, but reversed Crane's convictions for "kidnapping, attempted aggravated sodomy, and attempted rape" (Kansas v. Crane 1996, 234). But for the reversal, Crane would have served thirty-five years to life in prison.

Kansas then sought to refile charges of "attempted aggravated sodomy and attempted rape." Crane, however, agreed to a plea bargain, in which he pleaded guilty "to the single offense of aggravated sexual battery. He pled guilty in August 1997, and his conditional release date was January 6, 1998" (In re Crane 2000, 589). On December 11, 1997, Kansas filed a petition charging Crane as a sexual predator. The state, however, released Crane on parole on January 6, 1998 (In re Crane 2000, 592).

Two psychiatrists, on separate occasions, diagnosed Crane with ASPD and exhibitionism (In re Crane 2000, 578). Exhibitionism alone would not qualify Crane for Kansas's sexual violent predator commitment statute. But the psychiatrists noted that Crane is a sexually violent predator, and, as a result of the combination of his crimes, ASPD, and exhibitionism, the state believed he qualified for civil commitment. Dr. Leonardo Mabugat, a psychiatrist, stated that "Crane's behavior was a combination of willful and uncontrollable behavior" (In re Crane 2000, 585).

To commit Crane under the SVPA,

> [T]he jury was instructed that in order to establish that Crane is a sexually violent predator, the State had to prove (1) that Crane had been convicted of aggravated sexual battery and (2) that he "suffers from a mental abnormality or personality disorder which makes the respondent likely to engage in future predatory acts of sexual violence, if not confined in a secure facility." "Likely" was defined as "more probable to occur than not to occur." "Mental abnormality" was defined for the jury . . . as a "condition affecting the emotional or volitional capacity which predisposes a person to commit sexually violent offenses in a degree constituting such person a menace to the health and safety of others." "Personality disorder" was defined for the jury as a "condition recognized by the . . . [*DSM* IV], and includes antisocial personality disorder." (In re Crane 2000, 581)

The district court ordered Crane committed and the Kansas supreme court reversed, in part because "Crane suffers from a 'personality disorder,' which by definition does not include a volitional impairment" (In re Crane 2000, 586; Kansas v. Crane 2002, 417; Kansas v. Hendricks 1997, 358). Crane raised one important constitutional question: "whether it is constitutionally permissible to commit [him] as a sexual predator absent a showing that he was unable to control his dangerous behavior" (In re Crane 2000, 580). Neither in *Crane* nor in *Hendricks* did the Supreme Court define the inability to control; nor has anyone been able to quantify, by way of a mental status test, what that means. As Scott Henderson has written, "quantification of capacity to resist carrying out an act is not at present possible by any psychometrically established method" (2005, 273). Moreover, if Justice Breyer, writing for the Court, wants judges to rely on diagnoses of personality disorders that breakdown into emotional and behavioral disorders, he should be made aware that such diagnoses "have the least clinician-to-clinician reliability among the psychiatric diagnostic categories" (Sparr 2009, 169).

At the Supreme Court, Kansas argued that the state supreme court's holding, that a committee be "*completely* unable to control his behavior," was the wrong standard, though this was not the state supreme court's holding. The Supreme Court's 7–2 decision disagreed with Kansas's contention regarding requiring a finding of complete inability to control one's behavior. But it held that *Crane* requires a separate finding of an inability to control one's behavior

(Kansas v. Crane 2002, 412; Pfaffenroth 2003, 2249–50; Plucker 2003). Justices Thomas and Scalia dissented. The Supreme Court's ruling vacated Crane's sentence but did not overrule *Hendricks*. It did, however, add a new standard for commitment. The "State must show not merely a likelihood that the defendant would engage in repeat acts of sexual violence, but also an inability to control violent behavior" (Kansas v. Crane 2002, 417). The *Crane* Court was uncomfortable allowing a standard for commitment without setting some kind of volitional standard for commitment that involved the subject's emotional state. But it refused to create the distinctions it felt necessary to impose upon the states:

> The Court in *Hendricks* had no occasion to consider whether confinement based solely on "emotional" abnormality would be constitutional, and we likewise have no occasion to do so in the present case. (Kansas v. Crane 2002, 415)

Breyer's addition to *Hendricks*—requiring a separate finding of an inability to control one's impulses—raises two questions: One, what will the volitional standard be? Will it be a medical or a juridical standard? And two, why is an additional standard necessary, given that the Court had, only five years prior, ruled on the constitutionality of the SVPA without establishing such a standard?

Justice Breyer intended his decision in *Crane* to heighten the mental abnormality standard the Court set forth in *Hendricks*. The key sentence is: "It is enough to say that there must be proof of serious difficulty in controlling behavior" (Kansas v. Crane 2002, 413). Breyer was concerned that the standard of mental abnormality or personality disorder plus dangerousness, without more, was insufficient to prevent the commitment of the "typical recidivist" (Kansas v. Crane 2002, 413). Scalia addressed this point in dissent; it is called the "causal link" model (Maizel 2015, 729, n. 199). For Scalia, to establish the "difficulty if not impossibility" standard for controlling behavior, courts must find a "*causal connection* between the likelihood of repeat acts of sexual violence and the existence of a 'mental abnormality'" (Kansas v. Crane 2002, 419; italics in original).

Scalia has the law on his side. The Kansas law in question "does not specify" that a separate finding of volitional impairment "is [a] required element to be proven" (In re Crane 2000, 581). Rather, the Kansas law (too loosely, in the *Crane* majority's view, but not so in *Hendricks*) defined mental abnormality "as a condition that affects an individual's emotional *or* volitional capacity" (Kansas v. Crane 2002, 411; italics in original). Breyer argued that the Court in *Hendricks* did not "draw a clear distinction between the purely 'emotional' sexually related mental abnormality and the 'volitional.'" Indeed, the Court failed to delineate the distinction among "the volitional, emotional, and cognitive impairments" (Kansas v. Crane 2002, 415).

What Breyer does not say is that this is so not because of a weakness in constitutional law but because "there has been little scientific evidence to show how volition operates, leaving the exploration of volition to be mostly theoretical in nature" (Mercado, Schopp, and Bornstein 2005, 304). There is no such thing as an emotional disorder that is separate from a behavioral or personality disorder. *Crane*, then, does this much: it requires the state to prove that the offender suffers from "(1) a mental abnormality that causes sex offending behavior, (2) a difficulty controlling the behavior that the mental abnormality drives," and (3) that there is "a risk that the individual will similarly offend in the future" (Maizel 2015, 729). By bringing up questions of emotions and volition, Breyer requires courts to rely on psychiatry and the neurological sciences (Maizel 2015, 716), which undermines deliberative outcomes at the state level. In *Crane*, the Court intended the "control test" to be independent of the "mental abnormality and dangerousness elements established in *Hendricks*" (Maizel 2015, 729).

Between 1930 and 1960, twenty-six states and the District of Columbia had some kind of sexual psychopath law that allowed for the civil commitment of sexual predators (Blacher 1995). None of those states had a separate criterion regarding volition or control. By the 1980s, at least half the states with civil commitment laws had repealed them; by 1990, they had replaced them with the type of law Kansas used in *Hendricks*, that is, without a separate volitional component. A separate criterion is neither an integral part of the due process clause of the Fourteenth Amendment, nor can it claim to be part of the concept of ordered liberty (Kansas v. Hendricks 1997, 357). Given the civil nature of the SVP Act, Justice Breyer's volitional addition is problematic. The civil nature of the act means that Kansas regards committees as mentally disordered, not as criminally culpable. Mental disorder in this case means that committees have trouble controlling their behavior, according to the variable "nature of the psychiatric diagnosis, and the severity of the mental abnormality itself" (Kansas v. Crane 2002, 413).

Unfortunately, Justice Breyer's opinion does not go into detail regarding how a jury can determine "that the subject suffers from an inability to control [his or her] behavior," and this is the key failure of the opinion. Nor did he explain the distinction between volitional and emotional impairments, or what a "purely" emotional mental abnormality is. The normal distinction in law regarding responsibility—the conflict between the *McNaughtan* rules and irresistible impulse—is usually between the cognitive and the volitional, knowing and doing. Breyer introduces the emotional sense without telling us if it is separate from cognition or volition.

In the literature on the mind in the nineteenth century, the emotional faculty was something like a moral sense, attached to right and wrong. Its true objects were "duties, obligations, or moral responsibilities" (Pierce 1895, 127). The emotions were thought to be unschooled. Left to themselves, they could lead to private vices. Throughout the nineteenth century, the emotions were not understood to be part of an autonomous faculty, largely because they were associated with passions, and passions could be crude or unrefined. The true meaning of a sensual experience could not be fully understood unless the intellect interpreted it. Thus the Scottish moral philosopher Alexander Bain (1865, 35) said that the emotions are "secondary, derived, or compound feelings." The emotions are dependent upon the intellectual faculty for will power and understanding. Each faculty, during the nineteenth century, was thought to have its own aims or goals—"The intellect sees, the emotions feel" was a common expression (LaMartine 1884, 5)—but the provinces were blurred. The process of understanding the feelings required intellectual assessment; the two faculties were thought to be symbiotic.

By the twentieth century, scientists had abandoned the idea that the emotions were connected to the moral sense and replaced it with pleasure and pain. Although the definition of the emotions remained elusive to twentieth-century thinkers, overall there was general agreement among philosophers and scientists that some emotions are "mechanical results of the way in which our nervous centres are framed" (James 1918, 484), while other emotions are the products of accident. According to William James (1918, 473), the emotions constitute a third performative function of the faculties, after cognition and volition. James did not think that a precise classification of the emotions was possible, given their subjective and sensual nature.

Modern scholarship tends to regard emotions in ways not dissimilar to the late nineteenth century, that is, the emotions are dependent upon cognition for understanding. Emotions, Eric Posner (2001, 1980) has written, have "an irreducibly mental component" to them. Breyer is correct to note that there is no "bright line" rule that the Court can create regarding emotions, because "the Constitution's safeguards of human liberty in the area of mental illness and the law are not always best enforced through precise bright-line rules" (Kansas v. Crane 2002, 413). But if there is no bright-line rule, why create an additional standard, particularly one that may not be reachable by juries? The requirement of medical certainty regarding emotions and behavior can and probably will impede judicial or legislative action. This is important, given Breyer's observation that psychiatry "is an ever-advancing science, whose distinctions do not seek precisely to mirror those of the law" (Kansas v. Crane 2002, 413).

Crane establishes that the standard in *Hendricks* is insufficient from the standpoint of science and, perhaps, due process, and that an additional element—volition tied to emotional status—is necessary. But the Court (wisely in principle, but to its detriment in terms of jurisprudence) refrains from delineating what constitutes volition. As Cynthia Calkins Mercado and her colleagues have noted, "On the whole, there has been little scientific evidence to show how volition operates, leaving the exploration of volition to be mostly theoretical in nature" (Mercado, Schopp, and Bornstein 2005, 304). Thus not only did the *Crane* Court add a criterion to the *Hendricks* standard that appears to be procedurally unnecessary, it "left open the constitutional meaning of lack of control" (Morse 2002, 1033). The states then might feel compelled to rely on scientific evidence for understanding control, or they could ignore them entirely (Pierson 2012; Thomas v. Missouri 2002). The *Hendricks* decision failed to clarify a crucial problem in sex offender legislation regarding deterrence and sanity, determination and free agency. The *Crane* decision confounded matters by creating and then not specifying the contours of volition and the meaning of the emotions in their relationship to cognition and volition.

The Supreme Court handed down its ruling in January 2002. Kansas then released Crane "after doctors concluded that his mental condition had changed and that he was no longer a threat" (New York Times 2003). In June 2003, Crane was arrested for raping a woman. The authorities were able to match the semen on the victim to Crane, whose DNA was on file in the national database for convicted felons.

Conclusion

Leroy Hendricks, a pedophile, admitted that he was unable to control his desires. Michael Crane, a sexual offender of adults, did not admit that he was unable to control his desires, yet Kansas committed Crane under the same law used in *Hendricks*. In both cases, mental health professionals testified in court that both men suffered from ASPD and other assorted mental and personality disorders and that both were unlikely to control their desires, though both were capable, at times, of doing so. In *Crane*, for no compelling constitutional reasons, which had the effect of subverting the deliberative intentions of legislators regarding public safety and individual treatment, the Court created a standard above what *Hendricks* had created. *Crane* does not hold that a state has to prove that a criminal defendant cannot totally control his or her sexual or violent impulses to be committed. It requires that states demonstrate "proof of serious difficulty in controlling behavior" (Kansas v. Crane 2002, 413).

Given the scientific and legal problems associated with volition, the emotions, and cognition, Breyer's opinion in *Crane* comes across as wholly unwarranted. *Crane* has forced courts (1) to rely more extensively on medical and psychological factors in the assessment of dangerousness, and (2) to delve into the gray zone that separates voluntary from involuntary actions. These two additional prongs do not facilitate the governance of sex offenders. In the attempt to make determinations of commitment more scientific, the Supreme Court has increased the burdens on courts to determine, through the due process clause, the boundaries of science and public safety. As I have argued throughout, the deliberative sense of the community is directed at a more important horizon, the ability of legislators to choose the "*appropriateness* of competing policies" that comports with "our conception of ourselves as a people" (Kendall 1971, 336; italics in original).

The complexity and conflicts over legal needs and psychological wants demonstrate the limits of interdisciplinary jurisprudence. Stephen Morse writes that substituting the control standard with a rationality defects test

> will permit mental health professionals readily to explain and legal decision-makers easily to understand the precise behavioral grounds for inferring that an agent suffers from rationality defects. . . . Experts evaluating the rationality standard will be able to avoid the type of unscientific, conclusory reasoning that marks conclusions about control defects, and legal evaluation will be uncontaminated by confusing, metaphorical evidence . . . the irrationality standard will provide a morally, politically, and legally justifiable limiting condition for the massive deprivation of liberty that results. (2002, 1075)

A rationality standard has the virtue of focusing on the deliberative intentions of legislators and jurors and granting the committee the respect of his own agency. "It is strange to define a mental abnormality," Morse writes, "by reference to the penal code" (2002, 1050). Doing so corrupts and diminishes both jurisprudence and medicine. The law of civil commitment will function with more clarity if jurors assess the potential committee's responsibility level—his "lack of capacity for rationality" (Morse 2002, 1077)—rather than debate whether or not a mental abnormality contributed to, but did not overwhelm, the sex offender's ability to choose the wrong way to behave.

NOTES

1. Kansas defines a child as someone "who is 14 or more years of age but less than 16 years of age." Indecent liberties with a child include the following acts: "fondling," "touching," or "soliciting" with the "intent to arouse or to satisfy the sexual desires of either the child or the offender, or both" (Kansas v. Hendricks 1996b, appendix).

2. A very short list of cases that rejected irresistible impulse: *State v. Miller* (1892); *Thomas v. State* (1894); *Wilcox v. State* (1894).

3. Breyer thought that the lack of treatment was a substantive violation of due process. The state supreme court, however, noted discrepancies over Hendricks's treatment. Justice Thomas admitted that Hendricks's treatment was "meager" but noted that Hendricks was Kansas's first committee (In re Hendricks 1996, 258; Kansas v. Hendricks 1997, 367–68, n. 5, and 374).

4. The four pillars of punishment are: deterrence, retribution, rehabilitation, and incarceration or incapacitation (Doe v. Pataki 1996, 605).

REFERENCES

Ahluwalia, Aman. 2006. "Civil Commitment of Sexually Violent Predators: The Search for a Limiting Principle." *Cardozo Public Law, Policy and Ethics Journal* 4 (3): 489–538.

Alexander, Rudolph. 2004. "The United States Supreme Court and the Civil Commitment of Sex Offenders." *Prison Journal* 84 (3): 361–78.

Appelbaum, Paul, and Thomas Grisso. 1995. "The MacArthur Treatment Competence Study I: Mental Illness and Competence to Consent to Treatment." *Law & Human Behavior* 19 (2): 105–26.

Bain, Alexander. 1865. *The Emotions and the Will.* 2nd ed. London: Longsman, Green, and Company.

Bannister, H. M. 1894. "The Prendergast Case." *American Law Register and Review* 42: 545–64.

Blacher, Raquel. 1995. "Historical Perspective of the 'Sex Psychopath' Statute: From the Revolutionary Era to the Present." *Mercer Law Review* 46 (2): 889–920.

Bodine, Brian. 1990. "Washington's New Violent Sexual Predator Commitment System: An Unconstitutional Law and Unwise Policy Choice." *University of Puget Sound Law Review* 14 (1): 105–41.

Brakel, Samuel Jan, and James Cavanaugh. 2000. "Of Psychopaths and Pendulums: Legal and Psychiatric Treatment of Sex Offenders in the United States." *New Mexico Law Review* 30 (1): 69–94.

Buchanan, Alec, and Howard Zonana. 2009. "Mental Disorder as the Cause of Crime." *International Journal of Law and Psychiatry* 32 (3): 142–46.

Cornwell, John Kip. 1996. "Protection and Treatment: The Permissible Civil Detention of Sexual Predators." *Washington & Lee Law Review* 53 (4): 1293–1337.

Diagnostic and Statistical Manual. 2000. 4th ed. Washington, DC: American Psychiatric Association.

Diagnostic and Statistical Manual. 2013. 5th ed. Washington, DC: American Psychiatric Association.

Ely, John Hart. 1980. *Democracy and Distrust: A Theory of Judicial Review.* Cambridge, MA: Harvard University Press.

Fingarette, Herbert. 1970. "The Perils of Powell: In Search of a Factual Foundation for the Disease Concept of Alcoholism." *Harvard Law Review* 83 (4): 793–812.

Graeve, Christine. 2007. "An Exploratory Look at Career Criminality, Psychopathy, and Offending Persistence: Convergence of Criminological and Psychological Constructs?" Master's Thesis. Iowa State University.

Grisso, Thomas, and Paul Appelbaum. 1995. "The MacArthur Treatment Competence Study III: Abilities of Patients to Consent to Psychiatric and Medical Treatments." *Law & Human Behavior* 19 (2): 149–74.

Grisso, Thomas, Paul Appelbaum, Edward Mulvey, and Kenneth Fletcher. 1995. "The MacArthur Treatment Competence Study II: Measures of Abilities Related to Competence to Consent to Treatment." *Law & Human Behavior* 19 (2): 127–48.

Henderson, Scott. 2005. "The Neglect of Volition." *British Journal of Psychiatry* 16 (4): 273–74.

Horwitz, Allan. 2002. *Creating Mental Illness.* Chicago: University of Chicago Press.

Hughes, Graham. 1959. "The English Homicide Act of 1957: The Capital Punishment Issue, and Various Reforms in the Law of Murder and Manslaughter." *Journal of Criminal Law and Criminology* 49 (6): 521–32.

James, William. 1918. *The Principles of Psychology*. Vol. 2. New York: Dover.

Karasch, Meredith. 2003. "Where Involuntary Commitment, Civil Liberties, and the Right to Mental Health Collide: An Overview of California's Mental Illness System." *Hastings Law Journal* 54 (2): 493–523.

Kendall, Willmoore. 1971. "American Conservatism and the 'Prayer' Decisions." In *Willmoore Kendall Contra Mundum*, edited by Nellie Kendall, 326–46. New Rochelle, NY: Arlington House.

Kendell, R. E. 2002. "The Distinction between Personality Disorder and Mental Illness." *British Journal of Psychiatry* 180 (2): 110–15.

Klein, Susan. 1999. "Redrawing the Criminal-Civil Boundary." *Buffalo Criminal Law Review* 2 (2): 679–721.

Krueger, Richard. 2010. "The *DSM* Diagnostic Criteria for Sexual Sadism." *Archives of Sexual Behavior* 39 (2): 325–45.

LaMartine, Pierre. 1884. "The Mental Faculties and the Order and Means of Their Development." *Educational Weekly* 2 (10): 3–5.

Maizel, Michael. 2015. "Confining Control: Narrowing the 'Control' Standard under New York's Mental Hygiene Law." *Cardozo Law Review* 37 (2): 713–50.

Mercado, Cynthia Calkins, Robert Schopp, and Brian Bornstein. 2005. "Evaluating Sex Offenders under Sexually Violent Predator Laws: How Might Mental Health Professionals Conceptualize the Notion of Volitional Impairment?" *Aggression and Violent Behavior* 10 (3): 289–309.

Morse, Stephen. 2002. "Uncontrollable Urges and Irrational People." *Virginia Law Review* 88 (5): 1025–78.

New York Times. 2003. "Sex Offender in Predator Case Held in Rape after His Release." June 22.

Pfaffenroth, Peter. 2003. "The Need for Coherence: States' Civil Commitment of Sex Offenders in the Wake of *Kansas v. Crane*." *Stanford Law Review* 55 (6): 2229–66.

Pierce, Ray Vaughn. 1895. *The People's Common Sense Medical Advisor in Plain English; or Medicine Simplified*. 33rd ed. Buffalo: World's Dispensary Printing.

Pierson, Janine. 2012. "Construing *Crane*: Examining How State Courts Have Applied its Lack-of-Control Standard." *University of Pennsylvania Law Review* 160 (5): 1527–59.

Plucker, Nathaniel. 2003. "Debating the End of the World and other Pointless Endeavors: *Thomas v. State* and the Civil Commitment of Sex Offenders in Missouri after *Kansas v. Crane*." *St. Louis University Law Journal* 47 (4): 1151–84.

Porter, Gregory. 1997. "Uncivil Punishment: The Supreme Court's Ongoing Struggle with Constitutional Limits on Punitive Civil Sanctions." *Southern California Law Review* 70 (2): 517–90.

Posner, Eric. 2001. "Law and the Emotions." *Georgetown Law Journal* 89 (6): 1977–2012.

Ray, Isaac. 1838. *A Treatise on the Medical Jurisprudence of Insanity.* Boston: Charles Little and James Brown.

Schopf, Simeon. 1995. "'Megan's Law': Community Notification and the Constitution." *Columbia Journal of Law and Social Problems* 29 (1): 117–46.

Sparr, Landy. 2009. "Personality Disorders and Criminal Law: An International Perspective." *Journal of the American Academy of Psychiatry and the Law* 37 (2): 168–81.

Teir, Robert, and Keven Coy. 1997. "Approaches to Sexual Predators: Community Notification and Civil Commitment." *New England Journal on Criminal and Civil Confinement* 23 (2): 405–26.

Wechsler, Herbert. 1955. "The Criteria of Criminal Responsibility." *University of Chicago Law Review* 22 (2): 367–76.

Wharton, Francis. 1874. *A Treatise on the Criminal Law of the United States.* Vol. 1, 7th and rev. ed. Philadelphia: Kay and Brother.

World Health Organization. n.d. *The ICD-10 Classification of Mental and Behavourial Disorders.* https://www.who.int/classifications/icd/en/bluebook.pdf

Zander, Thomas. 2005. "Civil Commitment without Psychosis: The Law's Reliance on the Weakest Links in Psychodiagnosis." *Journal of Sexual Offender Civil Commitment: Science and the Law* 1: 17–82.

CASES

Addington v. Texas, 441 U.S. 418 (1979).
Ake v. Oklahoma, 470 U.S. 68 (1985).
Allen v. Illinois, 478 U.S. 364 (1986).
Atkins v. Virginia, 536 U.S. 304 (2002).
Bell v. Wolfish, 441 U.S. 520 (1979).
Brewer v. Quarterman, 550 U.S. 286 (2007).
Brown v. Dodd, 108 S.Ct. 33 (1987).
Calder v. Bull, 3 U.S. 386 (1798).
California v. Hubert, 119 Cal. 216 (1897).
Clark v. Arizona 548 U.S. 735 (2006).
Collins v. Youngblood, 497 U.S. 37 (1990).
Colorado v. Connelly, 479 U.S. 157 (1986).
Connecticut v. Johnson, 40 Conn. 136 (1873).
Davis v. U.S., 160 U.S. 469 (1895).

DeJarnette v. Virginia, 75 Va. 867 (1881).
Delling v. Idaho, 133 S.Ct. 504 (2012).
Doe v. Pataki, 940 F.Supp. 603 (1996).
Drope v. Missouri, 420 U.S. 162 (1975).
Fisher v. University of Texas, 570 U.S. 297 (2013).
Ford v. Wainwright, 477 U.S. 399 (1986).
Foucha v. Louisiana, 504 U.S. 71 (1992).
Greenwood v. U.S., 350 U.S. 366 (1956).
Hall v. Florida, 134 S.Ct. 1986 (2014).
Illinois v. Leroy, 357 Ill.App.3d 530 (2005).
Indiana v. Edwards, 554 U.S. 164 (2008).
In re Crane, 269 Kan. 578 (2000).
In re El-Rashad, Alleged Mentally Ill, 411 N.W.2d 567 (1987).
In re Gault, 387 U.S. 1 (1967).
In re Hendricks, 259 Kan. 246 (1996).
In re Linehan, 544 N.W.2d 308 (1996).
In the Matter of the Commitment of W.Z., 339 N.J.Super. 549 (2001).
Jackson v. Indiana, 406 U.S. 715 (1972).
Jones v. U.S., 463 U.S. 354 (1983).
Kansas v. Crane, 260 Kan. 208 (1996).
Kansas v. Crane, 534 U.S. 407 (2002).
Kansas v. Hendricks, WL 528985 (1996a).
Kansas v. Hendricks, WL 450661 (1996b).
Kansas v. Hendricks, 521 U.S. 346 (1997).
Madden v. Collins 18 F.3d. 304 (1994).
McNeil v. Director, Patuxent Institution, 407 U.S. 245 (1972).
M'Elroy's Case, WL 5177 (1843).
New York v. Donald DD, 24 N.Y.3d 174 (2014).
O'Connor v Donaldson, 422 U.S. 563 (1975).
Olmstead v. L.C. ex rel. Zimring, 527 U.S. 581 (1999).
Palko v. Connecticut, 302 U.S. 319 (1937).
Pennhurst State School and Hospital v. Halderman, 451 U.S. 1 (1981).
Pennsylvania v. Mosler, 6 Pa. L.J. 90 (1846).
Penry v. Lynaugh, 492 U.S. 302 (1989).
Reno v. Flores, 507 U.S. 292 (1993).
Salerno v. U.S., 481 U.S. 739 (1987).
San Antonio Independent School District v. Rodriguez, 411 U.S. 1 (1973).
Schall v. Martin, 467 U.S. 253 (1984).
Schweiker v. Wilson, 450 U.S. 221 (1981).

Smith v. Doe I, 538 U.S. 84 (2002).
Smith v. Spisak, 558 U.S. 139 (2010).
Specht v. Patterson, 386 U.S. 605 (1967).
State v. Miller, 111 Mo. 542 (1892).
Stewart v. U.S., 366 U.S. 1 (1961).
Thomas v. Missouri, 74 S.W.3d 789 (2002).
Thomas v. State, 71 Miss. 345 (1894).
U.S. v. Comstock, 560 U.S. 126 (2010).
U.S. v. Halper, 490 U.S. 435 (1989).
U.S. v. Ward, 448 U.S. 242 (1980).
Vincent v. Louisiana, 105 S.Ct. 928 (1985).
Washington v. Glucksberg, 521 U.S. 702 (1997).
West Virginia v. Harrison, 15 S.E. 982 (1892).
Wilcox v. State, 94 Tenn. 106 (1894).
Youngberg v. Romeo, 457 U.S. 307 (1982).
Zinermon v. Burch, 494 U.S. 113 (1990).

CHAPTER 5

The Nationalization of Civil Commitment

With the passage of the Adam Walsh Child Protection and Safety Act of 2006 (AWA),[1] Congress granted the federal government the power to commit any federal prisoner who has completed his prison term to a psychiatric facility, provided a federal court determines that the prisoner "suffers from a serious mental illness, abnormality, or disorder as a result of which he would have serious difficulty in refraining from sexually violent conduct or child molestation if released" (Congress 2006, sec. 302, 33–34; Hudson v. Florida 2002). The law tracked the language used (at the time) in twenty states. In effect, the AWA does at the federal level what the Kansas law does at the state level.

There are, however, differences between the state and federal statutes, and they raise vexing questions relating to law and politics. It is well established that states have the power of postconviction civil commitment. Does Congress have the same power over federal prisoners? If so, then Congress has police or *parens patriae* powers, derived either from Article I, section 8 of the Constitution or from an inherent notion of power or sovereignty. The idea that Congress has such power is controversial. It is said that ours is a government of limited or enumerated powers and the Constitution limits congressional powers explicitly under Article I, section 8. Supporters of this view begin with the Articles of Confederation, where the states remained sovereign in a "treaty of amity of commerce and of alliance" (Madison 1981, 60), and argue that the states never gave up their sovereignty when they ratified the Constitution. Today, some justices on the Supreme Court speak of "dual sovereignty" (Printz v. U.S. 1997, 918), of "express" congressional limits under Article I, section 8 (National Federation of Independent Business v. Sebelius 2012, 2577), and claim that the Tenth Amendment provides additional limits on congressional power. Only the states have police powers (U.S. v. Comstock 2010, 148, 153; U.S. v. Comstock 2009a, 278; U.S. v. Lopez, 1995, 1633; Tiedman 1886, 612–14 [sec. 201]).

The other view holds that it is the people who are sovereign, not the states. Article VI of the Constitution establishes congressional law as supreme and asserts that state judges are bound to uphold federal law, provisions lacking in the Articles of Confederation. Moreover, the Tenth Amendment speaks of "delegated" not enumerated powers and omits "expressly delegated" (Goldwin 1997, 130; Mikhail 2014, 1064; The Federalist 2001, 288 [no. 44]), a phrase the Constitution's opponents wanted to keep because it appeared in the Articles of Confederation. As a matter of constitutional history, the Tenth Amendment has not been thought to contain "terms that the courts can use to settle any legal case or controversy" (Berns 1963, 132). Chief Justice John Marshall, in his commerce clause rulings, "rejected the Tenth Amendment as an active principle of limitation" (Frankfurter 1964, 40; Gibbons v. Ogden 1824, 197). Justice Joseph Story thought that it was "plain" that the founders did not intend to "to give [the Tenth Amendment] effect, as an abridgment of any of the powers granted under the constitution" (1858, 2: 3: 44, 682–83 [sec 1908]).

The line between state and federal jurisdictions is not clearly marked, a point Publius recognized (The Federalist 2001, no. 17), and the Supreme Court agrees with. In *Garcia v. San Antonio Metropolitan Transit Authority* (1985), the Court held that it is the preserve of the political process, in combination with the makeup of our legislative configuration, to police the boundaries of federal-state relations. The political process and a bicameral legislature create a "built-in restraint" on federal overreach (1985, 556). Chief Justice John Marshall offers a different view of national supremacy. He wrote that the federal government has the power to punish federal crimes, and "the power of punishment appertains to sovereignty, and may be exercised, whenever the sovereign has a right to act, as incidental to his constitutional powers" (McCulloch v. Maryland 1819, 418; The License Cases 1849, 583). This way of thinking about federal power is no longer common. But the federal government has federalized "traditional" state crimes, such as "carjacking" (Congress 1992; Coyle 1996) under the commerce clause, without raising constitutional problems. Today, there are "more than 3,000 federal crimes on the books" (Brickey 1995, 1135, n. 1). These laws require federal police agents to enforce federal police powers (U.S. v. Comstock 2010, 156–57). As Jay Bybee (1997, 41) has noted, "the [Crimes] Act of 1790 itself suggest[s] that Congress did not take seriously the position, held by some Framers [i.e., the opponents of the Constitution, the Anti-Federalists], that Congress had limited power to define crime." Without settling this important matter, the Supreme Court, in *U.S. v. Comstock* (2010), upheld the constitutionality of the AWA.

I do not address in this chapter the collateral consequences of registration and notification laws associated with the AWA, a point that should not be interpreted to mean that they are unimportant. Rather, my focus is on constitutional interpretation and institutional powers as a way to draw attention to the deliberative and institutional aspects of lawmaking. My aim is threefold. First, I will examine the AWA's aim and scope, with a focus on institutional issues AWA raises. Second, I look at how civic groups advocated for sex offender legislation, revealing a concerted effort by parents, victim groups, and other interested parties to shape legislation to make communities safe. An examination of constitutional law cannot be indifferent to the role played by public opinion and interested citizens. My third aim is to emphasize the formal, institutional, deliberative, and procedural aspects of constitutionalism at work in the AWA, *Comstock*, and sex offender legislation in general. My idea is that the more we take the Constitution, the institutions it created, and the processes that support it seriously, the less need we will have to focus on rhetoric, narrative, the social and natural sciences, and abstract questions of right and morality in deciding complex cases. I am not making a case for the "autonomy" of the law or legislatures as much as I am trying to emphasize that "we cannot avoid constitutional politics." As George Edwards has noted, focusing on constitutional politics "might help make us more appreciative of constitutional forms" (2008, 6–7). This has been my explicit aim since the introduction to this book. Informal and noninstitutional emphases about rights and justice not only deflect from the important procedural aspects of law and politics, they exacerbate political divisions by hardening questions of right and wrong, creating ontological categories of majorities and minorities that are immune to negotiated settlements. A more process-based and institutional focus on constitutionalism (not just law) should restrain these democratic (and undemocratic) impulses.

The Aims and Scope of AWA

The AWA is also known as the Sex Offender Registration and Notification Act (SORNA). It is a multipurpose act, and its main goal is "to create a comprehensive nationwide registry system to regulate the movement and activities of sex offenders across jurisdictions" (Miner 2011, 88). Congress named the law after Adam Walsh, a six-year-old boy who was abducted, sexually abused, and killed in Florida in 1981. Adam's father, John Walsh—not yet known as a TV personality advocating for missing persons—worked tirelessly with other parents who had lost children to sex offenders and with organizations interested in the protection of children to get a law through Congress.[2]

SORNA ties registration to levels of dangerousness, called tiers. The purpose of tiers is to allow the public to understand degrees of dangerousness. Without a tiered system, a state's registration law could be open to the misperception that all sex offenders are equally dangerous. This is called "stigma-plus," and it could violate a person's "liberty interest" in being free from stigma (Doe v. Lee 2001a; 2001b). Registration, however, "is a common and long-standing regulatory technique with a remedial purpose" (Artway v. Attorney General of New Jersey 1996, 1264). Under SORNA, registration is for "(1) 15 years, if the offender is a tier I sex offender; (2) 25 years, if the offender is a tier II sex offender; and (3) the life of the offender, if the offender is a tier III sex offender" (Congress 2006, secs. 115–116). Offenders have to keep their registration current (annually for tier 1, every six months for tier 2, and every three months for tier 3). SORNA does not require states to follow the same registration and notification requirements, but the states' tiered system cannot impose registration requirements less than what the federal government has created (E.B. v. Verniero 1997; U.S. v. Madera 2007).

Through various sections of the act, many named after those mostly but not exclusively children who were sexually violated by previously convicted sex offenders, the AWA incorporates a host of federal and state provisions regarding the registration and notification of convicted sex offenders. The AWA requires that all sex offenders register with their local police and that the police notify communities of a sex offender's return from prison. Part of the reason for these requirements can be found in the Dru Sjodin story:

> Dru Sjodin was murdered by a man named Alphonso Rodriguez, Jr. He was a level three sex offender. He was a sexual predator who had been in prison for 23 years, and prior to being released from prison, was judged to be a high risk for another violent offense, by psychiatrists and others who evaluated him. Despite that, he was released from prison without notification of the local State's attorney, without notification of local law enforcement authorities. (Congress 2008, 2–3)

Rodriguez abducted Sjodin in North Dakota but hid her dead body in Minnesota. Because he crossed state lines to commit his crime, he was tried in federal court, which sentenced him to death (U.S. v. Rodriguez 2009). When Congress passed the AWA, it created the Dru Sjodin National Sex Offender Public Website, which links "public state, territory, and tribal sex offender registries from one national search site" (U.S. Department of Justice).

Those opposed to sex offender legislation make many criticisms of interest groups and civic associations: that they are not mom and pop organizations but highly organized interests with political agendas inimical to the rights of sex offenders; that they clog the administration of justice with narrow interests; and that they reflect elite wants at the expense of those who lack the time and money to get involved (Einstein, Palmer, and Glick 2019, 30). Murray Edelman (1988, 4) has made a career suggesting that interests are not reflections of organic individual and group desires but are processes of "rationalization." Ben Berger offers a more thoughtful critique. He makes the important point that "social engagement" should not be "divorced from state-sanctioned political processes and institutions" (2009, 342), lest they become unmoored from the restraints imposed by processes and institutions.

Civic involvement has a long and storied legacy in American politics. Civic associations reflect both a desire by citizens for more engagement with the political process and a recognition that we govern through representation. As Theda Skocpol (1997, 468) has written, by the beginning of the twentieth century, civic associations "became good at simultaneously influencing and reflecting popular opinion in localities and at lobbying legislators and government administrators at local, state, and national levels." I see nothing in the interests that pushed for sex offender legislation in the 1990s to suggest that they thought only symbolically, or acted punitively, or had only narrow, vengeful instincts. To dismiss the civic-mindedness of interests and associations dedicated to passing sex offender legislation is to fail to grasp how important civic engagement is for large portions of the population interested in developing "political skills" and cultivating "social capital" (Clemens 1999, 82). John Walsh and Dru Sjodin's parents, along with many others, are the heirs to this tradition of civic engagement.

What prompted Congress to act: symbolism or moral panic? These are the common charges. A closer look reveals ordinary concerns, such as child and community safety. The states began passing legislation directed at protecting children in 1962, after the publication of a pediatric paper called "The Battered Child Syndrome." Congress took action the same year, amending the Social Security Act to include child protective services (Myers 2008–2009, 455). In 1974, Congress passed the Child Abuse Prevention and Treatment Act (CAPTA). In 1982, Congress passed the Missing Children's Act; in 1984, Congress created the National Center for Missing and Exploited Children (Child Welfare Information Gateway 2016). In 1994, Congress created the Morgan P. Hardiman Task Force on Missing and Exploited Children, which relies on "agents from seven Federal law enforcement agencies, headed by the FBI, working with the [National Center for Missing and Exploited Children] in difficult cases" (Congressional Record 1995, H11682). This is path dependency, not moral panic. These laws go back fifty years; these concerns have infiltrated both state and federal lawmaking for a half century.

In 1990, following two sex crimes by repeat offenders, and the release of a habitual sex offender and murderer, Washington became the first state to require registration and postconviction civil commitment of sexual offenders.[3] Senator David Durenberger and Congressman Jim Ramstad (both of Minnesota, which had just passed a registration law) were working on a federal registration bill when "another highly publicized crime was committed" in Indiana. "On July 15, 1993, ten-year-old Zachary Snider was molested and murdered, and his body and bicycle were thrown off a bridge. A neighbor who had befriended the child was charged with the crime. Unbeknownst to the community, the neighbor was a released child sex offender" (Earl-Hubbard 1996, 795). The next year, Indiana passed "Zachary's law," creating a state registry for sex offenders. As Lori McPherson (2016, 748) has written, "In the midst of the enactment of these state laws, the U.S. Congress started considering measures that would encourage the implementation of sex offender registration programs in the remaining states, as well as the standardization of registration programs across the country."

By 1994, twenty-five states had registration laws for sex offenders (Houston 1994, 731), though only two required community notification (Cierzniak 1995, 716). In 1994, Congress made both a national requirement, passing the Jacob Wetterling Crimes Against Children and Sexually Violent Offender Registration Act, which was part of an omnibus bill called the Violent Crime Control and Law Enforcement Act (Congress 1994, Title XVII; Eisen and Chettiar 2016; McPherson 2016, 765–68). Congress named the law after Jacob Wetterling, who was eleven years old when a sex offender killed him in Minnesota, in 1989. By the end of the 1990s, every state was in compliance with the Wetterling Act

(Agan 2011, 210). In 1996, Congress amended the Wetterling Act with Megan's Law, named after Megan Kanka, a seven-year-old New Jersey resident who was raped and murdered by a convicted sex offender, mandating community notification of convicted sex offenders who were released into communities.

According to the FBI, between 1990 and 2009, "the number of rape/sexual assault victimizations for those age 12 and older" declined (Wiseman and Lobanov-Rostovsky). While sex offenses were decreasing, there was an "increase in articles relating to sexual offending" (Justice Policy Institute). John Gramlich, of the PEW research center, has noted, for example, that "in 18 of 22 Gallup surveys since 1993 that have asked about national crime, at least six-in-ten Americans said there was more crime in the U.S. compared with the year before, despite the generally downward trend in national violent and property crime rates during most of that period" (Gramlich 2019). An overall decline in sexual offending, and a corresponding increase in news about sex offending, leads to the charge that elected representatives, in passing sex offender legislation, were burdened by social and psychological problems, such as "misplaced anxiety" (Walshe 2012), causing them to pass "draconian" legislation based on "myths, misinformation, moral panic, and public hysteria" (Dubin and Horowitz 2017, 21). Critics of sex offender legislation consider sex offender laws to be examples of a puritanical culture incapable of thinking rationally about sex, and as a set of impulsive "legislative reactions to sensational sexual crimes" (Lieb, Quinsey, and Berliner 1998, 61–62).

The reason for sex offender legislation in the states in the 1990s is much more basic than the psychological analyses social scientists offer. The modern movement to register sex offenders began in Washington State, when Ida Ballasiotes "sat down at her typewriter" and wrote a letter to state officials following the rape and death of her daughter, Diane, by a released convicted sex offender, who authorities admitted was "too dangerous" for a mental hospital (Siegel 1990). By the late 1980s, the citizens in Washington were so concerned about sexual murders of children they organized themselves into groups, one called "the Tennis Shoe Brigade," and another called the "Friends of Diane and Trish Tobias's Family and Friends of Missing Persons and Violent Crime Victims." Their fears were not misplaced.

Earl Shriner, a resident of Washington State, "had a 24-year history of killing, sexual assault, and kidnapping." Prior to his release from prison, in May of 1987,

> prison officials learned that he intended to torture children after he was released, and tried vigorously to detain him through the civil commitment laws covering mental illness. Unable to demonstrate the required "the recent overt act" to prove dangerousness, the state had no option but to release Shriner. Two years after his release, he raped and strangled a seven-year-old boy in Tacoma, Washington, severed his penis, and left him in the woods to die. (Lieb 1996, 1)

Days after the assault, "more than 300 people attended a public forum on child sexual assault in Tacoma. Within a week, more than 1,000 people had called or written to the governor about the public safety issue, and two state senators called for a public hearing. Within two weeks, citizens had raised $335,000 for the boy's medical care and were still demanding the state government take action" (Post 1999, 189). As the *Los Angeles Times* reported, the Friends of Diane and the Tennis Shoe Brigade

> marched on the state capitol in Olympia, where they dumped thousands of tennis shoes—a symbol of children's vulnerability, they explained—in Gov. Gardner's outer office. . . . "These are the shoes of a beautiful 18-year-old girl who was murdered last summer," read the unsigned note attached to a pair of white exercise shoes. . . . People who'd never before written public officials now lifted pens. Employees in restaurants organized fund drives. . . . Thousands called elected officials to demand change. Plans were formed to convert the site of Shriner's attack into a park named after his victim. . . . The degree of outrage and mobilization . . . is unprecedented in recent history, prosecutor [Norm] Maleng observed of this uprising. (Siegel 1990)

In 1993, Polly Klaas, in California, and Jacob Wetterling, in Minnesota, were abducted, sexually abused, and killed. With the help of organized interests in those two states, the movement began toward the passage of the nation's first three-strikes law and the second sex offender law. Washington passed a three-strikes law in 1993 by a ballot initiative first posted by Mrs. Ballasiotes, who became a member of the Washington House of Representatives after the death of her daughter. New Jersey named its Registration and Community Notification Laws, known as "Megan's Law," after Megan Kanka (Office of the Attorney General 1998). The death of Megan Kanka "was the fourth young girl in just a little more than a year to be sexually abused and killed in New Jersey. In each instance the person charged with the crime had a prior record for sex-related crimes" (Doe v. Poritz 1995). New Jersey's law is the most prominent of the laws named after dead children, but there are others,[4] and at that point national media attention turned to sex offending. The Klaases and the Wetterlings became activists for legislative changes in their home states, joining Adam Walsh's father in Florida, Ida Ballasiotes in Washington, and families in other states.

Critics do not regard sex offender laws as instances of interest group mobilization or policy setting at the state and local levels. They follow the lead of political theorists who say that deliberation masks "dominance and inequality" (Sanders 1997, 362). These critics condemn the participatory and process approach as partisan and vengeful. In these dismissals of demonstrations of democratic governance, there is a reluctance to address the indispensable relationship that exists between civic groups and legislators, in terms of knowledge acquisition and political strategies that lead to the formation of laws. There is the implication that laws not derived from scientific studies lack legitimacy, as seen in the critics' unwillingness to accept Mrs. Ballasiotes's contribution to democratic thought and practice. They see no spirit of republican self-government in the fact that sex offender legislation is mostly the product of those not previously politicized. And they fail to see the importance for the study of politics the connection between crime victims and the rise of victims' rights groups. As Alan Abramowitz (2010, 19) has written, "Americans today are more interested in politics, better informed about public affairs, and more politically active than at any time during the past half century." This increase in civic engagement has, no doubt, put off those who look to the courts, or social science, or both, to resolve the tensions that democracy, majority rule, and rights claims create in society.

The solution to the problems that arise in a democracy is not to shut down democratic practices by imposing ill-timed judicial judgments or calling for more scientific studies about sex offenders' behavior. Rather, a greater dedication to democratic deliberation is required by channeling the deliberative instincts of the American people into effective lawmaking. The problem facing sex offender legislation is that the focus on the narrative and discursive aspects of sex offender legislation blinds critics to the common-sense notion that sex offender legislation is the product of increased civic engagement and legislative deliberation about public safety. Narratives of social injustice regarding sex offending legislation obscure the indispensable idea "that self-government on a small scale is a legitimate . . . portion of the American political inheritance" (Derthick 1999a, 10).

The work of constitutional construction is, as Keith Whittington has noted, "creative." It relies upon the text of the Constitution, but not exclusively. The "text" is "brought into being" by processes, institutions, and interpretation (Whittington 1999, 5). A focus on narrative, and the emphasis on the vengeful sentiments of crime legislation, by contrast, means that critics fail to appreciate the nuances of constitutional law; the grassroots origins of interest groups; the importance of constituency representation; the structure of local and state governments; the linkage between public opinion and public policy, where support for sex offender laws is high; party competition within states; gubernatorial influences on policy and agenda-setting; levels of consensus and dissensus in the states; and why states innovate (Lieberman and Shaw 2000; Barrilleaux and Berkman 2003). The perception of sex offender legislation as vengeful and not scientific also misses important political and institutional practices. Sex offender laws are not the result of state-wide referenda (except California), where minorities tend to lose (Lewis 2013; Hume 2013). Legislators, not the people directly, deliberate about the content of these laws (Logan 2008, 113–14), which fosters moderation. At the national level, critics have failed to account for the influence of the separation of powers, checks and balances, and the evolving practices of federalism on national legislation for sex offenders. For almost two hundred years, Martha Derthick has noted (1999b, 130), the "bedrock of American domestic government was local." SORNA reflects that principle, as it combines laws from across the nation.

SORNA was not passed in a political vacuum. It builds upon and consolidates numerous federal and state laws dealing with interstate crimes such as sex offending, kidnapping, and pornography. I have already noted the Wetterling Act and Megan's Law. In 1996, Congress passed the Pam Lychner Tracking and Identification Act, named after Pam Lychner, an adult who was sexually assaulted by a previously convicted sex offender who had "moved to Texas after committing his crimes out-of-state" (Logan 2008, 72). Lychner survived the attack and subsequently created a lobbying organization for the registration of sex offenders. The Lychner Act, now part of the AWA, requires, among other things, that federally convicted sex offenders "register, and keep the registration current, in each jurisdiction where the offender resides, where the offender is an employee, and where the offender is a student. For initial registration purposes only, a sex offender shall also register in the jurisdiction in which convicted if such jurisdiction is different from the jurisdiction of residence" (Congress 2006, sec. 113).

In 1998, Congress passed the Jacob Wetterling Improvement Act, part of the Appropriations Act of 1998. This act amended provisions of the Wetterling and Lychner acts. The Wetterling Act required "registered offenders who change their state of residence to register under the new state's laws," and "to register in the states where they worked or went to school if those states were different from their state of residence." It also "[d]irected states to participate in the National Sex Offender Registry"; and "[r]equired each state to set up procedures for registering out-of-state offenders, federal offenders, offenders sentenced by court martial, and non-resident offenders crossing the border to work or attend school" (SMART). Also in 1998, Congress passed the Protection of Children from Sexual Predators Act, which requires "the Director of the Bureau of Justice Assistance to carry out the Sex Offender Management Assistance (SOMA) program" to help eligible states comply with registration requirements (Congress 1998a). In 2000, Congress passed, as part of the Victims of Trafficking and Violence Protection Act, the Campus Sex Crimes Prevention Act. This act requires, in part, that registered sex offenders notify the college or university they are attending, including noting changes in enrollment and employment (Congress 2000, sec. 1601). Finally, in 2003, Congress created the Amber Alert system, which is part of the Prosecutorial Remedies and Other Tools to End the Exploitation of Children Today (PROTECT) Act. This act requires the states to maintain a website containing registry information and the Department of Justice "to create a national Internet site that links all such State Internet sites" (Congress 2003, sec. 604). In various forms, Congress included these provisions in the AWA.

To dismiss these laws as punitive and self-serving is to misunderstand the institutional complexity of American politics, including the important role played by public opinion and local, state, and national lawmakers in constructing a constitutional narrative about sex offending. There are many reasons why people join interest groups and why states pass laws. Some interest groups want recognition, such as the naming of a park or a bridge, to honor the deceased's legacy. Others have political agendas. More important than a focus on hysteria and panic, however, is to acknowledge that state and local interest groups have to work within existing legislative structures to formulate their goals, moderating them through a process of deliberation. As Vanessa Barker (2007; 2009b, 10–11) has shown, the passage of laws depends to a great extent on the political makeup of an individual state—its history and structure, the relationship between the legislature and the governor, and the strength of the political parties. Barker argues that some states tend to view crime as a matter of safety and health and others as a matter of restoration and rehabilitation. To regard all state regulation of sex offenders as the product of vengeance, symbolism, or fear is to misunderstand gravely the institutional and popular aspects of American politics.

The idea that laws are symbolic has come to mean that they are without purpose, except for the rhetoric that legislators use to get reelected (Edelman 1960; King 1997; Mayhew 1974, 119). Murray Edelman, for example, has characterized policymaking as the "formation of myths, rites, and other symbolic forms." For Edelman (1964, 4–6; 1971), politics is the displacement of "private emotions," which are real and thus have primacy over the public interest, which, he argues, is constructed for our amusement. Applied to sex offender legislation, the idea suggests that sex offenders are not dangerous but misunderstood (Human Rights Watch 2007), and that legislators are irrational (except in the electoral sense) in thinking they can contain this problem through law or politics. The symbolism of all laws, however, wears thin. Neither SORNA nor its state versions are symbolic in the sense that their only intent is to "allow lawmakers to portray themselves favorably to the public" (Grattet and Jenness 2008, 502; Hennessy 1998, chaps. 5, 8). These laws are designed to redress omissions in the care and treatment of sex offenders and provide for the public safety by detaining those who cannot control their behavior. Claims to the contrary misread the legislative history and the deliberative intentions of the individuals, families, and legislators involved. They also ignore the complexities that beset interest groups and political parties in trying to pass legislation at the state and federal levels (Boehmke, Osborn, and Schilling 2015). The charge, then, that sex offender policy is symbolic misses a set of important facts about lawmaking, specifically during the 1990s (Thorson 1998; Schneider 1979).

There is, for example, ample evidence that criminals seek out crime in states based upon jurisdictional differences in criminal justice. Doron Teichman (2005, 1833) speaks of "profit-driven criminals" who make decisions based on jurisdictional differences in criminal justice. As numerous witnesses pointed out in congressional hearings over SORNA, sex offenders leave one state and turn up in another with regularity. After sexually abusing and then killing Jessica Lunsford (age nine) in Florida, John Evander Couey traveled to Georgia, where he was arrested, but not before he had bought a bus ticket to

Tennessee. Couey's probation officer did not know that Couey was a convicted sex offender (Congress 2009, 86). When debating the AWA, senators included the horrific story of Joseph Duncan, who was a registered tier 3 sex offender in South Dakota, but who committed sex crimes and murder in four states; South Dakota officials did not know about his prior crimes (Miner 2011, 54–57; Congressional Record 2006). In *Smith v. Doe* I (2002, 105), the Supreme Court cited a study that noted that "38% of recidivist sex offenses in the State of Washington took place in jurisdictions other than where the previous offense was committed."

By the 1990s, Morris Fiorina (1999, 408) has noted, Americans had "more opportunities than ever before to influence the actions of their government." During that decade, the states and Congress were responding to interests coalescing around the idea of child protection and public safety. As Dale Krane (2007, 462) has argued, "[s]tate policy activism has always been a feature of American federalism," but it increased "at an accelerating pace" during the 1990s.[5] Krane (2007) and Paul Posner (2007) make the same point about the increase in state policy activism during the 1990s, and the increasing nationalism of public policy during that decade (an overlooked point by all critics of sex offender laws). SORNA is a reflection of the fact that we have been nationalizing our politics at a great pace. As Daniel Hopkins demonstrates in *The Increasingly United States: How and Why American Political Behavior Nationalized* (2018, 236), "the debates in states and even some localities have taken on a national hue, as state political conflicts become an extension of national conflicts, albeit with a different balance of forces."

For a variety of reasons, then, as Krane, Posner, Hopkins, and others (Grumbach 2018) have shown, the states began legislating in the 1990s more than in the past. And as Hopkins notes, states began enacting policies that reflected national concerns. The family of a murdered child in California shared their concerns with the family of a murdered child in New Jersey. Such crimes called for national legislation or, at least, legislation that facilitated national problem solving. Sex offender legislation, rather than the product of symbolism or hysteria, is an example of this understandable trend.

In the 1990s and 2000s, Congress was partly concerned with rising recidivism rates for sex offenses,[6] and that the protections for personal and public safety had become porous. What motivated Congress to pass the AWA was the sense that the parameters of public safety had changed since the 1930s, that sex offending was no longer the preserve of a particular type of person meeting at the city's limit, luring unsuspecting victims into prostitution or sex trafficking. Today, offending is more widespread, reliant upon the Internet, and generally easier to engage in. The abduction and killing of Polly Klaas, twelve years old at the time, from inside her home in California had an important effect on the debate over repeat sexual offenders, as well as three-strikes laws.

A second factor should also be mentioned that provided critical support for the AWA. As Michael Petrunik (2002) has noted, there were changes in approaches to crime and rehabilitation in the 1980s, from a clinical approach, which relied on the expertise of mental health professionals, to a justice approach, which stressed punishment and confinement. The justice approach did not entirely supplant the clinical. Since the 1990s, regarding criminal justice policy, Congress and the states adapted to a changed medical, psychological, cultural, and technological landscape regarding crime. Congress and the states thought it possible to meliorate the effect of sexual violence and to rehabilitate sex offenders through a combination of medications and psychotherapy (Daly 2008). Unlike the 1930s, the era of so-called moral panic, by the 1990s, those with psychological and sexual disorders were no longer stigmatized by their disorders (Smith 2008; Doe v. Lee 2001a). Also unlike the 1930s, treatment programs for sex offenders have become more available and are thought to reduce recidivism (McKune v. Lile 2001; Mancini 2014; Yates and Kingston 2016). While it is true that prisoners since the 1990s have served longer stays in prison than prisoners in any prior decade (Pew Center on the States 2012, 16; Cahalan 1986, 43, table 3–16), some sex offenders, often with tragic results, have been released early because of the perception that they do not pose a continuing danger to the public. The Megan Kanka story and the *Linehan* cases are unfortunate examples.

Morris Fiorina (1977, 177) once noted that "political processes and events are easier to describe than to explain." Those focused on rhetoric, symbolic politics, and moral panic describe one aspect of American politics, but they do not explain the totality of what constitutes sex offender legislation or what governance requires. They ignore the relationship among institutions, ideas, and interests in the production of policy. More than that, they want to do away with political struggles and constitutional conflicts. While it is true that members of Congress engage in symbolic activities to get reelected (Hill and Hurley 2002), there are myriad reasons why they get reelected (pork barreling, fundraising, gerrymandered districts, and so on). To say that sexually violent predator (SVP) laws are only symbolic, without understanding the institutional nature and deliberative components of American politics, demonstrates a refusal to acknowledge how sexually violent predator laws are infused with a combination of local concerns about security, state and national moral outrage, procedural concerns for the rights of the accused and convicted, and the betterment of sex offenders through treatment. The implication that SVP laws are the product of mass hysteria and moral panic can only mean that elected representatives can only act irrationally, and it is the duty of the Supreme Court to correct them, following good science. This is not an edifying contribution to democratic politics, and it posits an empty claim about the connection between science and policy. For good democratic and republican reasons, the Constitution set up a system in which majority rule is the primary vehicle through which laws are passed.

Comstock and the Problem of Federalism

The Supreme Court's decision in *United States v. Comstock* reminds us of the importance of institutions, principles, and constitutional structures in thinking about the passage of laws. The AWA may be about registering offenders and reducing sex crimes through treatment and incapacitation, but the way to do that goes through deliberative institutions at the state and national levels and institutional checks on power across national institutions.

The vexing issue in *Comstock* is section 4248 of the AWA, entitled the "civil commitment of a sexually dangerous person." The constitutional question section 4248 raises is whether Congress has the power, either under Article I, section 8, clause 3, the "commerce clause," or clause 18, the "necessary and proper" clause, to impose a postconviction civil sanction of possibly indefinite detention on someone whose conviction is about to expire because that person remains dangerous to the community (U.S. v. Kebodeaux 2013).

Federal Courts and Section 4248 in Context

The AWA is not a law concerned with the intimate relationship "between government and economic enterprise" (Frankfurter 1964, 1); its connection to the commerce clause is questionable, but not without possibility (Gonzales v. Raich 2005, 27–28; Heart of Atlanta Hotel 1964, 270–72; Katzenbach v. McClung 1964, 299). The AWA addresses Internet pornography, kidnapping, the registration of sex offenders across the United States, and the transportation of illicit material across state lines (Congress 2006, secs. 2250, 3299 [sec. 213]; Title V, sec. 501; sec. 503 [sec. 2257A]).[7] The question presented to the Court was not based on a connection between economic activity and the postconviction confinement of sex offenders suffering from mental abnormalities. Rather, it was "'whether the means chosen are "reasonably adapted" to the attainment of a legitimate end under the commerce power' or under other powers that the Constitution grants Congress the authority to implement" (U.S. v. Comstock 2010, 135).

In 2000, the federal government indicted Graydon Comstock for "[r]eceipt [by computer] of materials depicting a minor engaging in sexually explicit conduct" (U.S. v. Comstock 2007, 526). He was sentenced to thirty-seven months in federal prison, and "[s]ix days prior" to the completion of his sentence, "the Attorney General certified Comstock as a sexually dangerous person, staying his release from prison" (U.S. v. Comstock 2009a, 277). According to the AWA, "the Government (acting through the Department of Justice) must certify to a federal district judge that the prisoner meets the conditions just described, *i.e.*, that he has engaged in sexually violent activity or child molestation in the past and that he suffers from a mental illness that makes him correspondingly dangerous to others." The statute allows the defendant to obtain counsel "to subpoena witnesses on his behalf, and to confront and cross-examine" witnesses. The government must prove its case in a federal court by clear and convincing evidence, the standard the Court set for state civil commitment cases in *Addington v. Texas.* If the government proves its case, it must then request the state in which the crime was committed to civilly commit the defendant. If not, then "the Attorney General shall place the person for treatment in a suitable [federal] facility." Release occurs if the committee's "mental condition improves to the point where he is no longer dangerous." The law requires "ongoing psychiatric and judicial review of the individual's case, including judicial hearings at the request of the confined person at six-month intervals" (U.S. v. Comstock 2010, 130–31; Vars 2013, 860 nn. 29–30).

Where did Congress get its authority to authorize "the Department of Justice to detain a mentally ill, sexually dangerous federal prisoner beyond the date the prisoner would otherwise be released"? (U.S. v. Comstock 2010, 129). Civil commitment is not an enumerated power.

Finding that Congress had exceeded its authority under Article I, section 8, the federal district court in North Carolina, in *U.S. v. Comstock* (2007), concluded that section 4248 is unconstitutional. When the government's appeal landed in the federal court of appeals for the fourth circuit in 2008, it was the first case involving the AWA to appear in an appellate court. Five district courts in five states had already addressed the question of congressional power to civilly commit sexual offenders postconviction. Two district courts—the eighth, in *U.S. v. Tom* (Minnesota), and the fourth, in *U.S. v. Comstock* (North Carolina)—held that Congress lacked the authority under Article I, section 8 to pass the legislation. Three district courts in four different cases—the ninth, in *U.S. v. Abregana* (Hawaii); the tenth, in *U.S. v. Dowell* (Oklahoma); and the first, in *U.S. v. Shields* and *U.S. v. Carta* (Massachusetts)—held the opposite.

Just prior to the release of Comstock and Roger Tom, a sex offender from Utah held in federal custody in Minnesota, the U.S. Attorney General's office, in the respective jurisdictions, initiated proceedings to stay their release and have both men civilly committed, pending psychiatric reviews to determine whether they were sexually dangerous as defined by federal law. Tom was in prison for "aggravated sexual abuse of a minor" (U.S. v. Tom 2009, 498). In *Tom*, the district court found that section 4248 is of a "'noneconomic, criminal nature' and therefore of the type that the Court has identified as being 'a province of the States'" (U.S. v. Tom 2008, 936). The *Tom* court found nothing in Article I, section 8 to grant Congress the power to detain persons (1) after conviction; (2) in lieu of a not guilty by reason of insanity verdict; or (3) in lieu of a finding of mental incompetence. The district court conceded that one plausible reading of the statute was that it was based on a "'costs of crime' rationale" (U.S. v. Tom 2008, 937)—Tom's crime involved interstate travel. The court rejected that argument on its reading of *U.S. v. Lopez* (1995) and *U.S. v. Morrison* (2000).

In *U.S. v. Darby* (1941, 114), the Court declared:

> The power of Congress over interstate commerce is complete in itself, may be exercised to its utmost extent, and acknowledges no limitations other than are prescribed by the Constitution, and that power can neither be enlarged nor diminished by the exercise or non-exercise of state power.

The *Darby* decision represents the difference between the pre-New Deal Court, which refused to protect economic regulation in the states, and the Roosevelt Court under Chief Justice Charles Evans Hughes and Harlan Fiske Stone, which did.

Lopez and *Morrison* are instances of the Court's abandonment of the New Deal Court's *Darby* jurisprudence; these cases held that congressional acts that do not "substantially affect" (U.S. v. Morrison 2000, 609) interstate commerce are unconstitutional. Chief Justice William Rehnquist began his *Lopez* opinion with what he called "first principles": "The Constitution creates a Federal Government of enumerated powers" (U.S. v. Lopez 1995, 552). A constitution that enumerates all legislative powers cannot, in the opinion of the Court, allow Congress to do something that is "not enumerated" (U.S. v. Lopez 1995, 567).

In *Comstock*, the Supreme Court sidestepped Congress's commerce powers in relation to civil commitment and upheld the fourth circuit court of appeals' decision that the law in question was constitutional under the necessary and proper clause. There is precedent for the Court's decision. In 1956, the federal government charged Earl Greenwood with "armed robbery of a United States Post Office and jeopardizing the life of a postal clerk" (U.S. v. Greenwood 1954, 778). He waived his right to a jury trial, and his counsel asked for a sanity hearing. A psychiatrist found Greenwood incapable of making reasoned judgments. The Board of Examiners recommended permanent commitment. Greenwood was then transferred to a state facility, where his psychosis was found to be in remission. At a subsequent hearing, Greenwood was found to be psychotic, incompetent to stand trial, and potentially dangerous to the United States. The Attorney General of the United States then assumed custody over Greenwood. Greenwood's crime occurred in Ohio, and it was the position of the federal government that Ohio should incarcerate Greenwood. Ohio refused, which meant that there were two alternatives: (1) either turn Greenwood loose on society, or (2) the federal government should assume jurisdiction and hold Greenwood in a federal mental facility.

In *Greenwood*—the case most directly linked to *Comstock*—the Supreme Court took for granted that the necessary and proper clause had a plain meaning about congressional powers, and it unanimously held that a federal civil commitment power was "auxiliary to incontestable national power" (Greenwood v. U.S. 1956, 375). That power is presumably criminal activity related to commerce (Congress 1910; Congress 1968a; 1968b; Tot v. U.S. 1943; U.S. v. Bass 1971). Justice Felix Frankfurter in *Greenwood* never clarified this point, but he wrote: Greenwood "came legally into the custody of the United States. The power that put him into such custody—the power to prosecute for federal offenses—is not exhausted" (Greenwood v. U.S. 1956, 375). What was not exhausted was the federal government's right to try Greenwood at some future time when (and if) he returned to sanity. Frankfurter noted, however, that Greenwood may never return to sanity, so the detention could be indefinite.

In the meantime, the Court held that the federal government had the power to continue to detain Greenwood in a federal forensic facility despite the fact that he had not gone to trial.

The district courts in *Tom* and *Comstock* did not see *Greenwood*'s relevance to the cases at hand. The district court in *Tom* held that Congress has no plenary power over criminal activity. The district court in *Tom* attacked the AWA at its source and followed the lead of the district court in *Comstock*: The "federal government simply does not have broad power generally to criminalize sexually dangerous conduct and child molestation" (U.S. v. Comstock 2007, 538; U.S. v. Tom 2008, 940). In fact, section 4248 is civil, not criminal, so it does not "criminalize" any behavior. Only the "failure to register" requirement criminalizes conduct that crosses state lines or in some way affects interstate commerce. That, however, was not the issue in *Comstock*.

Under the Mann Act (1910), also known as the White-Slave Traffic Act, the government has the power to criminalize sexually dangerous conduct and child molestation that crosses state lines. The Mann Act is not a usurpation of state authority; it is an aid to the states' administration of criminal justice. As with the AWA, the Mann Act works best when the FBI lets state authorities prosecute Mann Act offenders (Pliley 2014, 7, 67, 117; Bell 1910, 316–17; Congress 1914; 1919; 1932).

The Mann Act makes three points about the power of Congress to regulate behavior through the commerce clause that buttresses the claim that the AWA is constitutional: (1) the power of Congress is extensive regarding the trafficking of persons across state lines; (2) congressional laws that are derived from enumerated powers can also encompass other clauses of Article I, section 8, including the general welfare provision (Champion v. Ames 1903; U.S. v. Dotterweich 1943; Congress 1938); and (3) it is possible for the Supreme Court to demonstrate its fidelity to the Constitution without engaging in endeavors that shed no light on the congressional purpose of a given act.

> [I]f the facility of interstate transportation can be taken away from the demoralization of lotteries, the debasement of obscene literature, the contagion of diseased cattle or persons, the impurity of food and drugs, the like facility can be taken away from the systematic enticement to and the enslavement in prostitution and debauchery of women, and, more insistently, of girls. (Hoke v. U.S. 1913, 322)

The Mann Act's constitutionality is unquestioned (Athanasaw v. United States 1913; Caminetti v. United States 1917).

The AWA's focus is much narrower than the Mann Act's. The AWA does not usurp state power over the prosecution of sexual crimes in the name of a general police power. Section 142 states: "The Attorney General shall use the resources of Federal law enforcement, including the United States Marshals Service, to assist [state] jurisdictions in locating and apprehending sex offenders who violate sex offender registration requirements." The next section calls for greater integration among federal, state, and local law enforcement. Indeed, the civil commitment of the insane and infirm at the federal level in no way is of a local character that the founders would have thought to be essential to the administration of justice among the states. What Justice Anthony Kennedy wrote in *U.S. v. Lopez* (1995, 583) applies to the *Comstock* case: "This is not a case where . . . federalism has been violated by a formal command from the National Government directing the State to enact a certain policy, or to organize its governmental functions in a certain way." The law, moreover, cannot be connected to a commercial enterprise that does not intend to engage in interstate commerce but that may affect interstate commerce (Gonzalez v. Raich 2005).

Yet according to the district courts in *Tom* and *Comstock*, Congress, in lieu of an explicit grant of power over the mentally ill, has no general police power to confine them. Article I, section 8, clause 18 cannot grant to Congress what the Constitution forbids by its silence. Moreover, the district court in *Tom* found compelling the argument that the Tenth Amendment prohibits Congress from entering into areas that are the traditional preserve of the states. Citing the Supreme Court's decision in *U.S. v. Morrison,* the district court in *Tom* wrote (2008, 940): the "'suppression of violent crime and vindication of its victims' are police powers that are 'reposed in the States.'" This misses an important point. The AWA's main focus is the creation of a national registration list of sex offenders, to facilitate states in the surveillance and apprehension of sex offenders who cross state lines. This is a legitimate congressional power because, as the New York court of appeals (New York v. Parker 1976, 25) held, "crimes committed in other jurisdictions . . . with differing social mores and standards of conduct take on added significance in our highly mobile society." The act includes penalties and creates guidelines for federal judges to determine dangerousness. Other sections enhance penalties for federal criminal offenses. Insofar as the law criminalizes conduct, such as pornography and human trafficking, Congress has tied those criminal offenses to legitimate interstate commerce concerns. As the court of appeals noted in *U.S. v. Tom* (2009, 506), "'When the federal government exerts any of its constitutional powers, no valid objection can be based upon the fact that such exercise' may be accomplished by a state through the use of its police power."

The district court's opinion in *Tom* is incomplete as a statement of the extent of congressional powers under the Constitution (Elliot 1827, 2: 325–37, esp. 335; The Federalist 2001, no. 44; Story 1858, 2: 3, 27 [sec. 1287], 170). As Herbert Storing (1985, 24) has noted, when the first Congress refused to put the words "expressly delegated" into the Tenth Amendment, the advocates of state sovereignty "lost the battle over the basic character of the Constitution." The AWA reflects that character by providing the states with national resources. It does not usurp state power. It seeks to suppress dangerous criminals who engage in the channels and instrumentalities of interstate commerce (Carr v. U.S. 2010). The failure to register requirement, the only new crime the AWA creates, implicates interstate commerce because convicted sex offenders move to other states and do not register with the local police. As the court of appeals in *U.S. v. Tom* noted (2009, 506), it is "not unreasonable to assume that upon completion of any prison term convicted sex offenders will travel outside of the state of incarceration." Section 2250 of the AWA requires that state prisoners must travel by the instrumentalities of interstate commerce to be eligible for this provision (Congress 2006, 2250(a); 2250(a)(2)(B); Morse 2009, 1760, n. 56).

In *U.S. v. Comstock* (2009a, 278), the fourth circuit court of appeals echoed the opinion of the district court in *U.S. v. Tom*: "Unlike the states, the federal government has no general police or *parens patriae* power." The court said this despite knowing that the federal government has had a custodial power over insane federal criminals—*parens patriae*, in other words—since 1857. In 1855, Congress created the Government Hospital for the Insane, so named until 1916, when it became St. Elizabeths, "to provide 'the most humane care and enlightened curative treatment of the insane of the army and navy of the United States, and of the District of Columbia'" (U.S. v. Comstock 2009b, 24). While Congress claimed this power under Article I, section 8, clause 17, which gives Congress exclusive jurisdiction over the nation's capital, it strains constitutional logic to associate a custodial concern for the infirm with a mere jurisdictional power. In 1927, the District of Columbia circuit court held, in *White v. Treibly*, that the government has the power to "commit a retired naval officer" to an asylum because "his 'care and protection' were a 'concern and duty of the government'" (U.S. v. Comstock 2009b, 25). Traditionally, "the state governments have a full superintendence and control over the immense mass of local interests in their respective states" (Story 1851, I: 3, 6 [sec. 510], 358). But section 4248 does not usurp a traditional state power in the same manner as the post-Civil War Amendments and Enforcement Acts do. Section 4248 claims a power for the federal government without disrupting the same power among the states.

In *U.S. v. Carta* (2007, 407 n. 5), a federal district court in Massachusetts acknowledged that section 4248 "is not linked to specific crimes," but it still found that section constitutional. In *U.S. v. Shields* (2007, 326), another federal district court in Massachusetts held that "Congress has the authority to enact section 4248 pursuant to the federal government's power under the commerce clause to prevent the commission of federal sex crimes." And in *U.S. v. Dowell* (2007, 6–7), a federal district court in Oklahoma concluded that section 4248 is not unlike section 4246 (used in the *Greenwood* case), which various federal courts have held to be constitutional. Congress passed section 4246 in 1949. Prior to that, "the federal government had to release criminal defendants if they were insane" (Note 1955, 1070).

The differences between sections 4246 and 4248 are minor. Section 4246 is "triggered by the prospect of generalized danger arising from mental illness," whereas section 4248 "is triggered by discrete dangers arising from a particular manifestation of mental illness: sexually dangerous proclivities" (U.S. v. Volungus 2010, 7). Section 4246 prohibits federal civil commitment proceedings unless "suitable arrangements for State custody and care are not available." Section 4248 allows the attorney general to initiate civil commitment proceedings after a district court has found the defendant "sexually dangerous"; at that point, the attorney general is "authorized to initiate civil commitment proceedings" (U.S. v. Tom 2009, 499–500). Finally, under section 4246, "the Attorney General is required to seek state placement for the individual as long as he is in federal custody. . . . In contrast, under § 4248 this requirement is merely implicit." Both sections "express a preference" (U.S. v. Tom 2009, 508) for state commitment, and section 4248 requests the attorney general to "defer to available state custody" (Congress 20006, sec. 4248(g); U.S. v. Volungus 2010, 3; U.S. v. Tom 2009, 507; U.S. v. Abregana 2008, 1133–34). One important difference is that section 4246 does not grant the federal government the power to commit persons postconviction. What they have in common is of utmost significance: both require the government to protect the public from those in custody who pose a threat to society. Section 4248 "allows the government to retain custody of a prisoner who would be dangerous to others if released. That step seems to be plainly adapted to the proper discharge of the government's custodial duty" (U.S. v. Volungus 2010, 8; U.S. v. Abregana 2008, 1131).

Following the fourth circuit court of appeal's affirmation of the district court's ruling in *Comstock*, the government appealed to the Supreme Court. Before the Court decided *Comstock*, two courts of appeals had decided the constitutionality of section 4248. In *U.S. v. Volungus* (2010), the court of appeals for the first circuit upheld section 4248; the court found no substantial differences between sections 4246 and 4248. In *U.S. v. Tom* (2009), the court of appeals for the eighth circuit overruled the district court's holding and concluded (2009, 502): "That Congress has the authority under the Necessary and Proper Clause to criminalize and punish certain activities as a means of effectuating its enumerated powers is beyond dispute." With the fourth circuit's *Comstock* ruling having created a division among three circuits, the Supreme Court accepted the government's appeal in *Comstock*. The government's burden was to prove that section 4248 properly grants to the government the power to regulate "sex-related crimes" (U.S. v. Comstock 2009a, 282) postconviction. In a 7–2 decision, with Justices Kennedy and Samuel Alito concurring and Justices Clarence Thomas and Antonin Scalia dissenting, the Supreme Court upheld section 4248.

The Supreme Court Decides

In upholding section 4248, Justice Stephen Breyer made five points about its constitutionality. First, the section is constitutional under the necessary and proper clause. Second, the section is "a modest addition to a set of federal prison-related mental-health statutes that have existed for many decades." Third, "the Federal Government is the custodian of its prisoners." Fourth, the section does not violate the Tenth Amendment or state interests. And fifth, section 4248 is narrow in scope (U.S. v. Comstock 2010, 137, 142, 143–44, 146).

The Court did not address the problem whether section 4248 creates the proper standard for confinement ("clear and convincing" or "preponderance of evidence"). Nor did it address the problem of custody. It remains unclear whether section 4248 applies "to all persons in the custody of the [Bureau of Prisons] regardless of the basis for that custody" (U.S. v. Comstock 2009c, 18).

Unlike the statute in *Kansas v. Hendricks*, which "applied only to persons previously 'convicted of or charged with' at least one of twelve specifically-defined sexually violent offenses" (U.S. v. Comstock 2009c, 21), the federal commitment law has no such restriction. While this is an interesting jurisdictional problem, there is less here than meets the eye, as there is no reason not to extend the holding in *Greenwood* to postconviction civil confinement, given that Frankfurter noted that Greenwood's condition was most likely permanent. As the court of appeals held in *U.S. v. Carta* (2010, 44), section 4248 restricts the government's commitment power to those "individuals already in its custody." Nor did the Court address the civil-criminal problem. Finally, it did not address questions about the "equal protection of the laws, procedural or substantive due process, or any other rights guaranteed by the Constitution" (U.S. v. Comstock 2010, 149–50).

Regarding the necessary and proper clause, Breyer relied on Chief Justice John Marshall's opinion in *McCulloch v. Maryland* (1819, 421; U.S. v. Comstock 2010, 134):

> Let the end be legitimate, let it be within the scope of the constitution, and all means which are appropriate, which are plainly adapted to that end, which are not prohibited, but consist with the letter and spirit of the constitution, are constitutional.

This overused phrase nevertheless gets to the heart of congressional power regarding sex offending. First, it sets up a "means-ends" relationship for the Supreme Court to judge the constitutionality of legislation (Burroughs v. United States 1934, 547–48; Charles 2010). Rather than inviting judicial activism, the connection between means and ends reduces the possibility that the Court will engage in maximal policymaking because it acknowledges that congressional power is not without limitations. In Cass Sunstein's terms (1999, chap. 1), recognizing institutional constraints increases the possibility for democratic deliberation and reduces the likelihood that the judiciary will engage in framing new principles. Second, it grants to Congress a wide latitude in passing laws without requiring Congress to pass laws with "scientific exactitude" (Gonzales v. Raich 2005, 17). Marshall's means-end relationship means that "Congress must show a reasonable connection between what it regards as expedient and an enumerated power" (Dry 1987, 242). It allows representatives to think for themselves about governance and to regard legislation as expressions of popular opinion, rather than of nondemocratic and scientific or abstract inclinations. And third, it removes from consideration a formalistic straightjacket that suggests that Congress has no implied powers. This is why Congress, "in furtherance of its enumerated powers, 'can cause a prison to be erected at any place within the jurisdiction of the United States, and direct that all persons sentenced to imprisonment under the laws of the United States shall be confined there'" (U.S. v. Comstock 2010, 136).

Justice Breyer's second point is that Congress has long been involved in criminal law, specifically the "delivery of mental health care to federal prisoners" (U.S. v. Comstock 2010, 137).

> In 1874 . . . Congress provided for civil commitment in federal facilities (or in state facilities if a State so agreed) of "*all* persons who have been or shall be convicted of any offense in *any* court of the United States" and who are or "shall become" insane "during the term of their imprisonment." (U.S. v. Comstock 2010, 138; italics in original)

A problem in understanding federal power in criminal law is that history suggests a robust interpretation of congressional power, as the 1790s Crimes Act demonstrates (Elliot 1827, 2: 325–37). In 1789, Congress passed a law requesting the states to hold federal prisoners because there were no federal prisons, a request that held until 1891, when Congress passed the "three prisons act," creating federal prisons in Leavenworth, Kansas; Atlanta, Georgia; and MacNeil Island, Washington (Congress 1891; U.S. v. Ramirez 1977; Cosgrove v. Smith 1983, 1138; White 1948, 402). Congress then increased the number of federal prisons to seven. In 1930, Congress created the Bureau of Prisons to supervise the care and custody of federal prisoners (Congress 1930; Morris 1998, chap. 8). In 1948 and 1949, Congress again intervened in this area, passing two laws that "provided for the civil commitment of individuals who are, or who become, mentally incompetent at any time after their arrest and before the expiration of their federal sentence." In 1984, Congress, in passing an insanity law, provided for "civil commitment if, in addition to the other conditions, the prisoner's 'release would create a substantial risk of bodily injury to another person or serious damage to the property of another'" (U.S. v. Comstock 2010, 140–41).

Breyer's third point required him to expand upon his second. Given that the federal government is the "custodian of its prisoners" (U.S. v. Comstock 2010, 142), it necessarily follows that the government has a duty to control prisoners under its jurisdiction. Such a power must come from the "necessary and proper" clause. Breyer reasoned by analogy, equating mental illness and dangerousness to an infectious disease, which Congress has the power to protect against. "And if confinement of such an individual is a 'necessary and proper' thing to do, then how could it not be similarly 'necessary and proper' to confine an individual whose mental illness threatens others to the same degree?" (U.S. v. Comstock 2010, 142–43).

Breyer's fourth point is an attempt to dampen criticism that section 4248 usurps the states' *parens patriae* and police powers. Section 4248 implicates congressional power over interstate commerce because that clause empowers Congress to prevent the channels and instrumentalities of interstate commerce from being used for "immoral and illegal purposes" (U.S. v. Tom 2009, 506; Caminetti v. U.S. 1917, 484). Section 4248 implicates interstate commerce in two ways. One, sex offenders can commit an array of crimes. "As a Senate report indicates, by one estimate more than 50% of child molesters possessed child pornography at the time of arrest" (U.S. v. Tom 2009, 506). Congress has jurisdiction over Internet pornography (Congress 1998b; Ashcroft v. American Civil Liberties Union 2004). Second, it is not unlikely that a convicted sex offender can be incarcerated in a state other than of his own origin, having committed a second offense in a different state (U.S. v. Comstock 2010, 143). Section 4248 does not replace state civil commitment with federal civil confinement; it facilitates state interagency cooperation.

Finally, Breyer clarified Congress's power under the necessary and proper clause. For Breyer, the power to incarcerate those who violate federal law derives from a specific enumerated power plus the commerce clause.

> Indeed even the dissent acknowledges that Congress has the implied power to criminalize any conduct that might interfere with the exercise of an enumerated power, and also the additional power to imprison people who violate those (inferentially authorized) laws, and the additional power to provide for the safe and reasonable management of those prisons, and the additional power to regulate the prisoners' behavior even after their release. (U.S. v. Comstock 2010, 147)

Congress's power is limited under the necessary and proper clause because section 4248's reach is only over those "already 'in the custody of the' Federal Government" (U.S. v. Comstock 2010, 149). *Comstock* adheres to precedent and to proper constitutional construction because the necessary and proper clause permits

> Congress to create federal criminal laws, to punish their violation, to imprison violators, to provide appropriately for those imprisoned, and to maintain the security of those who are not imprisoned but who may be affected by the federal imprisonment of others. The Constitution consequently authorizes Congress to enact the statute. (U.S. v. Comstock 2010, 149)

The Dissent and American Constitutionalism

"Under the Court's precedents," Justice Thomas wrote, "Congress may not regulate noneconomic activity (such as sexual violence) based solely on the effect such activity may have, in individual cases or in the aggregate, on interstate commerce" (U.S. v. Comstock 2010, 164). Thomas found a stark difference between a state's police or *parens patriae* powers and a federal police power or an implied power derived from an enumerated one.

Thomas wrote the majority opinion in *Kansas v. Hendricks*, upholding a state postconviction civil commitment statute, and dissented in *Kansas v. Crane*, in which the Court added language about control of impulses to the state's requirement for commitment. In *Crane* and *Hendricks*, Thomas was a forceful defender of the legislature's power to protect citizens from dangerous and mentally abnormal sexual offenders and a forceful critic of the judiciary's power to overturn valid legislation. Thomas's dissent in *Comstock* suggests that he prefers to use the Court's power to check large-scale majorities but resists the invitation to check smaller majorities, which is an ironic position, given that states are more homogeneous and potentially more tyrannical toward minority interests than national interests (The Federalist 2001, no. 10).

Thomas misses the point about what a limited government is under the Constitution. The founders did not create a government of "unlimited" (U.S. v. Comstock 2010, 161) powers. As Charles Pinckney of South Carolina noted at the constitutional convention, the broad grants of power to the federal government did not mean that Congress would be all-powerful; Congress is constrained by the democratic nature of the Constitution and the institutional design of Congress. Thomas loses sight of this in his *Comstock* dissent. Under Article I, section 8, clauses 11–13, for example, Congress has the power to declare war and raise an army and a navy. That Congress has the power to grant pensions to those who serve in the armed forces, and their dependents, is an implied power, as the Court noted in *U.S. v. Hall* (1878). Or as John Marshall noted in *McCulloch v. Maryland* (1819, 37):

> Take, for example, the power "to establish post-offices and post-roads" . . . from this has been inferred the power and duty of carrying the mail along the post-road, from one post-office to another. And from this implied power, has again been inferred the right to punish those who steal letters from the post-office, or rob the mail.

As Comstock was rightfully in federal custody, the Constitution grants the federal government the authority to extend its custody over him until he is no longer mentally ill and dangerous.

As Publius points out, the barrier to an "unlimited government" (The Federalist 2001, 343 [no. 53]) is not judicial review but biennial elections, the separation of powers, what is now called federalism, staggered elections, and finally an extensive sphere that allows for commercial activities. The political process, not judges, determines the extent of our liberties (Weiner 2019, 74). Thomas forgets what critics of sex offender legislation ignore—namely the importance of understanding the Constitution in its totality, as a framework of governance. By granting no meaning to the necessary and proper clause other than that it allows for the implementation of clauses one through seventeen (U.S. v. Comstock 2010, 178 n. 16), Thomas shifts power away from Congress and to the federal judiciary, which acts not as an arbiter of federal power but as a censor for minority interests. Because of this limitation, he cannot see section 4248 as an extension of a legitimate federal power over insane criminals.[8]

Conclusion

My aim in this chapter has been to demonstrate the complexity of lawmaking in the face of criticism that sexually violent predator laws are products of hysteria, moral panic, and symbolic gestures. The AWA is a reflection of the wisdom of the founders' vision of a federal republic and a testament to the power of groups concerned about the public interest to influence policy. The problems the AWA raises reach back not to the 1930s, the so-called era of moral panic, but to the founding era. The search for "a middle ground" (Derthick 2001, 1) between local and national power is the theme of American constitutionalism, and the AWA draws our attention to that issue. Federalism and concerns about national governmental power are the twin pillars of the AWA. Without considering the contours of federalism and national governmental power, there is no way to understand the AWA's attempt to provide safety to communities or treatment for those in need.

Those who argue that SVP laws are products of hysteria and panic ignore the deliberative aspects of lawmaking, downplay the moral strength and courage of Ida Ballasiotes to alter her state's laws, and misunderstand the necessary limits of judicial review. How can they favor judicial resolution over legislative decision-making without first arguing about democratic accountability, and second, without taking into account that "a kind of legislation seems to be resorted to when Courts exercise judicial review in developing substantive rights while policing the activities of legislatures" (Anastaplo 1995, 94)? Dismissing the Constitution as an effect of power without providing an alternative understanding of governance represents a massive failure by the critics of sex offender legislation to explain why legislators and Supreme Court justices discuss at length a law's institutional problems.

The AWA is not without historical precedent. It has two important features: (1) it assists the states in funding programs for the civil commitment of sexual offenders; and (2) it requires the civil commitment of sexually dangerous federal offenders. The latter point is the more controversial, as it dredges up the idea that the federal government not only has a police power, but that its police power will overtake the states' police powers. I have shown that this concern is misplaced. In 1790, Congress authorized revenue collectors "to assist in enforcing the state quarantine laws," despite protests that "this was an unconstitutional interference with the powers of the states." The AWA demonstrates the equal necessity of "cooperative relations between the two separate systems of administration" (White 1948, 401).

Finally, I have demonstrated that there are multiple reasons why the states enacted civil commitment laws in the 1990s. State governments became more active than in the past, and the states began responding to federal legislation and national trends in ways they had not before. There was also an increasing mixture of state and federal functions developing over crime in the 1990s, and postconviction civil commitment is an instance of this trend. As Sara Sun Beale (1995, 997–98) has written:

> Dual federal-state criminal jurisdiction is now the rule rather than the exception. Federal law reaches at least some instances of each of the following state offenses: theft, fraud, extortion, bribery, assault, domestic violence, robbery, murder, weapons offenses, and drug offenses. In many instances, federal law overlaps almost completely with state law, as is the case with drug offenses.

The point of constructing a constitutional narrative that is not simply a legal exegesis is not to understand federalism concerns narrowly, or to dismiss the processes that help construct constitutional law, but to demonstrate the felt need for congressional help regarding interstate sex offending—a congressional concern since the beginning of the twentieth century—and to highlight the national importance of laws and institutions that seek to limit the danger of sex offenders.

NOTES

1. The AWA has been amended to include Keeping the Internet Devoid of Predators Act (KIDS Act 2008); Military Sex Offender Reporting Act (2015); and International Megan's Law (2016). Congress (2017) reauthorized the AWA in 2017.

2. John Walsh's advocacy for children goes back to Congress's passage of the Missing Children's Act of 1982 and the Missing Children's Assistance Act of 1984 (Waxman 2016).

3. California created a sex offender registry in 1947, followed by "Arizona (1951), Nevada (1961), Ohio (1963), and Alabama (1967)." Then, between "1984 and 1996, all other states enacted sex offender registrations statutes" (McPherson 2016, 747).

4. The list is not exhaustive: Zachary's Law 1994 (Indiana); Jessica's Law 2005 (Florida); Ashley's Law 1995 (Texas); Jimmy Ryce 1999 (Florida); Kendra's Law 1999 (New York); Laura's Law 2004 (California). In 2018, Congress (2018) passed the Amy, Vicky, and Andy Child Pornography Victim Assistance Act, which provides restitution to child victims of pornography.

5. Federalism is alive and well in the AWA, as a number of states are noncompliant, because of financial considerations (Clark 2012).

6. This turned out not to be completely accurate, though recidivism is difficult to measure. I discuss this in the next chapter.

7. The AWA extends federal jurisdiction over kidnappers who do not cross state lines but who "use a channel or instrumentality of interstate commerce in the

commission of the kidnapping." A kidnapper who never leaves a state with a victim is in violation of the commerce clause (Ram 2008, 767–87).

8. Thomas's dissent draws our attention to one interesting omission in the majority opinion. The "definition of 'sexually dangerous person' contains no element relating to the subject's crime" (U.S. v. Comstock 2010, 170). It is theoretically possible for a federal court to accept a request from the Attorney General's office to civilly commit an individual "without finding that he was ever charged with or convicted of a federal crime involving sexual violence" (U.S. v. Comstock 2010, 170; Morse 2009, 1757–58; Barker 2009a, 164). The concern, though, is overstated. While the term "sexual predator" has different meanings according to different statutes, "most definitions require a sexually dangerous individual who the court deems is likely to be a risk for sexual re-offending in the future" (Fabian 2003, 390). As noted earlier in the chapter, section 4248 has a number of procedures to ensure that the person being committed is sexually dangerous to the community.

REFERENCES

Abramowitz, Alan. 2011. *The Disappearing Center: Engaged Citizens, Polarization, and American Democracy.* New Haven: Yale University Press.

Agan, Amanda. 2011. "Sex Offender Registries: Fear without Function?" *Journal of Law and Economics* 54 (1): 207–39.

Anastaplo, George. 1995. *The Amendments to the Constitution: A Commentary.* Baltimore: John Hopkins University Press.

Barker, Vanessa. 2007. "The Politics of Pain: A Political Institutionalist Analysis of Crime Victims' Moral Protests." *Law & Society Review* 41 (3): 619–63.

Barker, Emily. 2009a. "The Adam Walsh Act: Un-Civil Commitment." *Hastings Constitutional Law Quarterly* 37 (1): 141–66.

Barker, Vanessa. 2009b. *The Politics of Imprisonment: How the Democratic Process Shapes the Way America Punishes Offenders.* Oxford: Oxford University Press.

Barrilleaux, Charles, and Michael Berkman. 2003. "Do Governors Matter? Budgeting Rules and the Politics of State Policymaking." *Political Research Quarterly* 56 (4): 409–17.

Beale, Sara Sun. 1995. "Too Many and Yet Too Few: New Principles to Define the Proper Limits for Federal Criminal Jurisdiction." *Hastings Law Journal* 46 (4): 979–1018.

Bell, Ernest Albert. 1910. *Fighting the Traffic in Young Girls; or, War on the White Slave Trade.* Chicago: G. S. Ball.

Berger, Ben. 2009. "Political Theory, Political Science, and the End of Civic Engagement." *Perspectives on Politics* 7 (2): 335–50.

Berns, Walter. 1963. "The Meaning of the Tenth Amendment." In *A Nation of States: Essays on the American Federal System,* edited by Robert A. Goldwin, 126–48. Chicago: Rand McNally & Company.

Boehmke, Frederick, Tracy Osborn, and Emily Schilling. 2015. "Pivotal Politics and Initiative Use in the American States." *Political Research Quarterly* 68 (4): 665–77.

Brickey, Kathleen. 1995. "Criminal Mischief: The Federalization of American Criminal Law." *Hastings Law Journal* 46 (4): 1135–74.

Bybee, Jay. 1997. "Insuring Domestic Tranquility: Lopez, Federalization of Crime, and the Forgotten Role of the Domestic Violence Clause." *George Washington Law Review* 66 (1): 1–83.

Cahalan, Margaret Werner (with the assistance of Lee Anne Parsons). 1986. *Historical Corrections Statistics in the United States, 1850–1984.* Washington, DC: U.S. Department of Justice, Bureau of Justice Statistics. https://www.bjs.gov/content/pub/pdf/hcsus5084.pdf

Charles, Patrick. 2010. "Originalism, John Marshall, and the Necessary and Proper Clause: Resurrecting the Jurisprudence of Alexander Addison." *Cleveland State Law Review* 58 (3): 529–74.

Child Welfare Information Gateway. 2016. *Major Federal Legislation Concerned with Child Protection, Child Welfare, and Adoption.* Washington, DC: U.S. Department of Health and Human Services, Children's Bureau. https://www.childwelfare.gov/pubPDFs/majorfedlegis.pdf

Cierzniak, Elizabeth Kelley. 1995. "There Goes the Neighborhood: Notifying the Public When a Convicted Child Molester is Released into the Community." *Indiana Law Review* 28 (3): 715–54.

Clark, Maggie. 2012. "States Still Resisting National Sex Offender Law." Pew. https://www.pewtrusts.org/en/research-and-analysis/blogs/stateline/2012/10/01/states-still-resisting-national-sex-offender-law

Clemens, Elisabeth. 1999. "Organizational Repertoires and Institutional Change: Women's Groups and the Transformation of American Politics, 1890–1920." In *Civic Engagement in American Democracy*, edited by Theda Skocpol and Morris Fiorina, 81–110. Washington, DC: Brookings Institution Press.

Congressional Record. 1995. Proceedings and Debates of the 104th Congress, 1st sess: 141(171).

Congressional Record. 2006. Children's Safety and Violent Crime Reduction Act. Senate. Proceedings and Debates, 109th Cong., 2d sess.: S8012–02.

Coyle, Kevin. 1996. "The Anti Car Theft Act of 1992: Federal Cops, Highway Robbers, and the Constitution." *North Carolina Central Law Journal* 22 (2): 137–76.

Daly, Reagan. 2008. *Treatment and Reentry Practices for Sex Offenders: An Overview of States.* New York: Vera Institute of Justice.

Derthick, Martha. 1999a. “Introduction.” In *Dilemmas of Scale in America’s Federal Democracy*, edited by Martha Derthick, 1–13. Cambridge: Cambridge University Press.

Derthick, Martha. 1999b. “How Many Communities? The Evolution of American Federalism.” In *Dilemmas of Scale in America’s Federal Democracy*, edited by Martha Derthick, 125–53. Cambridge: Cambridge University Press.

Derthick, Martha. 2001. *Keeping the Compound Republic: Essays on American Federalism*. Washington, DC: Brookings Institution Press.

Dry, Murray. 1987. “Federalism and the Constitution: The Founders’ Design and Contemporary Constitutional Law.” *Constitutional Commentary* 4 (2): 233–50.

Dubin, Lawrence, and Emily Horowitz. 2017. “Caught in the Web of the Criminal Justice System: Autism, Developmental Disabilities, and Sex Offenses.” In *Caught in the Web of the Criminal Justice System: Autism, Developmental Disabilities, and Sex Offenses*, edited by Lawrence Dubin and Emily Horowitz, 21–33. London: Jessica Kingsley Publishers.

Earl-Hubbard, Michele. 1996. “Child Sex Offender Registration Laws: The Punishment, Liberty Deprivation, and Unintended Results Associated with the Scarlet Letter Laws of the 1990s.” *Northwestern University Law Review* 90 (2): 788–862.

Edelman, Murray. 1960. “Symbols and Political Quiescence.” *American Political Science Review* 54: 695–704.

Edelman, Murray. 1964. *The Symbolic Uses of Politics*. Urbana: University of Illinois Press.

Edelman, Murray. 1971. *Politics as Symbolic Action: Mass Arousal and Quiescence*. Chicago: Markham Publishing Company.

Edelman, Murray. 1988. *Constructing the Political Spectacle*. Chicago: University of Chicago Press.

Edwards, George. 2008. *The Madisonian Constitution*. Baltimore: Johns Hopkins University Press.

Einstein, Katherine Levine, Maxwell Palmer, and David Glick. 2019. “Who Participates in Local Government? Evidence from Meeting Minutes.” *Perspectives on Politics* 17 (1): 28–46.

Eisen, Lauren-Brooke, and Inimai Chettiar. 2016. “The Complex History of the Controversial 1994 Crime Bill.” MSNBC. http://www.msnbc.com/msnbc/analysis-the-complex-history-the-controversial-1994-crime-bill

Elliot, Jonathan. 1827. *The Debates in the Several State Conventions of the Adoption of the Federal Constitution. Vol. 2*. https://oll.libertyfund.org/titles/elliot-the-debates-in-the-several-state-conventions-vol-2

Fabian, John. 2003. “Kansas v. Hendricks and Beyond: ‘Mental Abnormality,’ ‘Volition,’ ‘Dangerousness,’ and the Debate between Community Safety and Civil Liberty.” *University of West Los Angeles Law Review* 35 (4): 389–439.

The Federalist. 2001. Ed. Robert Scigliano. New York: The Modern Library.

Fiorina, Morris. 1977. "The Case of the Vanishing Marginals: The Bureaucracy Did It." *American Political Science Review* 71 (1): 177–81.

Fiorina, Morris. 1999. "Extreme Voices: A Dark Side of Civic Engagement." In *Civic Engagement in American Democracy*, edited by Theda Skocpol and Morris Fiorina, 395–425. Washington, DC: Brookings Institution Press.

Frankfurter, Felix. 1964. *The Commerce Clause under Marshall, Taney, and Waite*. Chicago: Quadrangle Books.

Goldwin, Robert. 1997. *From Parchment to Power*. Washington, DC: American Enterprise Institute Press.

Gramlich, John. 2019. Five Facts about Crime in the U.S. PEW Research Center. Pew. http://www.pewresearch.org/fact-tank/2018/01/30/5-facts-about-crime-in-the-u-s/

Grattet, Ryken, and Valerie Jenness. 2008. "Transforming Symbolic Law into Organizational Action: Hate Crime Policy and Law Enforcement Practice." *Social Forces* 87 (1): 501–27.

Grumbach, Jacob. 2018. "From Backwaters to Major Policymakers: Policy Polarization in the States, 1970–2014." *Perspectives on Politics* 16 (2): 416–35.

Hennessy, David (Lord Windlesham). 1998. *Politics, Punishment, and Populism*. Oxford: Oxford University Press.

Hill, Kim Quaile, and Patricia Hurley. 2002. "Symbolic Speeches in the U.S. Senate and Their Representational Implications." *Journal of Politics* 64 (1): 219–31.

Hopkins, Daniel. 2018. *The Increasingly United States: How and Why American Political Behavior Nationalized*. Chicago: University of Chicago Press.

Houston, Julia. 1994. "Sex Offender Registration Acts: An Added Dimension to the War on Crime." *Georgia Law Review* 28 (3): 729–70.

Human Rights Watch. 2007. *No Easy Answers: Sex Offender Laws in the U.S.* https://www.hrw.org/report/2007/09/11/no-easy-answers/sex-offender-laws-us

Hume, Robert. 2013. *Courthouse Democracy and Minority Rights: Same-Sex Marriage in the States*. Oxford: Oxford University Press.

Justice Policy Institute. *Registering Harm: A Briefing Book on the Adam Walsh Act*. http://www.justicepolicy.org/images/upload/08-11_BRF_WalshActRegistries_JJ-PS.pdf

King, Anthony. 1997. "The Vulnerable American Politician." *British Journal of Political Science* 27 (1): 1–22.

Krane, Dale. 2007. "The Middle Tier in American Federalism: State Government Policy Activism during the Bush Presidency." *Publius* 37 (3): 453–77.

Lewis, Daniel. 2013. *Direct Democracy and Minority Rights: A Critical Assessment of the Tyranny of the Majority in the American States*. London: Routledge.

Lieb, Roxanne. 1996. *Washington's Sexually Violent Predator Law*. Olympia: Washington State Institute for Public Policy. http://www.wsipp.wa.gov/ReportFile/1244/Wsipp_Washingtons-Sexually-Violent-Predator-Law-Legislative-History-and-Comparisons-With-Other-States_Full-Report.pdf

Lieb, Roxanne, Vernon Quinsey, and Lucy Berliner. 1998. "Sexual Predators and Social Policy." *Crime and Justice* 23: 43–114.

Lieberman, Robert, and Greg Shaw. 2000. "Looking Inward, Looking Outward: The Politics of State Welfare Innovation under Devolution." *Political Research Quarterly* 53 (2): 215–40.

Logan, Wayne. 2008. "Criminal Justice Federalism and National Sex Offender Policy." *Ohio State Journal of Criminal Law* 6 (1): 51–122.

Madison, James. 1981. "Vices of the Political System of the United States." In *The Mind of the Founder: Sources of the Political Thought of James Madison*, edited by Marvin Meyers, 57–65. Hanover, NH: University Press of New England.

Mancini, Cristina. 2014. *Sex Crime, Offenders & Society.* Durham, NC: Carolina Academic Press.

Mayhew, David. 1974. *Congress: The Electoral Connection.* New Haven: Yale University Press.

McPherson, Lori. 2016. "The Sex Offender Registration and Notification Act at 10 Years: History, Implementation, and the Future." *Drake Law Review* 64 (3): 741–96.

Mikhail, John. "The Necessary and Proper Clauses." *Georgetown Law Journal* 102 (4): 1045–1132.

Miner, Matthew. 2011. "The Adam Walsh Act's Sex Offender Registration and Notification Requirements and the Commerce Clause: A Defense of Congress's Power to Check the Interstate Movement of Unregistered Sex Offenders." *Villanova Law Review* 56 (1): 51–96.

Morris, Norval. 1998. "The Contemporary Prison: 1965-Present." In *The Oxford History of the Prison: The Practice of Punishment in Western Society*, edited by Norval Morris and David Rothman, 202–31. Oxford: Oxford University Press.

Morse, Robin. 2009. "Federalism Challenges to the Adam Walsh Act." *Boston University Law Review* 89 (5): 1753–94.

Myers, John. 2008–2009. "A Short History of Child Protection in America." *Family Law Quarterly* 42 (3): 449–64.

Note. 1955. "Federal Hospitalization of Insane Defendants under Section 4246 of the Criminal Code." *Yale Law Journal* 64 (7): 1070–80.

Office of the Attorney General. 1998. Attorney General Guidelines for Law Enforcement for the Implementation of Sex Offender Registration and Community Notification Laws. https://www.nj.gov/oag/dcj/megan/meganguidelines-2-07.pdf (revised February 2007).

Petrunik, Michael. 2002. "Managing Unacceptable Risk: Sex Offenders, Community Response, and Social Policy in the United States and Canada." *International Journal of Offender Therapy and Comparative Criminology* 46 (4): 483–511.

Pew Center on the States. 2012. *Time Served: The High Cost, Low Return of Longer Prison Terms.* https://www.pewtrusts.org/-/media/assets/2012/06/06/time_served_report.pdf

Pliley, Jessica. 2014. *Policing Sexuality: The Mann Act and the Making of the FBI.* Cambridge, MA: Harvard University Press.

Posner, Paul. "The Politics of Coercive Federalism in the Bush Era." *Publius* 37 (3): 390–412.

Post, Dawn. 1999. "Preventive Victimization: Assessing Future Dangerousness in Sexual Predators for Purposes of Indeterminate Civil Commitment." *Hamline Journal of Public Law & Policy* 21 (1): 177–246.

Ram, Colin. 2008. "Regulating Intrastate Crime: How the Federal Kidnapping Act Blurs the Distinction Between What is Truly National and What is Truly Local." *Washington & Lee Law Review* 65 (2): 767–806.

Sanders, Lynn. 1997. "Against Deliberation." *Political Theory* 25 (3): 347–76.

Schneider, Jerrold. 1979. *Ideological Coalitions in Congress.* Westport, CT: Greenwood Press.

Siegel, Barry. 1990. "Locking Up 'Sexual Predators': A Public Outcry in Washington State Targeted Repeat Violent Sex Criminals. A New Preventive Law Would Keep Them in Jail Indefinitely." *Los Angeles Times* (May 10). https://www.latimes.com/archives/la-xpm-1990-05-10-mn-1433-story.html

Skocpol, Theda. 1997. "The Tocqueville Problem: Civic Engagement in American Democracy." *Social Science History* 21 (4): 455–79.

SMART (Office of Sex Offender Sentencing, Monitoring, Apprehending, Registering, and Tracking). http://ojp.gov/smart/legislation.htm

Smith, Douglas. 2008. "The Constitutionality of Civil Commitment and the Requirement of Adequate Treatment." *Boston College Law Review* 49 (5): 1383–1429.

Storing, Herbert. 1985. "The Constitution and the Bill of Rights." In *How Does the Constitution Secure Rights?*, edited by Robert Goldwin and William Schambra, 15–35. Washington, DC: American Enterprise Institute.

Story, Joseph. 1851. *Commentaries on the Constitution of the United States.* 2nd ed. Boston: Charles C. Little and James Brown.

Story, Joseph. 1858. *Commentaries on the Constitution of the United States.* 3rd ed. Boston: Little, Brown and Company.

Sunstein, Cass. 1999. *One Case at a Time: Judicial Minimalism on the Supreme Court.* Cambridge, MA: Harvard University Press.

Teichman, Doron. 2005. "The Market for Criminal Justice: Federalism, Crime Control, and Jurisdictional Competition." *Michigan Law Review* 103 (7): 1831–76.

Thorson, Gregory. 1998. "Divided Government and the Passage of Partisan Legislation, 1947–1990." *Political Research Quarterly* 51 (3): 751–64.

Tiedman, Christopher. 1886. *A Treatise on the Limitations of the Police Power in the United States.* St. Louis: F. H. Thomas Law Book Company.

U.S. Congress. 1891. Three Prisons Act. 26 Stat. 839.

U.S. Congress. 1910. The White-Slave Traffic Act. (The Mann Act). 36 Stat. 825; codified as amended at 18 U.S.C. §§ 2421–2424.

U.S. Congress. 1914. The Harrison Narcotics Tax Act. 38 Stat. 785.

U.S. Congress. 1919. The Dyer Act. 41 Stat. 324.

U.S. Congress. 1930. An Act to Reorganize the Administration of Federal Prisons. 46 Stat. 325.

U.S. Congress. 1932. Federal Kidnapping Act. 18 U.S.C. § 1201.

U.S. Congress. 1938. Federal Food, Drug, and Cosmetic Act. 52 Stat. 1040.

U.S. Congress. 1968a. Gun Control Act of 1968. 82 Stat. 1213.

U.S. Congress. 1968b. Omnibus Crime Control and Safe Streets Act. 82 Stat. 197.

U.S. Congress. 1992. Anti Car Theft Act. 106 Stat. 3384.

U.S. Congress. 1994. The Violent Crime Control and Law Enforcement Act. 108 Stat. 1796.

U.S. Congress. 1998a. Protection of Children from Sexual Predators Act. 112 Stat. 2974.

U.S. Congress. 1998b. Child Online Protection Act. 112 Stat. 2681–736.

U.S. Congress. 2000. Victims of Trafficking and Violence Protection Act. 114 Stat. 1464.

U.S. Congress. 2003. The Protect Act. 117 Stat. 650.

U.S. Congress. 2006. The Adam Walsh Child Protection and Safety Act. U.S.C. 42 secs. 16911 et seq.

U.S. Congress. 2008. Tracking Sex Offenders in Indian Country: Trial Implementation of the Adam Walsh Act. Hearing before the Committee on Indian Affairs. Senate Hearing 110–557, 110th Cong., 2d sess. https://www.govinfo.gov/content/pkg/CHRG-110shrg44800/html/CHRG-110shrg44800.htm

U.S. Congress. 2009. Sex Offender Notification and Registration Act (sic) (SORNA): Barriers to Timely Compliance by States. Hearing before the Subcommittee on Crime, Terrorism, and National Security. 111th Cong., 1st sess. (Testimony of Mark Lunsford).

U.S. Congress. 2018. Amy, Vicky, and Andy Child Pornography Victim Assistance Act. Public Law No: 115–299.

U.S. Department of Justice. n.d. Dru Sjodin National Sex Offender Public Website. https://www.smart.gov/pdfs/NSOPWFactSheet.pdf

Vars, Frederick. 2013. "Delineating Sexual Dangerousness." *Houston Law Review* 50 (3): 855–98.

Walshe, Sadhbh. 2012. "The Counterproductive Catch-All of Supposed Sex Offenders." *The Guardian.* https://www.theguardian.com/commentisfree/cifamerica/2012/apr/18/counterproductive-catchall-sex-offenders

Waxman, Olivia. 2016. "The U.S. Is Still Dealing with the Murder of Adam Walsh." *Time.* https://time.com/4437205/adam-walsh-murder/

Weiner, Greg. 2019. *The Political Constitution: The Case against Judicial Supremacy.* Lawrence: University Press of Kansas.

White, Leonard. 1948. *The Federalists: A Study in Administrative History.* New York: Macmillan.

Whittington, Keith. 1999. *Constitutional Construction: Divided Powers and Constitutional Meaning.* Cambridge, MA: Harvard University Press.

Wiseman, Jane, and Chris Lobanov-Rostovsky. n.d. "Chapter 1: Incidence and Prevalence of Sexual Offending." Sex Offender Management Assessment and Planning Initiative. https://www.smart.gov/SOMAPI/sec1/ch1_incidence.html

Yates, Pamela, and Drew A. Kingston. 2016. "The Shortcomings of Sexual Offender Treatment: Are We Doing Something Wrong?" In *Treatment of Sex Offenders: Strengths and Weaknesses in Assessment and Intervention*, edited by D. Richard Laws and William O'Donohue, 261–79. Switzerland: Springer.

CASES

Artway v. Attorney General of New Jersey, 81 F.3d 1235 (1996).

Ashcroft v. American Civil Lziberties Union, 542 U.S. 656 (2004).

Athanasaw v. U.S., 227 U.S. 326 (1913).

Burroughs v. U.S., 290 U.S. 534 (1934).

Caminetti v. U.S., 242 U.S. 470 (1917).

Carr v. U.S., 560 U.S. 438 (2010).

Champion v. Ames, 188 U.S. 321 (1903).

Cosgrove v. Smith, Attorney General of the U.S., 697 F. 2d 1125 (1983).

Doe v. Lee, 132 F.Supp.2d 57 (2001a).

Doe v. Lee, 271 F.3d 38 (2001b).

Doe v. Poritz, 142 N.J. 1 (1995) (unpublished text).

E.B. v. Verniero, 119 F. 3d 1077 (1997).

Garcia v. San Antonio Metropolitan Transit Authority, 469 U.S. 528 (1985).

Gibbons v. Ogden, 22 U.S. 1 (1824).

Gonzales v. Raich, 545 U.S. 1 (2005).

Greenwood v. U.S., 350 U.S. 366 (1956).

Heart of Atlanta Motel, Inc. v. U.S., 379 U.S. 241 (1964).
Hoke v. U.S. 227 U.S. 308 (1913).
Hudson v. Florida, 825 So. 2d 460 (2002).
Katzenbach v. McClung, 379 U.S. 294 (1964).
The License Cases, 48 U.S. 283 (1849).
McCulloch v. Maryland, 17 U.S. 316 (1819).
McKune v. Lile, WL 802194 (2001).
National Federation of Independent Business v. Sebelius, 567 U.S. 519 (2012).
New York v. Parker, 41 N.Y. 2d 21 (1976).
Printz v. U.S., 521 U.S. 898 (1997).
Smith v. Doe I, 538 U.S. 84 (2002).
Tot v. U.S., 319 U.S. 463 (1943).
U.S. v. Abregana, 574 F.Supp. 2d 1123 (2008).
U.S. v. Bass, 404 U.S. 336 (1971).
U.S. v. Carta, 503 F.Supp. 2d 405 (2007).
U.S. v. Carta, 592 F. 3d 34 (2010).
U.S. v. Comstock, 507 F.Supp. 2d 522 (2007).
U.S. v. Comstock, 551 F. 3d 274 (2009a).
U.S. v. Comstock, WL 4247966 (2009b).
U.S. v. Comstock, WL 3727683 (2009c).
U.S. v. Comstock, 560 U.S. 126 (2010).
U.S. v. Darby, 312 U.S. 100 (1941).
U.S. v. Dotterweich, 320 U.S. 277 (1943).
U.S. v. Dowell, F.Supp. 2d (2007) (not reported).
U.S. v. Greenwood, 125 F.Supp. 777 (1954).
U.S. v. Kebodeaux, 133 S.Ct. 2496 (2013).
U.S. v. Lopez, 514 U.S. 549 (1995).
U.S. v. Madera, 474 F.Supp. 2d 1257 (2007).
U.S. v. Morrison, 529 U.S. 598 (2000).
U.S. v. Ramirez, 556 F.2d (1977).
U.S. v. Rodriguez, 581 F.3d 775 (2009).
U.S. v. Shields, 522 F.Supp. 2d 317 (2007).
U.S. v. Tom, 558 F.Supp. 2d 931 (2008).
U.S. v. Tom, 565 F. 3d 497 (2009).
U.S. v. Volungus, 595 F. 3d 1 (2010).

CHAPTER 6

Residency Restrictions and the Limits of Social Science

The purpose of this chapter is to examine residency restrictions through the lens of the social scientific critique of these restrictions. In the next chapter, I examine the problem of residency restrictions by discussing whether they "banish" individuals from their homes and thus constitute punishment that offends the Eighth Amendment.

In this chapter, I address the two most important conflicts facing judges over residency restrictions: one, the scientific uncertainty of the data about dangerousness and recidivism; and two, the democratic implications of laws that restrict where convicted sex offenders can live, which I view as legitimate expressions of the democratic character of local and state politics. I argue in this chapter for judicial deference or minimalism because judicial intervention in this area is fraught with enormous difficulties, such as having judges sort out different and difficult scientific conclusions about recidivism. The application of empirical findings to law and democratic practices clearly has its limits. As J. Harvie Wilkinson has written, "The more volatile the issue, the less justification there often is for constitutionalizing it" (2012, 108).

Criticisms of sex offender legislation embody the following two complaints of normative-based legal understandings: the first is that sex offender laws and regulations are too general. These laws fail to consider the "gender and socioeconomic status" of sex offenders, thus undermining "the principle that sentences should be individualized" (Collins 2018, 4). Second, these laws are counterproductive. Amanda Agan, an economist who has studied sex offender registration, writes (2011, 208; Agan and Prescott 2014):

> I find little evidence to support the effectiveness of sex offender registries, either in practice or in potential. Rates of sex offense do not decline after the introduction of a registry or public access to a registry via the Internet, nor do sex offenders appear to recidivate less when released into states with registries.

Jill Levenson (2005, 3) argues that the "media" propagate three myths about sex offenders and residency restrictions: "1) all sex offenders reoffend; 2) treatment does not work; and 3) the concept of 'stranger danger.' Research does not support these myths, and in fact, there is research to suggest that exclusionary housing policies may ultimately be counterproductive."

These critics' surface argument suggests that all knowledge is the product of ideological constructs, which raises the question whether knowledge of what makes a law good is possible. Meloy, Miller, and Curtis (2008, 220) argue that only empirical findings can lead to "rational" solutions to social problems, which suggests that the only knowledge that is possible is of the functional variety. Knowledge about morality or values, in other words, is not knowledge but speculation. The buried premise of this critique is that sex offender legislation that is not based on empirical findings harms democracy. Social scientific critiques of sex offender legislation criticize the undemocratic aspects of the legislation but lack a defense of democratic practices.

A democratic defense of residency restrictions can be found in Lewis Powell's concurrence in *Keyes v. School District No. 1* (1973, 246), a case about desegregation:

> Neighborhood school systems, neutrally administered, reflect the deeply felt desire of citizens for a sense of community in their public education. . . . Many citizens sense today a decline in the intimacy of our institutions—home, church, and school—which has caused a concomitant decline in the unity and communal spirit of our people. I pass no judgment on this viewpoint, but I do believe that this Court should be wary of compelling in the name of constitutional law what may seem to many a dissolution in the traditional, more personal fabric of their public schools.

To take democracy seriously, a full understanding of residency restrictions has to take into account the intimacies of democratic institutions, the public's concern with safety, and communities' desire to shape a good society. Neighborhoods matter in shaping citizens' behavior and worldview (Sharkey and Faber

2014). While residency restrictions can be onerous, to turn decision-making authority regarding public safety over to the courts (and to the social scientists who study residency restrictions) would be an abdication of constitutional responsibility. Courts should follow the lead of the Iowa supreme court, which declared that no "particular procedure violates [due process] merely because another method may seem fairer or wiser" (Bowers v. Polk County Board of Supervisors 2002, 691).

On one side of the sex offender divide is the argument for the democratic process, for the chance to let the "deliberate sense of the community" determine a community's sense of safety, within the limits of due process. On the other is the argument for the application of the social sciences to lawmaking, which stands for the knowledge of general human behavior that, over time, reveals nuanced facts about individual and group preferences but that can say nothing about the quality of life of the democracy it is trying to understand. The social sciences are the sciences of "empirical reality," yet (for complex philosophical reasons) social scientists cannot say that their models or constructs are "representative of [the] truth about social reality" (Bergner 1981, 3, 136). If the limits of social science reside in its methodological formalism, what does that say about the lack of regard social scientists have for democratic and popular forms of governance, to say nothing of democratic ends these forms are supposed to further? The resolution of this conflict is at the heart of this chapter and the next.

Residency Restrictions: Democracy or Social Science?

Residency restrictions refer to the patchwork of state laws and local ordinances that regulate the places sex offenders can go and the distance sex offenders can live from schools, parks, and other commercial, residential, and public places. Delaware and Florida passed residency restrictions in 1995, following the abduction and murder of Megan Kanka in New Jersey, in 1994. A second wave occurred between 2005 and 2007, "following the highly publicized killings of Jessica Lunsford (age 9) and Sarah Lunde (age 13), in unrelated events by two different convicted sex offenders." By 2008, thirty states had residency restrictions (Meloy, Miller, and Curtis 2008, 210, 214–15). By and large, social scientists dismiss these laws as value laden, regarding them as "public policy narratives" that are the products of "instinctual and visceral response[s]" that encourage political and legal extremism (Harris and Socia 2014, 2, 6; Ellman and Ellman 2015, 496). Meloy, Miller, and Curtis (2008, 219, 222) believe that residency restrictions have a "deleterious impact on factors statistically predictive of criminal desistance." Equating social science data with democratic dogma, they call upon legislators to halt the passage of these laws "until empirical evidence suggests practices are associated with a decrease in or at least a null effect on sexual recidivism." Meloy, Miller, and Curtis argue that "singular legislative 'solutions' to complex social problems should be avoided."

The main thrust of the criticism against legislative "solutions" is that they fail to understand how the social scientific evidence supports greater individual rights. According to Jacqueline Berenson and Paul Appelbaum (2011, 236; italics in original):

> The theoretical basis for residence restrictions can be explained in terms of the general criminological principle of *distance decay*, i.e., that on average criminals commit their crimes with decreasing frequency the greater the distance from their place of residence. Applied to sexual offenses, this theory suggests that children in closer proximity to an offender's home are more likely to be chosen as victims. . . . Thus, the goal of sex offender residence restrictions is to distance offenders from potential victims by limiting access to and contact with children.

The problem, as Berenson and Appelbaum and countless others point out, is that the underlying legislative aim of residency restrictions is at odds with the data's conclusions.

The data show, for example, that most sexual offenses occur between family relations and among acquaintances. Residency restrictions are useless when the offender lives with or knows the victim. Moreover, residency restrictions can create collateral consequences, such as homelessness and despair, increase shame, and exacerbate other psychological disorders, all of which can increase violence among those susceptible to that impulse. Paul Zandbergen, Jill Levenson, and Timothy Hart (2010, 485) have summarized research that has found that among registered sex offenders

> in Oklahoma and Kansas, 54% reported that a housing restriction law forced them to relocate. In Indiana, 26% of sex offenders surveyed said that they were unable to return to their homes after incarceration, 37% were not allowed to

> live with family members, and nearly a third experienced a landlord's refusal to rent to them or to renew a lease.

Residency restrictions can also harm urban life. A Florida Sexual Offender and Sexual Predator Residence Task Force (Broward County, Florida 2009, 6) found that "[c]lustering of sexual offenders may lower property values and unfairly burdens the unincorporated areas of Broward County." A PEW study revealed that 82 percent of all sex offenders in Milwaukee county live in the city of Milwaukee, creating "a dumping ground" (Fifield 2016; Carpenter 2016) for sex offenders. Other consequences of residency restrictions include increasing the burdens on police, the risk of vigilantism, the possibility of arbitrary enforcement across counties (Doe I v. Marshall 2019), and "an increase in the number of sex offenders who have stopped registering with local authorities and gone missing" (Human Rights Watch 2013, 48).

In 2015, *The New York Times* criticized residency restrictions in an editorial entitled, "Pointless Banishment of Sex Offenders."

> It's a chilling image: the sex predator skulking in the shadows of a swing set, waiting to snatch a vulnerable child.
>
> Over the past two decades, that scenario has led to a wave of laws around the country restricting where people convicted of sex offenses may live—in many cases, no closer than 2,500 feet from schools, playgrounds, parks or other areas where children gather. In some places, these "predator-free zones" put an entire town or county off limits, sometimes for life, even for those whose offenses had nothing to do with children. (New York Times 2015)

The *Times* viewed these laws as vague, overbroad, and ill informed. The editorial turned to the facts of residency requirements, which show that residency restrictions do not prevent sex offenders from harming those closest to them; the editorial was silent about the values expressed by local communities in relying upon residency restrictions.

> Protecting children from sexual abuse is, of course, a paramount concern. But there is not a single piece of evidence that these laws actually do that. For one thing, the vast majority of child sexual abuse is committed not by strangers but by acquaintances or relatives. And residency laws drive tens of thousands

> of people to the fringes of society, forcing them to live in motels, out of cars or under bridges. The laws apply to many and sometimes all sex offenders, regardless of whether they were convicted for molesting a child or for public urination. (New York Times 2015)

One could imagine the *Times* speaking directly to state legislators to address this issue. Majority rule has its limits, the *Times* could have said, and we ask legislators to think hard about these errors of law and passion. But the editorial did not mention legislatures. Instead the editorial referred to three state courts that have found these laws unconstitutional and suggested that the Supreme Court may do so as well. (It has not.) If the *Times* had legislators in mind, it was only to remind them that judges are their superior, and above judges are scientific findings.

> It is understandable to want to do everything possible to protect children from being abused. But not all people who have been convicted of sex offenses pose a risk to children, if they pose any risk at all. Blanket residency-restriction laws disregard that reality—and the merits of an individualized approach to risk assessment—in favor of a comforting mirage of safety. (New York Times 2015)

As the *Times* believes that residency restrictions are balm for the public, the turn to an "individualized approach to risk assessment" is nothing more than a call for courts to resolve this political issue scientifically.

This is precisely what has happened. In *Doe v. Cooper* (2016), the fourth circuit court of appeals struck down a North Carolina residency restriction that made it

> unlawful for any registered offender whose registration follows a conviction for a violent sex offense or any offense where the victim was younger than sixteen at the time of the offense ("restricted sex offenders") to "knowingly be" at any of the following locations:
>
> (1) On the premises of any place intended primarily for the use, care, or supervision of minors, including, but not limited to, schools, children's museums, child care centers, nurseries, and playgrounds.
> (2) Within 300 feet of any location intended primarily for the use, care, or supervision of minors when the place is located on premises that are not intended primarily for the use, care, or supervision of minors,

including, but not limited to, places described in subdivision (1) . . . that are located in malls, shopping centers, or other property open to the general public.

(3) At any place where minors gather for regularly scheduled educational, recreational, or social programs. (2016, 838)

The court of appeals took issue with North Carolina's contention that the prohibition against sex offenders knowingly being at particular locations "where minors gather" was a legitimate constitutional prohibition. The court of appeals held that the law could not differentiate between a gathering of only minors and adults and minors. Courts frown upon this kind of legislative ambiguity, as they pose problems for both law enforcement and individual rights. The court of appeals also found that the law interfered with the First Amendment rights of individuals. John Does 1, 4, and 5 claimed that the restriction interfered with religious practices, as well as access to "public streets, parks, and other public facilities" (Doe v. Cooper 2016, 845).

Doe v. Cooper is a good case to introduce the problem of residency restrictions because (1) it involves a conflict between the associational rights of a group of convicted sex offenders and the state's understanding of its regulatory power over a dangerous subset of the population; (2) it pits the state's interest in public safety against rights claims involving nondangerous quotidian functions, such as church going; (3) it creates a clear distinction between facts and values, articulating a preference for facts derived from social science over community values; and (4) it draws attention to the potentially sweeping aspects of laws of this kind and thus to the need for courts to scrutinize such legislation.

The court of appeals took issue with the state's argument that sex offenders are dangerous because the state said they are dangerous. The court of appeals noted that the district court had asked the state to provide the court with evidence that offenders of nonminors need to be prevented from areas where minors congregate, but the state provided the court with no expert witnesses. According to the court of appeals, this was insufficient from a scientific point of view.

> The State tries to overcome its lack of data, social science or scientific research, legislative findings, or other empirical evidence with a renewed appeal to anecdotal case law, as well as to "logic and common sense." But neither anecdote, common sense, nor logic, in a vacuum, is sufficient to carry the State's burden of proof. Thus, while the State's argument *may be conceptually plausible,*

> it presented no evidence or data to substantiate it before the district court. . . . *Without empirical data or other similar credible evidence, it is not possible to tell whether subsection (a)(2)—and specifically its application to offenders with only adult victims—responds at all to the State's legitimate interest in protecting minors from sexual assault.* (Doe v. Cooper 2016, 846–47; italics added)

This is a remarkable commentary on the requirements for the assessment of a law's constitutionality. It is one thing to "characterize legal rules as mathematically derived" (Barzun 2004, 1054) in an attempt to claim that law is a science, that it is empirical, not normative, and based on "certainty and predictability" (Cook 2012, 23). It is another to say that a law has no validity outside of data that reinforce a judge's legislative preferences. Law as a science is rule-bound and can be a conservative idea. Law as a science used to mean, among other things, the protection of precedent. The scientific critique of law is that rather than focusing on facts, "[c]ourts 'feel,' 'sense' or by some process of intuition or imagination reach their conclusions. . . . The point is that the rationalization does not produce the result, the result produces the rationalization" (Goble 1934, 297, 305–6). In *Doe v. Cooper*, we have both critiques rolled into one. The judge requires the law to depend upon scientific facts, but there is no conserving function. A judge determined what scientific conclusions determine the law's meaning. The law is paradoxically scientific and sensual, requiring the judge to reject common sense—or public opinion, or the deliberations of a state legislature—because it is not verifiable (Doe v. Cooper 2016, 847). The fact that it is common makes it suspect scientifically (Bergner 1981, 127). Unfortunately, the court of appeals (1) never defined conceptual plausibility; (2) never said what the content of the scientific evidence has to be to overcome the law's conceptual plausibility problems; and (3) came close to arguing that laws that do not pass the bar of scientific evidence are not laws at all.

The idea that resorting to scientific (or social scientific) data to render legislation constitutional is problematic for four reasons, the first being the general idea that the "social sciences conduct an undemocratic inquiry into society. Democracy is an unscientific way of governing it" (Basbøll 2016). The complexity and messiness of democracy—that decision-making relies on moral, psychological, historical, and comparative analyses formed by elites and ordinary citizens, over time, and within different configurations of majorities and minorities—makes it a difficult object of study. To isolate one part of a democratic practice and assume it is fundamental to the nature or fabric of democratic practices not only misses the point about democratic practices, it requires that judges become neopositivists who see "no *logical* difference between explanations in the natural and cultural sciences" (Ringer 1997, 3; italics in original). When all behavior is thought to be determined, because it is the product of ideological constructions masquerading as knowledge, there is no need for legislators, and judges will have cleared a path for themselves to say what is constitutional and what is not.

Second, we do no service to the legislative process if we expect judges to rely on scientific data and disregard competing factors that clearly influence both legislation and peoples' attitudes about politics, such as the self-interest of individuals and parties and their ideas about the public interest. One problem confronting judges in scientific cases is which and whose data to use. There is a big difference between clinical assessments and actuarial assessments of dangerousness. Clinical assessments are much less likely to be respected, given the fallibility of judgment and what is called "treatment bias" (Brooks 2010, 274). But actuarial assessment tools, such as the Psychopathy Checklist Revised (PCL-R), are hardly models of accuracy (R. v. Aziga 2011; Jalava, Griffiths, and Maraun 2015, 121; Wisconsin v. Loomis 2016; Martens 2008).

The difference between what science requires and what the law demands is science's ability to predict future behavior. Yet studies show that juries "are unable to perform with any degree of accuracy the violence prediction task assigned to them by legislatures and the courts" (Cunningham et al. 2011, 20). The constitutional law scholar David O'Brien has summed up the problem of courts trying to resolve policy disputes involving scientific data analysis. They pose, he writes (O'Brien 1987, 1–2):

> a trilemma in the regulation of risk. That is, policymakers must respond in ways that (1) satisfy demands for a scientific basis for regulation; while (2) arriving at politically responsive and acceptable policies; and at the same time (3) guaranteeing some measure of procedural fairness for those contesting the scientific and normative basis for regulations.

If the "estimation or assessment of risk is itself political" (O'Brien 1987, 7), then judges have to understand judicial review's purpose to mean that courts have to connect constitutional principles to legislation seemingly lacking such facts. Judges cannot turn social scientific facts into constitutional trump cards to encourage efficiency in lawmaking. It is detrimental to democratic practice and theory to assume that judges have greater insight into the progress of decency or fairness and that legislators lack this insight because they are beholden to public opinion. It is unscientific to assume that judges can assess risk better than legislators. And it is hubristic to say that courts alone should be the engines of social change (Rosenberg 1991).

Third, the Supreme Court has never adopted a requirement that data are essential to the establishment of a law's constitutionality, or that a law's effectiveness is superior to its constitutionality. Consider *U.S. v. Lopez* (1995), in which the Supreme Court rejected congressional testimony about the relationship between the regulation of guns near schools and the purpose of the commerce clause because of an absence of "legislative findings" (i.e., "facts") that supported Congress's general idea (i.e., "values") that there is a relationship between guns near public schools and public safety. When Congress added "findings" about violence against women to a law that allowed women to seek civil damages in federal courts when confronted by violence, the Court, in *U.S. v. Morrison* (2000), struck down that legislation, too, holding (1) that Congress is not required to supply findings; but also that (2) when it does, the findings cannot be contrary to the Court's commerce jurisprudence (U.S. v. Lopez 1995, 563; U.S. v. Morrison 2000, 614).

Neither *Lopez* nor *Morrison* solves the problem of what data to use or how the judiciary should interpret the data Congress assembles. A charitable interpretation of *Lopez* and *Morrison* is that constitutional principles of limited government that emanate from Article I, section 8 trump the factfinding that tries to solve a social problem. A less charitable interpretation is that these are instances of rank activism. *Morrison* shows the difficulty courts have separating constitutional principles from what a majority of justices do not want Congress to do. In *Gonzales v. Raich* (2005), the Court reversed course and held that the commerce clause allows Congress to regulate intrastate activities that have an effect on interstate commerce. More important, for our purposes, the Court in *Raich* noted that the absence of particularized findings does not call into question Congress' authority to legislate (2005, 21).

It cannot be said that either behavioralists or quantitative analysts have solved the core questions of political science regarding governance. Indeed, the Court in its commerce clause jurisprudence has exposed the weakness of applying social science to jurisprudence because it cannot tell us precisely what the law needs to tell us: what is the right way to live, what are the limits of violence against women, and how far from schools must drug-dealing occur. Only democratic practices can answer these questions.

Fourth, in the same way that "a constitution is not intended to embody a particular economic theory, whether of paternalism and the organic relation of the citizen to the State or of *laissez faire*" (Lochner v. New York 1905, 75), nor should constitutional law be made dependent upon the findings of social scientists to determine who is dangerous, for not just the methodologies of law and social science differ, their application is different as well (Winch 1990, 93; Berns 1963). Courts make determinations about a law's constitutionality on a host of reasons, and not all of them on whether the law is scientifically valid or on what effect scientific evidence would have on political practice.

The assumption of the court of appeals in *Doe v. Cooper* and *The New York Times* editorial on sex offending is that the right assemblage of facts leads to the right conclusion about the value of a law. The assumption is that "right in a scientific sense" (Kendall 1971, 100) means right in a democratic sense. Neither lawmaking nor democracy work that way. A certain degree of "discretion, equity, and flexibility" needs to be factored into "the legal system" (McCleskey v. Kemp 1987, 311) because laws deal with actual human beings in their self-interested pursuit of happiness, safety, and the common good, while social science methods rely on statistical analyses that can only abstract from experience or opinion something less than pure knowledge (Weber 1949, 15). The focus on facts to determine policy values means "the legal standard cannot be the standard" (Berns 1963, 203) by which law is judged. Things outside of law determine a law's meaning. Law, according to this thesis, is an empty vessel that must be joined to sociology or psychology (especially to their data-collecting, quantitative aspects) to gain validity. But then law is no longer law and is no longer democratic. "Society" replaces "law" without regard for the interconnectedness of the term. By disconnecting law from society, empiricists strip consent, once the backbone of democratic lawmaking, of its legitimacy. Not wisdom or principle but facts reduced to data points replace consent. If the court of appeals in *Doe v. Cooper* is right and "conceptual plausibility" can no longer be the ground upon which laws are passed, then we must conclude that only social scientists can save us from ourselves.

Residency Restrictions, Social Science, and Due Process

Residency restrictions first came into focus as a constitutional question with the registration and notification requirements required under New Jersey's Megan's Law.[1] In *Doe v. Poritz* (1995), the New Jersey supreme court upheld the nation's first Megan's Law, which required offenders to register with their local police departments. Registration can be quite burdensome. In Washington State:

> If [Elbert] Williamson moves within the same county, he must notify the county sheriff in writing 14 days before moving. If he moves to a new county, he must notify the new sheriff 14 days before moving and must register within 24 hours of moving. If he moves out of Washington, he must notify the county sheriff in Washington within 10 days of the move. If Williamson attends an institution of higher education, he must notify the sheriff of his residence of his intent to attend that institution, and the sheriff must notify the institution's department of public safety.
>
> Failing to register within the time required by law is either a felony or a gross misdemeanor, depending on the nature of the underlying conviction. Finally, if Williamson desires to change his name in the future, he must follow the same procedures used for changing his address. (Williamson v. Gregoire 1998, 1181)

The New Jersey registration law did not initially contain a residency restriction, but it did require that any organization that cares for women or children and is "likely to encounter" (E.B. v. Verniero 1997, 1085) a tier 2 or tier 3 sex offender must be notified of the sex offender's presence. The New Jersey supreme court understood this restriction to include "schools and other institutions in adjacent municipalities depending upon their distance from the offender's residence, place of work, or school." The law prevented these organizations from disseminating such information (Doe v. Poritz 1995, 36).

In 2005, the New Jersey township of Lower (also known as Lower Township) passed an ordinance prohibiting "registered sex offenders from residing or loitering within 500 feet of any school, park, playground, recreation area, or day care facility or within 25 feet of a school bus stop located in Lower Township . . . or adjacent municipalities" (Elwell and Elwell v. Township of Lower 2006, 1). In 2008, there were at least one hundred municipalities throughout New Jersey with such laws (G.H. v. Township of Galloway 2008, 399). Restrictions vary with each municipality (some municipalities exclude tier 1 offenders from residency restrictions, others do not). Lower Township defines a sex offender as anyone required to register under Megan's Law.

Steven Elwell, a registered tier 1 sex offender (for aggravated sexual assault) in New Jersey, made four complaints against the ordinance, after he, his wife, and their two children moved to Lower Township:

> (1) The Ordinance is preempted by state law; (2) it deprives plaintiffs of substantive due process under the New Jersey Constitution; (3) it violates the *ex post facto* and double jeopardy clauses of the New Jersey Constitution; and (4) the Ordinance is *ultra vires* and unconstitutionally vague. (Elwell and Elwell v. Township of Lower 2006, 1)

According to the town council, the purpose of the law is "'to protect and insure the health, safety and welfare of children within the Township and not to penalize registered sex offenders'" (Elwell and Elwell v. Township of Lower 2006, 2). Elwell, by contrast, charged that the ordinance unduly burdened his daily activities, such as taking his children to school. It is possible that the state could find Elwell in violation of the ordinance if he were to buy a house within an approved buffer zone or a new bus stop were to appear twenty-five feet from his new home. In that case, he would be forced to move at a moment's notice. Moreover, he argued that Megan's Law precludes municipalities from passing legislation that either conflicts with, or is preempted by, the provisions of Megan's Law. Preemption means that a municipality is prevented from "exercising a police power 'when the Legislature has restricted such an exercise by preempting the area of regulation'" (New York v. Diack 2015, 679). Elwell suggested that Megan's Law requires uniform regulations for sex offenders at the state level and demonstrates the unconstitutional status of residency restrictions at the local level.

Residency restrictions vary by state. As a general rule, "a local government's police power is not absolute" (New York v. Diack 2015, 676; Monjeau 2011). New Jersey's residency restriction only applies to parolees and probationers (McKinstry 2012). Some ordinances prohibit sex offenders from living or being near any institution that deals with children from 500 to 2,500 feet. Some include bus stops, others do not. Some ban sex offenders from all parks within a city's limits. And some states allow localities broad public safety powers. In a New York residency challenge on the subject of preemption, the supreme court held that "local governments are better situated to promote the welfare of their citizens by enacting legislation restricting the residency of sex offenders who are no longer on parole, probation, subject to a conditional discharge or seeking public assistance" (New York v. Diack 2013, 39). New York's highest court, the court of appeals, however, overturned that decision, noting that "[l]ocal residency restriction laws also hinder statewide uniformity concerning sex offender placement" (New York v. Diack 2015, 686). The conflict between state law and local ordinance over safety concerns highlights the constitutional and personal challenges of residency restrictions in a federal republic.

In *Elwell*, the New Jersey superior court found the ordinance in violation of the state constitution on all the challenged grounds. The court found that the ordinance made no distinction regarding the tiered status of sex offenders because it did not "assess the actual risk posed by a particular offender" (Elwell and Elwell v. Township of Lower 2006, 15; Tewksbury and Mustaine 2013). Although the New Jersey supreme court had held, in *Doe v. Poritz*, that Megan's Law is not a criminal statute, the superior court in *Elwell* found Lower Township's ordinance criminal, and thus in violation of the ban on ex post facto legislation (Bains 2007, 485).

> Its sole purpose is deterrence, to keep sex offenders away from certain areas of the Township. It limits residency and movement of all Megan's Law registrants without distinction as to the sex offender's tier ranking, nature of offense, or whether the offender's victim was an adult or a minor. (Elwell and Elwell v. Township of Lower 2006, 17)

The court also found the ordinance, because of its criminal status, to be in violation of the prohibition against double jeopardy, although the court did not specifically address this issue. Finally, the court ruled that the law was vague.

> Vagueness "is essentially a procedural due process concept grounded in notions of fair play." . . . In interpreting words used in a statute, "the basic rule is that the statutory language should be given its ordinary meaning absent specific intent to the contrary." When examining statutory language for vagueness, the test is whether a person of average intelligence comprehends the meaning of the words. (In the Matter of the Commitment of W.Z. 2001, 112–13)

The narrow tailoring of a law provides protection against vagueness (Papachristou v. Jacksonville 1972; Winters v. New York 1948, 524). Lower Township's "[o]rdinance does not provide clear notice to a sex offender as to what behavior is permitted and what behavior is prohibited" (Elwell and Elwell v. Township of Lower 2006, 19).

In *G.H. v. Township of Galloway* (2008), the New Jersey superior court again struck down a local sex offender ordinance. The court consolidated two cases from two different townships. One involved a college student, convicted of a sex offense during his youth, in Galloway Township, who could not live in a college dormitory. The other involved two impoverished young adults who could not live in a motel, in Cherry Hill Township.

Finding that "The Cherry Hill ordinance prohibits CSOs [convicted sex offenders] from residing in virtually the entire township [and the] Galloway ordinance bans CSOs from living in about two-thirds of Galloway Township" (G.H. v. Township of Galloway 2008, 406–7), the court held that state law preempts the two ordinances. The ordinances are not merely "zoning regulations," which would fall within the constitutional province of municipalities, provided the regulation is "designed to serve a substantial governmental interest" (Renton v. Playtime Theatres 1986, 47). The New Jersey superior court stressed, for example, that a zoning regulation that prohibited an adult theater from operating within so many feet of a school or church is within a municipality's jurisdiction because it is governed by land-use regulations (although this is not the only reason). Such regulations are necessary for municipalities to arrange business districts and thus do not interfere with the First Amendment (Giorkaris 1987; Paris Adult Theater I v. Slaton 1972; Young v. American Mini Theatres 1976; Schad v. Mt. Ephraim 1981). As Virginia Giokaris (1987, 277) has noted, "Courts have generally adopted a deferential attitude toward zoning ordinances." Giokaris is referring to the regulation of pornography and obscenity, not to sex offenders. In turning to regulations that touch upon family life, the Court has raised the bar for what a local or state government can rightfully do. (I discuss this in the next chapter.) Thus Giokaris (1987, 277–78) writes that "when the exercise of a fundamental right is burdened by a zoning ordinance, the ordinance will be strictly scrutinized."

Residency restrictions, however, do not fall under the Court's strict scrutiny analysis, and it strains constitutional logic to suggest that a convicted sex offender, even one without an interest in minors, has a fundamental right to visit a park. To be sure, residency restrictions can involve questions relating to so-called liberty interests, such as maintaining family relationships and engaging in other First Amendment practices. But such interests are clearly incidental to the more necessary regulation over public safety. In any case, the superior court in *Galloway* held that the goal of Megan's Law is rehabilitation, and residency restrictions are not commercial zoning regulations because residency restrictions interfere with the state's stated intention to rehabilitate sex offenders. Total exclusion of a class of persons (such as in Galloway Township) or near exclusion (such as in Cherry Hill Township) serves no rehabilitative goals, the court said. Moreover, local residency regulations can fail to take into consideration the sudden need for bus stops or day-care centers, and they can exclude too many offenders (e.g., sex offenders who do not violate minors) (Bains 2007; Grubesic, Murray, and Mack 2011; Socia et al. 2014). For this reason, the court held that Megan's Law preempts local residency ordinances.

In November 2006, California voters passed Proposition 83, formally called "The Sexual Predator Punishment and Control Act: Jessica's Law," named after Jessica Lunsford, a nine-year-old Florida native who was raped and murdered by a convicted sex offender in 2005. Proposition 83 prohibits probation, mandates "longer prison terms," eliminates "early release credits," and extends "the period of parole." It imposes "compulsory lifetime GPS monitoring on persons required to register as sex offenders because of where they were imprisoned" and expands "the reach of the laws governing the civil commitment of sexually violent predators." It also limits "the rights of parolee sex offender registrants, while on parole, to live with other registered sex offenders" (California v. Mosley 2015, 1063, 1048). Finally, the law includes a provision prohibiting paroled sex offenders from living within 2,000 feet of "any public or private school, or park where children regularly gather" (In re Taylor 2015, 1023; D'Orazio et al. 2009).

Soon after the passage of Proposition 83, the California Department of Corrections and Rehabilitation (CDCR) began to enforce the law against paroled sex offenders living in San Diego. Four sex offenders who were not compliant with residency requirements filed suit. William Taylor suffers from "throat cancer, AIDS, and diabetes. He has had a heart attack and several strokes, suffers from chronic depression and paranoid schizophrenia, and is addicted to cocaine." After being admitted to a drug clinic, Taylor was told that the clinic was not compliant with the residency restriction. A stay in the hospital proved his downfall, as he was unable to establish his residency there. He subsequently moved into a compliant hotel. Jeffrey Glynn's residence was also not compliant, so he and his wife moved into a van. Subsequently, he was found to be living at a noncompliant address. Julie Briley, convicted of "lewd and lascivious" acts against her daughter, was directed by her parole officer to live in an alley, which she did for one and a half years. Briley suffers the effects of "hepatitis C, high blood pressure, thyroid problems and osteoarthritis that is aggravated by exposure to cold temperatures." At the time of the suit, she was living in a recreational vehicle in a noncompliant part of San Diego. Finally, Stephen Todd, a juvenile offender of other juveniles (but an adult at the time of the suit), with a long history of criminal activity, "suffers from bipolar disorder, is diabetic and subject to seizures, is a recovering heroin addict, and has been addicted to methamphetamine for 18 years." Unable to find compliant housing, a parole agent suggested that Todd live "in the riverbed of the San Diego river" (In re Taylor 2015, 1026–29).

The trial court held that the mandatory residency restriction was unconstitutional as applied (In re Taylor 2015, 1039; Kreit 2010). The decision was affirmed on appeal, and the California supreme court affirmed, holding that residency restrictions increase homelessness, hinder medical treatment, and interfere with rehabilitation strategies. According to the supreme court, residency restrictions infringe upon sex offenders' "liberty and privacy interests, however limited, while bearing no rational relationship to advancing the state's legitimate goal of protecting children from sexual predators" (In re Taylor 2015, 1023).

While California, New Jersey, and other courts (Mann v. Georgia Department of Corrections 2007, 755; Doe v. Baker 2006; West 2007, 241 n. 10) have found state and local residency restrictions punitive, vague, and unconstitutional, other courts have not. In 2003, Arkansas "enacted a residency restriction for Level 3 'high risk' offenders and Level 4 'sexually violent predators.' Offenders in these classes are not permitted 'to reside within two thousand feet (2,000') of the property on which any public or private elementary or secondary school or daycare facility is located'" (Weems v. Little Rock Police Department 2006, 1013). The Arkansas legislature determined that "'sex offenders pose a high risk of reoffending after release from custody,' [and] that 'protecting the public from sex offenders is a primary governmental interest'" (Weems v. Little Rock Police Department 2006, 1012).

In *Weems v. Little Rock Police Department* (2006), the eighth circuit court of appeals rejected a claim by a level 3 registered sex offender that he had "a constitutional right 'to reside in a certain place, i.e., with family members.'" As disruptive as the Arkansas law was, the court reasoned "that because the statute did not 'operate directly on the family relationship,' the residency restriction did 'not infringe upon a constitutional liberty interest relating to matters of marriage and family in a fashion that requires heightened scrutiny'" (Weems v.

Little Rock Police Department 2006, 1015). In *Illinois v. Leroy* (2005), the Illinois supreme court upheld Illinois's 500-foot restriction. Leroy argued that the law "effectively renders him homeless" because the house was his mother's and that he had lived with his mother all of his life. The supreme court disagreed, holding that the law "does not prevent the defendant from living with his mother; rather, it merely prevents him from living with her at her present location, because that location is within 500 feet of a school." Indeed, other states, the Illinois supreme court noted, have upheld more extensive restrictions.

> Although it is not clear from the record how the distance of 500 feet was decided upon, we believe that 500 feet is a reasonable distance. We note that among the 13 states that have enacted some form of residency restriction applicable to sex offenders, the 500-foot restriction of subsection (b–5) is the least restrictive in geographical terms. (Illinois v. Leroy 2005, 534–35)

Why do some courts uphold these regulations and others do not? In the cases that have struck down residency restrictions, courts have held the laws insufficiently respectful of the due process rights convicted sex offenders have, such as a right to individualized assessment of their dangerousness. Courts have also found due process violations because the laws have prevented released convicts from living in places of their choice (Berlin v. Evans 2011; Williams v. Department of Corrections 2014). Courts have also focused on the harm done to the psychological status of the individuals involved, finding that they can suffer from "isolation, disempowerment, shame, depression, anxiety, and a disconnection from social supports" (Human Rights Watch 2007, 62; Levenson and Hern 2007; Millard v. Rankin 2017). They have also acknowledged the burdens the law has created through unintended consequences, such as increased homelessness (In re Taylor 2015; California Sex Offender Management Board 2011; Williams v. Department of Corrections 2016; Vann v. Alabama 2013). And they have suggested that these restrictions involve fundamental rights, such as privacy and intrastate travel (Iowa v. Williams 2001) (which I discuss in the next chapter).

In the cases that have upheld restrictions, we find a greater focus on procedure and deference to legislative initiatives. These courts have taken a more expansive view of state and local legislative power and a dimmer view of the claim that the rights involved are fundamental. Judges in these cases have also stressed the need to balance rights claims against public safety concerns. And while the courts in these cases have not disregarded the enormous burdens imposed by residency restrictions, they have relied on the fact that each defendant had options to live other than where he or she preferred (Williams v. Department of Corrections 2014). These courts have also denied categorically that there is a right to live where one wants.

There is no doubt that residency restrictions create problems without clear judicial solutions. The Illinois supreme court upheld a 500-foot restriction, but that implies that a longer distance may prove constitutionally questionable, though under what state and federal constitutional provisions remains an open question. If the California supreme court ruled that a 2,000-foot restriction was too burdensome, why did the Iowa supreme court rule otherwise on a 2,000-foot restriction?

In *Iowa v. Seering* (2005), the Iowa supreme court heard a challenge to Iowa's residency restriction of 2,000 feet. Seering claimed a fundamental right "to the privacy and freedom of association in one's family." The statute, he asserted, infringed on "the ability to live with spouses and the right to carry on a daily routine and make basic determinations about child care" (Iowa v. Seering 2005, 662–63).

For the court, however, "The crux of Seering's constitutional claims is an alleged violation of a private interest in freedom of choice in residence. While this is an important interest, it is not a fundamental one." The focus of this chapter is on the procedural problems raised by residency restrictions. In the next chapter, I will address the fundamental issues involved in residency restrictions. For now, it is worth emphasizing that the Iowa supreme court believed that the 2,000-foot restriction did not invade any fundamental right. So the court held: "Although additional testimony revealed that the two-thousand-foot restriction was not necessarily a perfect protection against this threat, perfection is not necessary to meet the rational basis standard" (Iowa v. Seering 2005, 665–66).

After a federal district court ruled Iowa's 2,000-foot restriction unconstitutional, the court of appeals, in *Doe v. Miller* (2005), reversed. *Miller* is the first federal case to uphold residency restrictions. *Miller* involved eighteen plaintiffs, all under the guise of John Doe, contending that Iowa's residency restriction deprived them of due process "because some cities in Iowa are unable to provide sex offenders with information about the location of all schools and registered child care facilities, and because it is difficult to measure the restricted areas, which are measured 'as the crow flies' from a school or child care facility."

The Does also argued that the residency restriction infringed on the fundamental right "to travel and to 'privately choose how they want to conduct their family affairs'" (Doe v. Miller 2005, 708, 706–7).

The twin problem of measuring distances and the law's lack of a classification of individual dangerousness is a problem of procedural due process. On the matter of procedural due process, the court of appeals in *Miller* held that Iowa's residency restriction "applies to all offenders who have been convicted of certain crimes against minors, regardless of what estimates of future dangerousness might be proved in individualized hearings" (Doe v. Miller 2005, 709). What the Does want is for the court of appeals to create a substantive rule that says that a law that ignores an individual's level of dangerousness violates due process because it is not based on scientific evidence about an individual's past, present, and future dangerousness (Doe v. Miller 2005, 721; Connecticut Department of Public Safety v. Doe 2003). The charge is that the failure to take into account levels of dangerousness implicates due process because it denies each John Doe an opportunity to be heard. The Does complain that a law regulating residency must take into consideration the different tiers of dangerousness outlined by psychological research, which show that sex offenders are not a homogeneous group. The Does' due process claim, then, is a request that courts turn to scientific data in an effort to differentiate individual sex offenders. Other petitioners have made similar claims.

In *Indiana v. Pollard* (2009, 1153), for example, the Indiana supreme court struck down an Indiana residency restriction as applied to Pollard, holding that the law was punitive insofar as it disregarded "the seriousness of the crime, the relationship between the victim and the offender, or an initial determination of the risk of re-offending." In *Kentucky v. Baker* (2009, 446), the Kentucky supreme court struck down a 1,000-foot restriction in part because the law did not require an individual assessment of dangerousness. The Kentucky court held the law to be punitive in effect even though its intent was not punitive. And in *Doe v. Otte*, a 2001 case involving an Alaska registration, notification, and residency restriction law, the ninth circuit court of appeals held the law to violate the ex post facto provision of the Constitution. "The Ex Post Facto Clause expresses our commitment to constrain the manner in which legislatures can address intense fears of the type evoked by the return to the community of convicted sex offenders" (Doe v. Otte 2001, 836; Doe v. Pataki 1997, 1272; Weaver v. Graham 1981).

On the question of residency restrictions, dangerousness, and risk, the court of appeals in *Doe v. Otte* declared (2001, 848): "With only one exception, every sex offender registration and notification law that has been upheld by a federal Court of Appeals has tailored the provisions of the statute to the risk posed by the offender." The ruling in *Otte* focused on ex post facto problems, so it did not deal extensively with the problem of due process and classification of risk and dangerousness. But holding that the Alaska statute was "exceedingly broad"—a reference, in part, to the law's lack of a classification scheme—the court of appeals declared the law punitive in effect. Among some federal and state courts, to treat one John Doe as all John Does violates due process; stated otherwise, the imposition of equal treatment violates individual fairness.

In *Smith v. Doe* (2002) (which overturned the court of appeals' decision in *Doe v. Otte*), the Supreme Court held that a "State's determination to legislate with respect to convicted sex offenders as a class, rather than require individual determination of their dangerousness, does not make the statute a punishment." Addressing the issue of ex post facto, the Court held that that clause does not prevent a state from "making reasonable categorical judgments that conviction of specified crimes should entail particular regulatory consequences" (Smith v. Doe 2002, 104, 103). Fairness, the Supreme Court suggests, is not the equivalent of due process. In rejecting the Does' claims, the Court upheld the idea that due process of law is the imposition of both fairness and equality; references to scientific data were noticeably missing.

The charge of a denial of a right to be heard, which is tied to the law's omission of individual levels of dangerousness, is an important one, particularly as some individuals can show, through statistical analyses and classification schemes that rank dangerousness, that they are either not dangerous or less dangerous than other sex offenders. To rule in their favor would demonstrate the importance and necessity of social science data informing legal analyses, while diluting deliberative principles of legislation focused on public safety. In *Connecticut Department of Public Safety v. Doe* (2003), the Supreme Court was confronted with a sex offender registry law that required all convicted sex offenders, regardless of their dangerousness levels, to register. When the case was in the court of appeals, that court held that:

> the plaintiff and the members of the due process class are entitled to the opportunity to have a hearing consistent with due process principles to determine

> whether or not they are particularly likely to be currently dangerous before being labeled as such by their inclusion in a publicly disseminated registry. (Doe v. Lee 2001, 62)

When that case reached the Supreme Court, it held:

> The fact that respondent seeks to prove that he is not currently dangerous is of no consequence under Connecticut's Megan's Law. As the DPS Website explains, the law's requirements turn on an offender's conviction alone. (Connecticut Department of Public Safety v. Doe 2003, 7)

Although *Connecticut Department of Public Safety* was not a case about residency restrictions, its logic could have an effect on any case involving residency restrictions and social science data that might come to the high court.

A law that is facially neutral is constitutional unless it can be shown that the provisions of the law conflict with other constitutional provisions or values (Yick Wo v. Hopkins 1886; Lukumi Babalu Aye v. Hileah 1993). The Does in *Miller* could not refute the facially neutral content of the law for two reasons: (1) they were not a protected class; and (2) the law was not administered in an unequal way. The more fundamental question the Does raised is whether the exclusion of social science research that points to the heterogeneity of sex offenders offends due process? (Williamson v. Lee Optical 1955, 488). For the Does, due process is always substantive.

The Does seem to think that judges (not legislators) should assess specific levels of dangerousness, and that the presentation of facts requires an interpretation of facts by neutral judges, not partisan legislators. There is, however, an indeterminateness to the historical assessments of danger that makes determinations of danger less than objective. There are, for example, eighteenth-, nineteenth-, twentieth- and twenty-first century notions of dangerousness. And though they differ in their conceptions of what danger is and can be, the ideas contained within each century are not discrete; they build upon each other. They start with the body of the criminal and branch out into analyses of class and social structure (Pinel 1806; Rosenberg 1989; Foucault 1990; Harcourt 2003). What the historical study of dangerousness reveals is that dangerousness is not the province of one disciplinary understanding. There are medical and legal conceptions of dangerousness, which are more likely to work in opposition than in concert (Federman 2012). Moreover, quantitative studies of the future dangerousness of violent criminals are inexact (Estelle v. Smith 1981; Barefoot v. Estelle 1983). Unlike the Does, we know that "dangerousness is overpredicted. The highest rate of accurate prediction of future dangerous behavior has been approximately 35%—in other words, only 35% of the persons labeled dangerous actually exhibited dangerous behavior in the future" (Groethe 1977, 583). Because we know that dangerousness cannot be accurately linked with the presence of white matter in the prefrontal cortices of psychopaths, dangerousness is a judgment that legislators are capable of making.

To succeed in the claim that dangerousness is measurable (that is, measurable in the same way that carcinogenic elements in food are measurable; see O'Brien 1987, chap. 2) would require a court to seek the resolution of conflicting constitutional claims in the annals of medical literature and not in the nation's principles, history, and traditions, as shaped by legal concepts and the political process over time. It would, as J. Harvie Wilkinson writes (2012, 78), provide a "general warrant" to judges "to insert themselves into the political process." The Does want courts to purge the political content of legislation from the political process that fashions legislation. Their view of law and politics is scientific and untainted by the give-and-take of the political process.

Residency restrictions are clearly popular in numerous communities throughout the United States.

> [A] 2005 survey of Florida citizens revealed that 76.3% of respondents supported community notification for all sex offenders, and only 6.3% favored exempting low-risk sex offenders with no history of violence. A national phone survey conducted in 2006–2007 produced higher levels of support for such policies, with 92% of respondents expressing support for making the names and addresses of convicted sex offenders available to the public. In addition, 76% of respondents to that survey supported policies that restrict where sex offenders can live. (Harris and Socia 2014, 5)

Amy Anderson, Lisa Sample, and Calli Cain (2015, 272) have found "widespread public support for exclusionary zones contained within residency restriction laws, suggesting that exclusionary zones could be enacted in most municipalities irrespective of their utility or instrumental value."

Residency restrictions got a boost from Justice Anthony Kennedy's opinion in *Smith v. Doe* (2002), when he altered a phrase he wrote in *McKune v. Lile* (2002, 33–34): "The risk of recidivism posed by sex offenders is 'frightening and high.'" He then relied upon a Department of Justice study that declared: "When convicted sex offenders reenter society, they are much more likely than any other type of offender to be rearrested for a new rape or sexual assault" (Smith v. Doe 2002, 103).[2] Ira Mark Ellman and Tara Ellman (2015, 497) have noted that the phrase "frightening and high" has appeared "in 91 judicial opinions, as well as briefs in 101 cases." The Ellmans have gotten the Department of Justice to retract its figure of an 80 percent recidivism rate.

Recidivism "refers to a person's relapse into criminal behavior, often after the person receives sanctions or undergoes intervention for a previous crime" (U.S. Sentencing Commission 2019, 4). Sex offender recidivism is not nearly as high as is generally supposed (Tekle-Johnson 2009, 612, n. 14; Bedarf 1995, 895–99; Miller, Amenta, and Conroy 2005). Two prominent studies have come to similar conclusions regarding recidivism and sex offending.

> Hanson and Bussiere (1998), which synthesized 61 individual recidivism studies and found a mean sexual recidivism rate of 13.4% within four to five years. A nearly-identical rate (13.7%) was reported in a follow-up analysis by Hanson and Morton-Bourgon (2005), although the rates of individual studies vary, with some finding considerably lower rates of recidivism. (Scurich and John 2019, 4)

As Nicholas Scurich and Richard John have noted, "the rate of *actual* sexual recidivism is substantially larger than the rate of *observed* sexual recidivism" (2019, 25; italics in original). Clearly, research on recidivism is not without serious methodological shortcomings (Doren 1998; Quinsey et al. 1993; Furby, Weinrott, and Blackshaw 1989; Henderson and Kalichman 1990). Scurich and John (2019, 7; italics in original) note, for example, that "[b]ecause not all crime is reported to the authorities, one should not assume that the 74% of offenders who were not *charged* with a new sexual offense did not *commit* a new sexual offense." As Judge Richard Posner has written, not only is there "serious underreporting of sex crimes, especially sex crimes against children," but one study found "that 86 percent of sex crimes against adolescents go unreported to police or any other authority, such as a child protective service" (Belleau v. Wall 2016, 933). Indeed, let's admit that recidivism is hardly a science with mathematical certainty.[3] Then let's admit that even if sex offender recidivism is low, it is not so low that laws against sex offending serve no purpose. Every "year there are between 1,600 and 2,300 stranger abductions of children under the age of 12 in the United States" (Congressional Record 1995, H11678). A septuagenarian sex offender who has "aged out" of sex offending can—and did—sexually harm a child (Berlin v. Evans 2011).

Recidivism does not refer to one type of reoffending. Recidivism rates for higher-tiered sex offenders are higher than for lower-tiered sex offenders. The highest rate of reoffending occurs among those with preferences for young males. Recidivism is higher for those who engage in contact sexual offending than for those who do not (Cohen and Spidell 2016, 23). In one study, Amanda Agan (2011, 229) has written, 229 "registered offenders" had "higher rates of recidivism" than nonregistered offenders. Those with ties to a community recidivate less than those with no such ties (Levenson and Hern 2007, 61). "States with harsher sentences for rape tend to have less recidivism for sex offenses but more recidivism for other crimes" (Agan 2011, 229).

There are four problems with the study of recidivism and its application to sex offenders. One is that sex offender laws clearly have an effect on recidivism rates. Provided that the "public has a substantial and compelling interest in protecting children from sex offenders," Chief Judge Sandra Beckwith has written, "the legislature is entitled to conclude that protecting or trying to protect a small number of victims justifies imposing burdens on the larger number of individuals who will not reoffend" (Doe v. Petro 2005, 4). Another problem is with statistics and reporting. Underreporting gets us to the 13 percent figure, cited above. Scurich and John note that underreporting can be supplemented by polygraphs. In "a sample of 127 sexual offenders with no official history of contact offenses," researchers found that "4.7% of the sample admitted to sexually abusing a child. However, after being polygraphed about their previous sexual behavior, an additional 52.8% disclosed that they had in fact committed a contact sexual offense that was never detected" (2019, 9). According to the Bureau of Justice Statistics (2012), "On average, an estimated 211, 200 rapes and sexual assaults went unreported to police each year between 2006 and 2010."

A third problem is that recidivism refers to reconviction not reoffending. A Department of Justice report on child sexual molestation noted that "child abusers have been known to reoffend as late as 20 years following release into the community" (Prentky, Knight, and Lee 1997, vi). Rapists have a fairly high recidivism rate for rape; they also commit and recommit (at higher levels than for rape) other crimes, such as "robbery, assault, burglary" (Bedarf 1995, 897), drug offenses, and public order offenses (Doe v. Pataki 1997, 1266). A 2006 study by the California Research Bureau stated that "Pedophiles that molest boys and rapists of adult women are among those most likely to recidivate. . . .

There is also substantial evidence that sex offenders commit many undetected offenses" (California Research Bureau 2006, 4). Robert Teir and Kevin Coy (1997, 408) report that, on average, there are "twenty-three child victims per sex offender." A General Accounting Office study reveals that "about 1 in every 5 girls and 1 in every 7 to 10 boys are sexually abused" (GAO 2013, 2). Another "study of 453 pedophiles, funded by the National Institute of Mental Health, reported that each pedophile molested an average of 52 girls or 150 boys. Another study reported an average of 72 victims per pedophile" (Teir and Coy 1997, 408). It is worth pointing out that "juveniles commit more than 25 percent of all sex offenses and more than 35 percent of all sex offenses against children" (In re C.P. 2012, 541).

A fourth problem is that part of the problem of recidivism is structural, which is beyond the reach of judges. Research on sex offenders has revealed that what makes neighborhoods unsafe is not the presence of sex offenders as such but "housing instability," which is "strongly correlated with increased criminal recidivism and absconding. In a sample of more than 6,000 criminal offenders in Georgia, each time a parolee relocated, the risk of being rearrested increased by 25%, doubling the odds of recidivism by moving three times while on parole" (Zandbergen, Levenson, and Hart 2010, 485). Must judges, vested with the power to analyze social science data, also restructure neighborhoods, as they once took over prisons and school districts?

Studies show that legislators rely on the idea that criminals engage in rational behavior and do not behave in abstract ways as models (Zandbergen, Levenson, and Hart 2010, 483; Wilson 1977, chap. 3). One study in Arkansas "found that 48% of child molesters lived in close proximity to schools, day care centers, or parks compared with 26% of perpetrators convicted of sex crimes against adult victims." According to Jill Levenson and Leo Cotter (2005, 169), "[t]he authors [of the Arkansas study] speculated that molesters who were motivated to reoffend might be more likely to purposely place themselves in close access to potential child victims." In other studies, researchers have found that sex offenders were "randomly scattered throughout the study area and did not seem to live closer than nonrecidivists to schools or child care centers." But there is research suggesting "a direct link between geographic patterns of offending and crime-related decision making, perhaps involving a rational calculus process that considers factors such as target attractiveness and spatial opportunity" (Nobles, Levenson, and Youstin 2012, 493).

Registered and convicted sex offenders, for example, are more likely to live in poor neighborhoods.

> Less-affluent neighborhoods tend to be densely populated, and residential dwellings are therefore naturally in close proximity to schools and daycare centers. Although sex offenses occur more frequently in census tracts with larger proportions of young children, the number of schools in a neighborhood is not associated with a greater frequency of sex offenses. (Nobles, Levenson, and Youstin 2012, 494)

Proximity matters, but it is not determinative of sexual offending. As Paul Zandbergen, Jill Levenson, and Timothy Hart demonstrate, child abusers in Pulaski County, Arkansas, are "more likely than other sex offenders to live near schools, daycares, and parks." But child abusers in Newark, New Jersey, are less likely to live near schools. These researchers note, however, that "Newark sex offenders lived significantly closer (on average 1,094 feet closer) to schools than did other community members; in Camden County, New Jersey, 88% of sex offenders lived within 2,500 feet of schools, parks, daycares, or churches, compared to 80% of households in general" (Zandbergen, Levenson, and Hart 2010, 483).

If the purpose of social science research is to make lawmaking efficient and rational, and less dependent upon people's irrational fears, it faces an uphill climb on the subject of sex offending and residency restrictions. What conclusions, in other words, should be drawn from conflicting social science findings? Should judges in Newark decide child abuse cases differently than judges in Pulaski County, Arkansas, because the data suggest different offending patterns? There are, also, different sexual offending patterns among blacks and whites (Prescott and Rockoff 2011; Post 1999; Monahan 2006). Should judges rule by racial concerns? There is no doubt that residency laws have unintended consequences, most of which fall upon the economically disadvantaged. It behooves legislators to pay attention to the collateral consequences of these laws. But we should be wary of suggestions that there can be laws without unintended consequences (Rozansky and Lerner 2012, 97; Nelson 1982).

Legislators can learn a lot from social science research. Jill Levenson and Andrea Hern are correct in alerting "society" to problems social scientists have exposed (2007, 68), though a study by the Department of Justice in 2010 revealed that the public has a pretty good understanding of the patterns of offending (Center for Sex Offender Management 2010). It might be better to ask: what are judges and legislators to make of these studies? Is a 2,000-foot restriction inherently unconstitutional? Does the science behind the criticism of residency restrictions jibe with due process, with the feelings of security communities must have? At the least, a more pointed argument can be made for alerting legislators to these findings, rather than connecting the claims of social science research to judicial interpretations of constitutional law.

For example, states and localities can "provide a safe, structured re-entry for offenders, using monitoring, stable housing and access to treatment" (Fifield 2016). And while treatment for sex offending remains uncertain, some studies "have found that rates of sexual reoffending drop by about 40% after participation in contemporary cognitive-behavioral therapies" (Levenson 2008, 4). Another alternative is for states and localities to enact "child safety zones," which prevent released sex offenders from entering or loitering around "parks, schools, daycare centers, playgrounds, and other places where children congregate" (McKay 2002, 18). Time (and constitutional challenges) can only tell if such regulations can be effective. They have the benefit of not making worse the prospects for reintegration of sex offenders into their home communities.

Finally, not all residency restrictions need be "draconian." New York state's residency restriction, for example, does not "impose strict liability," something other states should follow.

> Incidental contact with the 1000 foot zone of exclusion, when walking between two permissible places (e.g., home and subway) does not alone constitute a violation. First, a violation would require proof that the parolee knowingly violated the statute. The State has the burden of proving any parole violation, including the knowledge element. Second, if a parolee knows that he or she would be traversing the zone, it is not unreasonable to require the parolee to detour to avoid it. (Williams v. Department of Corrections 2014, 375–76)

There are, in short, reasonable measures that states can take that both protect public safety and the rights of parolees and former convicts without having to turn law into a subset of the social sciences. Perhaps, above all, should constitutional infractions occur, courts can decide these cases on an "as applied" basis, which allows courts to say that the law as applied in one particular instance is unconstitutional, but that the law itself is constitutionally sound (Chicago v. Morales 1999).

Conclusion

The presupposition of critics of sex offender legislation is that scientific analyses provide better, because more efficient, solutions to social problems than political institutions can. Yet there is no way to know if science will always defend civil liberties and minority rights in the way its defenders expect. "[T]ime has overtaken some of *Roe*'s factual assumptions," Justice Sandra Day O'Connor wrote in *Planned Parenthood of Southeastern Pennsylvania v. Casey* (1992, 860). Why wouldn't it do the same with the softer sciences? The scientific method is not obligated to follow the Constitution's fundamental principles.

I have sought in this chapter to present an understanding of residency restrictions through a critique of social scientific data. The standard analysis yields the following results. Residency restrictions do more harm than good and should be abolished based on their inability to control those they explicitly seek to control. I have found that analysis wanting for three reasons: First, the scientific data do not conclusively demonstrate the conclusions researchers try to draw. Second, other conclusions can be inferred from the data, such as the necessity for residential exclusion zones, mandatory treatment regimes, chemical castration, or resort to penile plethysmography (Weems v. Little Rock Police Department 2006, 1013; Harlow and Scott 2007), ideas at odds with the general tenor of those who advocate for the fairness of social scientific research. Third, the resort to social science runs up against the general aims and scope of the democratic process, the states' police power, and constitutional analyses of what constitutes public safety. Alterations in laws and regulations are best left to legislatures, not courts. Finally, I have argued that scientific facts applied to the tumultuous world of democratic politics is not an easy fit with American political practices, a point rarely mentioned by social science's supporters. Indeed, they operate without a commitment to the democratic process. The upshot of the findings about the harms of residency restrictions raise serious questions about the role of democratic deliberation in shaping a free society.

NOTES

1. California was the first state to require the registration of felons. The Supreme Court declared the law unconstitutional. Felix Frankfurter, in dissent, wrote: "The present laws of the United States and of the forty-eight States are thick

with provisions that command that some things not be done and others be done, although persons convicted under such provisions may have had no awareness of what the law required or that what they did was wrongdoing. The body of decisions sustaining such legislation, including innumerable registration laws, is almost as voluminous as the legislation itself" (Lambert v. California 1957, 230).

2. In *McKune*, Kennedy used the phrase in the context of making a point about what prisoners should learn about the reason for their incarceration. "[T]o identify the traits that cause such a frightening and high risk of recidivism" (McKune v. Lille 2002, 34). In *Smith*, that idea is missing.

3. In U.S. v. Carta (2009, 220), Dr. Amy Phenix estimated that Carta's potential for recidivism was 13.4 percent to 27.7 percent "after five years." Dr. Leonard Bard thought it was 13.8 percent.

REFERENCES

Agan, Amanda. 2011. "Sex Offender Registries: Fear without Function?" *Journal of Law and Economics* 54 (1): 207–39.

Agan, Amanda, and J. J. Prescott. 2014. "Sex Offender Law and the Geography of Victimization." *Journal of Empirical Legal Studies* 11 (4): 786–828.

Anderson, Amy, Lisa Sample, and Calli Cain. 2015. "Residency Restrictions for Sex Offenders: Public Opinion on Appropriate Distances." *Criminal Justice Policy Review* 26 (3): 262–77.

Bains, Chiraag. 2007. "Next-Generation Sex Offender Statutes: Constitutional Challenges to Residency, Work, and Loitering Restrictions." *Harvard Civil Rights-Civil Liberties Law Review* 42 (2): 483–500.

Barzun, Charles. 2004. "Common Sense and Legal Sense." *Virginia Law Review* 90 (4): 1051–91.

Basbøll, Thomas. 2016. "The Liberal Arts of Being Ruled." *Research as a Second Language* (blog). http://secondlanguage.blogspot.com/2016/11/the-liberal-arts-of-being-ruled.html

Bedarf, Abril. 1995. "Examining Sex Offender Community Notification Laws." *California Law Review* 83: 885–939.

Berenson, Jacqueline, and Paul Appelbaum. 2011. "A Geospatial Analysis of the Impact of Sex Offender Residency Restrictions in Two New York Counties." *Law and Human Behavior* 35 (3): 235–46.

Bergner, Jeffrey. 1981. *The Origin of Formalism in Social Science*. Chicago: University of Chicago Press.

Berns, Walter. 1963. "Law and Behavioral Science." *Law and Contemporary Problems* 28 (1): 185–212.

Brooks, William. 2010. "The Tail Still Wages the Dog: The Pervasive and Inappropriate Influence by the Psychiatric Profession on the Civil Commitment Process." *North Dakota Law Review* 86 (2): 259–319.

Broward County, Florida. 2009. "Final Report: Sexual Offender & Sexual Predator Residence Task Force." https://ccoso.org/sites/default/files/import/Final-Report---Sexual-Offender-Sexual-Residence-Task-Force.pdf

California Research Bureau. 2006. "The Impact of Residency Restrictions on Sex Offenders and Correctional Management Practices: A Literature Review." California Agencies. Paper 303. http://digitalcommons.law.ggu.edu/caldocs_agencies/303

California Sex Offender Management Board. 2011. "Homelessness Among California's Registered Sex Offenders: An Update."http://www.casomb.org/docs/Residence_Paper_Final.pdf

Carpenter, Jacob. 2016. "Sex Offender Ordinance Hasn't Worked as Planned, Putting Public at Greater Risk." *Milwaukee Journal Sentinel*. https://www.jsonline.com/story/news/local/2016/08/20/sex-offender-ordinance-worked-planned-putting-public-greater-risk/88948028

Center for Sex Offender Management. 2010. "A Project of the U.S. Department of Justice, Office of Justice Programs. Exploring Public Awareness and Attitudes about Sex Offender Management: Findings from a National Public Opinion Poll." https://www.csom.org/pubs/CSOM-Exploring%20Public%20Awareness.pdf

Cohen, Thomas, and Spidell, Michelle. 2016. "How Dangerous Are They: An Analysis of Sex Offenders under Federal Post-Conviction Supervision." *Federal Probation* 80 (2): 21–32.

Collins, Erin. 2018. "Punishing Risk." *Georgetown Law Journal* 107 (1): 57–108.

Congressional Record. 1995. Proceedings and Debates of the 104th Congress, 1st sess: 141 (171).

Cook, Nancy. 2012. "Law as Science: Revisiting Langdell's Paradigm in the 21st Century." *North Dakota Law Review* 88 (1): 21–50.

Cunningham, Mark, Jon Sorensen, Mark Vigen, and S. O. Woods. 2011. "Life and Death in the Lone Star State: Three Decades of Violence Predictions by Capital Juries." *Behavioral Sciences & the Law* 29 (1): 1–22.

D'Orazio, Deidre, Steven Arkowitz, Jay Adams, and Wesley Maram. 2009. "The California Sexually Violent Predator Statute: History, Description, and Areas of Improvement. The California Coalition on Sexual Offending." https://ccoso.org/sites/default/files/CCOSO%20SVP%20Paper.pdf

Doren, Dennis. 1998. "Recidivism Base Rates, Predictions of Sex Offender Recidivism, and the 'Sexual Predator' Commitment Laws." *Behavioral Sciences & the Law* 16 (1): 97–114.

Ellman, Ira Mark, and Tara Ellman. 2015. "Frightening and High: The Supreme Court's Crucial Mistake about Sex Crime Statistics." *Constitutional Commentary* 30 (3): 495–508.

Federman, Cary. 2012. "Assessing Dangerousness." In *(Re)Thinking Violence in Health Care Settings: A Critical Approach*, edited by Dave Holmes, Trudy Rudge, and Amélie Perron, 297–314. Surrey, England: Ashgate.

Fifield, Jen. 2016. Pew. "Despite Concerns, Sex Offenders Face New Restrictions." https://>www.pewtrusts.org/en/research-and-analysis/blogs/stateline/2016/05/06/despite-concerns-sex-offenders-face-new-restrictions

Foucault, Michel. 1990. "The Dangerous Individual." In *Michel Foucault: Politics, Philosophy, Culture: Interviews and Other Writings, 1977–1984*, edited by Lawrence Kritzman, 125–51. London: Routledge.

Furby, Lita, Mark Weinrott, and Lyn Blackshaw. 1989. "Sex Offender Recidivism: A Review." *Psychological Bulletin* 105 (1): 3–30.

Giorkaris, Virginia. 1987. "Zoning and the First Amendment: A Municipality's Power to Control Adult Use Establishments." *University of Missouri-Kansas City Law Review* 55 (2): 263–83.

Goble, George. 1934. "Law as a Science." *Indiana Law Journal* 9 (5): 294–313.

Groethe, Reed. 1977. "Overt Dangerous Behavior as a Constitutional Requirement for Involuntary Civil Commitment of the Mentally Ill." *University of Chicago Law Review* 44 (3): 562–93.

Grubesic, Tony, Alan Murray, and Elizabeth Mack. 2011. "Sex Offenders, Residence Restrictions, Housing, and Urban Morphology: A Review and Synthesis." *Cityscape: A Journal of Policy Development and Research* 13 (3): 7–31.

Harcourt, Bernard. 2003. "The Shaping of Chance: Actuarial Models and Criminal Profiling at the Turn of the Twenty-First Century." *University of Chicago Law Review* 70 (1): 105–28.

Harlow, Michael, and Charles Scott. 2007. "Penile Plethysmography Testing for Convicted Sex Offenders." *Journal of the American Academy of Psychiatry and the Law* 35 (4): 536–37.

Harris, Andrew, and Kelly Socia. 2014. "What's in a Name? Evaluating the Effects of the 'Sex Offender' Label on Public Opinions and Beliefs." *Sexual Abuse* 28 (7): 660–78.

Henderson, Margit, and Seth Kalichman. 1990. "Sexually Deviant Behavior and Schizotypy: A Theoretical Perspective with Supportive Data." *Psychiatric Quarterly* 61 (4): 273–84.

Human Rights Watch. 2007. *No Easy Answers: Sex Offender Laws in the U.S.* https://www.hrw.org/report/2007/09/11/no-easy-answers/sex-offender-laws-us

Human Rights Watch. 2013. *Raised on the Registry: The Irreparable Harm of Placing*

Children on Sex Offender Registries in the U.S. https://www.hrw.org/report/2013/05/01/raised-registry/irreparable-harm-placing-children-sex-offender-registries-us

Jalava, Jarkko, Stephanie Griffiths, and Michael Maraun. 2015. *The Myth of the Born Criminal: Psychopathy, Neurobiology, and the Creation of the Modern Degenerate.* Toronto: University of Toronto Press.

Kendall, Willmoore. 1971. "The Majority Principle and the Scientific Elite." In *Willmoore Kendall Contra Mundum*, edited by Nellie Kendall, 93–102. New Rochelle, NY: Arlington House.

Kreit, Alex. 2010. "Making Sense of Facial and As-Applied Challenges." *William & Mary Bill of Rights Journal* 18 (3): 657–708.

Levenson, Jill. 2005. "Sex Offender Residence Restrictions: A Report to the Florida Legislature." https://ccoso.org/sites/default/files/residencerestrictionsFL.pdf

Levenson, Jill. 2008. "Sex Offense Recidivism, Risk Assessment, and the Adam Walsh Act." https://www.researchgate.net/profile/Jill_Levenson/publication/242471123_Sex_offense_recidivism_risk_assessment_and_the_Adam_Walsh_Act/links/5592facf08ae16f493ee4b5b/Sex-offense-recidivism-risk-assessment-and-the-Adam-Walsh-Act.pdf

Levenson, Jill, and Leo Cotter. 2005. "The Impact of Sex Offender Residence Restrictions: 1,000 Feet from Danger or One Step From Absurd?" *International Journal of Offender Therapy and Comparative Criminology* 49 (2): 168–78.

Levenson, Jill, and Andrea Hern. 2007. "Sex Offender Residence Restrictions: Unintended Consequences and Community Reentry." *Justice Research and Policy* 9 (1): 59–73.

Martens, Willem H. J. 2008. "The Problem with Robert Hare's Psychopathy Checklist: Incorrect Conclusions, High Risk of Misuse, and Lack of Reliability." *Medicine and Law* 27 (2): 449–62.

McKay, Brian. 2002. "The State of Sex Offender Probation Supervision in Texas." *Federal Probation* 66 (1): 16–20.

McKinstry, Lohr. 2012. "Essex County Again Considers Sex-Offender Residency Law." *Press-Republican* (September 13). https://www.pressrepublican.com/news/local_news/essex-county-again-considers-sex-offender-residency-law/article_9ba68c73-81c9-57a1-9429-071828af32cc.html

Meloy, Michelle, Susan Miller, and Kristin Curtis. 2008. "Making Sense out of Nonsense: The Deconstruction of State-Level Sex Offender Residence Restrictions." *American Journal of Criminal Justice* 33 (2): 209–22.

Miller, Holly, Amy Amenta, and Mary Alice Conroy. 2005. "Sexually Violent Predator Evaluations: Empirical Evidence, Strategies for Professionals, and Research Directions." *Law and Human Behavior* 29 (1): 29–54.

Monahan, John. 2006. "A Jurisprudence of Risk Assessment: Forecasting Harm among Prisoners, Predators, and Patients." *Virginia Law Review* 92 (3): 391–435.

Monjeau, Caitlin. 2011. "All Politics is Local: State Preemption and Municipal Sex Offender Residency Restrictions in New York State." *Boston University Law Review* 91 (4): 1569–96.

Nelson, Michael. 1982. "A Short, Ironic History of American National Bureaucracy." *Journal of Politics* 44 (3): 747–78.

New York Times. 2015. "The Pointless Banishment of Sex Offenders." (September 8). https://www.nytimes.com/2015/09/08/opinion/the-pointless-banishment-of-sex-offenders.html

Nobles, Matt, Jill Levenson, and Tasha Youstin. 2012. "Effectiveness of Residence Restrictions in Preventing Sex Offense Recidivism." *Crime & Delinquency* 58 (4): 491–513.

O'Brien, David. 1987. *What Process Is Due? Courts and Science-Policy Disputes.* New York: Russell Sage.

Pinel, Phillipe. 1806. *A Treatise on Insanity.* London: Sheffield.

Post, Dawn. 1999. "Preventive Victimization: Assessing Future Dangerousness in Sexual Predators for Purposes of Indeterminate Civil Commitment." *Hamline Journal of Public Law and Policy* 21 (1): 177–246.

Prentky, Robert, Raymond Knight, and Austin F. S. Lee. 1997. "National Institute of Justice. Research Report, Child Sexual Molestation: Research Issues." https://www.ncjrs.gov/pdffiles/163390.pdf

Prescott, J. J., and Jonah Rockoff. 2011. "Do Sex Offender Registration and Notification Laws Affect Criminal Behavior?" *Journal of Law and Economics* 54 (1): 161–206.

Quinsey, Vernon, Grant Harris, Marnie Rice, and Martin Lalumière. 1993. "Assessing Treatment Efficacy in Outcome Studies of Sex Offenders." *Journal of Interpersonal Violence* 8 (4): 512–23.

Ringer, Fritz. 1997. *Max Weber's Methodology: The Unification of the Cultural and Social Sciences.* Cambridge, MA: Harvard University Press.

Rosenberg, Charles. 1989. *The Trial of the Assassin Guiteau: Psychiatry and Law in the Gilded Age.* Chicago: University of Chicago Press.

Rosenberg, Gerald. 1991. *The Hollow Hope: Can Courts Bring About Social Change?* Chicago: University of Chicago.

Rozansky, Jeremy, and Josh Lerner. 2012. "The Political Science of James Q. Wilson." *The New Atlantis* 35: 84–98.

Scurich, Nicholas, and Richard John. 2019. "The Dark Figure of Sexual Recidivism." U.C. Irvine School of Law Research Paper No. 2019–09. https://ssrn.com/abstract=3328831

Sharkey, Patrick, and Jacob Faber. 2014. "Where, When, Why, and For Whom Do Residential Contexts Matter? Moving Away from the Dichotomous Understanding of Neighborhood Effects." *Annual Review of Sociology* 40: 559–79.

Socia, Kelly, Jill Levenson, Alissa Ackerman, and Andrew Harris. 2014. "'Brothers under the Bridge': Factors Influencing the Transience of Registered Sex Offenders in Florida." *Sexual Abuse* 27 (6): 559–86.

Teir, Robert, and Kevin Coy. 1997. "Approaches to Sexual Predators: Community Notification and Civil Commitment." *New England Journal on Criminal and Civil Confinement* 23 (2): 405–26.

Tekle-Johnson, Asmara. 2009. "In the Zone: Sex Offenders and the Ten-Percent Solutions." *Iowa Law Review* 94 (2): 607–63.

Tewksbury, Richard, and Elizabeth Ehrhardt Mustaine. 2013. "Law-Enforcement Officials' Views of Sex Offender Registration and Community Notification." *International Journal of Police Science and Management* 15 (2): 95–113.

U.S. Bureau of Justice Statistics. 2012. "Lynn Langton, Marcus Berzofsky, Christopher Krebs, Hope Smiley-McDonald, Victimizations Not Reported to the Police, 2006–2010." *RTI International.* https://www.bjs.gov/index.cfm?ty=pbdetail&iid=4962

U.S. General Accounting Office. 2013. "Sex Offender Registration and Registration and Notification Act: Jurisdictions Face Challenges to Implementing the Act, and Stakeholders Report Positive and Negative Effects. Report to the Subcommittee on Crime, Terrorism, and Homeland Security, Committee on the Judiciary, House of Representatives." https://www.gao.gov/assets/660/652032.pdf

U.S. Sentencing Commission. 2019. "Recidivism among Federal Violent Offenders." https://www.ussc.gov/sites/default/files/pdf/research-and-publications/research-publications/2019/20190124_Recidivism_Violence.pdf

Weber, Max. 1949. "The Meaning of 'Ethical Neutrality' in Sociology and Economics." In *The Methodology of the Social Sciences*, translated by Edward Shils and Henry Finch, 1–47. Glencoe, IL: Free Press.

West, Amanda. 2007."The Georgia Legislature Strikes with a Vengeance–Sex Offender Residency Restrictions and the Deterioration of the Ex Post Facto Clause." *Catholic University Law Review* 57 (1): 239–68.

Wilkinson, J. Harvie. 2012. *Cosmic Constitutional Theory: Why Americans are Losing Their Inalienable Right to Self-Governance.* Oxford: Oxford University Press.

Wilson, James Q. 1977. *Thinking About Crime.* New York: Vintage.

Winch, Peter. 1990. *The Idea of a Social Science and its Relation to Philosophy.* 2nd ed. London: Routledge.

Zandbergen, Paul, Jill Levenson, and Timothy Hart. 2010. "Residential Proximity to Schools and Daycares: An Empirical Analysis of Sex Offense Recidivism." *Criminal Justice and Behavior* 37 (5): 482–502.

CASES

Barefoot v. Estelle, 463 U.S. 880 (1983).
Belleau v. Wall, 811 F.3d 929 (2016).
Berlin v. Evans, 31 Misc. 3d 919 (2011).
Bowers v. Polk County Board of Supervisors, 638 N.W. 2d 682 (2002).
California v. Mosley, 60 Cal. 4th 1044 (2015).
Chicago v. Morales, 527 U.S. 41 (1999).
Connecticut Department of Public Safety v. Doe, 538 U.S. 1 (2003).
Doe v. Baker, WL 905368 (2006).
Doe v. Cooper, 842 F.3d 833 (2016).
Doe v. Lee, 271 F.3d 38 (2001).
Doe v. Miller, 405 F.3d 700 (2005).
Doe v. Otte, 248 F.3d 832 (2001).
Doe v. Pataki, 120 F.3d 1263 (1997).
Doe v. Petro, WL 1038846 (2005).
Doe v. Poritz, 142 N.J. 1 (1995).
Doe I v. Marshall, WL 539055 (2019) (slip copy).
E.B. v. Verniero, 119 F.3d 1077 (1997).
Elwell and Elwell v. Township of Lower, 2006 WL 3797974 (2006) (unpublished opinion).
Estelle v. Smith, 451 U.S. 454 (1981).
G.H. v. Township of Galloway, 401 N.J. Super. 392 (2008).
Gonzalez v. Raich 545 U.S. 1 (2005).
Illinois v. Leroy 357 Ill.App. 3d 530 (2005).
Indiana v. Pollard, 908 N.E. 2d 1145 (2009).
In re C.P., 131 Ohio St.3d 513 (2012).
In re Taylor, 60 Cal.4th 1019 (2015).
In the Matter of the Commitment of W.Z., 773 A.2d 97 (2001).
Iowa v. Seering, 701 N.W.2d 655 (2005).
Iowa v. Williams, 628 N.W. 2d 447 (2001).
Kentucky v. Baker, 295 S.W. 3d 437 (2009).
Keyes v. School District No. 1, Denver, 413 U.S. 189 (1973).
Lambert v. California, 355 U.S. 225 (1957).
Lochner v. New York, 198 U.S. 45 (1905).

Lukumi Babalu Aye v. Hileah, 508 U.S. 520 (1993).

Mann v. Georgia Department of Corrections, 282 Ga. 754 (2007).

McCleskey v. Kemp, 481 U.S. 279 (1987).

McKune v. Lile, 536 U.S. 24 (2002).

Millard v. Rankin, WL 3767796 (2017).

New York v. Diack, 41 Misc. 3d 36 (2013).

New York v. Diack, 24 N.Y. 3d 674 (2015).

Papachristou v. Jacksonville, 405 U.S. 156 (1972).

Paris Adult Theater I v. Slaton, 414 U.S. 49 (1972).

Planned Parenthood of Southeastern Pennsylvania v. Casey 505 U.S. 833 (1992).

R. v. Aziga, ONSC 4592 (2011).

Renton v. Playtime Theatres, Inc., 475 U.S. 41 (1986).

Schad v. Mount Ephraim, 452 U.S. 61 (1981).

Smith v. Doe, 538 U.S. 84 (2002).

U.S. v. Carta, 620 F.Supp 2d 210 (2009).

U.S. v. Lopez, 514 U.S. 549 (1995).

U.S. v. Morrison 529 U.S. 598 (2000).

Vann v. Alabama, 143 So. 3d 850 (2013).

Weaver v. Graham, 450 U.S. 24 (1981).

Weems v. Little Rock Police Dept., 453 F.3d 1010 (2006)

Williams v. Department of Corrections and Community Supervision, 43 Misc.3d 356 (2014).

Williams v. Department of Corrections and Community Supervision, 136 A.D. 3d 147 (2016).

Williamson v. Gregoire 151 F.3d 1180 (1998).

Williamson v. Lee Optical Co., 348 U.S. 483 (1955).

Winters v. New York, 333 U.S. 507 (1948).

Wisconsin v. Loomis, 371 Wis. 2d 235 (2016).

Yick Wo v. Hopkins, 118 U.S. 356 (1886).

Young v. American Mini Theatres, 427 U.S. 50 (1976).

CHAPTER 7

Banishment, Deliberation, and the Meaning of Punishment

In 1905, Justice David Brewer—writing in dissent in a case that upheld the administrative decision to exclude a Chinese national claiming to be an American citizen from entering the United States—defined banishment as "punishment inflicted on criminals by compelling them to quit a city, place, or country for a specified period of time, or for life" (U.S. v. Ju Toy 1905, 269–70). Brewer meant by banishment two things: one, that legislatures cannot banish an individual beyond a state's borders, as that would violate comity among the states (Snider 1998; Michigan v. Baum 1930); and two, courts cannot impose banishment as a condition of a criminal sentence (Armstrong 1963; Brilliant 1989; Saxer 2009; U.S. v. Abushaar 1985). The Georgia supreme court has upheld, however, as a condition of probation, the placement of a convicted felon in one county, effectively banning him from the other 158 Georgia counties (Terry v. Hamrick 2008; Alloy 2002). To be sure, probation has historically "been regarded as punishment" (Shaw v. Patton 2015, 8), but the Georgia supreme court saw no need to address that issue, as Terry's "banishment" involved probation's historic supervisory function (Terry v. Hamrick 2008, 28).[1]

Federal and state courts have upheld conditions of parole that have banned convicted criminals from returning to their home states; they have upheld conditions of parole that have prevented convicted criminals from leaving the state; and they have upheld executive pardons involving banishment (Snider 1998, 471–74). As Wm. Garth Snider (1998, 471-72, 486) has written, "Most jurisdictions have held that any condition, so long as it is not illegal, immoral, or impossible to perform, may be attached to a parole or a pardon." This is because sentencing judges are "afforded the widest latitude in the imposition of conditions" (Snider 1998, 456, n. 6; 465, n. 78). Legislation that singles out an individual or a group for banishment, however, is unconstitutional (Dick 2011).

The final problem confronting the regulation of sex offenders is this: conceding that residency restrictions are not banishment in Brewer's sense, do residency restrictions "resemble" banishment (Olson 2010, 423) and "essentially 'banish' sex offenders" (Janicki 2007, 300) or "result in de facto banishment" (Logan 2006, 4), thus violating the Eighth Amendment's cruel and unusual clause? The New York supreme court has stated, in a sex offender case, that "if the [residency] statute is applied to prevent [Ariel] Berlin from living in his apartment, or anywhere else within 1,000 feet of a school, he is effectively banished from New York County" (Berlin v. Evans 2011, 923). And the supreme court of Oklahoma has held, also in a sex offender case, that "[t]he expulsion from one's residence is . . . analogous to the traditional punishment of banishment" (Starkey v. Oklahoma 2013, 1026). Banishment, Earl Warren once wrote, is "a fate universally decried by civilized people" (Trop v. Dulles 1958, 102; Kennedy v. Mendoza-Martinez 1963, 168, n. 23). What began as an attempt at risk management in the public interest, akin to quarantine and curfew, has become associated with ancient and medieval practices unsuitable for a modern people.

In this final chapter, I will do three things. First, I will address the variety of theories of what punishment is and see if we can apply those insights to post-conviction sex offender legislation. Second, I will analyze the Supreme Court's understanding of punishment, focusing on three-strikes laws and conditions of confinement cases, in an attempt to discover if the Court's punishment jurisprudence has a unifying principle that could be applied to sex offender legislation. Finally, I will consider the claim that residency restrictions interfere with a right to travel, and thus violate the Eighth and Fourteenth Amendments. Banishment and the interference with a right to travel are the most substantive claims made against residency restrictions, and they need to be addressed to understand fully the arguments over sex offender regulations.

Theories of Punishment

The idea that restricting where sex offenders can go is punishment or cruelty in an Eighth Amendment sense reflects an uncertainty of purpose about the goals of punishment under modern liberalism. Contemporary social scientists and theorists regard punishment not as an act of sovereignty against willful citizens, or as a reaffirmation of "moral values" (von Hirsch 1976, 49), but as "dependent upon a wide array of . . . social forces" (Garland 1993, 20) that diminish individual responsibility but increase the state's role in crime control. Jonathan Simon, for example, denies that punishment can be explained as a "relationship of sovereignty between the state and the citizen." He regards the state's sovereignty over a population as a "semimystical assumption" and argues that punishment is meted out "amid patterns of nonstate actions" (1993, 10–11), such as parole supervision. Theodore Caplow and Jonathan Simon write that the penal system is "focused on managing a seemingly permanent criminal population" (1999, 98). The focus on managerialism, risk, and danger, Caplow and Simon write, is politically opportunistic, the result of the anxiety legislators and the public feel as a result of the collapse of "racial and gender hierarchies" (1999, 65). These "[s]hifts in political ideology" (Caplow and Simon 1999, 69) require collapsing the "boundary between [civil] legislative regulation and [criminal] punishment" (Notes 1959, 231; Klein 1999). Caplow and Simon highlight the informal ways in which the federal and state governments engage with cruelty through crime control.

Whatever insight this critique might have regarding how power works under neoliberalism, it focuses too much on indeterminate factors acting on the state and individuals, creating a self-fulfilling prophecy that the state only engages in reactionary policies. It fails to take seriously the argument that punishment is informed by concerns for individual responsibility, law abidingness, public safety, and even justice. Stanley Brubaker (1988, 821) offers a far more insightful understanding of punishment's meaning under liberalism. He writes, "Liberalism is a doubting philosophy of politics. It doubts that the human good, or human excellence, exists." By doubting that the highest good exists, liberals cast doubt on the limited purposes of punishment, because punishment involves a judgment that it is good to punish the bad. Punishment "invokes a vision of the moral order where the virtuous flourish and the wicked suffer" (Brubaker 1988, 825). Punishment has political and moral components to it. Arthur Shuster (2016, 140) writes that punishing the guilty is the clearest expression of "the moral demands of . . . political life." Brubaker suggests, however, that modern-day liberals disdain moral and political judgments regarding punishment. Liberals prefer to rely on social science data, which purport to show that individuals, though not wholly responsible for their actions, can be rehabilitated. It is this uncertainty about modern punishment—(1) what its purpose is; and (2) how the state justifies imposing it—and not its perceived reactionary status that lies at the core of the constitutional problem of postconviction sex offender legislation.

According to Brubaker, the inability of liberals to punish rests on four ideas, which I will reduce to three. First, Brubaker argues that anger is a legitimate component of punishment (but not its raison d'être); liberals want to dampen the passions that lead from anger to cruelty (Brubaker 1988, 831; Terchek and Brubaker 1989, 1313; Kekes 1993, 183–92; Shklar 1982). Second, punishment has a strong connection to the public good. It "vindicates the community in its standard of right" (Brubaker 1988, 825). Liberals prefer the individual to the community, and individual rights to the common good. In Michael Sandel's phrase (1982, 1), liberalism asserts the "priority of the right over the good." Brubaker's third and fourth points are related. For Brubaker, the inner core of liberalism is self-preservation. Therefore liberals cannot account for an understanding of punishment that is "expressive of reprobation and resentment" (Brubaker 1988, 825). Pain, Brubaker writes (1988, 825), "bears a statement about the human good." Deterrence, Brubaker argues, is not enough to satisfy the public's need for justice.

Legal theorists divide punishment theories into four categories: retribution, deterrence, rehabilitation, and incapacitation. For retributivists, "punishment is justified by the desert of the offender" (Moore 1997, 87). If retributivism is backward looking, based on what one has done, deterrence is forward-looking. "Men are not hanged for stealing horses, but that horses may not be stolen," Lord Halifax allegedly said. Rehabilitation is the idea that convicted criminals can return to society as nondangerous through psychological and behavioral therapies that treat criminals as patients (Schopp 1995). Incapacitation is the removal of an offender from society. Incapacitation, rehabilitation, and deterrence are subsets of utilitarianism, whose central idea is usually stated as the greatest good for the greatest number of people (Bentham 1988, 2). Retributivism and deterrence are the two dominant theories of punishment. As the Supreme Court has noted, the "traditional" understanding of punishment includes "retribution and deterrence" (Kennedy v. Mendoza-Martinez 1963, 168).

Mixed theories of punishment combine attributes of retribution and deterrence (Hart 1988; von Hirsch 1976, chap. 6). H. L. A. Hart's view is the classic mixed view. Punishment for Hart contains the following five ideas: (1) "It must inflict pain" or impose some unpleasantness; (2) it can only be imposed on those who violate legal rules; (3) the punishment imposed must be on the person thought to be the criminal; (4) those who administer punishment must not be the offender; and (5) those who administer punishment must be duly constituted by a legal authority (Hart 1988, 4–5). Despite his criticisms of retribution and deterrence, Hart remains committed to understanding punishment in utilitarian terms. As Richard Wasserstrom has noted (1967, 111), "The actual punishment of persons is necessary only to keep the threat of punishment credible." Hart regards punishment not as a good to be enforced but as an evil to avoid.

According to Émile Durkheim, however, punishment does more than deter and impose desert; it unites a community. It neither seeks to satisfy the greatest number within a society or community, as utilitarianism does, nor does it attempt to establish justice on the basis of desert. Durkheim's understanding of punishment as a form of social solidarity is complex and need not be recounted in depth, though one point is important to stress. The "real function" of punishment, he writes, "is to maintain inviolate the cohesion of society by sustaining the common consciousness in all its vigor" (Durkheim 1984, 63). For Durkheim, the value of punishment lies in social solidarity. Punishment for Durkheim imposes a stigma on the criminal, and so its effect on society is positive not negative. Punishment is the tribute vice pays to virtue for violating social norms. Punishment for Durkheim is normative and relativistic. "The criminal is simply the man . . . who has refused to obey the laws of the city" (Aron 1970, 19).

In somewhat modified form, Durkheim's view is called expressivism, which Thom Brooks defines as "the emphatic denunciation by the community of a crime" (Brooks 2012, 102). Expressivism provides a link, however imperfect, between deterrence and retribution because the criminal law cannot be indifferent to the "sentiments of the law-abiding population" (Berns 1979, 136). Expressivists take from retribution the idea that the criminal is to be punished for what he or she did, but they abandon the idea of desert. There is no underlying principle behind expressivism except to reclaim communal solidarity. At the same time, expressivists take from utilitarianism the idea that reforming the criminal is in society's best interest. Expressivists draw attention to the role of public opinion as a valid source for laws. Moreover, expressivists, unlike retributivists, tend to follow positivistic social science—the science of the emotions—in fashioning the outlines of their theory. Joel Feinberg, for example, criticizes retributivism in the name of expressivism for failing to consider "an assessment of the character of the offender" over his "whole life" (Feinberg 1994, 88; Primoratz 1990, 2). What we gain from expressivism is the idea that the law cannot be limited to deterring behavior because humans are subject to more than just the sensations of pleasure and pain. Expressivism, however, runs the risk that, in the attempt to understand all, we must forgive all.

At their core, registration and residency restrictions are civil regulations that promote public safety (Doe v. Pataki 1997, 1283–84; Shaw v. Patton 2016, 572), and thus do not constitute punishment in any Eighth Amendment sense. But they contain aspects of expressivism (moral condemnation) and retribution and deterrence (punitiveness) that some scholars interpret as cruel. Judith Shklar defines cruelty as the "deliberate infliction of physical, and secondarily of emotional, pain upon a weaker person or group by stronger ones in order to achieve some end, tangible or intangible, of the latter" (1989, 29; Kekes 1996, 836). This definition is broader than how the Supreme Court has defined cruelty under the Eighth Amendment. For the Court, emotional pain is not part of Eighth Amendment jurisprudence. Incidental effects do not constitute punishment, the New Jersey supreme court declared in a sex offender case. Rather, the question is "whether punishment is 'the *purpose*[ ] that the [sanction] may *fairly* be said to serve'" (Doe v. Poritz 1995, 54; italics in original). According to the Supreme Court, a punishment "out of all proportion to the offense" constitutes cruelty and violates the Eighth Amendment. So, too, is a cruel and unusual method of punishment (Robinson v. California 1962, 676; Scalia 1989, 864).

John Stinneford narrows and clarifies Shklar's understanding of punishment. "When a given punishment is challenged as cruel and unusual," Stinneford writes, "the question is not whether it inflicts pain that is unduly harsh as an abstract and absolute matter, but rather whether it inflicts pain that is unduly harsh in comparison to the traditional punishments it has replaced" (2017, 447). Clearly, residency restrictions, which may exacerbate the emotional problems sex offenders suffer from, do not inflict unduly harsh pain and are in no way untraditional forms of regulation. Their deterrent effects are "distinct from any punitive purpose" (Bennis v. Michigan 1996, 452). Deterrence, after all, "may serve civil as well as criminal goals" (U.S. v. Ursery 1996, 292). In *Hudson v. U.S.* (1997, 105), a case involving the imposition of monetary penalties and debarment for violating federal banking rules, the Court denied that monetary penalties made the law criminal. "To hold that the mere presence of a deterrent purpose renders such sanctions 'criminal' for double jeopardy purposes would severely undermine the Government's ability to engage in effective regulation of institutions such as banks." A regulation that includes deterrent effects can be constitutional because deterrence does not define the Eighth Amendment's parameters. "Any number of governmental programs might deter crime without imposing punishment," the Court declared in *Smith v. Doe* (2003, 102).

Expressivism provides the Court with a democratic and deliberative basis for upholding sex offender legislation. But it cannot be the sole justification for residency restrictions. Brubaker's concern for the moral basis of punishment cannot be ignored. Courts must look to the role that deliberative majorities play in formulating laws and generating values about punishment, as well as our principles, history, and traditions, to determine a law's purpose and punitiveness. My focus on deliberative majorities in legislatures is an acknowledgment that public opinion can be cruel toward sex offenders (California v. Steele 2004). But if we avoid the talk about structural forces that eliminate agency and the possibility of knowledge, and understand punishment as a real-world consequence of willful criminal actions, filtered through a system of separation of powers and checks and balances, then the constitutionality of postconviction sex offender legislation is premised not upon its fit with various punitive theories (or social science data) but because it conforms to the aims of a limited and moderate constitutional government. In the next section, I will analyze how the Supreme Court understands punishment, in an attempt to see if residency restrictions are punitive in an Eighth Amendment sense.

The Supreme Court Defines Punishment

In *Kansas v. Hendricks* (1997, 361), the Court held that (1) deference to a legislature's intent should guide judicial decisions to punitive challenges; and (2) only the "clearest proof" that the regulation is punitive either in purpose or effect will render the law criminal rather than civil. Justice Anthony Kennedy, concurring, expressed concern about the blurred line that sex offender laws create between civil regulation and criminal punishment, although he did not propose an alternative approach to determining a law's punitive intent or effect. In *Smith v. Doe* (2003, 92), Justice Kennedy wrote the majority opinion upholding Alaska's sex offender registration law. There, he created a two-part test to determine whether a law is punitive. Kennedy wrote that the Court would first look at legislative intent. Then, if the intent proved nonpunitive, it would decide "whether the statute's effects are so punitive in nature as to deem legislative intent null and void." In *Smith v. Doe* (2003), the Court held that the purpose of Alaska's notification and registration law was to enhance public safety, and "humiliation is but a collateral consequence of a valid regulation" (2003, 99).[2]

In *Kennedy v. Mendoza-Martinez* (1963), the Supreme Court created a test for determining whether a congressional act is "penal or regulatory in character." That test included seven factors:

> [1] Whether the sanction involves an affirmative disability or restraint, [2] whether it has historically been regarded as a punishment, [3] whether it comes into play only on a finding of scienter, [4] whether its operation will promote the traditional aims of punishment—retribution and deterrence, [5] whether the behavior to which it applies is already a crime, [6] whether an alternative purpose to which it may rationally be connected is assignable for it, and [7] whether it appears excessive in relation to the alternative purpose assigned are all relevant to the inquiry, and may often point in differing directions.[3] (1963, 168–69)

Courts call this the "intent-effects" test (U.S. v. One Assortment of 89 Firearms 1984; Doe v. Poritz 1995, 131) and it appears in *Hendricks* and *Smith v. Doe*. It is essentially a balancing test, where courts look first to the legislative intent and then determine if the effect of the law is so punitive as to render a civil regulation criminal (Wisconsin v. Muldrow 2018, 508; Shaw v. Patton 2016, 577). In *Doe v. Pataki* (1997), a case that challenged New York's notification and registration requirements, the second circuit court of appeals used a four-part test—"(1) legislative intent, (2) statutory design, (3) historical analogies, and (4) effect of the statute" (Doe v. Pataki 1997, 1271; 1996, 616)—to determine punishment.[4] The "effects" prong has two parts. First, courts inquire into the "resemblance to historical forms of punishment," then they determine whether the regulation imposes an "affirmative disability or restraint" (Logan 2018, 441). "Intent-effects" does not always lead a court to uphold a law, as historical inquiry can take into account "evolving conceptions" of punishment. In 2017, a federal district court held Colorado's registration requirement for sex offenders unconstitutional as applied to David Millard, Eugene Knight, and Arturo Vega. Each defendant had been convicted of sexual assault against minors. The district court differentiated the cases under review from *Smith v. Doe* by noting that information that appears on the Internet is no longer "merely informational," as *Smith* suggests, but causes "humiliation" (Millard v. Rankin 2017,

13, n. 9). For the district court, societal changes regarding the power of social media to influence viewpoints about others requires changing constitutional conceptions of punishment. The district court did not explain why or how humiliation became part of Eighth Amendment analysis. One suspects that the judge in *Millard* meant by humiliation something along the lines of stigma and ostracism, though he never connected the dots that extend from humiliating an innocent person to blaming a guilty one.[5]

The *Mendoza-Martinez* test is less a reflection of rational analysis about the meaning of constitutional punishment than a "grab-bag of many individual tests" (Artway v. Attorney General of New Jersey 1996, 1263); as such, the Court has made a number of changes to it. In the 1980s, the Court revised the *Mendoza-Martinez* criteria by calling for greater legislative deference. The Court held that *Mendoza-Martinez* is "helpful," but its criteria are "neither exhaustive nor dispositive" (U.S. v. Ward 1980, 249). The Court expanded upon this idea in three cases, *United States v. Halper* (1989), *Austin v. United States* (1993), and *Montana Department of Revenue v. Kurth Ranch* (1994). "In the *Halper* line [of cases], the Court seems to focus exclusively on whether the sanction serves the dual aims of statutory sanctions, namely retribution and deterrence" (Goodman 1996, 786). In the latter-half of the 1990s, the Court revisited the punitive criteria in use in cases that are either civil, criminal, or both. Recognizing the intractability of the conflicts over what constitutes punishment, the Court chose to emphasize legislative intent in such cases as *Salerno v. United States* (1987), *United States v. Ursery* (1996), *Bennis v. Michigan* (1996), *Kansas v. Hendricks* (1997), *Hudson v. United States* (1997), and *United States v. Bajakajian* (1998). In *U.S. v. Salerno* (1987, 747), the Court's aim was clear: "To determine whether a restriction on liberty constitutes impermissible punishment or permissible regulation, we first look to legislative intent." In *California Department of Corrections v. Morales* (1995), the Court rejected the contention that a law was punitive that lowered the plaintiff's chances of being paroled. But it noted, as Daniel Feldman (1997, 1097) has written, that the effect of a "severe burden or sanction could constitute punishment, notwithstanding" the nonpunitive intention of the law.

In cases involving civil regulations and forms of punishment, the meaning of punishment remains vague and somewhat contradictory (Klein 1999, 702). Because of this ambiguity, it is worth looking at Supreme Court cases that involve laws that aim specifically to inflict punishment, rather than at laws that incidentally may determine what punishment is. We can begin with a hypothesis: that criminal justice cases that specifically refer to the state's power to punish infractions will lead to clarity about what punishment is, rather than to what punishment is not, and therefore provide guidance to understand whether sex offender regulations constitute punishment.

Three-Strikes Laws

The "primary goals" of three-strikes laws "are to deter repeat offenders and . . . to segregate that person from the rest of society for an extended period of time" (Rummel v. Estelle 1980, 284). Three-strikes laws are antirecidivism statutes that raise two important questions, the first relating to deterrence, the second to retribution: (1) whether it is proper for the state to sentence someone based on the accumulation of prior convictions and a new conviction to deter the future behavior of the accused and of others; and (2) what is the relationship in equity between the punishment of a crime and the crime itself? The first point is utilitarian because it treats offenders as means to a public safety end without regard for the proportionality of the punishment to the crime. The second point implicates retribution because the sentence is longer than what the individual would have received for the final crime judged by itself (Ewing v. California 2003, 31; Primoratz 1990, 162–64).

In *Graham v. Florida* (2010), a case about juveniles and life imprisonment, Justice Kennedy wrote: "The concept of proportionality is central to the Eighth Amendment" (2010, 59). The Court's proportionality review includes two areas of law. The first "involves challenges to the length of term-of-years sentences given all the circumstances in a particular case. The second comprises cases in which the Court implements the proportionality standard by certain categorical restrictions on the death penalty" (Graham v. Florida 2010, 59). In *Graham*, the Court held that attacks against sentences must show that "the punishment is not grossly disproportionate in light of the justification offered" (2010, 72). Proportionality, however, is a principle of retribution and not of utilitarianism, because "any punishment in excess of what is deserved for the criminal conduct is punishment without guilt" (Gross 1979, 436). Because the production of pleasure and the elimination of pain define utilitarianism, utilitarians can ignore punishing criminals for what they have done (i.e., desert) and sanction punishing the innocent to increase the happiness of the greatest number (Primoratz 1990, 9; Bagaric 1999). To be clear, proportionality review applies only to sentences attached to convictions and not to postconviction regulations, such as parole and probation (Rummel v. Estelle 1980, 295). The only justification for proportionality in such cases (including postconviction sex offender cases) is as a moral principle to limit deterrence-based punishments. It is an especially awkward fit in sex offender cases, coming as it does after sentencing (Primoratz 1990, 37; Ohio v. Blankenship [2015]; Kansas v. Mossman [2012]; Kansas v. Proctor [2012]; Iowa v. Oliver [2012]; Minnesota v. Christie [1993]; Minnesota v. Combs [1993]).

In *Rummel v. Estelle* (1980), the Court's first foray into three-strikes legislation, the Court upheld Texas's sentence of life in prison to William James Rummel for his third felony offense, all of which were nonviolent. The Court rejected the idea that the punishment was disproportionate to the offense because "[o]utside the context of capital punishment, successful challenges to the proportionality of particular sentences have been exceedingly rare" (Rummel v. Estelle 1980, 272). Since 1976, when the Court reinstated capital punishment, a majority of justices have been willing to apply proportionality to death penalty cases because "death is different" (Gregg v. Georgia 1976, 188). But the criteria for comparison in noncapital cases are difficult to assess, something that should be considered in the context of sex offender legislation (Lee 2008). William Rehnquist, writing for the Court in *Rummel*, pointed out that the Court had an institutional "reluctance to review legislatively mandated terms of imprisonment" (Rummel v. Estelle 1980, 274), on the idea that it is not the purpose of the justices to impose their notions of just punishments. There is also federalism to consider in when resorting to proportionality.

> That a State is entitled to treat with stern disapproval an act that other States punish with the mildest of sanctions follows *a fortiori* from the undoubted fact that a State may criminalize an act that other States do not criminalize *at all.* (Harmelin v. Michigan 1991, 989; italics in original)

In the next three-strikes case, *Solem v. Helm* (1983), the Court held that a South Dakota law that allowed for life imprisonment without the possibility of parole for repeat offenders was unconstitutional because it was disproportionate to the offense. *Solem* does not overturn *Rummel.*[6] It distinguishes it by noting the differences between the two states' parole possibilities (Solem v. Helm 1983, 288, 297). Jerry Buckley Helm committed seven felonies, including grand larceny and driving while intoxicated. For those offenses, plus "uttering a 'no account' check for $100," he was sentenced to life in prison. The Court held that proportionality analyses "should be guided by objective criteria, including (i) the gravity of the offense and the harshness of the penalty; (ii) the sentences imposed on other criminals in the same jurisdiction; and (iii) the sentences imposed for commission of the same crime in other jurisdictions" (1983, 281, 292). The Court's three-part analysis provided no guidance to determine how many crimes constitute disproportionality. Moreover, the Court applied proportionality as a limiting principle to a law that seeks only to deter, demonstrating the weakness of proportionality principles when attached to utilitarian criminal policies (Lacey 1988, 119, 176–77, 198–201).

It is possible to acknowledge a role for proportionality in Eighth Amendment analyses without increasing the role of judges' subjective value systems. Justice Kennedy's position, in *Harmelin v. Michigan* (1991), focuses on "the primacy of the legislature, the variety of legitimate penological schemes, the nature of our federal system, and the requirement that proportionality review be guided by objective factors." Kennedy then added that the "Eighth Amendment does not require strict proportionality between crime and sentence. Rather, it forbids only extreme sentences that are 'grossly disproportionate' to the crime" (Harmelin v. Michigan 1991, 1001). The different outcomes in *Rummel* and *Solem*, however, may be a sign that not all judges understand grossly disproportionate in the same way as Justice Kennedy.

This was Justice Antonin Scalia's opinion. He rejected an Eighth Amendment proportionality principle. "Proportionality . . . is inherently a concept tied to the penological goal of retribution," he wrote in *Ewing v. California* (2003, 31). In *Harmelin v. Michigan* (1991), Scalia wrote that proportionality becomes meaningless "once deterrence and rehabilitation are given significant weight" (1991, 989) in a law that also punishes based on desert. Moreover, Scalia rejected any resort to proportionality in noncapital cases because of the legislature's reliance on heterodox punitive concepts. For Scalia, the Eighth Amendment "disables the Legislature from authorizing particular forms or 'modes' of punishment—specifically, cruel methods of punishment that are not regularly or customarily employed" (Harmelin v. Michigan 1991, 976). To be sure, Scalia's position may result in some harshness toward defendants and can be considered constitutionally rigid—it may even be an abdication of the necessary role that judgment plays in deciding cases—but Scalia was trying to be both faithful to originalism (but see Stinneford 2008, 1819–20) and to prevent judges from making policy based upon subjective factors and transhistorical events, as Justice John Paul Stevens did when he spoke of the "world community" in the death penalty case *Atkins v. Virginia* (2002, 316 n. 21). When judges decide what is "grossly out of proportion" (Roper v. Simmons 2005, 589), and where the arc of history bends, they turn themselves into legislators and subvert democratic practices.

In the next three-strikes cases, *Ewing v. California* (2003) and *Lockyer v. Andrade* (2003), decided the same day, the Court upheld the three-strikes laws in question. In *Ewing v. California*, Justice Sandra Day O'Connor, writing for a plurality, upheld a "narrow proportionality principle" that "applies to noncapital sentences" (Ewing v. California 2003, 20). While on parole, Gary Ewing committed his last felony offense (he had three others, plus burglary offenses), walking out of a sporting goods store with "three golf clubs, priced at $399 apiece" (Ewing v. California 2003, 28). The prosecutor charged Ewing under California's three-strikes law. The court sentenced Ewing to twenty-five years to life.

In upholding California's law, Justice O'Connor turned to legislative deference as a priority, which she married to the Court's agnosticism regarding the aims of punishment: "Our traditional deference to legislative policy choices finds a corollary in the principle that the Constitution 'does not mandate adoption of any one penological theory'. . . . Selecting the sentencing rationales is generally a policy choice to be made by state legislatures, not federal courts" (Ewing v. California 2003, 25). In *Lockyer v. Andrade* (2003, 77), the Court upheld Lockyer's sentence of twenty-five years to life for stealing $150 worth of videotapes in California, holding that the "gross disproportionality principle reserves a constitutional violation for only the extraordinary case."

Rather than defining punishment, these cases turn on the meaning of proportionality. Proportionality, however, is difficult to define, and more suitable to death penalty cases, given their finality.[7] In *Coker v. Georgia* (1977), *Enmund v. Florida* (1982), *Ford v. Wainwright* (1986), *Thompson v. Oklahoma* (1988), *Atkins v. Virginia* (2002), *Roper v. Simmons* (2005), and *Kennedy v. Louisiana* (2008), all capital punishment cases, the Court used proportionality principles to limit the application of the death penalty, holding that punishments that are "grossly disproportionate" (Coker v. Georgia 1977, 592); "totally without penological justification" (Gregg v. Georgia 1976, 183); which "involve the unnecessary and wanton infliction of pain" (Gregg v. Georgia 1976, 173); and which do not comport with "evolving standards of decency" (Atkins v. Virginia 2002, 312) violate the Eighth Amendment. In no capital case, however, including *Furman v. Georgia* (1972), has the Court held that capital punishment itself is disproportionate to the crime it purports to deter.

The hypothesis has failed. We have not learned what punishment is in these cases. We know what it is not: the Court will not interfere with the "legislative prerogative" (Rummel v. Estelle 1980, 274) over punishments unless such laws reveal gross violations of what is cruel and unusual punishment. But we remain uncertain of the meaning of grossly disproportionate and of what constitutes cruel and unusual punishment. Originalist methodologies reveal greater insight into the meaning and use of cruel and unusual than those who advocate for evolving standards of decency, if only because the former provides a more principled basis for judgment than the latter. Nevertheless, resorting to a proportionality principle in sex offender cases risks interfering with the "appropriate level of deference to state legislative policymaking" (Sheketoff 2010, 2217) that is so important to our constitutional system. To examine further our hypothesis, I turn to conditions of confinement cases.

Conditions of Confinement

Conditions of confinement cases concern challenges by prisoners (and pretrial detainees) to prison conditions and regulations. Unlike three-strikes cases, conditions of confinement cases tell us something positive about punishment. In conditions of confinement cases, punishment is not just an evil, it is an indignity. According to dignity's advocates, dignity is an ethical maxim of contemporary life and a foundational idea in Eighth Amendment law, undergirded by the idea of progress in human affairs (Rao 2011; Pillsbury 1982, 1117). Dignity appears "in most treaties banning torture, slavery, inhuman and degrading treatments, and discriminations of all sorts" (Andorno 2009, 227; Barroso 2012, 342–43). Dignity is less a positive right than a universal norm, a categorical imperative of constitutional government. Dignity stands in opposition to imprisonment and punishment as such because it is an expression of the fundamental sameness of human beings. "The basic concept underlying the Eighth Amendment is nothing less than the dignity of man" (Trop v. Dulles 1958, 100).

Dignity took on its present form as a critique of power during the 1970s, when federal judges began resorting to dignity as a way to criticize prison management and conditions, in light of the historic lack of constitutional protections for prisoners (Ruffin v. Virginia 1871; Jackson v. Bishop 1968). As Judge Donald Lay, of the eighth circuit court of appeals wrote, regarding deplorable prison conditions in Arkansas, "The Eighth Amendment prohibiting 'cruel and unusual punishment' relates to 'evolving standards of decency that mark the progress of a maturing society.' The present record reflects the prison system at Cummins Prison Farm to be not only shocking to 'standards of decency,' but immoral and criminal as well" (Holt v. Sarver 1971, 309–10). In an earlier incarnation of this case, Chief Judge Jesse Smith Henley, of the eighth circuit federal district court, stated that the meaning of cruel and unusual "cannot be defined with specificity. It is flexible and tends to broaden as society tends to pay more regard to decency and dignity" (Holt v. Sarver 1970, 380). And in *Brown v. Plata* (2011), a case about prison overcrowding, Justice Kennedy stated, "A prison that deprives prisoners of basic sustenance . . . is incompatible with the concept of human dignity" (2011, 1928).

Strip searching prisoners and nonprisoners (who enter prisons and jails for visits or until their trial dates are set) has come under attack for violating the dignity of those being searched (Laaman v. Helgemoe 1977, 323; Florence v. Board of Chosen Freeholders 2012). In *Bell v. Wolfish* (1979), Justices John Paul Stevens and William Brennan held that strip searches must be "judged against our historic respect for the dignity of the free citizen." In the same case, Justice Thurgood Marshall argued that body cavity searches "represent one of the most grievous offenses against personal dignity and common decency." He went so far as to say that the regulations themselves, regardless of context or necessity, are an "affront to the dignity of the detainee as a human being" (Bell v. Wolfish 1979, 595, 576–77, 592). And in *Bull v. San Francisco* (2010), Judge Sidney Thomas, of the ninth circuit court of appeals, writing in dissent in a case that required the strip-searching of all arrestees in the San Francisco jail system, held:

> The indignity of the strip search is great. And is not a minor or incidental humiliation. It's a serious intrusion [on] a person's personal right to privacy, in my view. And I don't think there's a large amount of argument over that point. . . . It is not any more complicated than that, I think. (2010, 995)

When an individual's understanding of an indignity is thought to come from a universal standard of behavior, disregarding context,[8] then the emphasis is not on what is prudent in terms of punishment and rehabilitation but on the individual's experience of indignity.[9] If indignity is a violation of our status as human beings, with an emphasis on our sensual natures, then there is no limit to what constitutes indignity, and, more important, there is no possibility of constitutional dialogue among institutions and between institutions and persons regarding the means and ends of responsibility and public safety. Dignity is unabashedly result-oriented. Dignity in conditions of confinement cases makes sense only if there is no distinction between prison and society, responsibility and irresponsibility. Let's see how the Supreme Court has tried to make this work.

J. W. Gamble was an inmate in Texas who was injured performing prison work. After numerous doctor visits and prescribed medications, Gamble insisted that he was not fit for work and that the work he continued doing, while in pain, was cruel and unusual punishment. Prison administrators disagreed and imposed penalties upon him for his failure to work.

Traditionally, for punishment to be unconstitutional, it must (1) be state imposed; and (2) reach or go beyond the historical meaning of "cruel and unusual" (Stinneford 2017; 2008; Granucci 1969). Gamble's work requirement would not normally fall under the Eighth Amendment. But the Court in *Estelle v. Gamble* (1976) held that, since *Trop v. Dulles* (1958), the Eighth Amendment embodies "'broad and idealistic concepts of dignity, civilized standards, humanity, and decency' against which we must evaluate penal measures" (Estelle v. Gamble 1976, 102). Consequently, the Court held in *Estelle* (1976, 103) that "[t]hese elementary principles establish the government's obligation to provide medical care for those whom it is punishing by incarceration." The Court, however, ruled against Gamble and created a test of "deliberate indifference" to determine if prison authorities unconstitutionally punished Gamble by forcing him to work through pain (Estelle v. Gamble 1976, 104).

In *Hutto v. Finney* (1978, 685), the Court declared that "[c]onfinement in a prison or in an isolation cell is a form of punishment subject to scrutiny under Eighth Amendment standards," in part because punishments that are "grossly disproportionate to the offense" violate the "broad and idealistic concept[] of dignity" (1978, 685) found in the Eighth Amendment. But it was not until *Rhodes v. Chapman* (1981, 335) that the Court "considered a disputed contention that the conditions of confinement at a particular prison constituted cruel and unusual punishment." In *Rhodes*, the challenge was that double-celling inmates violated the Eighth Amendment. Although the Court declared that "the task of the courts in cases challenging prison conditions is 'to determine whether a challenged punishment comports with human dignity'" (1981, 361), the Court refused the challenge and created the "totality of conditions" test for determining deliberate indifference. In *Whitley v. Albers* (1986), the Court heard a challenge from an inmate who was shot during a prison riot, seemingly accidentally, by an officer firing a warning shot. This case is not a conditions of confinement case, but it addressed deliberate indifference. The Court ruled that although "deliberate indifference" applies to a "prisoner's serious illness or injury," this was not the case here. Instead, "a deliberate indifference standard does not adequately capture the importance of such competing obligations . . . necessarily made in haste, under pressure, and frequently without the luxury of a second chance" (1986, 320).

In *Wilson v. Seiter* (1991), Pearly Wilson alleged that an assortment of prison conditions—"overcrowding, excessive noise, insufficient locker storage space, inadequate heating and cooling, improper ventilation, unclean and inadequate restrooms, unsanitary dining facilities and food preparation, and housing with mentally and physically ill inmates"—violated the Eighth Amendment's prohibition against cruel and unusual punishments (1991, 295). Justice Scalia, for the majority, held that a prisoner claiming that conditions of confinement violate the cruel and unusual clause "must show a culpable state of mind on the part of prison officials," as well as significant injury (1991, 296). The Court defined cruelty by certain objective conditions and not by the "subjective intent of government officials" (1991, 309).

In *Hudson v. McMillian* (1992, 4), Keith Hudson, an inmate in Louisiana, claimed that two prison guards, Jack McMillan and Marvin Woods, beat him while another guard, the supervisor on duty, Arthur Mezo, watched but did nothing to stop the beating. Although Hudson did not experience "serious injury," he claimed that the beating constituted cruel and unusual punishment. "For generations," Justice Scalia noted in dissent, "judges and commentators regarded the Eighth Amendment as applying only to torturous punishments meted out by statutes or sentencing judges, and not generally to any hardship that might befall a prisoner during incarceration" (Hudson v. McMillian 1992, 18). The majority decision, however, accepted the idea that punishment does not have to be state sanctioned to be considered cruel and unusual under the Eighth Amendment, and it downplayed *Wilson v. Seiter*'s holding that the pain inflicted should be substantial. Justice O'Connor, writing for the Court, held that "When prison officials maliciously and sadistically use force to cause harm, contemporary standards of decency always are violated" (Hudson v. MacMillian 1992, 9).

Finally, in *Farmer v. Brennan* (1994), the Court confronted a challenge to the Eighth Amendment by Dee Farmer (born Douglas Coleman Farmer), who was in the middle of receiving treatment for sex reassignment when Farmer was convicted of credit card fraud. After transferring Farmer to a high security penitentiary, prison officials placed Farmer in the general population of a men's prison. Farmer made no objection to the transfer or to being placed in the general population. Farmer was subsequently raped and beaten. Farmer sued, arguing deliberate indifference on the part of prison officials.

The Court took the case to resolve a conflict among federal courts over the meaning of deliberate indifference. Some federal courts had stressed the subjective test, others more objective factors (Farmer v. Brennan 1994, 836). The Court rejected Farmer's argument for an objective test. Justice David Souter, writing for the Court, held that:

> a prison official cannot be found liable under the Eighth Amendment for denying an inmate humane conditions of confinement unless the official knows of and disregards an excessive risk to inmate health or safety; the official must both be aware of facts from which the inference could be drawn that a substantial risk of serious harm exists, and he must also draw the inference. (1994, 837)

The Court held that prison officials can be held liable for deliberate indifference to prisoners' health and safety and that prison officials have a constitutional duty to provide humane conditions. But the Court stated that a state actor's deprivation of an inmate's liberty must be "sufficiently serious," and must "result in the denial of 'the minimal civilized measure of life's necessities.'" The inmate must show that he or she is living under conditions which pose "a substantial risk of serious harm." Moreover, the prison official must have a "culpable state of mind" (1994, 825, 834). Deliberate indifference now "means recklessness" on behalf of prison officials (Stinneford 2017, 457), an equally vague concept that can only lead to more court challenges. The Supreme Court remanded the case to the federal district court.

The Supreme Court has not come to a conclusion regarding what constitutes punishment in cases involving conditions of confinement. Justices Scalia and Thomas have argued that punishment refers only to sentencing and never to the actions of state actors; all other justices believe that punishment can be imposed by state actors, where the criteria for evaluation turns on evolving standards of decency, violations of dignity, and a combination of objective and subjective factors. Neither three-strikes cases, which focus on proportionality, nor conditions of confinement cases, which stress dignity and deliberate indifference, tell us what punishment is under the Eighth Amendment. For John

Stinneford, cruelty "refers to the effect of the punishment, not the intent of the punisher" (2017, 471; Baze v. Rees 2008; Wilkerson v. Utah 1879). Unusual, according to Stinneford, "means 'contrary to long usage' . . . [and] almost certainly was intended to cover grossly disproportionate punishments" (Stinneford 2008, 1820). Stinneford's understanding would bring clarity to three-strikes and conditions of confinement cases. But we cannot apply Stinneford's definition to residency restrictions. In conditions of confinement cases, cruelty and indignity are used as substitutes for traditional Eighth Amendment analysis, which is not the case with residency restrictions, which rely upon individual risk assessments.[10] While a claim could be made that residency restrictions are disproportionate to the original crime, these are postconviction regulations and residency restrictions are not contrary to long usage by state governments to protect the public.

The question that weighs on courts deciding residency restriction cases is whether or not such restrictions impose unfair burdens (the "effect of the punishment," as Stinneford writes) on a host of rights that convicted sex offenders have as free or semi-free citizens, for example, intrastate travel, privacy, the right to work in areas of one's choosing, and the right to be free from stigma. What remains to examine is what courts and legislators regard as punishment in cases involving residency restrictions and to see, perhaps, if the regulation is excessive to the point that it constitutes cruelty under the Eighth Amendment.

Banishment, Travel, and Fundamental Rights

Thomas Hobbes regarded punishment as an "evil" (Hobbes 1994, chap. 28, para. 1; Bentham 1830, 1) because he recognized that in a liberal state, founded on a social contract dedicated to self-preservation and public safety, punishment is necessary to maintain order, even if it is philosophically incompatible with other liberal ideas (Schrock 1991). For Hobbes, punishment is the expression of the state's agreement to protect the public under the terms of the social contract. Punishment is also the outcome of the deliberate sense of the community because punishment under liberalism is not strictly imposed—it requires notice, information, a trial and judgment about punishment's extent. Punishment in a liberal but not strictly Hobbesian sense comports with democratic practices. If, however, punishment is not rooted in public safety but is an indignity rooted in evolving conceptions of human and civilizational decency, then there is no purpose to punishment except state-sanctioned vengeance. Dignitarian jurisprudence erodes the political, democratic, and contractual basis for punishment. In this final section, I will focus on banishment, residency restrictions, and intrastate travel to see if each individually or collectively violates the Eighth Amendment's prohibition against cruel and unusual punishment or the due process clause of the Fourteenth Amendment.

The argument that residency restrictions are punitive and violate substantive due process is based on a set of assumptions about constitutional law as expansive (Porter 1992; Saenz v. Roe 1999; Dunn v. Blumstein 1972). It requires substituting majority rule and the institutional limits of our constitutional structure for the "deep" and "wide" (Sunstein 1999, 16; Chapman and McConnell 2012) understanding of due process as an absolute protection for minority rights, based on conceptions of fairness or universal principles of dignity. Catherine Carpenter and Amy Beverlin (2012, 1122) capture this idea when they write, "At its heart, substantive due process was 'intended to secure the individual from the arbitrary exercise of the powers of government.'" This is not the meaning of substantive due process. This is what due process does in its ordinary function (Fay v. Noia 1963, 402). Indeed, the internal quote Carpenter and Beverlin rely on is from *Hurtado v. California* (1884), a procedural due process case. Due process is respectful of human and institutional limitations, including judicial traditions, and is minimalistic in scope. The Supreme Court requires those making substantive claims to be "specific and concrete" in their descriptions and avoid "sweeping abstractions and generalities" (Doe v. Lafayette 2004, 769). The conflating of due process with substantive due process reflects the state of jurisprudential thinking regarding punishment: that substantive due process is the normal application of due process; it is not.

According to the anonymous plaintiffs in *Doe v. Miller* (2005, 709), residency restrictions interfere with a "fundamental right to live where you want." Presumably, the denial of that right results in banishment. The Supreme Court requires that "'[s]ubstantive due process' analysis must begin with a careful description of the asserted right, for '[t]he doctrine of judicial self-restraint requires us to exercise the utmost care whenever we are asked to break new ground in this field'" (Reno v. Flores 1993, 302). Were the right to live where one wants a fundamental right, then other concerns, such as community safety, could not overcome the claim that a residency restriction banishes a person or a set of persons from a particular part of a city. Such laws or regulations would be subject to heightened scrutiny. Civil peace would be made subordinate to the individual right to live or go where one pleases, regardless of one's status as a threat to the community (Doe v. Lafayette 2004, 774). And, as this right is not explicitly mentioned in the Constitution, it must be extrapolated from a right (also not explicitly mentioned) to interstate travel and the "right to live in the political subdivision of [one's] choice" (Edgerton 2007, 1024).

In *U.S. v. Guest* (1966, 757), the Supreme Court held that the "constitutional right to travel from one State to another, and necessarily to use the highways and other instrumentalities of interstate commerce in doing so, occupies a position fundamental to the concept of our Federal Union." The Court admitted that the "right finds no explicit mention in the Constitution," but it noted that the right was "elementary" (U.S. v. Guest 1966, 758). In *Shapiro v. Thompson* (1969, 633), the Court reaffirmed the right to travel, holding that "a State may not" interfere with this right "by invidious distinctions between classes of its citizens."

In *Washington v. Glucksberg* (1997), the Supreme Court outlined a two-part test to establish whether or not a rights claim that is new falls under the Fourteenth Amendment's substantive understanding of the due process clause. First, the asserted right must be "objectively, deeply rooted in this Nation's history and tradition, and implicit in the concept of ordered liberty, such that neither liberty nor justice would exist if it were sacrificed." Second, the Court requires a "careful description of the asserted fundamental liberty interest" (1997, 720–21). The reason for the high regard the Court has placed on careful description of the asserted right and the need for objectively rooted traditions is because, by granting a fundamental right, the Court effectively shuts down the political process.

> By extending constitutional protection to an asserted right or liberty interest, we, to a great extent, place the matter outside the arena of public debate and legislative action. We must therefore exercise the utmost care whenever we are asked to break new ground in this field, lest the liberty protected by the Due Process Clause be subtly transformed into the policy preferences of the members of this Court. (1997, 720)

In *Lawrence v. Texas* (2003, 571–72), Justice Kennedy noted that the "events" of "the last half century" are equally determinative of substantive due process claims as are history and tradition, but he did not tell judges or the American people how to think about these unstated changes and their relationship, if any, to the Constitution's history and traditions. His opinion blurs what

Glucksberg clarifies because it does not elucidate what events of the past half-century matter. Nor does he explain why the *Glucksberg* majority was unaware of the import of these events (Conkle 2006). Despite the break with *Glucksberg's* emphasis on the political process, *Lawrence* in no way diminishes *Glucksberg's* value. In the context of this contested understanding of due process and substantive due process, we are forced to confront three questions: (1) are residency restriction laws that are applied to convicted sex offenders banishment; (2) is banishment of this type a punishment that violates the due process clause; and (3) whether banishment means only expulsion from the state or does it include expulsion from a neighborhood or county? (Georgia v. Collett 1974; Terry v. Hamrick 2008). As the law stands now, the only test for banishment in residency restriction cases is whether the restriction is rationally related to a governmental objective. That objective is usually understood to stem from a government's "compelling interest to promote, protect and improve the public health, safety and welfare" (Ryals v. City of Englewood 2016, 904) of its citizens. Consequently, state and federal courts have dismissed claims that residency restrictions are the same as laws that prevent a person from living with a relative who receives public funds, which are unconstitutional (Bains 2007, 492).

Banishment is an ancient punishment, but ancient cities had neither prisons as we would call them today nor the institutions that form the administration of justice (Peters 1998). The concept of ancient banishment is not easily assimilated into modern banishment statutes. Montesquieu tells us that in Athens banishment was only for "great personages" (1949, 159) and resorted to only every five years. The Greeks used exile as a way to purify a community following a crime. The refusal of banishment meant death. For the ancients, banishment had a symbolic and practical meaning, something that residency restrictions lack. For the Greeks, crimes and especially murders were instances of too much anger (*thymos*), and exile was a way to "cure the community and . . . the wrongdoer" (Allen 2000, 82, 60, 201) of this excess. The punishment of banishment was based on desert and applied to those who, through their own actions, were no longer deemed fit to participate in the life of the city. The Greeks called this *atimia*, a loss of honor. One who was *atimos* was prevented from participating in civic life but could remain within the city itself (Allen 2000, 202, 61, 286; Forsdyke 2005, 7). Ancient banishment—that is, being exiled from a city for a crime or an act of moral turpitude—was necessary because life in the ancient city had meaning beyond mere self-preservation (de Coulanges 1980; Bauman 2012).

The contrast between ancient banishment and modern residency restrictions could not be clearer. Residency restrictions impose restrictions on where convicted sex offenders can live—extending anywhere from 500 feet to 2,500 feet. They do not, as the Romans did, strip citizens of their property or deny them civil offices. Nor do they, as the English did in the early modern period, impose death upon those who illegally return from banishment (Shaw v. Patton 2016, 568). Unlike ancient punishment, residency restrictions are not linked with every civil penalty (Friedman 1993, 32–34; Poodry v. Tonawanda Band of Seneca Indians 1996). Residency restrictions are not the equivalent of bills of attainder or civil death (Dick 2011). The alternative to residency restrictions is not execution. As the court of appeals held in *Illinois v. Leroy* (2005, 539–40):

> [A]lthough the defendant is prohibited from "residing" at the home his mother owns in East St. Louis because that home is located within 500 feet of a school, he is not precluded from visiting his mother at that home on a daily basis and thereby enjoying her support. Put simply, the restrictions placed on the defendant . . . in no way resemble the historical punishment of banishment, and only a tortured reading of the term banishment could lead us to conclude otherwise.

Because residency restrictions do not meet the standards set out in *Mendoza-Martinez* or its progeny, they cannot be considered punishment. Residency laws, Judge Diarmuid O'Scannlain of the ninth circuit court of appeals held, in *Russell v. Gregoire*, have "protective purposes" (1997, 1092; McAllister 1998). And because they seek the protection of vulnerable populations, courts cannot subject residency restrictions to strict scrutiny.

The residency law in Iowa, which has a 2,000-foot restriction, is comprehensive in its concerns. It "does not 'expel' the offenders from their communities or prohibit them from accessing areas near schools or child care facilities for employment, to conduct commercial transactions, or for any purpose other than establishing a residence." Nor does the statute "require a change of residence: the Iowa General Assembly included a grandfather provision that permits sex offenders to maintain a residence that was established prior to July 1, 2002, even if that residence is within 2000 feet of a school or child care facility" (Doe v. Miller 2005, 719). There is considerable constitutional difference between having "vast spaces" "declared off limits" to convicts and being banished to another county, city, state, or country (Shaw v. Patton 2016, 567; Vann v. Alabama 2013; Iowa v. Seering 2005).

If residency restrictions are not banishment, perhaps residency restrictions interfere with another right. Is there a right to travel that residency restrictions interfere with? In *Saenz v. Roe* (1999), which concerned residency requirements and receipt of welfare payments, the Supreme Court held that the right to interstate travel is based upon the privileges and immunities clauses found in Article IV, section 2, and the Fourteenth Amendment.

> The "right to travel" discussed in our cases embraces at least three different components. It protects the right of a citizen of one State to enter and to leave another State, the right to be treated as a welcome visitor rather than an unfriendly alien when temporarily present in the second State, and, for those travelers who elect to become permanent residents, the right to be treated like other citizens of that State. (1999, 500)

Article IV section 2 speaks of privileges and immunities that each citizen is entitled to (Anastaplo 1989, chap. 13; Story 1858, 2: 3, 40). The Article does not define the term. In the Fourteenth Amendment, privileges "and" immunities is changed to "or" (Ely 1980, 22–30; Curtis 1986, 160–68). Article IV contains a right of citizens to regress and ingress (Paul v. Virginia 1869; Doe v. Miller 2005). Is this a right to travel? If so, is this right a trump card over residency restrictions?

One understanding of Article IV is clear: "It has no effect, either substantive or equality-based, on the treatment a state gives its own citizens" (Harrison 1992, 1398). Article IV allows states to make distinctions regarding extending privileges and immunities, such as to those charged with treason, felonies, those fleeing justice, and those charged with other crimes (I leave aside the clause about those "held to service"). The Constitution does not allow such persons to move about freely among several states, evading the law. The right to travel under Article IV is bounded by concerns about criminal behavior. Indeed, the Constitution requires the states to "deliver up" such persons. The right to travel interstate, then, is not absolute or fundamental.

There is, of course, a "right of locomotion, the right to remove from one place to another according to inclination," and that such a right "is an attribute of personal liberty . . . secured by the 14th Amendment" (Williams v. Fears 1900, 274). But even in that case, *Williams v. Fears*, decided in 1900, the Court held that travel rights cannot dominate over a right, the taxing power of states, that the Constitution provides for. What "privileges or immunities" (taken from the Fourteenth Amendment) accomplishes, I believe, is an "*equality-based* protection," which John Harrison (1992, 1391; italics in original) defines as the requirement "that every state give the same privileges and immunities of state citizenship—the same positive law rights of property, contract, and so forth—to all of its citizens." What the Supreme Court has done in its travel cases since the 1960s is conflate the right to travel between or among states without fear or favor (Article IV) with the rights of citizenship (section 1 of the Fourteenth Amendment), creating a substantive right to travel, seemingly unconnected to community concerns and "bona fide residency requirements" (Saenz v. Roe 1999, 516).

Some federal courts have recognized a right to intrastate travel (Johnson v. Cincinnati 2002, 496 n. 3). In *King v. New Rochelle Municipal Housing Authority* (1971), the second circuit court of appeals held that a five-year residency requirement for admission to public housing violated the Equal Protection Clause. The court found a right to travel intrastate. "It would be meaningless to describe the right to travel between states as a fundamental precept of personal liberty and not to acknowledge a correlative constitutional right to travel within a state" (1971, 648–49).

Following the logic of this and other cases, the sixth circuit court of appeals held, in *Johnson v. Cincinnati* (2002), that a law that banned those either arrested or convicted of drug offenses from a "drug exclusion zone" was unconstitutional on substantive due process and freedom of association grounds. The Ohio supreme court defined a drug exclusion zone as an area of a city with a large number of drug arrests and "other drug-abuse related crimes" (Ohio v. Burnett 2001, 428–29). The purpose of the law was twofold: (1) to allow the public to move about the city free from drug trafficking; and (2) to deter those involved in drugs from returning to the scene of the crime.

> If the offender is subsequently convicted of the crime for which he or she was arrested, the offender is prohibited for one year from the date of conviction from being on any public street, sidewalk, or other public way in all drug-exclusion zones. If an excluded person is found within a drug-exclusion zone during the exclusion period, that person is subject to immediate arrest for criminal trespass. (Ohio v. Burnett 2001, 420)

The sixth circuit court of appeals, in *Johnson v. Cincinnati*, held that the ordinance violated the rights of those who want to assist in the raising of grandchildren, the right of those to intrastate travel, and the right of those to visit one's attorney. The "right to travel locally through public spaces and roadways—perhaps more than any other right secured by substantive due process—is an everyday right, a right we depend on to carry out our daily life activities" (2002, 495). *Johnson* relies on the Supreme Court's decision in *Apthetker v. Secretary of State* (1964), although Justice William Douglas in that case did not speak of a right to intrastate travel but of a "right to travel abroad" (1964, 521). The Court held similarly in *Kent v. Dulles* (1958, 127), where the Court upheld the right to travel abroad and explicitly declined to consider "the extent to which it can be curtailed." In the last year of the Warren Court, the Court struck down a one-year waiting period for welfare benefits of those who recently moved to the state because it "'has a chilling effect on the right to travel'" (Shapiro v. Thompson 1969, 623).

It would hardly be "meaningless," as the federal court of appeals in *King v. New Rochelle Municipal Housing Authority* declared, to give content to the right to travel, given that the right to intrastate travel clearly impinges upon the right of communities to prevent drug deals, or to have safe streets, or to restrict welfare benefits for a time, or to be free from pornography (Robinson v. California 1962, 666; Schall v. Martin 1984; Rise v. Oregon 1995). In *Johnson v. Cincinnati*, the court of appeals had to infer a fundamental right of intrastate travel from the right to travel abroad, which is quite a leap. The question the court of appeals raises is whether "a purely intrastate restriction" implicates a "right of interstate travel" (Bray v. Alexandria Women's Health Clinic 1993, 277).

In *Johnson v. Cincinnati*, two defendants, both convicted of drug offenses, were denied, in one instance visiting a lawyer (and therefore claiming interference with a right to petition the government for redress) and, in another, visiting grandchildren. The majority held that the drug exclusion zone interfered with the First and Fourteenth Amendments, which the court believed included a right to participate in the raising of one's grandchildren (Moore v. City of East Cleveland 1977). The constitutional issues involved here are too numerous to separate. For our purposes, the question *Johnson* raises is: does Cincinnati's restriction violate a "private realm of family life which the state cannot enter"? (Prince v. Massachusetts 1944, 166).

Though the court said yes, this is clearly not the case. As the Supreme Court held in *Village of Belle Terre v. Boraas* (1974), which tested a law that "restricted land use to one-family dwellings excluding lodging houses, boarding houses, fraternity houses, or multiple-dwelling houses":

> this case involves no procedural disparity inflicted on some but not on others. . . . It involves no "fundamental" right guaranteed by the Constitution, such as voting, the right of association, the right of access to the courts, or any rights of privacy. We deal with economic and social legislation where legislatures have historically drawn lines which we respect against the charge of violation of the Equal Protection Clause if the law be "reasonable, not arbitrary" and bears "a rational relationship to a (permissible) state objective." (1974, 2, 7–8)

This kind of analysis—one that focuses on three key concepts of democratic theory: (1) respect for the deliberative process; (2) a frank acknowledgment that the case involves liberty restrictions but no fundamental rights; and (3) respect for the limited reach of the judiciary in the face of historical patterns of state legislation concerning residency restrictions—is the key to solving the problem of residency restrictions for sex offenders.

Neither defendant in *Johnson v. Cincinnati* belonged to a suspect class. It strains the meaning of freedom of association to suggest that the regulation either interferes with attorney-client privileges or the right to petition the government for redress. It is true that the Supreme Court had previously admitted that the family is an institution "deeply rooted in this Nation's history and tradition" (Moore v. City of East Cleveland 1977, 503), and thus, by extension, a drug exclusion zone that prohibits a grandmother from *raising* her grandchildren *could* interfere with this right. But as the facts of *Johnson* show, the grandparent was not the primary guardian (Johnson v. Cincinnati 2002, 514). The court of appeals in *Johnson* made no attempt to explain the linkage between the necessary protections the family as such deserves under the Constitution and the right of local governments to protect the population it governs from drug dealers. Surely, the plague of drugs in American cities is a fact of the past half-century deserving of legislative oversight (Sasse 2000). Indeed, even the majority opinion recognized Cincinnati's "goal of eradicating the blight of drug-infested neighborhoods" as a "compelling governmental interest" (Johnson v. Cincinnati 2002, 516). Yet the majority rejected the argument the Supreme Court took in *Village of Belle Terre*, holding that the law's exclusion of (possibly innocent) individuals (i.e., those whose drug charges had been dropped) from an "entire metropolitan neighborhood of 10,000 people" (Johnson v. Cincinnati 2002, 503) was more than the Constitution could tolerate.

In *Lutz v. City of York* (1990), the third circuit court of appeals held that there was a right to intrastate travel in a case involving a York, Pennsylvania, ordinance that outlawed "cruising," that is, driving "repeatedly around a loop of certain major public roads through the heart of the city" (Lutz v. York 1990, 256). York passed the law after a study of traffic problems, including noting that cruising interfered with fire trucks on their way to putting out fires. The court was forced to admit that its reasoning was "ad hoc," as it strains credulity to associate blocking traffic with the right to travel. In any case, the court noted that there were possibly seven sources for a right to interstate travel in the Constitution: "the Article IV Privileges and Immunities Clause, the Fourteenth Amendment Privileges and [*sic*] Immunities Clause, a conception of national citizenship said to be implicit in the structural logic of the Constitution itself, the Commerce Clause, the Equal Protection Clause, and each of the Due Process Clauses" (Lutz v. York 1990, 260–61, 268). Ignoring the ambiguities and conflicts among these clauses, the court of appeals held that the right to intrastate travel was fundamental because it (1) belonged to the "concept of ordered liberty"; and (2) was "deeply rooted in our nation's history" (Lutz v. York 1990, 268). Rather than confront the legislature's concerns and the social science data about traffic flow, the court of appeals held that the right to intrastate travel is no different from the freedom of speech, which (in certain cases) can be limited by time, place, and manner restrictions, but is otherwise given wide latitude. The court then upheld the ordinance because it passed intermediate scrutiny analysis.

The cases that have found in favor of an intrastate right to travel have the following features in common: (1) the right to travel begins as a right to travel abroad, a right the Court initially found in the Fifth Amendment's due process clause; (2) the right to travel abroad is then connected to a right to travel interstate, but not attached to a specific constitutional provision or amendment; (3) the implicit right to travel interstate is then connected to the Fourteenth Amendment's privilege or immunities clause, but that clause, previously dormant (Slaughter-House Cases 1873), takes on a substantive aspect, allowing it to say what neither text nor history hitherto has (McDonald v. Chicago 2010, 805; Saenz v. Roe 1999, 511; Calabresi and Agudo 2008, 92–94). The complaints in residency cases then take on a more fundamental charge, that the right to travel is part of being human and no government can restrict travel without good cause. At which point: (4) the right to travel interstate must mean the right to travel intrastate. But the right to interstate and intrastate travel cannot be housed under the Fifth Amendment, so it has to lodge either in Article IV, the Ninth Amendment, the Fourteenth Amendment, or in the penumbra of the

Bill of Rights (Wilhelm 2010; Lash 2011, 425; 2005; Griswold v. Connecticut 1965, 484). In *Shapiro v. Thompson* (1969, 630), the Supreme Court admitted that "We have no occasion to ascribe the source of this right to travel interstate to a particular constitutional provision." Asserting that the right simply exists, the Court continued: "The constitutional right to travel from one State to another . . . occupies a position fundamental to the concept of our Federal Union." This broad assertion of judicial power means that the deliberative process that determines questions of public safety will be curtailed (Owens v. Maryland 1999, 56).

Not all courts have found a right to intrastate travel (Wright v. City of Jackson 1975; Hutchins v. District of Columbia 1999; Wardwell v. Board of Education 1976). These cases have held that "classifications" on travel "can only be subjected to low-level scrutiny under federal equal protection analysis" (Eddleman v. Center Township of Marion County 1989, 89 n. 8). For instance, in *Standley v. Town of Woodfin* (2012), the Georgia state court of appeals addressed a right to intrastate travel claim against the backdrop of sex offender legislation. Standley, while living in Florida, "was convicted of attempted sexual battery and aggravated assault against a woman." He then moved to North Carolina, "making him subject to the North Carolina Sex Offender & Public Protection Registry." While on probation, Standley was arrested for solicitation of a prostitute and the court revoked his probation. The Georgia court, following the federal court of appeals in *Johnson v. Cincinnati*, held that the right to intrastate travel is a "right of function." Neither the Georgia court of appeals nor the federal court of appeals in *Johnson* defined this right. Nevertheless, the *Standley* court held that a ban on entering a public park, in relation to limiting the movement of sex offenders, is not a violation of a right to intrastate travel because that right "does not impair . . . daily functions" (Standley v. Town of Woodfin 2012, 134, 136).

It is in the specificity of Standley's crime that his argument for substantive due process arises. That is to say, the law prevents Standley from entering public parks because he is a sex offender. The state passed the law, in large part, to protect minors in parks. These are legitimate constitutional concerns and functions. But Standley is not a child molester. He claimed that the law was too broad, that it lacked individualized risk assessment, and that it interfered with a right to travel. The Georgia supreme court, however, was reluctant to find a right to intrastate travel because of a lack of Supreme Court guidance and the rule, articulated in *Washington v. Glucksberg*, that courts should be "reluctant" to "transform[]" the vagaries of the due process clause "into the policy preferences of judges" (Willis v. Town of Marshall 2005, 265–66; Washington v. Glucksberg 1997, 720).

Perhaps one way to sort out a right to intrastate travel and sex offender residency restrictions is to mark the difference between those on parole or probation and those who are not, as New Jersey does. A "prisoner on parole is not free from legal restraint, but is constructively a prisoner in the legal custody of state prison authorities until officially discharged from parole" (Prison Law Office v. Koenig 1986, 566; Alloy 2002, 1089, n. 70). Parole serves as a way for society to ensure public safety, and the Supreme Court accepts that "[p]arolees have fewer constitutional rights than do ordinary persons" (In re Taylor 2013, 76; Morrisey v. Brewer 1972, 482). In *Williams v. Department of Corrections* (2014), Williams, a parolee, challenged New York's Sexual Assault Reform Act (SARA) on the ground that the 1,000-foot limitation was an infringement on a right to intrastate travel. And though the New York supreme court upheld the idea of a fundament right to interstate travel, it doubted that intrastate travel was such a right. It furthermore held that, as a parolee, Williams "does not enjoy an absolute right to travel" (2014, 375). Indeed, in a follow-up case, the same court made it clear that "an individual's constitutional right to travel . . . [is] legally extinguished by a valid conviction followed by imprisonment, [and] is not revived by the change in status from prisoner to parolee" (Williams v. Department of Corrections and Community Supervision 2016, 169).

State and local jurisdictions have the right to curtail the movements of probationers and parolees.[11] Such regulations do not run afoul of the Eighth or Fourteenth Amendments. In *Doe v. Petro* (2005, 1), a case in which a federal district court denied Doe's claim that an Ohio law that restricted convicted sex offenders from living within 1,000-feet of a school was an infringement upon a right to travel, the court ruled: "Even assuming there is a right of intrastate travel, convicted felons are properly subjected to many restrictions on their constitutional rights which would be objectionable if imposed on non-felons."

Conclusion

The attack against residency restrictions in the name of individual risk assessment, evolving standards of decency, dignity, and the social sciences denies the principle that a "minimalist court settles the case before it, but it leaves many things undecided" (Sunstein 1999, ix). Sunstein's "many things" means that communities get to say, with minimal constitutional intrusion, what constitutes safety and decency. "Narrow and incompletely theorized rulings," Sunstein writes (1999, 162), "allow room for public discussion and debate before obtaining a centralized national ruling that preempts ordinary political process." In *Paris Adult Theater I v. Slaton* (1973), the Supreme Court held that states can regulate pornography because of the "interest of the public in the quality of life and the total community environment," including "the public safety itself" (1973, 58). I see no reason why courts cannot apply that same logic to residency restrictions.

The problem I set up at the beginning of this book was this: what are the limits of popular sovereignty, majority rule, and deliberative legislative intent when confronted with the challenge that postconviction civil commitment, the registration of sex offenders' personal information, and residency restrictions violate fundamental liberty interests and social science data? I have shown that these regulatory forms, though they can be excessive and broad, do not violate due process or any other right challenged. Constitutionality and wisdom are not the same thing, though they can meet. As Keith Whittington writes, the Constitution's meaning "must be constructed from the political melding of the document with external interests and principles" (1999, 1). For me, these external interests and principles—legislative deliberation, majority rule, and the institutional configurations the Constitution has created (federalism, for example)—necessarily exclude a narrow and self-referential jurisprudence centered on an expansive reading of the Bill of Rights. They must also exclude extra-institutional considerations, such as dignity and a jurisprudence dependent upon "evolving standards of decency." Such views can only enhance judicial supremacy and diminish legislative deliberation.

If, as some believe, "Executions are brutal and inhumane" (Bessler 2012, 337) and therefore violate the Eighth Amendment's cruel and unusual clause, how is it possible that residency restrictions, registration requirements, and postconviction civil confinement are also cruel in an Eighth Amendment sense? Governance over a large republic, with federal principles and a separation of powers scheme, was the theme of Felix Frankfurter's jurisprudence. Frankfurter's advocacy of deference and respect for laws long on the books provides a clearer way to think of constitutional construction than any reliance on evolving standards of decency can. We can, then, alter Frankfurter's query from *Trop v. Dulles* (1958) only slightly to attain constitutional wisdom about sex offender legislation: "Is constitutional dialectic so empty of reason that it can be seriously urged that [residency restrictions are] a fate worse than death?" (1958, 125).

NOTES

1. For a detailed analysis of probation and punishment, see *Shaw v. Patton* (2016, 563–66), where the tenth circuit court of appeals rejected the contention that residency restrictions "resemble" probation and banishment. See *Smith v. Doe* (2003, 102) for the differences between probationary violations and registration and notification violations.

2. See *Shaw v. Patton* (2016, 568) for a number of cases in which courts have held that the collateral consequences of notification and registration requirements do not constitute punishment.

3. Legal scholars link *Mendoza-Martinez* (1963) with *De Veau v. Braistead* (1960) and *Trop v. Dulles* (1958). These three cases created the inquiry into the punitive elements of the civil-criminal distinction (Goodman 1996, 782–89; Steiker 1997).

4. Part of the problem with context independent of principle can be found in two federal district court cases that came to two different conclusions about notification and registration laws using the same analysis. In *Doe v. Pataki* (1996), a federal district court upheld New York's SORA law against an ex post facto challenge. In *Roe v. Office of Adult Probation* (1996), a different federal district court held Connecticut's community notification law unconstitutional, because it offended the Constitution's prohibition against ex post facto laws. The *Roe* court followed the same set of concerns—intent, design, history, and effects—the *Pataki* court had created. See also, *Doe v. Gregoire* (1997) and *Kansas v. Petersen-Beard* (2016, 197–98).

5. Courts that reject "intent-effects" can also use the "fundamental purpose" test, which eliminates the effect of the law or regulation from the intent-effects test (Wisconsin v. Muldrow 2018, 506).

6. Justice Harry Blackmun, who was in the majority in *Rummel*, joined *Rummel*'s dissenters to form a majority in *Solem*, though he did not explain why; in the interim, Justice Sandra Day O'Connor had replaced Potter Stewart, who had voted with the majority in *Rummel*. O'Connor joined the dissent in *Solem*.

7. In *Pulley v. Harris* (1984), the Supreme Court rejected the claim that the Eighth Amendment requires states to conduct comparative proportionality reviews in capital punishment cases (Pulley v. Harris 1984, 44; Harmelin v. Michigan 1991, 989).

8. According to the federal court of appeals in *Bull*, "searches of the San Francisco general jail population resulted in the discovery of 1,574 items of contraband, including 662 assorted controlled substance pills, 106 shanks and other weapons, 1 screwdriver, 17 jail-made handcuff keys, 42.88 grams of rock cocaine, 2.75 grams of powder cocaine, 6.70 grams of methamphetamine, 6.24 grams of tar heroine, 71.93 grams of marijuana, 4 ecstasy pills, 32 assorted pipes, 1 hypodermic needle, and 24 gallons of homemade alcohol known as 'Pruno'" (Bull v. San Francisco 2010, 966–67).

9. In *Department of Revenue of Montana v. Kurth Ranch* (1994, 777 n. 14), the Court held that "whether a sanction constitutes punishment is not determined from the defendant's perspective, as even remedial sanctions carry the 'sting of punishment.'"

10. It should be clear that the problem of individual assessment as a way to overturn an otherwise correct decision by a lower court is constitutionally troubling (Shaw v. Patton 2015, 11). It privileges a so-called scientific approach over a more general basis for the application of law. A case like Berlin v. *Evans* (2011) suggests the limits of such assessments. Ariel Berlin was in his early seventies when, searching online for homosexual companionship, he went to someone's house for sexual relations. The male who answered the door was dressed in women's clothing and was holding his five-year-old daughter's hand. She was naked. The two men then proceeded to fondle the child's vagina. Mr. Berlin had no criminal history. What is the point of a risk assessment in such a case?

11. In *Doe v. Lafayette*, Lafayette, Indiana, banned John Doe, a sex offender against minors, from entering "park property in the City of Lafayette, Indiana—including a golf course, sports stadium, and city pools" (2004, 774). Doe was not on probation when he challenged the law and lost. On the other hand, the tenth circuit court of appeals denied the city of Albuquerque's library ban of John Doe, a convicted sex offender, also not on probation (Doe v. Albuquerque 2012).

REFERENCES

Allen, Danielle. 2000. *The World of Prometheus: The Politics of Punishment in Democratic Athens.* Princeton: Princeton University Press.

Alloy, Jason. 2002. "'158-County Banishment' in Georgia: Constitutional Implications under the State Constitution and the Federal Right to Travel." *Georgia Law Review* 36: 1083–1108.

Anastaplo, George. 1989. *The Constitution of 1787: A Commentary.* Baltimore: Johns Hopkins University Press.

Andorno, Roberto. 2009. "Human Dignity and Human Rights as a Common Ground for a Global Bioethics." *Journal of Medicine and Philosophy* 34: 223–40.

Armstrong, Michael. 1963. "Banishment: Cruel and Unusual Punishment." *University of Pennsylvania Law Review* 111: 758–86.

Aron, Raymond. 1970. *Main Currents in Sociological Thought: Durkheim, Pareto, Weber.* Vol. 2. Trans. Richard Howard and Helen Weaver. New York: Anchor Books.

Bagaric, Mirko. 1999. "In Defence of a Utilitarian Theory of Punishment: Punishing the Innocent and the Compatibility of Utilitarianism and Rights." *Australian Journal of Legal Philosophy* 24: 95–144.

Bains, Chiraag. 2007. "Next-Generation Sex Offender Statutes: Constitutional Challenges to Residency, Work, and Loitering Restrictions." *Harvard Civil Rights-Civil Liberties Law Review* 42 (2): 483–500.

Barroso, Luis Roberto. 2012. "Here, There, and Everywhere: Human Dignity in Contemporary Law and in the Transnational Discourse." *Boston College International & Comparative Law Review* 35: 331–93.

Bauman, Richard. 2012. *Crime and Punishment in Ancient Rome.* London: Routledge.

Bentham, Jeremy. 1830. *The Rationale of Punishment.* London: Robert Heward.

Bentham, Jeremy. 1988. *The Principles of Morals and Legislation.* Amherst, NY: Prometheus Books.

Berns, Walter. 1979. *For Capital Punishment: Crime and the Morality of the Death Penalty.* New York: Basic Books.

Bessler, John. 2012. *Cruel & Unusual: The American Death Penalty and the Founders' Eighth Amendment.* Boston: Northeastern University Press.

Brilliant, Jon. 1989. "The Modern Day Scarlet Letter: A Critical Analysis of Modern Probation Conditions." *Duke Law Journal* 38 (5): 1357–85.

Brooks, Thom. 2012. *Punishment.* London: Routledge.

Brubaker, Stanley. 1988. "Can Liberals Punish?" *American Political Science Review* 82: 821–36.

Calabresi, Steven, and Sarah Agudo. 2008. "Individual Rights under State Constitutions When the Fourteenth Amendment Was Ratified in 1868: What Rights Are Deeply Rooted in American History and Tradition." *Texas Law Review* 87: 7–120.

Caplow, Theodore, and Jonathan Simon. 1999. "Understanding Prison Policy and Population Trends." *Crime and Justice* 26: 63–120.

Carpenter, Catherine, and Amy Beverlin. 2012. "The Evolution of Unconstitutionality in Sex Offender Registration Laws." *Hastings Law Journal* 63: 1071–1134.

Chapman, Nathan, and Michael McConnell. 2012. "Due Process as Separation of Powers." *Yale Law Journal* 121: 1672–1807.

Conkle, Daniel. 2006. “Three Theories of Substantive Due Process.” *North Carolina Law Review* 85: 63–148.

Coulanges, Numa Denis Fustel de. 1980. *The Ancient City: A Study of the Religion, Laws, and Institutions of Greece and Rome.* Baltimore: Johns Hopkins University Press.

Curtis, Michael Kent. 1986. *No State Shall Abridge: The Fourteenth Amendment and the Bill of Rights.* Durham, NC: Duke University Press.

Dick, Anthony. 2011. “The Substance of Punishment under the Bill of Attainder Clause.” *Stanford Law Review* 63: 1177–1212.

Durkheim, Émile.1984. *The Division of Labor in Society.* Trans. W. D. Halls. New York: Free Press.

Edgerton, Peter. 2007. “Banishment and the Right to Live Where You Want.” *University of Chicago Law Review* 74 (3): 1023–56.

Ely, John Hart. 1980. *Democracy and Distrust: A Theory of Judicial Review.* Cambridge, MA: Harvard University Press.

Feinberg, Joel. 1994. “The Expressive Function of Punishment.” In *A Reader on Punishment*, edited by Anthony Duff and David Garland, 73–91. Oxford: Oxford University Press.

Feldman, Daniel. 1997. “The Scarlet Letter Laws of the 1990s: A Response to Critics.” *Albany Law Review* 60 (4): 1081–1126.

Forsdyke, Sara. 2005. *Exile, Ostracism, and Democracy: The Politics of Expulsion in Ancient Greece.* Princeton: Princeton University Press.

Friedman, Lawrence. 1993. *Crime and Punishment in American History.* New York: Basic Books.

Garland, David. 1993. *Punishment and Modern Society: A Study in Social Theory.* Chicago: University of Chicago Press.

Goodman, Elga. 1996. “Megan’s Law: The New Jersey Supreme Court Navigates Uncharted Waters.” *Seton Hall Law Review* 26: 764–800.

Granucci, Anthony. 1969. “Nor Cruel and Unusual Punishments Inflicted: The Original Meaning.” *California Law Review* 57 (4): 839–65.

Gross, Hyman. 1979. *A Theory of Criminal Justice.* Oxford: Oxford University Press.

Harrison, John. 1992. “Reconstructing the Privileges or Immunities Clause.” *Yale Law Journal* 101: 1385–1474.

Hart, H. L. A. 1988. *Punishment of Responsibility: Essays in the Philosophy of Law.* Oxford: Clarendon Press.

Hobbes, Thomas. 1994. *Leviathan.* Ed. Edwin Curley. Indianapolis: Hackett Publishing.

Janicki, Megan. 2007. “Better Seen than Herded: Residency Restrictions and Global Positioning System Tracking Laws for Sex Offenders.” *Boston University Public International Law Journal* 16: 285–310.

Kekes, John. 1993. *Against Liberalism.* Ithaca: Cornell University Press.

Kekes, John. 1996. "Cruelty and Liberalism." *Ethics* 106 (4): 834–44.

Klein, Susan. 1999. "Redrawing the Criminal-Civil Boundary." *Buffalo Criminal Law Review* 2: 679–721.

Lacey, Nicola. 1988. *State Punishment: Political Principles and Community Values.* London: Routledge.

Lash, Kurt. 2011. "The Origins of the Privileges or Immunities Clause, Part II: John Bingham and the Second Draft of the Fourteenth Amendment." *Georgetown Law Journal* 99: 329–434.

Lee, Donna. 2008. "Resuscitating Proportionality in Noncapital Sentencing." *Arizona State Law Journal* 40: 527–84.

Logan, Wayne. 2006. "Constitutional Collectivism and Ex-Offender Residence Exclusion Laws." *Iowa Law Review* 92: 1–40.

Logan, Wayne. 2018. "Challenging the Punitiveness of New-Generation SORN Laws." *New Criminal Law Review* 21 (3): 426–57.

McAllister, Stephen. 1998. "Neighbors Beware: The Constitutionality of State Sex Offender Registration and Community Notification Laws." *Texas Tech Law Review* 29: 97–136.

Montesquieu, Baron de. 1949. *The Spirit of the Laws.* Trans. Thomas Nugent. New York: Hafner.

Moore, Michael. 1997. *Placing Blame: A General Theory of the Criminal Law.* Oxford: Oxford University Press.

Notes. 1959. "Punishment: Its Meaning in Relation to Separation of Power and Substantive Constitutional Restrictions and Its Use in the Lovett, Trop, Perez, and Speiser Cases." *Indiana Law Journal* 34: 231–95.

Olson, Michelle. 2010. "Putting the Brakes on the Preventive State: Challenging Residency Restrictions on Sex Offenders in Illinois under the Ex Post Facto Clause." *Northwestern Journal of Law & Social Policy* 5: 403–36.

Peters, Edward. 1998. "Prison before the Prison: The Ancient and Medieval Worlds." In *The Oxford History of the Prison*, edited by Norval Morris and David Rothman, 3–43. Oxford: Oxford University Press.

Pillsbury, Samuel. 1982. "Creatures, Persons, and Prisoners: Evaluating Prison Conditions Under the Eighth Amendment." *Southern California Law Review* 55: 1099–1131.

Porter, Andrew. 1992. "Toward a Constitutional Analysis of the Right to Intrastate Travel." *Northwestern University Law Review* 86 (3): 820–57.

Primoratz, Igor. 1990. *Justifying Legal Punishment.* Atlantic Highlands, NJ: Humanities Press International.

Rao, Neomi. 2011. "Three Concepts of Dignity in Constitutional Law." *Notre Dame Law Review* 86: 183–271.

Sandel, Michael. 1992. *Liberalism and the Limits of Justice.* Cambridge: Cambridge University Press.

Sasse, Benjamin. 2000. "Curfew Laws, Freedom of Movement, and the Rights of Juveniles." *Case Western Reserve Law Review* 50: 681–728.

Saxer, Shelley Ross. 2009. "Banishment of Sex Offenders: Liberty, Protectionism, and Alternatives." *Washington University Law Review* 86: 1397–1453.

Scalia, Antonin. 1989. "Originalism: The Lesser Evil." *University of Cincinnati Law Review* 57 (3): 849–66.

Schopp, Robert. 1995. "Sexual Predators and the Structure of the Mental Health System: Expanding the Normative Focus of Therapeutic Jurisprudence." *Psychology, Public Policy, and Law* 1: 161–92.

Schrock, Thomas. 1991. "The Rights to Punish and Resist Punishment in Hobbes's *Leviathan.*" *Western Political Quarterly* 44: 853–90.

Sheketoff, Julia Fong. 2010. "State Innovations in Noncapital Proportionality Doctrine." *New York University Law Review* 85: 2209–40.

Shklar, Judith. 1982. "Putting Cruelty First." *Daedalus* 111: 17–27.

Shklar, Judith. 1989. "The Liberalism of Fear." In *Liberalism and the Moral Life,* edited by Nancy Rosenblum, 21–38. Cambridge, MA: Harvard University Press.

Shuster, Arthur. 2016. *Punishment and the History of Political Philosophy: From Classical Republicanism to the Crisis of Modern Criminal Justice.* Toronto: University of Toronto Press.

Simon, Jonathan. 1993. *Poor Discipline: Parole and the Social Control of the Underclass, 1890–1990.* Chicago: University of Chicago Press.

Snider, Wm. Garth. 1998. "Banishment: The History of Its Use and a Proposal for Its Abolition under the First Amendment." *New England Journal on Criminal and Civil Confinement* 24: 455–509.

Steiker, Carol. 1997. "Punishment and Procedure: Punishment Theory and the Criminal-Civil Procedural Divide." *Georgetown Law Journal* 85 (4): 775–819.

Stinneford, John. 2008. "The Original Meaning of Unusual: The Eighth Amendment as a Bar to Cruel Innovation." *Northwestern University Law Review* 102 (4): 1739–1826.

Stinneford, John. 2017. "The Original Meaning of Cruel." *Georgetown Law Journal* 105 (2): 441–506.

Story, Joseph. 1858. *Commentaries on the Constitution of the United States.* 3rd ed. Boston: Little, Brown and Company.

Sunstein, Cass. 1999. *One Case at a Time: Judicial Minimalism on the Supreme Court.* Cambridge, MA: Harvard University Press.

Terchek, Ronald, and Stanley Brubaker. 1989. "Punishing Liberals or Rehabilitating Liberalism?" *American Political Science Review* 83: 1309–16.

Von Hirsch, Andrew. 1976. *Doing Justice: The Choice of Punishments.* New York: Hill & Wang.
Wasserstrom, Richard. 1967. "H. L. A. Hart and the Doctrines of Mens Rea and Criminal Responsibility." *University of Chicago Law Review* 35: 92–126.
Wilhelm, Kathryn. 2010. "Freedom of Movement at a Standstill? Toward the Establishment of Fundamental Right to Intrastate Travel." *Boston University Law Review* 90: 2461–99.

CASES

Aptheker v. Secretary of State, 378 U.S. 500 (1964).
Artway v. Attorney General of State of N.J., 81 F. 3d 1235 (1996).
Atkins v. Virginia, 536 U.S. 304 (2002).
Austin v. U.S. 509 U.S. 602 (1993).
Baze v. Rees, 553 U.S. 35 (2008).
Bell v. Wolfish, 441 U.S. 520 (1979).
Bennis v. Michigan, 516 U.S. 442 (1996).
Berlin v. Evans, 31 Misc.3d 919 (2011).
Bray v. Alexandria Women's Health Clinic, 506 U.S. 263 (1993).
Brown v. Plata, 131 S.Ct. 1910 (2011).
Bull v. San Francisco, 595 F.3d (2010).
California Department of Corrections v. Morales, 514 U.S. 499 (1995).
California v. Steele, WL 2897955 (2004) (Not Officially Published).
Coker v. Georgia, 433 U.S. 584 (1977).
De Veau v. Braisted, 363 U.S. 144 (1960).
Doe v. Albuquerque, 667 F.3d 1111 (2012).
Doe v. Gregoire, 960 F.Supp. 1478 (1997).
Doe v. Lafayette, 377 F. 3d 757 (2004).
Doe v. Miller, 405 F.3d 700 (2005).
Doe v. Pataki, 940 F.Supp. 603 (1996).
Doe v. Pataki, 120 F. 3d 1263 (1997).
Doe v. Petro, 2005 WL 1038846 (2005).
Doe v. Poritz, 142 N.J. 1 (1995).
Dunn v. Blumstein, 405 U.S. 330 (1972).
Eddleman v. Center Township of Marion County, 723 F. Supp. 85 (1989).
Enmund v. Florida, 458 U.S. 782 (1982).
Estelle v. Gamble, 429 U.S. 97 (1976).
Ewing v. California, 538 U.S. 11 (2003).

Farmer v. Brennan, 511 U.S. 825 (1994).
Fay v. Noia, 372 U.S. 391 (1963).
Florence v. Board of Chosen Freeholders of County of Burlington, 566 U.S. 318 (2012).
Ford v. Wainwright, 477 U.S. 399 (1986).
Furman v. Georgia, 408 U.S. 238 (1972).
Georgia v. Collett, 232 Ga. 668 (1974).
Graham v. Florida, 560 U.S. 48 (2010).
Gregg v. Georgia, 428 U.S. 153 (1976).
Griswold v. Connecticut, 381 U.S. 479 (1965).
Harmelin v. Michigan, 501 U.S. 957 (1991).
Holt v. Sarver, 309 F. Supp. 362 (1970).
Holt v. Sarver, 442 F. 2d 304 (1971).
Hudson v. McMillian, 503 U.S. 1 (1992).
Hudson v. U.S., 522 U.S. 93 (1997).
Hurtado v. California, 110 U.S. 516 (1884).
Hutchins v. District of Columbia, 188 F.3d 531 (1999).
Hutto v. Finney, 437 U.S. 678 (1978).
Illinois v. Leroy, 357 Ill.App.3d 530 (2005).
In re Taylor, 147 Cal.Rptr. 3d 64 (2013).
Iowa v. Oliver, 812 N.W. 2d 636 (2012).
Iowa v. Seering, 701 N.W.2d 655 (2005).
Jackson v. Bishop, 404 F. 2d 571 (1968).
Johnson v. Cincinnati, 310 F.3d 484 (2002).
Kansas v. Hendricks, 521 U.S. 346 (1997).
Kansas v. Mossman, 294 Kan. 901 (2012).
Kansas v. Petersen-Beard, 304 Kan. 192 (2016).
Kansas v. Proctor, 47 Kan.App. 2d 889 (2012).
Kennedy v. Louisiana, 554 U.S. 407 (2008).
Kennedy v. Mendoza-Martinez, 372 U.S. 144 (1963).
Kent v. Dulles, 357 U.S. 116 (1958).
King v. New Rochelle Municipal Housing Authority, 442 F. 2d 646 (1971).
Laaman v. Helgemoe, 437 F.Supp. 269 (1977).
Lawrence v. Texas, 539 U.S. 558 (2003).
Lockyer v. Andrade, 538 U.S. 63 (2003).
Lutz v. York, 899 F.2d 255 (1990).
McDonald v. Chicago, 561 U.S. 742 (2010).
Michigan v. Baum, 25 Mich. 187 (1930).
Millard v. Rankin, WL 3767796 (2017) (slip copy).

Minnesota v. Christie, 506 N.W. 2d 293 (1993).
Minnesota v. Combs, 504 N.W. 2d 248 (1993).
Montana Department of Revenue v. Kurth Ranch, 511 U.S. 767 (1994).
Moore v. City of East Cleveland, 431 U.S. 494 (1977).
Morrissey v. Brewer, 408 U.S. 471 (1972).
Ohio v. Blankenship, WL 6889360 (2015).
Ohio v. Burnett 193 Ohio St.3d 419 (2001).
Owens v. Maryland, 724 A.2d 43 (1999).
Paris Adult Theatre I v. Slaton, 413 U.S. 49 (1973).
Paul v. Virginia, 75 U.S. 168 (1869).
Poodry v. Tonawanda Band of Seneca Indians, 85 F.3d 874 (1996).
Prince v. Massachusetts, 321 U.S. 158 (1944).
Prison Law Office v. Koenig, 186 Cal.App. 3d 560 (1986).
Pulley v. Harris, 465 U.S. 37 (1984).
Reno v. Flores, 507 U.S. 292 (1993).
Rhodes v. Chapman, 452 U.S. 337 (1981).
Rise v. Oregon, 59 F.3d 1556 (1995).
Robinson v. California, 370 U.S. 660 (1962).
Roe v. Office of Adult Probation, 938 F.Supp. 1080 (1996).
Roper v. Simmons, 543 U.S. 551 (2005).
Ruffin v. Virginia, 62 Va. 790 (1871).
Rummel v. Estelle, 445 U.S. 263 (1980).
Russell v. Gregoire, 124 F.3d 1079 (1997).
Ryals v. City of Englewood, 364 P.3d 900 (2016).
Saenz v. Roe, 526 U.S. 489 (1999).
Schall v. Martin, 467 U.S. 253 (1984).
Shapiro v. Thompson, 394 U.S. 618 (1969).
Shaw v. Patton, WL 13134500 (2015) (slip copy).
Shaw v. Patton, 823 F.3d 556 (2016).
Slaughter-House Cases, 83 U.S. 36 (1873).
Smith v. Doe, 538 U.S. 84 (2003).
Solem v. Helm, 463 U.S. 277 (1983).
Standley v. Town of Woodfin, 186 N.C.App. 134 (2012).
Starkey v. Oklahoma, 305 P.3d 1004 (2013).
Terry v. Hamrick, 284 Ga. 24 (2008).
Thompson v. Oklahoma, 487 U.S. 815 (1988).
Trop v. Dulles, 356 U.S. 86 (1958).
U.S. v. Abushaar, 761 F.2d 954 (1985).
U.S. v. Bajakajian, 524 U.S. 321 (1998).

U.S. v. Guest, 383 U.S. 745 (1966).
U.S. v. Halper, 490 U.S. 435 (1989).
U.S. v. Ju Toy, 198 U.S. 253 (1905).
U.S. v. One Assortment of 89 Firearms, 465 U.S. 354 (1984).
U.S. v. Salerno, 481 U.S. 739 (1987).
U.S. v. Ursery, 518 U.S. 267 (1996).
U.S. v. Ward, 448 U.S. 242 (1980).
Vann v. Alabama 143 So.3d 850 (2013).
Village of Belle Terre v. Boraas, 416 U.S. 1 (1974).
Wardwell v. Board of Education, 529 F.2d 625 (1976).
Washington v. Glucksberg, 521 U.S. 702 (1997).
Whitley v. Albers, 475 U.S. 312 (1986).
Wilkerson v. Utah, 99 U.S. 130 (1879).
Williams v. Department of Corrections and Community Supervision, 43 Misc. 3d 356 (2014).
Williams v. Department of Corrections and Community Supervision, 136 A.D. 3d 147 (2016).
Williams v. Fears, 179 U.S. 270 (1900).
Willis v. Town of Marshall, 426 F.3d 251 (2005).
Wilson v. Seiter, 501 U.S. 294 (1991).
Wisconsin v. Muldrow, 381 Wis. 2d 492 (2018).
Wright v. City of Jackson, 506 F.2d 900 (1975).

Index

Printed and bound by CPI Group (UK) Ltd, Croydon, CR0 4YY
16/09/2026
14963491-0007